KU-316-392

EDITED BY SUSAN B. BOYD

Challenging the Public/Private Divide: Feminism, Law, and Public Policy

UNIVERSITY OF TORONTO PRESS
Toronto Buffalo London

© University of Toronto Press Incorporated 1997
Toronto Buffalo London
Printed in Canada

ISBN 0-8020-0703-1 (cloth)
ISBN 0-8020-7652-1 (paper)

Printed on acid-free paper

Canadian Cataloguing in Publication Data

Main entry under title:

Challenging the public/private divide : feminism, law, and
   public policy

Includes index.
ISBN 0-8020-0703-1 (bound)   ISBN 0-8020-7652-1 (pbk.)

1. Women – Government policy – Canada.   2. Women – Legal
status, laws, etc. – Canada.   3. Sex discrimination against
women – Canada.   I. Boyd, Susan B.

HQ1236.5.C2C42 1997   305.4'0971   C97-930441-5

LEEDS METROPOLITAN
UNIVERSITY
LEARNING CENTRE
1702738356
BL-B
1130934   3/3/00
305.42 CHA

University of Toronto Press acknowledges the financial assistance to its publishing
program of the Canada Council and the Ontario Arts Council.

To Marlène Cano
1955–1994
Friend, Colleague, Law Professor, and Mother

Contents

Preface and Acknowledgments

The idea for this book emanated from a group of British Columbia researchers funded by a three-year grant from the Social Sciences and Humanities Research Council of Canada, under the 'Women and Change' strategic theme (1993–6). When I arrived at the University of British Columbia in 1992 as the first incumbent of the Chair in Feminist Legal Studies, I envisioned the research project as a way to bring together feminist researchers who were working on different aspects of law and policy, but asking many of the same questions about privatization, the ideology of motherhood, the complex role of law in social change; and the intersectionality of race, class, gender, sexual identity, and (dis)ability. The women who eventually emerged as the research team were Nitya Iyer, Fiona Kay, Marlee Kline, Judith Mosoff, Katherine Teghtsoonian, Claire Young, and myself, and we represented the disciplines of political science, sociology, and law. Early in our collaboration, we identified the public/private divide as a unifying theme, although we were aware of the significant and interesting challenges to much theoretical work on the divide. As our collaborative research proceeded, we pondered the varying nature of the public/private divide and decided to explore it in the context of an edited collection. Virgil Duff of University of Toronto Press encouraged us in this decision in 1994, and he has been wonderfully supportive throughout.

We soon widened the scope of the collection by inviting graduate students and colleagues at universities in Australia and Ontario to contribute chapters. As is always the case in edited collections, choices of authors and topics were often serendipitous. My friend Marlène Cano, had she been alive to read this book, would point out that once again, in a collection from English-speaking Canada, Québec has been overlooked. British Columbia authors remain overrepresented in the collection, because of the location of the research project in that province. Despite the fact that the issues we chose to consider and our focus may have varied had we been living and working elsewhere, we feel that our analysis of most issues transcends in one way or another the geographic location in which we work. Moreover, we hope that this book offers a starting point for further conversations about the multiple and varying ways in which the public/private divide operates in our lives and our thoughts. To some extent, this process has already begun, because we have benefited from the helpful and constructive feedback of colleagues, friends, and the two anonymous reviewers. We also note a different form of conversation in the recent publication of an Australian collection edited by Margaret Thornton, *Public and Private: Feminist Legal Debates* (1995). Although some of the topics and themes parallel those in our collection (e.g., on outwork and international law), the Thornton collection includes chapters on some topics that we did not include (e.g., sexual harassment and family mediation). Similarly, ours includes topics (e.g., child welfare and taxation) not considered in the Australian book. Read together, the two collections complement one another nicely.

I want to acknowledge that in times of limited resources, we have been very fortunate to have the support of the Social Sciences and Humanities Research Council of Canada. This support enabled us to collaborate, to share research, to 'workshop' our papers, and, especially, to work with several wonderful students as research assistants. Indeed, our work could not have been completed as quickly or as effectively without the dedication over the years of our research assistants, who include Evelyn Ackah, Melanie Ash, Kim Brooks, Rachel Edgar, Kristin Graver, Chantal Morton, Amanda Ocran, and Carol Pakkala. In particular, Gillian Calder, as my research assistant throughout this book's genesis and completion, contributed excellent research skills, incisive editing suggestions, thoughtful and gentle critique, and organization of the manuscript's life on my computer. Finally, I want to thank the members of the SSHRCC project and the contributors to this book for their insights, energy, and collaboration.

SUSAN B. BOYD
VANCOUVER, 1996

Contributors

Pat Armstrong is a Professor and Director of the School of Canadian Studies at Carleton University. She has been writing about women and their work for more than twenty years. Her most recent publications include *The Double Ghetto: Canadian Women and Their Segregated Work* (3rd ed.); *Theorizing Women's Work*; *Vital Signs: Nursing in Transition*; *Wasting Away: The Undermining of Canadian Health Care*; and *Take Care: Warning Signals for Canada's Health System*.

Susan B. Boyd is Chair in Feminist Legal Studies and Professor of Law at the University of British Columbia. Her current research is on the role of family law in privatization trends, lesbian custody and support claims, and child custody and women's work.

Doris Elisabeth Buss is a Lecturer in Law at Keele University, England. Her chapter was written as part of her LLM thesis 'Crossing the Line: Feminist International Law Theory, Rape, and the War in Bosnia-Herzegovina' (UBC 1995). She is currently researching the growing activisim of the Vatican and the New Christian Right in the field of women's international human rights.

Dorothy E. Chunn is an Associate Professor of Criminology and a founding member of the Feminist Institute for Studies on Law and Society at Simon Fraser University. She is the author of *From Punishment to Doing Good: Family Courts and Socialized Justice in Ontario, 1880–1940* (1992) and other publications that deal with issues related to feminism, criminology, and family law. Her current research projects include historical analyses of violence against women and children, and of sex, sexuality, and reproduction in the Canadian welfare state.

Nitya Iyer is an Associate Professor at the Faculty of Law, University of British Columbia. Her current research includes critically examining medical and legal regulation of pregnancy and birth; inquiring into the utility of constitutional equality doctrines in addressing systemic racism; and monitoring the ability of human rights laws to address the social experience of discrimination.

Fiona M. Kay is an Assistant Professor of Sociology at the University of British Columbia. Her research interests include gender stratification in the legal profession, specifically gender differences in career mobility and salary differentials, and criminal patterns among young offenders. Together with John Hagan she is co-author of *Gender in Practice: A Study of Lawyers' Lives*. Her current research includes a comparative study of lawyers in Quebec and Ontario, focusing on the progress of women and minorities entering the legal profession (with John Hagan).

Marlee Kline is an Associate Professor at the Faculty of Law, University of British Columbia. Her research is focused on child welfare law (and social welfare law more generally), the ways that law is implicated in and can be relied on to challenge racism and anti-Semitism, and the impact of current neo-liberal restructuring. She is working on a book on child welfare law that will draw together her thinking in these areas.

Jennifer Koshan is the Legal Director of West Coast LEAF, the B.C. branch of the Women's Legal Education and Action Fund. Her LLM thesis at the University of British Columbia Faculty of Law is in the area of Aboriginal justice, the Charter, and violence against women. Before moving to B.C., she worked in the Northwest Territories as a Crown Prosecutor. She has also done work on gender equality issues in the legal profession, international human rights law, sexual assault, and genocide.

Jenni Millbank is a Lecturer in Law at the University of Sydney, Australia. Her current research is on lesbian and gay efforts to contest the meaning of 'family' in litigation and law reform.

Judith Mosoff is an Assistant Professor and Coordinator of the Clinical Program in the Faculty of Law at the University of British Columbia. She works in the area of law and policy in relation to persons with disabilities. She is currently looking at the way Canadian immigration policy affects people with disabilities.

Amanda Araba Ocran is a PhD Candidate in Geography, University of British Columbia. Her thesis research examines constructions of 'race,' ethnicity, and gender in the politics of economic restructuring. Her related publications include *Industrial Homework and Employment Standards: A Community Approach to 'Visibility' and Understanding* (1993), a report commissioned by the Ministry of Women's Equality, B.C.

Katherine Teghtsoonian is an Assistant Professor in the Multidisciplinary Master's Program in Policy and Practice in the Faculty of Human and Social Development at the University of Victoria, where she teaches courses on social policy and women in the human services. Her recent research has focused on a comparative analysis of the ideological construction of women, parenting, and families in Canadian and American child care policy debates.

Claire F.L. Young is a Professor of Law at the University of British Columbia. She researches and writes in the area of tax policy, and in particular, its impact on women. She is writing a book on women and tax policy, entitled *Taxing Times for Women: Critical Perspectives on Canadian Tax Policy.*

INTRODUCTION

1

Challenging the Public/Private Divide: An Overview

SUSAN B. BOYD

The practical consequence of non-regulation is the consolidation of the *status quo*: the *de facto* support of pre-existing power relations and distributions of goods within the 'private' sphere.

The ideology of the public/private dichotomy allows government to clean its hands of any *responsibility* for the state of the 'private' world and *depoliticizes* the disadvantages which inevitably spill over the alleged divide by affecting the position of the 'privately' disadvantaged in the 'public' world.

Lacey (1993, 97) (emphasis in original)

Since the 1960s notable shifts have occurred in the dynamics of both the paid labour force and familial relations in North America, and in the law and public policy relating to work and family relations. Some would say that, by enlarging the role of the public, these changes have transformed the divide between public and private spheres that informs liberal philosophy and capitalist states. The authors in this book agree that the public role *was* enlarged in the 1960s and 1970s; however, we show that these changes represented only part of a much longer history of shifts in the way that boundaries are drawn between public and private. This history forms a backdrop to our analysis of the current conjuncture and of the implications of the economic restructuring and (re)privatization that Canada is now undergoing. Although fundamental changes *are* now occurring in the perceived boundaries between public and private – changes that must be addressed by social movements such as feminism – it is equally apparent that the current reprivatization is not a new phenomenon. An appreciation of the history of shifts in the public/private divide, and an examination of the ways in which public/private discourse plays out in various contexts, is thus both crucial and timely.

This book examines some of the history and current dynamics of the public/private divide, with a focus on selected areas of law and public policy. We consider mainly the Canadian context, although some chapters (e.g., Buss, Millbank) relate to developments in other countries or internationally.[1] We explore various versions of the public/private divide, such as the way lines are drawn between state and family, state and market, market and family, and state and community. Our objectives are to elaborate and elucidate: the role of the state in articulating the boundary in different fields and at different historical moments; the relationship between the public/private divide and power relations connected to gender as it intersects with race, class, sexual identity, and disability; and the relative indeterminacy of the boundary between public and private.

We employ the public/private divide as an ideological marker that shifts in relation to the role of the state at particular historical moments, in particular contexts, and in relation to particular issues. Rather than demarcating actual spheres of activity that are either regulated by the state or not, we strive for an analysis that conceptualizes and recognizes the public/private divide as indeterminate and shifting, but at the same time connected to identifiable relations of power such as those based on class, gender, and race. While a rigid concept of public and private surely impedes useful analysis of women's oppression (Buss, Koshan this volume), a recognition of the ideological divisions between public and private within liberal legalism assists in resisting a descent into bottomless indeterminacy. An appreciation of the complex and shifting role of the state in relation to defining public/private boundaries is also of key importance.

In this Introduction, I identify some key changes relating to women, law, and policy over recent history, and question the extent to which these changes have fundamentally challenged the public/private divide and women's inequality. I then explore the insights of feminist literature on the public/private divide, raise questions about its explanatory capacity, and focus on the increasing complexity of feminist analyses that work within this paradigm. I also discuss some implications of the current restructuring trend for feminist strategies. Throughout I note how the chapters in this book, written by scholars in the fields of law, sociology, social history, geography, and public policy, contribute to the analysis of these issues.

Changes: Plus ça change ...

One of the most notable shifts in Canada over the past couple of decades has been the dramatic increase in the participation of women in the paid labour force, including women with young children (Armstrong this volume). This period has also been characterized by high numbers of single-parent families living in poverty, especially those headed by women, and an increase in the divorce rate (Statistics Canada 1995, 17, 85). Women's ability to live independently of men if they so choose has been enhanced by developments such as more effective and reliable mechanisms of reproductive control, increased demand for women in the labour force, greater access to divorce, and some improvement in the social acceptability of women living alone or with other women. Public attention to violence against women (and children) in intimate relationships has increased, accompanied by a fracturing of the image of the hitherto idealized hetero-patriarchal family.

Over this same period, major initiatives have been taken to rid law and social policy of assumptions based on stereotypical images of women as economically dependent wives and mothers. These efforts reflected not only the work of grassroots women's groups, but also the work of such state-funded bodies as the Royal Commission on the Status of Women (Canada 1970) and the Canadian Advisory Council on the Status of Women.[2] Although many of the formal barriers to women's participation in the labour force were removed in the 1950s in response to women's participation in the labour force during the Second World War, less formal barriers were not tackled until more recently. Assumptions that stereotypically female jobs such as secretarial work should be paid less than stereotypically male jobs such as janitorial work were addressed through legislation on equal pay for work of equal value and the more proactive pay equity schemes (Fudge and McDermott 1991). Attitudes that women were not suited to certain jobs were challenged through employment equity schemes such as the federal Employment Equity Act,[3] and cases such as *Action Travail des Femmes* v *Canadian National Railway Company*.[4] Although legislation on pay and employment equity does not exist uniformly across the country (Fudge 1996), and is being dismantled in Ontario under the Conservative Harris government, important ideological shifts in workplaces have occurred as a result of public debates on women's access to properly remunerated employment.

Family laws were amended in the 1970s and 1980s along liberal egalitarian lines to eradicate images of women as dependent wives and mothers in need of economic protection by men (Chunn 1995). Indeed, the language of many laws and policies (e.g., 'spousal assault') has been rendered gender neutral, and most 'protective legislation,' limiting women's work in certain fields, removed. Parental leave and other legal policy changes, such as custody laws that enable both fathers and mothers equally to claim custody, are geared towards facilitating and thereby encouraging the participation of men in the parenting of children (Boyd, Iyer this volume).

At the same time, law reforms related to family life have attempted to take into account the work that women traditionally have done in the home and to diminish the economic penalties incurred for performing such work (Mossman 1994c). Women's reproductive labour has been recognized through enhanced maternity leave and benefits policies in many Canadian workplaces (Iyer this volume). Efforts to facilitate the participation of women in the paid labour force (such as maternity leave provisions) have used public policy initiatives to try to alter the extent to which women are held to be 'privately' responsible for bearing the costs of 'choosing' to bear a child. By permitting a limited tax deduction and partially subsidizing the cost of day care spaces through federal–provincial cost-sharing programs such as the (now almost defunct) Canada Assistance Plan, the state has tendered public support for some private child care arrangements. Moreover, state funding of shelters and transition houses for battered women has represented public recognition that the private sphere is not necessarily a safe haven for women and children. Law and public policy no longer pretend, as they once did, that they play no role in the private sphere of 'family' and reproduction.

To some degree, then, the traditional 'public/private' divide between work and family, and between state intervention and the family, appears to have been challenged. Despite this progress, however, and the coming into force of the equality rights in section 15 of the Charter of Rights and Freedoms in 1985, the 1990s have revealed the persistence of inequality of women compared with men in various spheres, as well as the inequalities of some groups of women in relation to others (Iyer 1994, 1993). Access to the benefits and opportunities provided in Canadian society remains unequal and variable according to such factors as race, disability, class, and sexual identity as they intersect with gender. These inequalities persist *despite* significant shifts in social and legal policies geared towards ensuring the equality of women, promoting the sharing of familial responsibilities by women and men, and enhancing women's position in the labour force (Armstrong this volume; Boyd 1995; Chunn 1995; Mossman 1994c). In fact, the sexual division of labour remains largely intact, within both the heterosexual family and the paid labour force. Women continue to work mainly within 'job ghettos' for unequal wages, *and* they continue to assume the bulk of responsibility for domestic labour and child care in the home (Armstrong this volume). This division of labour prevails even for relatively privileged professional women such as lawyers (Brockman 1992, 1994; Kay this volume; Wilson 1993). Sexualized violence against women, both within and outside the family, persists despite the legal and policy changes introduced to address it (see, e.g., Roberts and Mohr 1994).

Given these contradictory effects of legal and policy changes, it is necessary to examine critically the roles that state, law, and public policy play in regulating women's lives and in restructuring the constraints within which women organize their lives in contemporary Canadian society. It is necessary, for example, to assess why the legal and policy shifts outlined above have not necessarily helped to ameliorate the difficulties that heterosexual women face in balancing labour force ('public') and family ('private') responsibilities, particularly where children are involved. The precise manner by which sociolegal policies regulate the private sphere and whether these same policies, perversely, contribute to the continuing inequalities that women experience must be considered. As well, the differential impact of particular reforms and legal regulation on certain groups of women, such as women of colour, lesbians, Aboriginal women, poor women, and women with disabilities, is a crucial part of such analyses (see, especially, chapters by Iyer, Koshan, Millbank, Mosoff, Ocran this volume). Legal and social policy initiatives must be investigated in order to develop an understanding of their inadequacies and contradictions, so as to point towards changes that might improve their efficacy. The extent to which state initiatives with regard to child care and economic dependency do not enhance public responsibility so much as privatize responsibility within family units is also an important element (Teghtsoonian, Young this volume), one that is exacerbated in the current restructuring processes that are occurring in Canada (Armstrong, Kline, Ocran this volume). Placing legal and policy debates and developments in their broader socioeconomic and cultural context helps to identify directions for overcoming barriers to the equality of women. Feminist literature on the public/private divide provides part of this context and assists in identifying strategies for change.

Feminist Analysis of the Public/Private Divide

A considerable body of literature now exists on the public/private divide, for example, Clark (1978), Elshtain (1981), Fineman and Mykitiuk (1994), Fudge (1987), Gavison (1992), Kerber (1988), Lacey (1993), O'Donovan (1985), Olsen (1985, 1983), Pateman (1983), Thornton (1995, 1991), Ursel (1992), Zaretsky (1976).[5] This divide, which has long informed dominant Western ways of knowing and being, denotes the ideological division of life into apparently opposing spheres of public and private activities, and public and private responsibilities. It has prevailed particularly over the past two centuries, as, with the industrialization of Western capitalist societies, people's lives were increasingly divided into public and private spheres at both material and ideological levels. Whereas households previously tended to constitute units of production with both men and women (and often people who might now be regarded as 'non-family' members) participating in work within these units, the spheres of home/family and paid work became physically and conceptually more separate in the nineteenth and early twentieth centuries (Anderson 1987, 21). The timing of the transition varied according to factors such as geographic region and level of industrial development. This phenomenon was highly gendered in that men tended to prevail over women in the public spheres of politics and work, which consequently gave them power in the private sphere of home/ family. Although public/private ideology was particularly obvious in the *laissez-faire* era of the nineteenth-century rise of industrial capitalism (Zaretsky 1976), it did not disappear with the rise of the regulatory welfare state in the twentieth century but rather assumed a different form (Chunn this volume). As Frances Olsen put it in her influential work on the public/ private divide, law, and gender: 'Just as the family was once seen as the repository for values being destroyed in the marketplace, the family may also be seen as the sanctuary of privacy into which one can retreat to avoid state regulation' (1983, 1504).

The public/private divide can be used to describe various interrelated phenomena (Olsen 1985, 1983), which must be considered together in order to gain a full understanding of their relevance to women's oppression. First, a distinction is often drawn between state regulation (government activity) and private economic activity (the market). In the liberal thought that accompanies and supports capitalism, it is often asserted that the market thrives when left unregulated by state and law (Brodie 1994, 52). Any economic or social inequalities that persist in the market are viewed as 'natural and beyond the proper scope of state activity' (Olsen 1983, 1502). It has, therefore, been more difficult to introduce regulatory measures that promote women's equality into non-government workplaces as compared with government workplaces. In consequence, women working in the public sector tend to receive somewhat better treatment than those in the private sector (Armstrong this volume). Fiona Kay (this volume) shows that women lawyers working in government, for example, as Crown prosecutors, have more access to workplace supports than women lawyers working in private practice. As another example, when the Ontario government passed wide-ranging employment and pay equity legislation in the late 1980s and early 1990s, the initiatives were met with outrage from business and government had to 'persuade the opponents of the equity initiatives that they would neither interfere with business's right to manage nor compromise its profits' (Fudge 1996, 73). The cost of these programs is perceived to be an unfair competitive burden, a perception that is exacerbated in times of deregulation and restructuring (Bakker 1991, 259). Yet the notion that the state is, or can be, neutral *vis-à-vis* the market is false: despite the rhetoric of neutrality and non-intervention in the market, capitalist states regularly promote the interests of entrepreneurs and big business at the expense of workers (Olsen 1983). Canada, in particular, has historically given such support to business (Wallace 1950).

A second aspect of the public/private divide is a distinction drawn between the market and the family. The market (or workplace) in this instance is viewed as 'public' in contrast to the 'private' sphere of family. This version of the public/private divide accounts for phenomena such as the usually unremunerated nature of labour performed (usually by women) in the home, in contrast to the remunerated labour performed (traditionally more by men than women) in the market (Armstrong and Armstrong 1994). As Marilyn Waring (1988) showed, the patriarchal assumptions that inform mainstream economics result in a failure to account for women's generally unpaid labour in both household and community. In addition to causing labour in the private sphere (primarily domestic labour and child care) to be invisible to marketplace mechanisms for valuing work, this version of the divide contributes to the undervaluing of work performed by women in the labour force. For example, work performed in the marketplace that resembles women's (unpaid) work in the home, such as child care or secretarial work, tends to be performed by women and is chronically underpaid (Armstrong and Armstrong 1994; Teghtsoonian this volume).

A third aspect of the public/private divide is the distinction between state regulation and family relations, with the family being viewed as a 'haven in a heartless world' (Lasch 1977) that should be protected from the public eye and from scrutiny by state and law. As feminist activists and scholars have shown, this version of the divide has a detrimental impact on women's ability to obtain compensation for their injuries or recognition of their work in the home (Graycar and Morgan 1990). Women's lives and women's issues have tended to be relegated to a separate, 'private' sphere that is considered immune from regulation (O'Donovan 1985; Olsen 1985). One example of this division is the state's failure to deal with men's violence against women in the 'private' sphere of family relations. This particular public/private boundary rests, therefore, on a ratification of unequal power relations between men and women in heterosexual families (Olsen 1985).

Considerable feminist energy has been directed to the deconstruction of especially the market/family and the state/family aspects of the public/private divide. For example, the links between women's oppression in the family and their inequality in the market have been highlighted. The objective has been to increase public attention to, and regulation of, social relations and sites that affect women, in the hopes of eliminating women's inequality. The 1970s rallying cry 'the personal is political' exemplified this type of initiative (MacKinnon 1989; Pateman 1983, 295–8; Prentice et al. 1988, 391). Social relations that hitherto were viewed as personal or private were to be politicized, analysed, exposed to scrutiny, and rendered an appropriate arena for regulation by state and law, especially where violence was concerned. As well, the first aspect of the divide, between state and market, is receiving increasing attention, as feminist scholars consider the impact on women of economic restructuring, deregulation of labour markets, and discourses of competition and technological change that increasingly displace the partial efforts of the state to regulate the market (e.g., Bakker 1994; Fudge 1996).

While most feminist theorizing on the public/private divide focuses on local or national laws and policies, recent scholarship has considered the public/private distinctions made within international law (Charlesworth, Chinkin, and Wright 1991). As Doris Buss shows (this volume), this work roughly parallels the three aspects of the divide delineated above. The state/market divide plays out in terms of distinctions drawn between public international law and the private world of international trade. Although international trade is subject to some regulation, this 'intervention' is usually justified as being necessary to free trade (Kennedy 1994). The second distinction, between market and family, plays out in the way that development policies generated in the West have assumed a gendered division of labour in which men work in the public world of commerce, while women stay at home. The role of women in activities such as subsistence farming is thus often ignored in development policies, so that women may effectively be denied access to these activities, leading to the impoverishment of themselves and their families (Goetz 1991, 137–8).

Finally, international law constructs a public world of interstate activity that is said to be separate from the 'private' world of domestic state affairs, a distinction analogous to that between state and family. At the international level, only relations between states, or issues that states have agreed to submit to regulation through international treaty or contract, are legitimate subjects for 'public' international legal regulation. Matters within a particular state are considered, in contrast, to be 'private' and therefore intervention by international law is inappropriate. This distinction may deny women the protection of international law, which is preoccupied with issues of national sovereignty and jurisdiction rather than the daily realities of women's struggle for food, shelter, and personal dignity.

Feminist activism and scholarship, then, have illuminated the disparate impact that the public/private divide has had on women and its role in diminishing the impact of efforts to eradicate women's oppression. Women's issues often are buried because of the layers of public and private. Women's issues are said to be located mainly within the private sphere of domestic law. Within the state, these are dismissed by the operation of the domestic state/family divide described earlier (see Olsen 1985). Outside of the state, within the international realm, they are overlooked as a result of the mandate of international law to deal only with 'external' or 'public' matters of the state.

Calls to bring relations previously constructed as private (such as the family) into the protection of the public sphere have arguably dominated much feminist activism at both national and international levels (Chunn 1995; Buss, Koshan this volume). In the period of growth connected with the postwar Keynesian welfare state, when regulation by the state was taken more for granted, it was also possible for feminists to argue, in many cases successfully, for state funding of women's groups and battered women's shelters (Findlay 1987; Ng 1988; Walker 1990). Despite the fact that the twentieth-century welfare state in Canada and other Western countries was based on many patriarchal assumptions (Andrew 1984; Chunn 1995; Ursel 1992), it provided openings for a realignment of the public/private divide that was more fair to women. Similarly, the post – Second World War system of international human rights, while problematic in many ways, provided an avenue for some women to pursue claims that challenged notions of public and private at the international level (Cook 1992).

Challenges to the Public/Private Metaphor: Indeterminacy and Difference

Challenges to some aspects of feminist analyses of the public/private divide have been mounted in recent years, often by feminist scholars themselves. Questions have been raised about the conceptualization of women's oppression and its causes within the public/private literature, the imagery of 'separate spheres,' and the strategy of bringing more private sphere relations into the realm of public regulation. For some authors, these challenges mean eschewing the public/private divide as a useful conceptual tool (e.g., Goodall 1990; Rose 1987). For others, including most authors in this book, such questions assist in determining more precisely how the divide operates in relation to different groups and issues and in different periods and locations. In other words, the analysis of public and private has been rendered more complex.

First, it has been shown that most feminist literature on the public/private divide tends to identify gender as the primary cause of women's oppression, thereby diminishing the potential of an analysis that examines the role of race, culture, class, sexuality, and disability (e.g., Buss, Koshan, Mosoff, Teghtsoonian this volume). It has become clear that the public/private dividing line is often drawn differently depending on factors such as race, class, and sexual identity. For example, women of classes and races 'other' than the protected, white, middle- or upper-class married woman were expected to work in both public and private spheres, even in the romanticized nineteenth century (Prentice et al. 1988, 123–8). Some did paid work in their homes for industries such as the garment trade (Ocran this volume). Others took boarders into their homes or did laundry for other households (Prentice et al. 1988, 121–2). Indeed, it was the work of 'othered' women, as maids for example, for women of the middle and upper classes that enabled the latter women to be viewed as 'protected' (from work) in the private sphere. Their labour also enabled some (mainly middle- or upper-class white) women to participate in limited ways in the public sphere, creating the new welfare state and engaging in charitable works (Chunn 1992; Prentice et al. 1988, 103–5; Ursel 1992; Valverde 1991, 29–30). Yet the historical image remains that women rarely performed paid labour in the domestic sphere or the public sphere. General statements about the 'experience of women' in the public and private spheres thus cannot be made, because gender-based dynamics are cross-cut by racialized and class-based social relations.

Second, it has been shown that it is inaccurate to portray the public/private divide as a natural or determinate division. Whereas white women might complain about a historical lack of legal protection in the private sphere of family, Black women or Aboriginal women might protest that, in their families, state intervention has been all too prevalent (see Koshan this volume). Canadian child welfare law and policy have been used to remove Aboriginal children from their homes and families (e.g., Kline 1993, 1992; Monture 1989) and family and social welfare law was used in an attempt to 'normalize' families that were viewed as marginal along class lines in early twentieth-century Canada (Chunn 1992).

In fact, the state always plays a role in regulating social and economic relations, even in its apparent absence (Chunn this volume). For example, even though the state may not intervene overtly in heterosexual family relations, it implicitly ratifies the unequal status quo between women and men by its regulatory absence (Olsen 1985). Through the state's failure to criminalize or prevent violence against women or children in the home, men have been accorded significant 'privatized' power by laws on marriage and family relations. The general logic of non-intervention in the family significantly impeded efforts to eradicate violence in the home, with wife rape, for instance, being legally permissible in many jurisdictions until very recently (Koshan this volume). Indeed, it is still more difficult to prosecute sexual assaults that occur in intimate relationships resembling marriage (e.g., Dawson 1993, 115–5).

Moreover, the public and private spheres, when they can be identified as such, exist not so much in opposition to one another, but rather *in reciprocal connection with* one another (Fudge 1987; Olsen 1985; Rose 1987; Thornton 1991). The ways in which the public sphere is organized – arguably along the lines of a presumed married man's lifestyle – *rely* on a particular way of organizing the private sphere. The ability of the unencumbered individual (man) to participate in the public sphere of work and politics assumes that someone, usually a woman, is preparing his food, cleaning his house, and raising the next generation of labourers through her reproductive labour. The 'sexual contract' under which women purportedly voluntarily agree to do these things supports men's ability to succeed in the public sphere and to have greater power than women both there and in the private sphere (Pateman 1988). Families that are not structured on this model have greater difficulty negotiating the demands of family and work (Iyer, Kay this volume; Mossman 1994a, 1994b). Although many individual men do not dominate the market sphere *per se*, this model enhances profit making by corporate capitalists because of the subsidization it offers to business through women's unpaid labour. Expectations that child care will be done 'for free' (by mothers in the home) are also reciprocally connected both to the underpaid nature of child care labour (often performed by women of colour: Macklin 1992) and to the lack of publicly funded day care that would enable women to work outside the home (see Teghtsoonian this volume). These relationships illustrate the complex connection between production (assumed to occur in the market) and reproduction (assumed to occur within the family) (Fudge 1987, 488; Ursel 1992).

Third, geographic imagery delineating separate spheres of market and family, with paid work occurring mainly in the market, fails to apply to the lives of many women. Many Aboriginal societies in Canada have not been organized along public/private lines at all, and the state/market, market/family, and state/family divisions may hold little resonance in this context. Rather, extended family structures were often supported by an economic infrastructure based on reciprocity, sharing, and production for the subsistence of the community (Bourgeault 1991; Das Gupta 1995; Koshan this volume; Monture-Angus 1995, 28, 37). In addition, in many women's lives, the home is not set apart from the market. Some immigrant women, for example, work for pay as domestic workers in other women's homes (Macklin 1992). For others, the market moves into the home: homework, or paid work done in the home, is not uncommon for immigrant women, and its prevalence is increasing in Canada and elsewhere (Mukhopadhyay 1994, 163). Despite its prevalence, this work is underpaid and effectively unregulated by employment standards, as Amanda Ocran demonstrates in her chapter on homework in the garment industry.

Race and class clearly play key roles in varying the gendered boundaries between public and private. Other social characteristics, such as sexuality, similarly interrupt the generality of any notion that state policy is to protect the privacy of families. Whereas white, heterosexual, middle- or upperclass families may be relatively insulated from public scrutiny, families that deviate from this norm for reasons of class, race, or sexual identity are regulated precisely because of their divergence from the norm. A clear example of state intervention in the supposed private sphere of sexuality is the alacrity with which the public eye invades the privacy of lesbian lives, often in a prurient fashion in the legal arena of child custody disputes (Arnup 1989; Millbank this volume). Dorothy Chunn (this volume) shows that early twentieth century state initiatives and reform campaigns dealing with sex and venereal disease attempted to regulate women's sexual and reproductive lives in different ways, depending on whether they were viewed as deviant, deviant but salvageable, or incorrigible. This determination of women's character and potential reproductive value was related in turn to factors such as class, race, and familial status.

As well, expert discourses on mental disability and sexuality play a role in varying the boundary between public and private. Sometimes, otherwise personal/private issues become public and subject to state action. For example, scientific expert discourses have played a key role in the regulation of women's sexuality through laws and policies on venereal disease (Chunn this volume). Judith Mosoff (this volume) argues that expert psychiatric discourses, when used in supposedly 'private' child custody cases in relation to mothers who are labelled as having mental disabilities, imbue the dispute with a public flavour not dissimilar to that in child welfare disputes. The boundary between public and private laws is thereby rendered illusory. Jenni Millbank (this volume) shows, however, that expert discourses can have contradictory effects: in lesbian custody cases, expert testimony about the benign nature of lesbian parenting is usually dismissed in favour of 'common sense' notions of the contagion of homosexuality. Expert discourses appear to hold less power when invoked in aid of interests that historically have been marginalized.

Attention is also directed in recent literature to the contradictory role of 'community' in the construction of the public/private divide (e.g., Mossman 1989). Sometimes community is considered private *vis-à-vis* the state: for example, Ralph Klein's neoliberal government in Alberta expects that community groups will assume responsibility for functions that previously were handled by the state (Kline this volume). It is assumed that this arrangement will be cheaper and involve less public money, although it has been shown that the savings will be generated out of further reliance on women's unpaid labour. 'Community' can, on the other hand, take on a public inflection as, for example, when progressive groups call for more community-based input and responsibility for public decisions over resources. Yet such promotion of grassroots input into public decision making by particular communities, such as Aboriginal communities, tends to be relied on only to buttress regressive initiatives to shift responsibility for social services to the private sphere (Kline this volume).

Is the State Important?

The above discussion has shown that the dividing line between ostensibly 'public' and 'private' spheres is unclear, and it shifts in a manner that is connected to the state's role in regulating power relations between various groups. To trace the operation of the divide and the role of the state accurately, the intersecting factors of race, class, gender, sexual identity, and disability must be carefully articulated. Some authors argue that it may be more useful to examine the multiple sites of power struggle that affect women's lives than to focus on the geographic imagery of 'public' and 'private' or an analysis of state action (e.g., Elliot 1989; Rose 1987).

Paying attention to the role of the state is, however, crucial to an understanding of current developments, even as analysis is shifted to multiple and local sites of struggle in order to challenge overly simplified approaches that considered the state to be either a neutral institution or an instrumentalist agent of capitalism or patriarchy (Brodie 1995, 23–8; Cooper 1993; Watson 1990). Liberal feminist expectations that legal change alone could deliver social equality between women and men have been revealed as overly optimistic (Boyd and Sheehy 1986). These expectations were based on a false assumption that the state was a relatively neutral institution that could be won over to a feminist cause that urged its use in dismantling discriminatory assumptions in laws and social policies. Moreover, powerfully evocative analyses of the state as an institution irretrievably captured by capitalist/patriarchal interests (e.g., Mac-Kinnon 1989), which feminists and other social activists could or should eschew in their struggles, have also been revealed as overly pessimistic and simplistic (Abner, Mossman, and Pickett 1990, 602). These insights mean that a more nuanced analysis of the state is necessary, rather than an abandonment of its place in regulating public and private relations.

Canadian feminists have been relatively pro-statist in their strategies compared with those in other countries (Vickers, Rankin, and Appelle 1993, 39–42). Some (middle class) women were active agents in the creation of the welfare state, so that it cannot be argued that state or law was imposed on them involuntarily (Chunn 1995). And, the role of the state in relation to women's work *has* provided employment opportunities to women, although these opportunities have been available to women to greater or lesser degrees depending on their race, immigrant status, (dis)ability, sexual identity, and so on (Armstrong this volume). Many of the (flawed) opportunities provided by this state action (such as employment and pay equity) are now under threat, as Pat Armstrong shows in this volume. Despite their inadequacies, their defence must be taken seriously, rather than adopting a position that dismisses all state action as patriarchal or capitalist. Although the overarching and limiting effect of dominant ideologies on the state and its institutions must be kept in mind, it is possible and necessary to engage in social struggle on the terrain of the state

(Cooper 1993; Findlay 1987; Herman 1994). It is therefore necessary to analyse its precise role in regulating family and work lives.

The Public/Private Divide and Familial Ideology

Feminist research on 'the family' has demonstrated how women and families deviating from the assumed white, middle-class, heterosexual norm have been differently regulated by sociolegal policies (Barrett and McIntosh 1982; Chunn 1992; Gavigan 1993; Kline 1993, 1992). Contemporary law and policy discourses need to be deconstructed by examining what kind of family, and what kind of mother, is assumed by various reform initiatives. Close study of the sociolegal treatment of familial forms that depart from the normative model reveals the inadequacy of the questions now being raised in mainstream public policy literature about 'the' changing family, and women's roles within it. Several chapters in this book suggest that these questions have left unchallenged underlying economic structures and their supporting ideological and cultural assumptions (e.g., Boyd, Iyer, Teghtsoonian, Young this volume). Consequently, efforts to eradicate barriers to the equality of women and other disempowered groups have been limited. Investigating how different women, and different types of families, are regulated by law and social policy, and examining the differential impact that these policies have on them (e.g., Iyer, Koshan, Millbank, Mosoff, Ocran this volume) assists in understanding why.

The public/private divide is intrinsically connected to the familial ideology that dominates capitalist societies.[6] A key ideological component of the division is the assumption that particular responsibilities will be taken care of in the private sphere of the family, which in turn rests on women's unpaid or poorly paid labour (Armstrong, Teghtsoonian this volume). Despite recent efforts to eliminate these assumptions by legislative initiatives such as parental leave (Iyer this volume), they continue to underpin law and social policy at a fundamental level, and they are experiencing a revival of sorts (Brodie 1994; Kline this volume). The current backlash against legislative initiatives such as employment and pay equity, while cloaked in the language of restructuring, financial restraint, and efficiency, relies partly on an assumption that women's place is in the home and men should be accorded all possible opportunities in the market. Ideological assumptions about women as the selfless caregivers, or mothers, of society thus continue to be reproduced in much legal and social policy regulation of work and family.

Sometimes these assumptions about women are contradictory, particularly in an economy that increasingly expects that women will work out-side the home. For example, although socioeconomic structures reinforce women's primary responsibility for child care, gender-neutral family laws tend not to acknowledge the continuing gendered nature of caregiving. The interaction between these contradictory norms makes it increasingly diffi-cult for mothers to assert custodial claims to their children as, increasingly, their caregiving work in the private sphere is rendered invisible (Boyd this volume; Fineman 1995).

Ideologies related to 'private lives' in families thus inform not only the private sphere, but also (public) laws and social policies (Chunn 1992; Ursel 1992). Public law is not, then, neutral or ungendered. For instance, lesbian or gay relationships that challenge the normative model of family have been excluded from state recognition until very recently, and recent changes that give partial recognition to same-sex relationships tend to do so mainly for those that mirror as closely as possible traditional heterosexual relationships (Boyd 1994a, 1994b; Herman 1994; Young 1994). Familial ideology has also influenced social welfare law, a field that is often regarded as 'public' law, through expectations that women will be dependent on men (Gavigan 1993, 616–23; Mossman and MacLean 1986). And pension regulation in Canada tends to reinforce women's dependency on men, with any subsidies through the tax system going mainly to men (Young this volume).

An important aspect of familial ideology is the normative model of motherhood. Several authors in this book investigate the ways in which expectations of 'good motherhood' and the application of legal principles such as 'best interests of the child' may vary with regard to different groups of women who deviate from the normative model, such as lesbian mothers (Millbank this volume), mothers with mental disabilities (Mosoff this volume), and 'ambitious' career-oriented mothers (Boyd this volume). Heightened scrutiny and criticism of these women's mothering and behav-iour occurs, as it also does in the case of Aboriginal women (Kline 1993). Discourses on child care are also influenced by the ideology of mother-hood. Teghtsoonian (this volume) shows that politicians influenced by neo-conservatism may regard publicly funded child care as necessary mainly for working-class women who are viewed as having no choice but to work outside the home; middle-class women should preferably assume responsibility for their children in the private sphere, supported by the het-erosexual patriarchal family. Iyer (this volume) argues that ostensibly uni-versal maternity benefits actually operate in race- and class-specific ways. Bringing issues like child care into the 'public' realm does not, therefore, necessarily succeed in challenging the ideology of motherhood or the (hetero)sexual division of labour, or in revaluing child care labour *per se*. Shifting the public/private divide requires a more fundamental reordering of gender relations, economic relations, and government regulation that challenges ideology at a more profound level.

Restructuring, Privatization, and Ideology

In the current period of restructuring, deregulation, and privatization, the historically contingent lines between public and private are being redrawn, with the private sphere being expected to assume greater responsibility for things that were once viewed as 'public' (Brodie 1994; Kline this volume). This realignment of public and private has highly gendered implications (Armstrong this volume; Brodie ibid.) and is intrinsically connected to the familial ideology outlined above. A renewed emphasis on the importance of the heterosexual patriarchal family as the fundamental building block in restructuring is evident. Families are expected to undertake caring functions for those who are ill, as hospitals cut back, as well as for children and the elderly (Armstrong this volume). As provinces such as Alberta shift responsibility for social assistance and child welfare to the private sphere, families and non-profit and for-profit organizations are expected to assume responsibility for certain aspects of that system (Kline this volume). Invocations of community responsibility are prevalent, and rather than 'community' assuming a public or collective meaning, in this context it is a tool of privatization. Given the high proportion of women in the ranks of those who perform volunteer, 'community,' and 'family' work in Canadian society (Armstrong this volume; Duchesne 1989), it is they who will be expected to assume the lion's share of low-paid and unremunerated work as society is restructured in the interests of capital.

Moreover, state policies (responding, in some cases, to feminist analysis) often promote privatized familial responsibility, for example, by heightening the responsibility of ex-spouses for their children through stricter child support enforcement (Pulkingham 1994). Claire Young demonstrates in her chapter that the tax system is used in a manner that reinforces expectations that the (already overburdened) private sphere will assume economic responsibility for such things as child care, the elderly, and children of separated parents. Thus, it is not sufficient to call for public action on such issues: the manner in which that public role is exercised is critical to assessing whether or not a shift in state policy is progressive in terms of redressing unequal social relations of power. It is also apparent that, while (re)privatization of economic responsibility is occurring, many intimate relations are encountering more public exposure as mechanisms develop that enhance surveillance of hitherto 'private' relations. For example, restrictions in eligibility for social assistance often are dependent on obtaining information about 'spousal' relationships, and in criminal law, therapeutic records are potentially available to defence counsel.[7]

We must be wary, then, of apparent state action that, in fact, does little to ameliorate the conditions of women's lives. For example, the Supreme Court of Canada decided in *Moge* v *Moge*[8] that an ex-husband who had lived apart from his wife for many years should continue to pay support to her. The Women's Legal Education and Action Fund (LEAF) successfully intervened in this case to show the systematic undervaluing of women's domestic labour and child care in the private sphere and to connect this phenomenon to the 'feminization of poverty' – the fact that women are (and always have been) disproportionately represented among the poor in Canada. In recognizing that women are not always able to achieve economic self-sufficiency at the same rate as men, and the connection between this problem and the sexual division of labour, the Supreme Court of Canada symbolically 'possessed' the field of the feminization of poverty by requiring men to pay for their ex-spouse and children. In a seemingly progressive decision, it appeared that the state was doing something to address the poverty of women and their children.

Despite the benefits that this approach offers to some women and children, it arguably helped to set the scene for further privatizing initiatives in public policy, such as child support guidelines (Pulkingham 1994). Feminist research has revealed the limits of this type of privatized family law approach under which responsibility for women's poverty rests wherever possible with a man with whom they have had a recognized relationship (Eichler 1990–1). Not only does it not effectively address poverty (ibid.), but responsibility for the costs of social reproduction and for economic hardship remains privatized, and the gendered relations of dependency are therefore reinforced (Boyd 1994a, 1994b; Sheppard 1995). American research has shown that privatized remedies for economic need particularly disadvantage Black women and single mothers (Beller and Graham 1993). The fledgling recognition of lesbian and gay relationships may also be motivated in part by the view that it is preferable to have individuals in intimate partnerships responsible for each other than to permit them to turn to the state when they are in financial need (Boyd 1994b).

In addition to this (re)privatization of the social costs of reproduction, privatization of the labour force is occurring. Industries increasingly rely on homeworkers, outsourcing, and subcontracting for labour, resulting in the physical and social isolation of workers within households and a decreased ability to obtain decent wages and conditions of work (Ocran this volume). For reasons such as women's responsibility for child care and domestic labour and the socioeconomic vulnerability of specific immigrant communities, homeworkers tend to be predominantly women, especially immigrant women (Ocran this volume). As well, public sector jobs in which women workers may have found somewhat more recognition and accommodation of their gendered lives, are being eroded (Armstrong, Kline this volume). Economic restructuring thus reinforces inequalities related to racial as well as gender oppression and diminishes the opportunities for collective organizing across such boundaries because of the fact that workers are increasingly separated from one another by the walls of their own homes.

Resistance and Sites of Struggle

Despite the pessimistic situation just outlined, restructuring that relies on an enlargement of the private sphere does contain spaces for resistance by social movements. For example, official reliance on progressive discourses (e.g., on 'community') has created some space for resistance to regressive restructuring of the child welfare system in Alberta (Kline this volume). To think about how to organize such resistance, insights gained from poststructuralism about the need for attention to local sites of struggle and resistance must be combined with structuralist/political economy approaches (Best and Kellner 1991; see also Ocran this volume).

Because domination based on direct coercion generally lasts only for short periods of time, an equally important focus of analysis is 'the "spontaneous" consent given by the great mass of the population to the general direction imposed on social life by the dominant fundamental group' (Gramsci 1971, 12; see also Hunt 1993, 229–32). 'Hegemony' is the concept used to describe the processes that create this spontaneous consent:

[Hegemony] entails the critical passage of a system of domination into the authority of a leading bloc, which is capable not only of organizing its own base through the construction of alliances between different sectors and social forces, but which has as a central feature of that process the construction and winning of popular consent to that authority among key sectors of the dominated classes themselves. (Hall 1988, 53)

This concept is useful in explaining the apparently widespread popular consent – across disparate social groups – to fiscal restraint policies. It may also assist in the identification of useful sites of struggle. Moreover, because the public/private divide itself is a hegemonic concept, it is important to examine the ways in which it is embraced or resisted in various sectors.

If hegemony is constructed through a complex process of struggle, the balance of social forces is subject to continuing evolution and development. Hegemony is not static, but rather 'must be constantly and ceaselessly renewed, reenacted' (ibid., 54). The use of law by progressive social movements may, then, represent an important form of resistance to oppression, even if these movements are participating in a process that often reinforces overall hegemonic forces. The exact outcome of a particular struggle over law or social policy is not predictable; rather it must be analysed to determine how, in combination with other struggles, it relates to the 'unstable equilibrium on which the authority of a social bloc is founded and that also defines its weak or unstable points' (ibid.). These struggles represent cultural battles to transform popular mentality. Thus, the importance of using struggles about law and social policy to convey alternative views of social problems and strategies emerges, with the specific result in any given struggle becoming somewhat less crucial.

In this period of restructuring, and given a seemingly more conservative Supreme Court of Canada (Pothier 1996) and legislatures, a realistic objective for social movements may be to keep alternative visions of social order in the collective memory, so that they may re-emerge at a later political moment. Contradictions in the privatized vision of the neo-liberal state provide a terrain for resistance even in the face of a seemingly intransigent restructuring impetus. Brodie pointed out that 'the patriarchal assumptions that inform the move to reprivatization also construct a vision of the private which is no longer sustainable' (1994, 57). In a society where many women in heterosexual relationships work outside the home, partly in order to sustain family life, and where single-parent families headed by women constitute a significant minority of families, it is not at all clear that state policies promoting privatization bolstered by traditional familial ideology can succeed. In the course of arguing for specific provisions (such as child support enforcement) that might benefit some women and children in the short term, it is also crucial to present a full picture of the social and economic difficulties facing them partly as a result of restructuring.

It must be noted that individualized, privatizing solutions, such as those promoted by tax and family law, have limitations in terms of achieving long-term social change (Young this volume). Moreover, as Judith Mosoff's chapter shows, strategies such as the primary caregiver presumption, which seeks to give greater weight to women's (often undervalued) private-sphere caregiving labour in child custody disputes, benefit only some women in the short term. This strategy may also reinforce larger trends towards privatization of the costs of social reproduction (Pulkingham 1994). Yet it may be possible to fashion arguments that place women's current inequalities (e.g., in the sexual division of labour) in the context of larger socioeconomic trends, in order to draw attention to the need both for laws that are sensitive to these inequalities *and* for wider socioeconomic change that will assist in eliminating these inequalities (Boyd 1995).

It is also necessary to challenge the technical and expert discourses of science (Chunn, Mosoff this volume), economics (Bakker 1994; Philipps 1996), efficiency, and restructuring, and the apparent inevitability of restraint policies. All of these tend to render the gendered, racialized, and class-based nature and impact of the policies invisible (Kline this volume). The notion that current economic restructuring is necessary and inevitable, with its corresponding diminishing of the few opportunities that have been gained for disadvantaged groups (e.g., Armstrong this volume), must be revealed as false. Similarly, the perceived inevitability of the public/private divide and the gendered division of labour must be deconstructed. As the impact of restructuring and privatization on a wide range of groups in Canadian society is felt, new opportunities for collective resistance may emerge as the contradictions in neoconservative policies are revealed.

The problem is how to sustain such struggle in the public eye when social movements are losing the limited economic support from the state that some groups benefited from in the 1970s and 1980s. Women's issues and gender now often disappear in public debates on economic crises (e.g., Human Resources Development Canada 1994). For example, child poverty is often characterized as a problem that is conceptually separate from gendered inequalities. In Alberta's child welfare debates, the interest of Aboriginal communities in achieving self-government is treated as though it were undifferentiated historically and at present from the desire of various other communities to have more autonomy from the state, thus obscuring the unique political position of Aboriginal peoples (Kline this volume).

Progressive social movements must try to avoid being co-opted by the use of progressive discourses in aid of regressive ends, as has happened to some extent in Alberta (Kline this volume). Analysis of the potential and strategies of social movements and progressive struggle must be linked to shifting economic policies more than has been the case recently. In the times ahead, it will be important to show that the various groups that are affected by retrenchment and deficit panic discourses (Ralph 1995) are connected in their struggles. Rather than the women's movement prioritizing gender in an analysis of the impact of privatization and the redrawing of the public/private divide, the intersections between gender, class, race, culture, disability, sexual identity, and other power relations inherent in Canadian society must be explored.

Furthermore, globalization and international relations must be part of feminist analysis: economic restructuring and privatization are occurring at local, national, and international levels. Over the past two decades, women's groups from around the world have met in the context of United Nations conferences to develop women's rights and development initiatives, culminating in the September 1995 Beijing World Conference on Women. These conferences have contributed to an appreciation of the extent to which women's lives in the 'Third' World have been detrimentally affected by 'structural adjustment' programs, and the role of the International Monetary Fund and the World Bank in imposing these programs since the 1970s (Brodie 1994, 47).[9] Canadian feminists struggling against the effects of current globalization and restructuring have much to learn from Third World women. Moreover, it is crucial for Western feminists to understand the power relations that prevail between First and Third World countries; the role that our countries play in perpetuating the economic subordination of countries in the Third World; the actual dependency of our countries on those of the Third World in economic terms; and the interrelatedness of the issues that women are facing worldwide (Buss this volume).

Working within a coalition of progressive struggles thus is crucial in keeping the multiplicity of women's interests front and centre in the debates about the role of the public and private spheres. We hope that this book contributes to this process.

Outline of This Book

The authors in this book explore various ways in which the public/private divide plays out in women's lives and the extent to which an analysis of the public/private divide assists in understanding the dynamics of women's oppression. We have organized the book as follows. The first part, 'The Role of the State: Some Histories,' includes three chapters dealing with how the state helps to define 'public' and 'private' and regulates both spheres. Pat Armstrong offers an analysis of the shifting role of the state in regulating women's paid and unpaid work in the labour force and in families, especially since the Second World War. At present, as she demonstrates, the role of the state is once again being restructured. Dorothy Chunn presents an historical perspective on state regulation of sexuality, focusing on the early twentieth-century reform campaigns dealing with venereal disease. Her work shows that the state has always played a role in regulating the private sphere, but it is a role that changed with the rise of the welfare state and that shifts when different groups of women are at issue. She highlights the complex and changing ways in which the state, in conjunction with other social institutions, affects gender relations. Jennifer Koshan's chapter deals with the historical relationship between the Euro-Canadian state (and law) and male violence against women in the family. She highlights the approach that feminists have taken to violence against women, drawing on analysis of the public/private divide, and questions the adequacy of this approach in the lives of Aboriginal women.

The second part, 'Family, Home, and Work,' offers four chapters dealing with various aspects of the market/family or work/family divide and the role of state and law in defining that divide. Katherine Teghtsoonian first subjects to careful scrutiny the discourses implicated in the failure of the federal government to develop a meaningful child care policy. She reveals problematic assumptions about women's roles in the family and the labour force. Amanda Ocran's analysis of the resurgence of homework in the garment industry and its relationship to gender, race, and class then raises questions about feminist analysis and strategies regarding the work/family version of the public/private divide. Nitya Iyer examines whether state-run maternity and parental leave are actually effective in reducing the conflict between work and family experienced by many women. Both Teghtsoonian and Iyer develop an analysis of how some women are encouraged by state and law to engage in full-time motherhood, whereas others are discouraged. Finally, Fiona Kay's chapter on women lawyers offers a perspective on the difficulties that women's responsibility for children and domestic labour presents even to professional women.

The third part, 'Legal Regulation of Motherhood: Child Custody and Child Welfare,' deals with the regulation of mothers who are viewed as different from the normative model. Judith Mosoff shows that when mothers who are labelled as having mental disabilities are involved, the differences between the ostensibly 'private' field of child custody and the 'public' field of child welfare law crumble. Such mothers are often constructed as 'unfit.' Mosoff demonstrates the ability of the modern state to monitor 'private behaviour' through the mental health professions, in conjunction with law.

Susan Boyd then offers a critical analysis of the gendered discourses in the *Tyabji* case. Tyabji, a female politician, lost custody of her children largely on the grounds that her career and ambition were perceived to preclude her from devoting sufficient time to her private sphere caregiving responsibilities. Finally, Jenni Millbank demonstrates that for lesbian mothers who claim custody of their children in judicial fora, privacy almost inevitably is foregone; moreover, the invocation of privacy arguments offers little purchase in convincing courts of a mother's competence. All three chapters raise questions about feminist strategies in the field of child custody law, such as the primary caregiver presumption. This strategy may not be capable of addressing the problems experienced by mothers who are lesbian or who have mental disability labels.

In the fourth part, 'Current Challenges: Restructuring, Privatization, and Globalization,' the first two chapters by Claire Young and Marlee Kline address the trends of privatization and restructuring that currently dominate Canadian public policy. Young's chapter addresses how taxation law (an ostensibly public field) contributes to women's inequality in the fields of child care, child support, and pensions. Far from offering public support for women's economic independence, taxation law tends to reinforce the privatization of the costs of supporting reproduction and the elderly. Kline's chapter provides a vision of the future of the welfare state in an age of fiscal conservatism, through a case study on restructuring by the Alberta government of the delivery of child welfare services. The manipulation of images of 'family' and 'community,' and the use of progressive discourses for regressive ends are highlighted. Doris Buss then engages critically with feminist scholarship on the public/private divide, with a view to identifying both its strengths and its weaknesses in analysing problems in international law, in particular, the construction of Third World women in feminist discourses. Given the increasing globalization of issues of concern to women, her insights are of critical importance.

We hope that this book will not only offer insights about the reshaping of the public/private divide that is now under way, but also open conversations about the strategies that need to be employed to address the inequalities related to the manipulation of the public/private divide.

NOTES

I owe many debts of gratitude regarding the writing of this chapter, a version of which was presented at Capilano College, Vancouver, 24 Jan. 1996. The collaborative process involved in this book's creation expanded my analysis of the public/

private divide immeasurably. The comments of Doris Buss, Gillian Calder, Dorothy Chunn, Kristin Graver, Nitya Iyer, Fiona Kay, Marlee Kline, Jennifer Koshan, Judith Mitchell, Judith Mosoff, Amanda Ocran, Lisa Philipps, Katherine Teghtsoonian, and Claire Young were of great assistance. The research and editing assistance of Gillian Calder and Kristin Graver was invaluable, as was the financial support of the Social Sciences and Humanities Research Council (Women and Change program).

1 Within Canada, we focus mainly on federal laws and policies, and those in common law provinces, especially Ontario, Alberta, and British Columbia. Readers may consult the special issue of *Les Cahiers de Droit* (1995) 36(1), 'L'influence du féminisme sur le droit au Québec,' to obtain a sense of Québécois feminist engagement with law.
2 The latter body, which existed from 1973 to 1995, was established on the recommendation of the royal commission and advised the federal government and informed the public on matters of concern to women. It published numerous research documents relating to women's interests in fields such as employment, family, and politics. Its abolition in 1995 by the Liberal government was widely viewed as an effort to diminish the actions and voices of women in the backyard of government, and as a hostile reaction to the successes of the women's movement over the past two decades.
3 RSC 1985 (2nd Supp.), c. 23.
4 [1987] 1 SCR 1114.
5 The edited collection by Margaret Thornton (1995) was published after our manuscript was completed. Consequently, our chapters contain no references to the important contributions in that book.
6 See the excellent review of feminist work on ideology (esp. familial ideology) by Philipps and Young (1995), at 247–50 and 274–80.
7 *R. v O'Connor* [1995] 4 SCR 411.
8 [1992] 3 SCR 813.
9 These trends and their relevance to Canadian women became clear to me at a talk called 'Beyond Beijing' about the Beijing conference by Gillian Calder and Frances Wasserlein, Centre for Research on Women's Studies and Gender Relations, University of British Columbia, 6 Dec. 1995 (in remembrance of the lives of the fourteen women killed by a man at the University of Montreal on 6 Dec. 1989).

REFERENCES

Abner, Erika, Mary Jane Mossman, and Elizabeth Pickett. 1990. 'No More Than

Simple Justice: Assessing the Royal Commission Report on Women, Poverty and the Family.' *Ottawa Law Journal* 22, 573–605

Anderson, Karen L. 1987. 'Historical Perspectives on the Family.' In Karen Anderson et al., eds. *Family Matters: Sociology and Contemporary Canadian Families.* Toronto: Methuen, 21–39.

Andrew, Caroline. 1984. 'Women and the Welfare State.' *Canadian Journal of Political Science* 17, 667–83

Armstrong, Pat, and Hugh Armstrong. 1994. *The Double Ghetto: Canadian Women and Their Segregated Work*, 3rd ed. Toronto: McClelland and Stewart

Arnup, Katherine. 1989. '"Mothers Just Like Others:" Lesbians, Divorce, and Child Custody in Canada.' *Canadian Journal of Women and the Law* 3(1), 18–32

Bakker, Isabella, ed. 1994. *The Strategic Silence: Gender and Economic Policy.* London: Zed Books

– 1991. 'Pay Equity and Economic Restructuring: The Polarization of Policy?' In Janine Brodie, ed., *Women and Canadian Public Policy.* Toronto: Harcourt Brace, 254–80

Barrett, Michèle, and Mary McIntosh. 1982. *The Anti-social Family.* London: Verso

Beller, Andrea H., and John W. Graham. 1993. *Small Change: The Economics of Child Support.* New Haven and London: Yale University Press

Best, Steven, and Douglas Kellner. 1991. *Postmodern Theory: Critical Interrogations.* New York: Guilford Press

Bourgeault, Ron. 1991. 'Race, Class and Gender: Colonial Domination of Indian Women.' In Jesse Vorst et al. eds., *Race, Class, Gender: Bonds and Barriers.* Toronto: Society for Socialist Studies and Garamond, 88–117

Boyd, Susan B. 1995. "Can Law Challenge the Public/Private Divide? Women, Work and Family.' *Windsor Yearbook of Access to Justice* 15

– 1994a. 'Expanding the "Family" in Family Law: Recent Ontario Proposals on Same Sex Relationships.' *Canadian Journal of Women and the Law* 7(2): 545–63

– 1994b. '(Re)Placing the State: Family, Law and Oppression.' *Canadian Journal of Law and Society* 9(1): 39–73

– and Elizabeth A. Sheehy. 1986. 'Feminist Perspectives on Law: Canadian Theory and Practice.' *Canadian Journal of Women and the Law* 2(1), 1–52

Brockman, Joan. 1994. 'Leaving the Practice of Law: The Wherefores and the Whys.' *Alberta Law Review* 32, 116–180

– 1992. 'Bias in the Legal Profession: Perceptions and Experiences,' *Alberta Law Review* 30, 747–808

Brodie, Janine. 1995. *Politics on the Margins: Restructuring and the Canadian Women's Movement.* Halifax: Fernwood

– 1994. 'Shifting the Boundaries: Gender and the Politics of Restructuring.' In

Isabella Bakker, ed., *The Strategic Silence: Gender and Economic Policy*. London: Zed Books, 46–60

Canada. 1970. *Report of the Royal Commission on the Status of Women*. Ottawa: Information Canada. Florence Bird (Chair)

Charlesworth, Hilary, Christine Chinkin, and Shelley Wright. 1991. 'Feminist Approaches to International Law.' *American Journal of International Law* 85, 613–45

Chunn, Dorothy E. 1995. 'Feminism, Law, and Public Policy: "Politicizing the Personal."' In Nancy Mandell and Ann Duffy, eds., *Canadian Families: Diversity, Conflict and Change*. Toronto: Harcourt Brace, 177–210

– 1992. *From Punishment to Doing Good: Family Courts and Socialized Justice in Ontario, 1880–1940*. Toronto: University of Toronto Press

Clarke, Lorenne M.G. 1978. 'Privacy, Property, Freedom, and the Family.' In Richard Bronaugh, ed., *Philosophical Law*. Westport, CT: Greenwood Press, 167–87

Cook, Rebecca. 1992. 'Women's International Human Rights: A Bibliography.' *International Law and Politics* 24, 857–88

Cooper, Davina. 1993. 'An Engaged State: Sexuality, Governance, and the Potential for Change.' *Journal of Law and Society* 20(3), 257–75

Das Gupta, Tania. 1995. 'Families of Native Peoples, Immigrants, and People of Colour.' In Nancy Mandell and Ann Duffy, eds., *Canadian Families: Diversity, Conflict and Change*. Toronto: Harcourt Brace, 141–74

Dawson, T. Brettel, ed. 1993. *Women, Law and Social Change*, 2nd ed. North York, ON: Captus Press

Duchesne, Doreen. 1989. *Giving Freely: Volunteers in Canada*. Ottawa: Statistics Canada (cat. no. 71-535, no. 4)

Eichler, Margrit. 1990–1. 'The Limits of Family Law Reform or, The Privatization of Female and Child Poverty.' *Canadian Family Law Quarterly* 7, 59–84

Elliot, Faith Robertson. 1989. 'The Family: Private Arena or Adjunct of the State?' *Journal of Law and Society* 16(4), 443–63

Elshtain, Jean Bethke. 1981. *Public Man, Private Woman: Women in Social and Political Thought*. Princeton: Princeton University Press

Findlay, Sue. 1987. 'Facing the State: The Politics of the Women's Movement Reconsidered.' In Heather Jon Maroney and Meg Luxton, eds., *Feminism and Political Economy: Women's Work, Women's Struggles*. Toronto: Methuen, 31–50

Fineman, Martha Albertson. 1995. *The Neutered Mother, the Sexual Family and Other Twentieth Century Tragedies*. New York: Routledge

– and Roxanne Mykitiuk, eds. 1994. *The Public Nature of Private Violence*. New York: Routledge

Fudge, Judy. 1996. 'Fragmentation and Feminization: The Challenge of Equity for

Labour-Relations Policy.' In Janine Brodie, ed., *Women and Canadian Public Policy.* Toronto: Harcourt Brace, 57–87

– 1987. 'The Public/Private Distinction: The Possibilities of and the Limits to the Use of Charter Litigation to Further Feminist Struggles.' *Osgoode Hall Law Journal* 25(3), 485–554

– and Patricia McDermott, eds. 1991. *Just Wages: A Feminist Assessment of Pay Equity.* Toronto: University of Toronto Press

Gavigan, Shelley A.M. 1993. 'Paradise Lost, Paradox Revisited: The Implications of Familial Ideology for Feminist, Lesbian, and Gay Engagement to Law.' *Osgoode Hall Law Journal* 31(3), 589–624

Gavison, Ruth. 1992. 'Feminism and the Public/Private Distinction.' *Stanford Law Review* 45(1), 1–45

Goetz, Anne Marie. 1991. 'Feminism and the Claim to Know: Contradictions in Feminist Approaches to Women in Development.' In Rebecca Grant and Kathleen Newland, eds., *Gender and International Relations.* Bloomington and Indianapolis: Indiana University Press, 133–57

Goodall, Kay. 1990. '"Public and Private" in Legal Debate.' *International Journal of the Sociology of Law* 18, 445–8

Gramsci, Antonio. 1971. *Selections from the Prison Notebooks.* Quintin Hoare and Geoffrey Nowell Smith, eds. New York: International Publishers

Graycar, Regina, and Jenny Morgan. 1990. *The Hidden Gender of Law.* Annandale, NSW: Federation Press

Hall, Stuart. 1988. 'The Toad in the Garden: Thatcherism among the Theorists.' In Cary Nelson and Lawrence Grossberg, eds., *Marxism and the Interpretation of Culture.* Urbana and Chicago: University of Illinois Press, 35–57

Herman, Didi. 1994. *Rights of Passage: Struggles for Lesbian and Gay Legal Equality.* Toronto: University of Toronto Press

Human Resources Development Canada. 1994. *Agenda: Jobs and Growth. Improving Social Security in Canada: A Discussion Paper.* Ottawa: Human Resources Development Canada

Hunt, Alan. 1993. *Explorations in Law and Society: Toward a Constitutive Theory of Law.* New York and London: Routledge

Iyer, Nitya. 1994. 'Categorical Denials: Equality Rights and the Shaping of Social Identity.' *Queen's Law Journal* 19, 179–207

Iyer (Duclos), Nitya. 1993. 'Disappearing Women: Racial Minority Women in Human Rights Cases.' *Canadian Journal of Women and the Law* 6(1), 25–65

Kennedy, David. 1994. 'Receiving the International.' *Connecticut Journal of International Law* 10(1), 1–26

Kerber, Linda K. 1988. 'Separate Spheres, Female Worlds, Women's Place: The Rhetoric of Women's History.' *Journal of American History* 75(1), 9–39

Kline, Marlee. 1993. 'Complicating the Ideology of Motherhood: Child Welfare
Law and First Nation Women.' *Queen's Law Journal* 18(2), 306–42
– 1992. 'Child Welfare Law, "Best Interests of the Child" Ideology, and First
Nations.' *Osgoode Hall Law Journal* 30(2), 375–425
Lacey, Nicola. 1993. 'Theory into Practice? Pornography and the Public/Private
Dichotomy.' *Journal of Law and Society* 20(1), 93–113
Lasch, Christopher. 1977. *Haven in a Heartless World: The Family Beseiged.* New
York: Basic Books
MacKinnon, Catharine A. 1989. *Toward a Feminist Theory of the State.* Cambridge
and London: Harvard University Press
Macklin, Audrey. 1992. 'Foreign Domestic Worker: Surrogate Housewife or Mail
Order Servant?' *McGill Law Journal* 37, 681–760
Monture, Patricia A. 1989. 'A Vicious Circle: Child Welfare and First Nations.'
Canadian Journal of Women and the Law 3(1), 1–17
Monture-Angus, Patricia. 1995. *Thunder in My Soul: A Mohawk Woman Speaks.*
Halifax: Fernwood
Mossman, Mary Jane. 1994a. 'Lawyers and Family Life: New Directions for the
1990's (Part One).' *Feminist Legal Studies* 2(1), 61–82
– 1994b. 'Lawyers and Family Life: New Directions for the 1990's (Part Two).'
Feminist Legal Studies 2(2), 159–182
– 1994c. '"Running Hard to Stand Still" The Paradox of Family Law Reform.' *Dal-
housie Law Journal* 17, 5–33
– 1989. 'Individualism and Community: Family as Mediating Concept.' In Allan
C. Hutchinson and Leslie J.M. Green, eds., *Law and the Community: The End of
Individualism?* Toronto: Carswell, 205–18
– and Morag MacLean. 1986. 'Family Law and Social Welfare: Toward a New
Equality.' *Canadian Journal of Family Law* 5(1), 79–110
Mukhopadhyay, Swapna. 1994. 'The Impact of Structural Adjustment Policies on
Women: Some General Observations Relating to Conceptual Bias.' In Isabella
Bakker, ed., *The Strategic Silence: Gender and Economic Policy.* London: Zed
Books, 158–64
Ng, Roxana. 1988. *The Politics of Community Services: Immigrant Women. Class
and State.* Toronto: Garamond Press
O'Donovan, Katherine. 1985. *Sexual Divisions in Law.* London: Weidenfeld and
Nicolson
Olsen, Frances E. 1985. 'The Myth of State Intervention in the Family.' *University
of Michigan Journal of Law Reform* 18(4), 835–64
– 1983. 'The Family and the Market: A Study of Ideology and Legal Reform.' *Har-
vard Law Review* 96(7), 1497–1578
Pateman, Carole. 1988. *The Sexual Contract.* Cambridge: Polity Press

- 1983. 'Feminist Critiques of the Public/Private Dichotomy.' In Stanley Benn and Gerald Haus, eds., *Private and Public in Social Life*. London: Croom Helm
Philipps, Lisa. 1996. 'Discursive Deficits: A Feminist Perspective on the Power of Technical Knowledge in Fiscal Law and Policy.' *Canadian Journal of Law and Society* 11(1), 141–76
- and Margot Young. 1995. 'Sex, Tax and the *Charter*: A Review of *Thibaudeau* v. *Canada*.' *Review of Constitutional Studies* 2(2), 221–304
Pothier, Dianne. 1996. 'M'aider, Mayday: Section 15 of the *Charter* in Distress.' *National Journal of Constitutional Law* 6(3), 295–345
Prentice, Alison, et al. 1988. *Canadian Women: A History*. Toronto: Harcourt Brace Jovanovich
Pulkingham, Jane. 1994. 'Private Troubles, Private Solutions: Poverty among Divorced Women and the Politics of Support Enforcement and Child Custody Determination.' *Canadian Journal of Law and Society* 9(2), 73–97
Ralph, Diana. 1995. 'Tripping the Iron Heel.' Paper presented at Canadian Social Welfare Policy Conference, Vancouver, B.C., 27 June 1995
Roberts, Julian V., and Renate M. Mohr, eds. 1994. *Confronting Sexual Assault: A Decade of Legal and Social Change*. Toronto: University of Toronto Press
Rose, Nikolas. 1987. 'Beyond the Public/Private Division: Law, Power and the Family.' *Journal of Law and Society* 14(1), 61–76
Sheppard, Colleen. 1995. 'Uncomfortable Victories and Unanswered Questions: Lessons from *Moge*.' *Canadian Journal of Family Law* 12(2), 283–329
Statistics Canada. 1995. *Women in Canada*, 3rd ed. Ottawa: Minister of Industry
Thornton, Margaret, ed. 1995. *Public and Private: Feminist Legal Debates*. Melbourne: Oxford University Press
- 1991. 'The Public/Private Dichotomy: Gendered and Discriminatory.' *Journal of Law and Society* 18(4), 448–63
Ursel, Jane. 1992. *Private Lives, Public Policy: 100 Years of State Intervention in the Family*. Toronto: Women's Press
Valverde, Mariana. 1991. *The Age of Light, Soap and Water: Moral Reform in English Canada, 1885–1925*. Toronto: McClelland and Stewart
Vickers, Jill, Pauline Rankin, and Christine Appelle. 1993. *Politics as if Women Mattered: A Political Analysis of the National Action Committee on the Status of Women*. Toronto: University of Toronto Press
Walker, Gillian A. 1990. *Family Violence and the Women's Movement*. Toronto: University of Toronto Press
Wallace, Elisabeth. 1950. 'The Origin of the Welfare State in Canada, 1867–1900.' *Canadian Journal of Economics and Political Science* 16, 383–93
Waring, Marilyn. 1988. *If Women Counted: A New Feminist Economics*. San Francisco: Harper and Row

Watson, Sophie, ed. 1990. *Playing the State: Australian Feminist Interventions.*
London: Verso

Wilson, Bertha (chair). 1993. Task Force on Gender Equality in the Legal Profession, *Touchstones for Change: Equality, Diversity and Accountability.* Ottawa: Canadian Bar Association

Young, Claire. 1994. 'Taxing Times for Lesbians and Gay Men: Equality at What Cost?' *Dalhousie Law Journal* 17(2), 534–59

Zaretsky, Eli. 1976. *Capitalism, the Family and Personal Life.* New York: Harper and Row

PART 1
THE ROLE OF THE STATE: SOME HISTORIES

2

Restructuring Public and Private: Women's Paid and Unpaid Work

PAT ARMSTRONG

The terms 'public' and 'private' have at least two meanings, both of which have significant implications for women and their work. At times, we use 'public' to refer to those services, supports, and regulations established by governments. The term 'private,' in this case, refers to what is not done by governments. Although this kind of 'private' can include both for-profit and not-for-profit organizations, as well as households, we are usually thinking of divisions within the formal economy when we talk of the private and the public sectors. At other times, we use 'public' to refer to the world outside the private household, to what is done in the public sphere. These two meanings of 'public' and 'private' often overlap, as do both kinds of private and public spheres.

The extent of the overlap is shaped in many ways by government initiatives. Governments frequently provide services and supports that would otherwise be the responsibility of individuals or households, especially of women in households. They also provide services that might otherwise be available from either for-profit or not-for-profit organizations. In providing services, governments are creating paid work for providers, most of whom are women. The form the service provision takes, then, has a profound impact on what gets done in and out of the household and on what kinds of jobs are open for women. Similarly, government regulations often set the conditions for women's employment in the labour force and for their work in the home. Indeed, they can heavily influence whether or not women work in the private or public sphere. Of course, the private in both senses of the term helps shape how and where governments intervene. Moreover, this structuring of private and public is both actual and ideological, involving an allocation of tasks and responsibilities in physical and ideological terms. The two are inseparable.

In the period following the Second World War, governments at the municipal, provincial, and national levels in Canada were faced with considerable pressure from unions, women's organizations, community groups, and returning veterans to provide services and supports that would allow individuals and families 'to meet the heavy disabilities of serious illness, prolonged unemployment, accident and premature death' (Marsh 1975). Keynesian economic theory taught that another depression could only be avoided through state support of individual purchasing power. War taught the importance of a healthy population and employers demanded not only a healthy but also an educated labour force. War also contributed to the enormous expansion in state intervention and made people accustomed to looking to the state for action (Panitch 1977).

In the aftermath of the war, in response to these pressures and guided by this theory, the state rapidly expanded in areas such as education, unemployment insurance, pensions, health, and welfare. Although some of these services and supports had been provided previously by the private sector, by charitable organizations, and by families, it was clear that this kind of support was insufficient. The depression had certainly demonstrated that unemployment was not primarily the fault of the individual. Many people did not have families, and many families did not have the necessary resources to purchase or otherwise provide the kinds of supports required to face severe illness, unemployment, or a lengthy old age. Many charitable organizations did not have the resources either. Those that did often restricted their services to particular groups, such as those with religious affiliation or those from certain cultural backgrounds, or set conditions, such as financial need or age, that excluded a wide range of individuals. Private services were expensive and also usually set conditions that excluded large numbers of people, particularly the many women who did not have income from paid work or other sources (see, e.g., Yalnizyan 1994).

Moreover, the nature of these services and of the economy changed significantly after the war. New technological developments in health care improved treatment at the same time as they rendered formal care increasingly beyond the means of many individuals and families, as machines such as X-rays and procedures such as heart surgery were introduced. Employers increasingly demanded a workforce that had formal education beyond what the majority could access. Improved conditions of work and living, along with compulsory retirement practices and new medical developments, meant that many more people lived into old age. The majority of the elderly were women, and most had no pensions from paid work. Many employers too had come to recognize the value of sharing the risks, especially those faced with strong unions demanding health care and protection against unemployment (see, e.g., Taylor 1978). The economic boom that was both a product of and contributor to what has come to be called the welfare state also helped women's groups to demand more regulation of relationships in the private and public spheres (Armstrong 1996; Armstrong and Armstrong 1988). The private and the public in both senses of the terms were restructured.

But as the economic boom began to fade in the late 1960s, attacks on the welfare state became more vociferous. Employers increasingly objected to the hard-won employment practices in the state sector and to state regulation of the private, for-profit sector, blaming both for the recession. Employers sought a more disciplined workforce and the right to invest in areas such as health care now dominated by the state. Financial institutions within and outside the country used the debt that they had helped create to demand that states downsize and deregulate (Martin 1993). There were increasing calls for a reduction in the public sector and for deregulation of the private sector. High unemployment levels weakened the claims of those defending extensive state intervention and meant employers faced weaker unions. In response, governments have been dismantling the welfare state, transferring much of the work to the private sector in the formal economy and to the private sphere. At the same time, they have been deregulating in ways that let private decisions of individuals govern the conditions of work and of relations in both the private and public spheres.

This chapter examines the consequences of restructuring for the conditions and relations of women's work, as well as for the construction of the public and private in the two senses of those terms. States have always intervened and regulated, but these take different forms at different times (see Chunn this volume). The impact on women also varies over time and for women from different groups and in different positions. Such state strategies both shape and are shaped by women's individual and collective efforts. However, women's strength not only varies with economic conditions but also with the structuring of public and private spheres and sectors and with their own organizing strategies. The restructuring that took place in the postwar period transformed women's lives and reflected their transformations. The current restructuring is once more altering women's lives, and cannot be understood without an analysis of what has gone before. This, then, is the purpose of this chapter.

The Public as Formal Economy

Education

The postwar period saw a dramatic growth in the number of women remaining in school beyond the elementary level. Between 1951 and 1991 the proportion of women 15 to 24 years of age who were students more than doubled from 21 per cent to 52 per cent (Armstrong and Armstrong 1994, Table 1). In the 1950s three times more men than women received bachelor or first professional degrees, six times more men than women graduated with master's degrees, and women accounted for only 6 per cent of those granted doctorates (Statistics Canada 1990, 47). By 1991 women accounted for the majority of those enrolled in bachelor and first professional degree courses, almost half of those in master's programs, and just over a third of those doing doctoral work (Statistics Canada 1994a, 6).

This change was the result of the large growth in public, post-secondary educational institutions, the increase in government economic support for students, and changes in admissions policies as well as in attitudes. Many of the new public colleges did not charge tuition fees, and tuition fees in universities were kept relatively low. The state covered the overwhelming majority of the costs. Moreover, most students were eligible for the federally funded Canada Student Loans and many were also eligible for bursaries. These developments reflected the government's belief that investment in human capital was necessary for economic growth. They also reflected demands from students based on studies demonstrating that the high costs meant access to education was based mainly on sex and class (see, e.g., Porter, Porter, and Blishen 1973). Few of the studies used to justify these changes considered race or disability; however, we now know that these groups had even more difficulty getting advanced education (Henry et al. 1995; Satzewich 1992).

A number of factors had discriminated against women entering post-secondary educational institutions. With low wages, young women could not earn as much working part-time as young men, so that women required higher loans and thus ended up with large 'negative dowries' (Porter, Porter, and Blishen 1973). Moreover, many faculties had quotas limiting the number of female students, quotas that were eliminated as a result of student research and demonstrations. Bursaries, and free or low tuition fees, along with other changes in funding and in admission policies made post-secondary institutions more accessible to women, although most women still needed part-time employment to meet their expenses. Nearly half of the women under age 24 had part-time employment in 1994, and almost two-thirds of them worked part-time because they were going to school (Statistics Canada 1995b, Tables 6.7 and 6.8). Together, these developments contributed to significant changes in women's educational attainment. By 1991, 32 per cent of the women aged 20 to 24 had a post-secondary diploma or a university degree compared with 22 per cent of the men in that age group (ibid., Table 5.2).

There were still differences among women that related to race, class, and region. And there may well be differences, not recorded in the data, related to sexual preference. However, women from all groups have significantly improved their position relative to that of men and relative to women's position in the 1950s. Both immigrant women and visible minority women are somewhat more likely than Canadian-born and white women to have university degrees. It is difficult to tell from the data to what extent this pattern reflects government immigration regulations favouring those with degrees as opposed to practices within Canada that have improved access for various groups (ibid., 120, 136). The data also indicate that just over half the Aboriginal women between the ages of 15 and 24 were in school in 1991, representing a significant increase in participation over the past thirty years. However, the participation rate of Aboriginal women remains below that of other women in Canada (ibid., 151). These data on Aboriginal women suggest that, although government intervention has contributed to improved access, it has not eliminated differences. In other words, state intervention in terms of economic support, investment, and regulation significantly influenced women's participation in educational institutions. Although this intervention certainly did not eliminate the influence of class, sex, race, or region, it did reduce their impact.

Paid Work

The postwar period has witnessed an enormous expansion not only in post-secondary education but also in women's participation in the paid workforce. In 1951 less than one in four women over age 15 was counted as part of the labour force. By 1991 this was the case for 60 per cent of women over 15 years of age (Armstrong and Armstrong 1994, Table 1). The increase was primarily accounted for by the movement of married women into paid work. The most dramatic increase has been among mothers with children under age 16 at home. In 1993 more than two-thirds of such mothers were in the labour force, and this was the case even for women who had children under 6 years of age, if they lived in two-parent families.

However, by contrast to the improving situation of married women, only 46 per cent of lone-parent women with young children were in the labour force (Statistics Canada 1994a, Table 6.3). A number of factors contributed to the increased number of women in the paid labour force.

Economic Need
The most important factor in the rising female participation rates was economic. In the case of single women, the need for earned income seems obvious and continuous. Few would challenge the notion that older single women, at least, need the earned income. Although some may argue that many younger single women can turn to their parents for economic support, the high proportion of young women who are both in school and in the labour force suggests that most need to at least supplement parental support (Armstrong 1995).

Economic need also seems an obvious reason for the labour force participation of separated and divorced women. Their numbers have increased over the past two decades, partly as a result of government regulation. Pressure, especially from women's groups, helped to create legislation that made it easier to divorce or separate, and gave women more access to the assets of the marriage (Mossman 1994). But these legal changes seldom left separated or divorced women free of economic need. Governments, and support enforcement agencies, have not been very effective in ensuring that men followed the rules, and only a minority of men make support payments after a marriage ends. 'In Ontario, for example, it has recently been estimated that there are 90,000 unpaid support orders' (Galarneau 1992, 10). Although some men choose not to pay, others may not be in a financial position to pay, given rising unemployment levels for men. Lone parenting is most common among Aboriginal and Black women (Lindsay 1992, Table 1.9), and the men from both of these groups have high levels of unemployment. The key point is that even when men can, and do, pay, the amounts are too low to support a family. In 1988 men who did provide support paid (per year) 'an average amount of $4,500 and a median amount of $3,000' (Galarneau 1992, 11). The inadequacy of such payments becomes obvious when compared with the total income of Ontario welfare recipients. In 1989 the Ontario government assumed that the absolute minimum income required for a woman living alone with one dependent child was $12,539 per year (National Council of Welfare 1990–1, Table 2).

Separated and divorced women certainly need money, but many of them have difficulty finding decent employment. If there are children from the marriage, they are most likely to be left in the custody of their mothers

(Statistics Canada 1995b). The high cost, scarcity, and low quality of day care services make it difficult for these women to take full-time paid work, although some are able to take advantage of government-subsidized day care. These subsidies may help to explain why a higher proportion of lone-parent families use day care services regularly, compared with two-parent families (Lindsay 1992, Table 2.13). Many lone-parent mothers have foregone their education in order to support their husbands, and many more have interrupted their paid employment career in order to care for husbands and children. Both factors make it more difficult for separated and divorced women to find decent work and help to explain why their participation rates are significantly lower than those of other women (Boyd 1977; Dulude 1984; National Council of Welfare 1990).

Government assistance at the federal, provincial, and municipal levels has allowed many of these women to survive, especially while their children are young. 'On average, transfer payments made up 30% of the income of these families, compared with 13% for lone-parent families headed by men and just 7% for two-parent families with children' (Lindsay 1992, 37). Although government support often limited women's alternatives and seldom kept them above the poverty line, it did provide for their basic needs. Moreover, pressure from a variety of groups helped reduce the surveillance that had once been a central feature of support and rules such as the one that cancelled payments if traces of a man were found in the house were removed in some jurisdictions (Gavigan 1996, 265–7). Education and language programs designed with such women in mind also improved their opportunities, although many of these programs were limited in scope and distribution. In short, government intervention permitted some women to leave their marriages with some assets and provided some support, but it left one in two single mothers living below the poverty line, many of them ill-equipped for the labour force (National Council of Welfare 1990).

Elderly women are also often in need of income, given that few have pensions from paid employment and many are widowed or married to men with no or low pensions. This pattern will not change significantly in the future because the number of men covered by employer-sponsored pension plans is declining, and the number of women covered by such plans is significantly below that of men (Frenken and Master 1992). The labour force participation of elderly women has not grown, however, in part because most have little labour market experience, and many have low levels of formal education. Another important reason for their low participation rate in the postwar period is universal government pension schemes.

Indeed, the major factor explaining the decline in poverty among elderly women is government transfer payments of various sorts. In 1990 the average income of women age 65 and over was $15,300 a year, and most of this came from federal pensions (Norland 1994, 46).

The economic need of married women is less obvious and more often challenged. However, study after study in the late 1960s and early 1970s demonstrated that there was a clear connection between husband's income and wife's labour force participation. The lower the husband's income, the more likely the wife was to be in the labour force (Gunderson 1976; Ostry 1968; Skoulas 1974; Spencer and Featherstone 1970). With less than 20 per cent of husband–wife households dependent on one male income earner, however, it is no longer possible to study the relationship in this way. But a great deal of other evidence indicates that married women's economic need has increased.

Since the 1960s there has been a growing income disparity among heterosexual families. The value of the male wage relative to prices started to decline then and has decreased more rapidly in recent years. Two things countered this growing inequality: increasing female labour force participation and government transfer payments (Armstrong and Armstrong 1994, Chapter 6; Morissette, Myles, and Picot 1993). In 1990 wives' income in dual-earner households accounted on average for just under 30 per cent of the household income, while husbands' income made up 56 per cent, and the rest was transfer payments (Statistics Canada 1992, 9). In 60 per cent of households the addition of a woman's income was not sufficient to keep the family income from declining. In many others a woman's income was what prevented household income from deteriorating further. Clearly economic need was a major factor in married women's growing labour force participation, even though governments contributed significantly to household income.

The rise in female labour force participation over the past thirty years, then, partly reflected the fact that the growing number of single women staying in school needed at least part-time income to support their studies. It also reflected the economic need of the increasing number of women who were separated and divorced. As well, as male wages failed to keep up with household economic requirements, it reflected married women's growing need for income. But to some extent this economic need was alleviated by government transfer payments and services in kind.

Demand

While women's economic need was increasing, so was the demand for their labour. Whether we look at industrial growth or occupational growth, the same picture emerges. Jobs grew where women have traditionally worked and where women are perceived to be most likely to have the skills considered necessary.

In 1951, 45 per cent of all employed men worked in mining, logging, agriculture, fishing, construction, and transportation. By 1991, however, jobs in these industries accounted for only 20 per cent of all employment and for less than 30 per cent of male work (Statistics Canada 1993, Table 1). Many men have found highly paid, unionized jobs in these industries. Indeed, to a large extent it was just such jobs that made it possible for many men to be the sole economic support for a family. But these jobs are disappearing. Meanwhile, jobs have been growing in the service industries, and a majority of these new jobs went to women. In 1951 more than two-thirds of employed women worked in the service sector. By 1991 this was the case for just over 80 per cent of them (Armstrong and Armstrong 1994, Table 2).

Although jobs have been growing throughout the service sector, the growth has been particularly strong in the public sector. In 1991 a third of all employed women worked in health and social services, education, or government services. Public sector employment was also important for men but only 16 per cent of them, just half the proportion of women, had jobs in these areas (Statistics Canada 1993, Table 1). The expansion of the public sector meant more paid jobs for women, especially when the work involved the provision of services to people.

Not surprisingly, the same kind of picture emerges if we look at occupations instead of industries. Growth was rapid in traditionally female jobs. Women were, and continue to be, highly concentrated in clerical, sales, and service work. While 55 per cent of women employed in 1993 worked in such jobs, this was the case for just over a quarter of the men (Statistics Canada 1994a, Table 2.8).

These broad industrial and occupational divisions hide even greater segregation. Women are not only segregated into certain industries and occupations, they are also segregated into female-dominated jobs. Of the 200 jobs selected in the 1991 Census summary, 35 are at least 70 per cent female and 81 are at least 70 per cent male. More than two-thirds of the women, 68 per cent of them, are employed in these 35 female-dominated jobs (Armstrong 1993, Tables 1 and 2). Among these are 15 jobs that could be described as belonging to the broader public sector and many of the others, such as those doing clerical or laundry work, may be paid by the state. Given that this is where so many employed women work and given the rise in female labour force participation, it seems clear that there was a significant growth in the demand for female labour. Some women did move into traditionally male-dominated work, but most responded to the growing demand for female-dominated jobs.

The gendered segregation is not limited to the kinds of work women do, however. It is also found in terms of wages. The salaries in the female-dominated jobs range from $13,037 to $37,694, while those for male-dominated occupations go from $16,135 to $111,261. The only female-dominated occupations paying $30,000 or more in 1990 were dieticians and nutritionists, elementary and kindergarten teachers, librarians, archivists and conservators, nurses, occupational therapists, physiotherapists, and radiological technologists and technicians (Armstrong 1993, Tables 1 and 2). Most of the women in these higher-paid occupations are paid directly or indirectly by governments.

The wage segregation is particularly evident if we look at the ten lowest and ten highest paid occupations. Women accounted for only 20 per cent of those in the ten highest paid occupations, but made up over 70 per cent of those in the ten lowest paid occupations. While nearly 5 per cent of employed males were in the ten highest paid occupations, this was the case for just under 2 per cent of the employed women. Meanwhile, nearly 6 per cent of women worked in the ten lowest paid jobs, while just over 1 per cent of the employed men were in such jobs (Armstrong and Armstrong 1994, Table 9). Clearly the demand in low wage jobs grew.

There is yet another kind of segregation in the labour force that also helps to explain the rising demand for female labour. Since 1975, the number of part-time jobs has more than doubled (Pold 1994). Young people are more likely than older people to work part-time. Nevertheless, the majority of part-time work is done by those between the ages of 25 and 54, and most of these part-time workers are women (ibid., 16). And although many women work part-time in the labour force in order to do their other job at home, a growing number are involuntary part-time workers who take part-time employment because these jobs are the only ones available (Noreau 1994). In 1993 nearly 70 per cent of all part-time workers were female, and close to 80 per cent of part-time employees 25 years of age or over were women. More than a quarter of employed women held part-time jobs, but only a third of these women said they did not want full-time work (Statistics Canada 1994b, Tables 10, 18, and 19).

Women are also more likely than men to do paid work at home, and this work has also been growing (see also Ocran this volume). In 1991, 56 per cent of those working some or all of their scheduled hours at home were

women. Whereas all of those giving family responsibilities as their reason
for taking such work were women, less than half of the women doing paid
work at home gave this reason. Women may do paid work at home for
other reasons, such as the lack of available jobs outside the home, health
hazards in the workplace, or cultural pressures to avoid workplaces, among
others. Three-quarters of the women doing homework were employed
full-time, and the overwhelming majority were not unionized (Siroonian
1993).

Overall, while women's labour force participation has grown dramatically, the segregation of the labour force has remained remarkably stable
throughout the postwar period. This pattern suggests that there was a
growing demand for workers in traditionally female areas and in low-paid
and part-time work. Much of the work was in the public sector, and more
of the work was homework.

Conditions of Paid Work and Ideas about Work
Rising female labour force participation was accompanied by growing
demands for better conditions of work. Women were brought together in
large workplaces, and more of them stayed in the job for a long period of
time. A significant number joined unions, even though the conditions set
by the state for union organizing often made this difficult (White 1980).
Less than a quarter of employed women belonged to unions in 1970; by
1992 close to a third were unionized (Statistics Canada 1985, Table 8, and
1995b, Table 6.12). Women's groups of various kinds were also important
in changing workplace conditions, especially in relation to state intervention. The Royal Commission on the Status of Women (Canada 1970) both
reflected and affected the efforts of these women's groups. Conditions
improved in a variety of ways.

In the period of consolidation in women's participation, women's average wages improved both absolutely and in relation to those of men.
'Between 1970 and 1980, the real average wage of men increased by 14%,
from $26,200 in 1970 to $29,900 in 1980, and that of women by 15% from
$13,700 to $15,700' (Rashid 1993, 17). While women employed full-time,
full-year averaged only 60 per cent of the equivalent male wage in the early
1970s, they were earning 72 per cent of the male wage in the early 1990s
(Statistics Canada 1994a, Table 4.1). Because so many women are employed
part-time, the overall wage gap is much larger. If all earners are taken into
account, women were paid only 64 per cent of what men were paid in 1992,
but this still represented an improvement over 47 per cent in 1971 (ibid.).

Of course, average wages hide inequalities among women. Unionized women did significantly better than those without a union. For example, in 1988 unionized professional women earned $101 more per week than did those without a union, and clerical workers with a union earned $108 more than non-unionized clerical workers (Statistics Canada 1992, Table 20). Although there was little difference between immigrant and non-immigrant women in terms of wages, visible minority women were paid less than other women. 'In 1990, the average employment income for visible minority women was $24,700, about $1,400 less than other women who earned an average of $26,000' (Statistics Canada 1995b, 123, 138). Aboriginal women averaged over $2,000 less than non-Aboriginal women (ibid., 152). However, women's wages in general are low, with nearly 60 per cent of women earners paid less than $20,000 a year in 1993 (Statistics Canada 1995c, Table 1). At the same time as so many women were at the bottom of the earnings categories, there was a small decrease in the number of women in the top income bracket. Moreover, the inequalities among women remain much smaller than those among men.

Unions clearly played a significant role in raising women's average wage, particularly in the public sector where more than half the women union members worked. Women's groups' successful demand for legislation requiring first equal pay for equal work and then equal pay for work of equal value was also important (Fudge and McDermott 1991). The prohibition of discrimination in determining benefits also helped improve women's economic position. Less obvious was the raising of the minimum wage and the requirement that this minimum be the same for women and men. Women are almost twice as likely as men to work at minimum wage, the only pay protection many women get. 'Close to a quarter of a million adult women worked for the minimum wage or less sometime in 1986' (Akyeampong 1989, 10). However, even minimum wage did not protect many women from poverty. 'Women accounted for 61% of adult low-paid workers who collected welfare' (ibid., 16).

Similarly, minimum employment standards legislation was particularly important for women, because for many the legislation is the only protection they have from employers who resist providing vacations or safe conditions of work. Those who are excluded from the legislation are especially vulnerable (Ocran this volume). Indeed, that the state specifically excludes some women from such protection indicates its contradictory role in relation to women. In the case of domestic workers, for example, the state has not only limited the application of minimum standards. It has also restricted their access to other employment if they come from other countries, as many do (Carty 1994).

In addition to pay and minimum standards legislation, the state introduced other measures that helped women obtain and keep employment. Human rights and employment equity legislation are obvious examples. Sexual harassment became recognized as sex discrimination, and employers were prohibited from discriminating on the basis of marital status and from laying off or dismissing pregnant women (Majury 1991). Indeed, the state went even farther, requiring that women be granted maternity leave and that unemployment insurance be paid to pregnant women who met particular employment requirements (see Iyer this volume). Unions, too, fought for additional rights for pregnant women, including fully paid and extended maternity leave, thus ensuring that some employers went beyond the minimum required by the state (White 1980). The state has not been willing, however, to extend full rights to lesbian women, particularly if it requires defining their relationships as 'family' (see Boyd 1994).

Many women continued to face workplace hazards and to receive low pay. Nevertheless, both collective bargaining and state intervention improved women's conditions of work in the labour force. In some cases the intervention by states and unions has served to increase differences among women; in others it had a very limited impact on women's work. As Mossman (1995, 211) so neatly put it, we have 'a legal system that feminists have used regularly and often successfully to advance women's claims, but which has, perhaps just as often, rejected or undermined such claims.'

Unquestionably, inequalities and barriers remain. For example, although immigrant women are only slightly underrepresented in professional and managerial work compared with other women, they are still disproportionately slotted into manufacturing work (Statistics Canada 1995b, 122). Visible minority women with university degrees are more likely than other women with university degrees to do clerical work and to be in sales, service, and manual jobs (ibid., 137). Aboriginal women are the least likely of all women to have professional or managerial jobs, and women with disabilities face higher rates of unemployment than other women. Moreover, some programs are administered in ways that perpetuate inequalities. But most women have been better off with state intervention and union support, even though they have not shared equally in the gains.

The Private as Household

The dramatic changes in education and in labour force participation in the postwar period were not accompanied by similarly dramatic changes in the household. Domestic work has remained primarily 'women's work,' whether or not they also work in the labour force. Research in the early 1970s (Clark and Harvey 1976) and in the early 1990s (Ornstein and Haddad 1991) demonstrated that the work of cleaning, cooking, shopping, and child care is primarily women's work. This is the case whether or not the research was done in Vancouver (Meissner et al. 1975), Sudbury (Wilkinson 1992), or the Great Northern Peninsula of Newfoundland (Sinclair and Felt 1992). Male contributions to household work have increased somewhat over time, and their contributions vary somewhat with education and class. Unemployed men help more than others, especially with child care. But most of the regular domestic work is still 'women's work.'

The same is true of care for elderly parents or for other adults who are ill or disabled. The number of people requiring such care has grown considerably in the postwar years as a result of new medical technologies and improved living conditions. A study undertaken for the Conference Board of Canada (MacBride-King 1990, 12) found that 16 per cent of the respondents provided care for an elderly or disabled family member. Another survey found that women accounted for two-thirds of those providing parent care (Stone 1994, 50).

Although women receive little support in their domestic chores from either their spouses or the state, they do receive some help in child care. A recent national survey found that 57 per cent of Canadian children 'under the age of 13 participate in at least one non-parental child care arrangement in a given week' (Goelman et al. 1993, 13). The federal, provincial, and municipal governments have not moved very far or very fast into the provision of day care (Teghtsoonian this volume), but they have provided some support in the form of subsidies to low-income mothers, in the form of capital subsidies to non-profit centres, and in the form of regulations for care. Some after-school and lunch programs, along with expanded public recreational facilities and publicly supported weekend events have also helped women with their parenting work.

The state became much more active during the 1960s and 1970s in terms of services for the elderly and the disabled. These services were appropriately criticized for the way they treated residents, for failing to be culturally sensitive, and for perpetuating some forms of inequality (see, e.g., Grant 1991; Northcott 1991). Nevertheless, state provision of these services meant both that more women with the required skills were paid to do the work in the labour force and that other women, many of whom did not have the necessary skills, the time, or the desire, were not required to do the work without pay in the home.

The state also intervened to offer some protection to women in the home. In response to pressure from women's groups and to pressure from those women working within government on women's issues, the state supported research on household relations. This research, along with that done by women's groups, accompanied by continued demands for intervention, resulted in the state making criminal laws more sensitive to wife battering and making wife rape illegal (Koshan this volume; Walker 1990). The state helped support women who left abusive relations through counselling services and group homes. Many women gained greater control over their own bodies, as both birth control and abortion became legal (Kleiber and Light 1978; McLaren 1992). But disabled women remained significantly disadvantaged in all respects, from protection from abuse to access to financial or emotional support and their right to decide about care (Statistics Canada 1995b). Although much of this state initiative has been criticized for its structure, content, and implementation (Koshan this volume), it did nevertheless help many women. State regulations on housing and household products also helped make the home safer, although many significant hazards remain (Rosenberg 1990).

Laws were also changed to ensure not only that women had a right to a division of the marital property on divorce, but also to some of the pensions earned by their spouse. Not all women were successful in acquiring the benefits that the law appeared to offer (Mossman 1995, 1994), even when they were helped by state-supported legal aid programs. Women whose first language was not English or French experienced particular problems in gaining access to such programs. Moreover, these family law rights were not, in general, extended to gay and lesbian couples (Boyd 1994).

Thus, the state has made the private sphere of family relations somewhat more of a public concern. This development is in many ways consistent with the old feminist slogan claiming that the personal is political. In some cases, such as social welfare and child welfare, this approach has meant that the state invaded the privacy of the home and served to perpetuate unequal relations (Mosoff this volume). State intervention also has often meant more protection for women and less unpaid work for women.

Redefining the Public/Private Divide

In the postwar period, then, the state expanded enormously in terms of services. Some of these services were provided directly by governments at various levels. Others were provided mainly by non-profit organizations that were paid by the state. In both cases the services were primarily delivered by women. And these women were much more likely than other women to be unionized and to have decent conditions of work.

At the same time the state increasingly regulated the for-profit and not-for-profit sectors. A range of legislation and regulations helped protect women from various hazards and types of exploitation. Some of this intervention required that women be treated like men, while other measures recognized women's unequal position in the market and their different roles in reproduction. Although not all women were protected by such state initiatives as labour codes, and although much of the legislation remained unenforced, poorly enforced, or inappropriately interpreted, many women did benefit from minimum protections. Moreover, women working within the legal system often helped overcome such problems in the legislation or used it to push for additional reform.

In both providing services and regulating other industries, the state was redefining what was public and what was private. In the process, it was altering the power structure. Certainly, the state was often far from democratic and egalitarian in process, content, or even intent, but at least it opened possibilities for women and provided some protections against employers and spouses and against extreme poverty and illness. The for-profit sector had been limited to some extent already by unions, but the state further limited the capacity of employers to treat women unfairly and required that some publicly determined standards be kept. It established a different kind of level playing field, one that required employers to accept some non-market rules and where an attempt was made to reduce inequality between the players.

Restructuring Public and Private Today

From the 1950s to the 1980s the public sphere grew enormously, both in terms of the state expanding what it did and how it intervened in the market and in terms of what the state did in relation to the home. Recently, however, this kind of intervention has come under attack, primarily in the name of reducing the public debt and of making government more efficient. Yet it has also been defended with reference to feminist critiques of past practices. Indeed, feminist criticisms of many state initiatives are being used increasingly to justify cutbacks done in the name of reform. For example, sending women home hours after childbirth is explained in terms of feminist concerns over medicalization of birth.

In the wake of these developments, some feminists find themselves defending processes, such as deinstitutionalization, that may force many women with disabilities on to the street with little support, while others find themselves defending the very state intervention, such as social welfare law and policy, that they criticized in the past. What is beyond question is that the private and the public are being, once again, dramatically redefined in ways that will have a profound impact on women.

In the public arena the state is rapidly reducing what government does (see also Kline this volume). The civil services are being downsized dramatically. Some of this downsizing means longer hours, greater insecurity, and intensified work for those who remain. The rest means job loss and, most likely, unemployment. Such developments are already evident in the most recent labour force data (Statistics Canada 1995a). Given that so many women work in public administration, the downsizing will have an obvious effect on women. According to the Alberta Advisory Council on Women's Issues (now being phased out): 'Females have been hurt by cuts to programs and services, layoffs and public service wage rollbacks at a greater rate than men' (*Calgary Herald* 1995). Some women may manage to acquire jobs doing the work that has been transferred to the private sector. But this work is much less likely to be protected by a union contract and is much more likely to be low paid and short term.

It is not only jobs that are being eliminated in the public service. It is also the monitoring of what the civil service does for women. The agencies that were at least nominally established to protect women's interests within the state and to support research on women's issues have been cancelled or reorganized. For example, the Canadian Advisory Council on the Status of Women was dismantled in 1995. Financial support provided by government to non-governmental agencies is under attack and is increasingly defined as support for special interests. Such interests must be privately funded in the new state.

At the same time governments at all levels are significantly reducing funding for education, health, and welfare. These cutbacks have an impact on women as both providers and users, given that they are the majority of both. In terms of employment, jobs are being eliminated rapidly in these areas, and work is increasingly being contracted out to private sector firms that pay women less and offer less job protection (Armstrong and Armstrong 1996). New work organization techniques transferred from the private sector are transforming many of the public sector jobs that remain (Armstrong et al. 1994). In the name of improving quality, public sector employers are appealing to women's desire to provide high quality services, to participate in decision-making, and to work in teams as a way of re-engineering work. But too often these processes end up deskilling the job. At the same time these private sector techniques frequently pit women against each other, undermining their traditional ways of working together. With government cutbacks, private sector for-profit firms are moving in to fill the demand for services. These employers tend to be non-union. Moreover, they are more likely than public sector employers to rely on part-time and short-term work, to vary their hours in ways that make it difficult for women to arrange child care, and to pay low wages and benefits. Because women form the majority of this labour force, the impact will be greatest on them.

In terms of service reduction, women will be particularly disadvantaged. For example, the proposed hike in post-secondary education tuition fees will return us to the time when parents and students had to cover a significant part of the costs. In those times, parents forced to choose which children to support chose sons over daughters, and declining incomes mean that more parents will again be forced to choose (Porter, Porter, and Blishen 1973). Moreover, the proposed payback scheme based on earnings will mean that women will be paying back their student loans for much longer, given that they earn less than men.

The state is not only withdrawing from the provision of services, however. It is also withdrawing from the regulation of the non-profit and for-profit sectors. When Treasury Board President Art Eggleton announced the federal government's plan for regulatory reform, he stated that 'whenever possible, government has to get out of the way' (Eggleton 1994, 2). 'Getting out of the way' may well mean removing most of the hard-won protections for women.

Certainly this is the case in Ontario, where the election of the Harris Conservative government in 1995 made it clear that employment equity legislation as we know it is gone and that there will be no money for pay equity. Cutbacks will mean that those last hired will be first fired, and, without protection, the women who did benefit from employment equity legislation are likely to suffer disproportionately. Labour legislation that made it easier for some women to organize into unions is also slated for removal, as are many aspects of health and safety protection. Highway safety patrols, for example, have been eliminated, leaving women on the road to fend for themselves.

These changes in the public arena have a significant impact on women in the household and the community. Services not provided by women paid and trained for the work are being rapidly transferred to women in the home or to voluntary agencies. Some new techniques and technologies are eliminating or reducing the labour required in some areas, making it possible to significantly alter services. So, for example, day surgery has become possible as a result of new surgical techniques and new ways of relieving pain. However, much labour is still required and this necessary labour is skilled labour. Indeed, precisely because the labour is related to new techniques, most of it has never been done at home (Armstrong 1994; Glazer 1991). Yet a great deal of this work is being sent home, where it is expected that it will be done by women without pay. However, most women now have labour force jobs, few have the necessary skills, and many do not have the desire to do the work. Particularly disadvantaged are poor women who cannot hire assistance, single women who do not have partners to help, and women without relatives in Canada who can support them in this work.

Some of the work transfer has no relation to new techniques. In Ontario and Alberta, for example, kindergarten, and day care are being cut. In both cases governments indicate, both explicitly and implicitly, that this work should be done by mothers or female relatives rather than by the state. Such a position not only deprives women of services, it also directly challenges their right to employment and defines them as the people responsible for child care.

The transfer of work to the community (see Kline this volume) has similar consequences. Much of the community work is done by women volunteers. While men do fundraising and coaching in the community, women do most of the actual service work. In the late 1980s women accounted for two-thirds of the volunteers providing care or companionship and three-quarters of those preparing and serving food (Duchesne 1989, Table 16). With less and less done by the state, more and more is left to such voluntary organizations. But given their high participation in the labour force, women have less and less time to do this work.

Changes in social assistance will also have a significant impact on women, given that they form the majority of recipients. In Ontario, for example, the payments for welfare have been significantly reduced and the rules for eligibility altered to make it much more difficult for anyone, even the disabled, to claim benefits. Aboriginal women in particular will suffer because a high proportion of them have been eligible for assistance in the past (Statistics Canada 1995b, 151–3). Similarly, proposed federal changes in unemployment insurance regulations would make payments based on household income. This change would not only transform the program from an insurance scheme based on right to a welfare program based on need; it would also disproportionately affect women. Under the current scheme each worker is treated as an individual who has rights based on contributions and job search. Under the proposed scheme women would be assessed as spouses dependent on the men who usually earn more, or at least enough, to make the women ineligible.

As is the case in the public arena, the state is also deregulating the household. Services for battered women have been dramatically reduced, along with other kinds of support like counselling. Legal aid to support women's claims is very much under threat, making it difficult for women to find protection under the rules that remain. Environmental regulations that help reduce hazards in the home and on the street are being altered to reduce their impact. And the federal government has virtually refused to regulate the new reproductive technologies that may endanger many women's lives.

The restructuring currently under way thus means both more unpaid work and less protection for women, in terms of social support, unionization, or regulation. It also means more responsibility and less power. As more work is transferred to community and home, more state surveillance enters the household. But this surveillance, in such forms as new regulations for welfare and for home care services, means that what has been private becomes public, without the kinds of protection such a shift usually provides. Home care workers, for example, enter the home at their convenience, following rules made by others about what can be done for whom. The new intervention in the household is more about policing women than about making private troubles public issues.

Conclusion

What we are seeing, then, is a dramatic restructuring of the public and private spheres. Partly in response to women's gains in areas such as wages and access to jobs as well as to services, the state is busy dismantling both the services and protections that women have so painfully and slowly gained. The state seldom went as far and as fast as women wanted. Too many of the services mainly reinforced inequality rather than challenged it. Many institutional practices were oppressive rather than supportive to women. And some state legislation and regulation strengthened differences, in the process increasing inequalities among women related to race, class, region, age, sexual orientation, and disability. Moreover, not all state employers have been decent employers.

However, the postwar expansion of the public both in the sense of what the public sector took over from or regulated in the market, and in the sense of what the state did in and for the household, did have two distinct advantages for women. First, the state did help many women and did help reduce inequality in many instances. Second, the state is much more open to democratic influence than is the case within the private sector or when women have to fight battles within their individual households.

As many feminists have pointed out, the state has never been a neutral arbitor or primarily a defender of women. But the state can, and does, set rules or provide services that can protect the weakest. Private firms and individual households offer much more arbitrary and unreliable protections, especially for the weakest. As the public shrinks in the sense of regulating and servicing, the private prevails. The impact will be greatest on women. Women's labour force participation has already declined and their unemployment rate grown as a result of the shift from the public to the private sphere (Statistics Canada 1995a). The problems that will be increasingly hidden in the household will take longer to become evident in the data. Meanwhile, the shifts in public and private will be played out in women's lives.

REFERENCES

Akyeampong, Ernest. 1989. 'Working for Minimum Wage.' *Perspectives on Labour and Income* 3, 8–20

Armstrong, Pat. 1996. 'Unravelling the Safety Net: Transformations in Health Care and the Impact on Women.' In Janine Brodie, ed., *Women and Canadian Public Policy*. Toronto: Harcourt Brace, 129–50

– 1995. 'The Feminization of the Labour Force: Harmonizing Down in a Global Economy.' In Karen Messing, Barbara Neis, and Lucie Dumais, eds., *Invisible*. Charlottetown: Gynergy Books, 368–92

– 1994. 'Closer to Home: More Work for Women.' In Pat Armstrong, Hugh Armstrong, Jacqueline Choiniere, Gina Feldberg, and Jerry White, *Take Care: Warning Signals for Canada's Health System*. Toronto: Garamond, 95–110

– 1993. *Equal Pay for Work of Equal Value*. Report prepared for the Public Service Alliance of Canada in *Canadian Postal Workers* v. *Canada Post*. Canadian Human Rights Commission

– and Hugh Armstrong. 1996. *Wasting Away: The Undermining of Canadian Health Care*. Toronto: Oxford

– 1994. *The Double Ghetto*. Toronto: McClelland and Stewart

– 1988. 'Taking Women into Account: Redefining and Intensifying Employment in Canada.' In Elizabeth Hagen, Jane Jenson, and Trudi Kozol, eds., *Feminization of the Labour Force: Paradoxes and Promises*. New York: Oxford, 65–84

- Jacqueline Choiniere, Gina Feldberg, and Jerry White. 1994. *Take Care: Warning Signals for Canada's Health System*. Toronto: Garamond

Boyd, Monica. 1977. 'The Status of Immigrant Women in Canada.' In Marylee Stephenson, ed., *Women in Canada*. Toronto: General Publishing, 228–44

Boyd, Susan B. 1994. 'Expanding the "Family" in Family Law: Recent Ontario Proposals on Same Sex Relationships.' *Canadian Journal of Women and the Law* 7(2), 545–63

Calgary Herald. 9 November 1995. 'Study Finds Cuts Hurt Women Most: Deficit Elimination No Advantages for Female Residents.' A2

Canada. 1970. *Report of the Royal Commission on the Status of Women*. Ottawa: Information Canada

Carty, Linda. 1994. 'African Canadian Women and the State: "Labour only, please."' In Peggy Bristow et al., *'We're Rooted Here and They Can't Pull Us Up': Essays in African Canadian Women's History*. Toronto: University of Toronto Press, 193–229

Clark, Susan, and Andrew S. Harvey. 1976. 'The Sexual Division of Labour: The Use of Time.' *Atlantis* 2(1), 46–65

Duchesne, Doreen. 1989. 'Giving Freely: Volunteers in Canada.' Ottawa: Statistics Canada (cat. no. 71-535, no. 4)

Dulude, Louise. 1984. *Love, Marriage and Money: An Analysis of Financial Arrangements among Spouses*. Ottawa: Canadian Advisory Council on the Status of Women

Eggleton, Art. December 1994. *Statement on Regulatory Reform and Paper Reduction Package*. Ottawa

Frenken, Hubert, and Karen Master. 1992. 'Employer-Sponsored Pension Plans – Who Is Covered?' *Perspectives on Labour and Income* 4(4), 27–34

Fudge, Judy, and Patricia McDermott, eds. 1991. *Just Wages: A Feminist Assessment of Pay Equity*. Toronto: University of Toronto Press

Galarneau, Deane. 1992. 'Alimony and Child Support.' *Perspectives on Labour and Income* 4(2), 8–21

Gavigan, Shelley A.M. 1996. 'Familial Ideology and the Limits of Difference.' In Janine Brodie, ed., *Women and Canadian Public Policy*. Toronto: Harcourt Brace, 255–78

Glazer, Nona. 1991. *Women's Paid and Unpaid Work*. Philadelphia: Temple University Press

Goelman, Hillel, Alan Pence, Donna Lero, Lois Brockman, Ned Glick, and Jonathan Berkowitz. 1993. *Where Are the Children? An Overview of Child Care Arrangements in Canada*. Ottawa: Health and Welfare Canada (cat. no. 89-527E)

Grant, Karen. 1991. 'Health Care in an Aging Society: Issues, Controversies and

Challenges in the Future.' In B. Singh Bolaria, ed., *Social Issues and Contradictions in Canadian Society*. Toronto: Harcourt, Brace, Jovanovich, 196–222

Gunderson, Morley. 1976. 'Work Patterns.' In Gail C.A. Cook, ed., *Opportunity for Choice: A Goal for Women in Canada*. Ottawa: Information Canada, 93–142

Henry, Frances, Carol Tator, Winston Mattis, and Tim Rees. 1995. *The Colour of Democracy*. Toronto: Harcourt Brace

Kleiber, Nancy, and Linda Light. 1978. *Caring for Ourselves: An Alternative Structure for Health Care*. Vancouver: B.C. Public Health

Lindsay, Colin. 1992. *Lone-Parent Families in Canada*. Ottawa: Minister of Industry, Science and Technology (cat. no. 89-522E)

MacBride-King, Judith. 1990. *Work and Family: Employment Challenge of the '90s*. Ottawa: Conference Board of Canada

Majury, Diana. 1991. 'Equality and Discrimination According to the Supreme Court of Canada.' *Canadian Journal of Women and the Law* 4(2), 407–39

Marsh, Leonard. 1975. *Report on Social Security for Canada 1943*. Toronto: University of Toronto Press

Martin, Brendon. 1993. *In the Public Interest*. London: Zed Press

McLaren, Angus. 1992. *A History of Contraception*. Oxford: Blackwell

Meissner, Martin, Elizabeth Humphreys, Scott Meiss, and William Sheu. 1975. 'No Exit for Wives: Sexual Division of Labour and the Culmination of Household Demands.' *Canadian Review of Sociology and Anthropology* 12(4), 424–39

Morissette, Rene, John Myles, and W.G. Picot. 1993. *What Is Happening to Earnings Inequality in Canada?* Ottawa: Statistics Canada

Mossman, Mary Jane. 1995. 'The Paradox of Feminist Engagement with Law.' In Nancy Mandell, ed., *Feminist Issues: Race, Class, and Sexuality*. Scarborough: Prentice-Hall, 211–43

– 1994. '"Running Hard to Stand Still": The Paradox of Family Law Reform.' *Dalhousie Law Journal* 17, 5–33

National Council of Welfare. 1990–1. *Welfare Incomes 1989*. Ottawa: National Council of Welfare

– 1990. *Women and Poverty Revisited*. Ottawa: National Council of Welfare

Noreau, Nathalie. 1994. 'Involuntary Part-timers.' *Perspectives on Labour and Income* 6(3), 25–30

Norland, J.A. 1994. *Profile of Canada's Seniors*. Ottawa: Minister of Industry, Science and Technology (cat. no. 96-312E)

Northcott, Herbert. 1991. 'Health Status and Health Care in Canada: Contemporary Issues.' In B. Singh Bolaria, ed., *Social Issues and Contradictions in Canadian Society*. Toronto: Harcourt Brace Jovanovich, 178–95

Ornstein, Michael, and Tony Haddad. 1991. *About Time: Analysis of a 1986 Survey of Canadians*. North York: Institute for Social Research, York University

Ostry, Sylvia. 1968. *The Female Worker in Canada*. Ottawa: Queen's Printer

Panitch, Leo, ed. 1977. *The Canadian State: Political Economy and Political Power*. Toronto: University of Toronto Press

Pold, Henry. 1994. 'Jobs! Jobs! Jobs!' *Perspectives on Labour and Income* 6(3), 14–17

Porter, Marion, John Porter, and Bernard Blishen. 1973. *Does Money Matter?* Toronto: York University Institute for Behavioural Research

Rashid, Abdul. 1993. 'Seven Decades of Wage Changes.' *Perspectives on Labour and Income* 5(2), 9–21

Rosenberg, Harriet. 1990. 'The Home Is the Workplace.' In Meg Luxton, Harriet Rosenberg, and Sedef Arat-Koç, *Through the Kitchen Window*. Toronto: Garamond, 57–80

Satzewich, Vic, ed. 1992. *Deconstructing a Nation*. Halifax: Fernwood

Sinclair, Peter, and Lawrence Felt. 1992. 'Separate Worlds: Gender and Domestic Labour in an Isolated Fishing Region.' *Canadian Review of Sociology and Anthropology* 29(1), 55–71

Siroonian, Jason. 1993. *Work Arrangements*. Statistics Canada Labour and Household Survey Analysis Division. Ottawa: Statistics Canada (cat. no. 71-535, no. 6)

Skoulas, Nicholas. 1974. *Determinants of the Participation Rate of Married Women in the Canadian Labour Force: An Econometric Analysis*. Ottawa: Information Canada

Spencer, Byron, and Dennis Featherstone. 1970. *Married Female Labour Force Participation: A Micro Study*. Ottawa: Queen's Printer

Statistics Canada. 1995a. *Labour Force Annual Averages, 1989–94*. Ottawa: Minister of Industry, Science and Technology (cat. no. 71-529)

– 1995b. *Women in Canada*, 3rd ed. Ottawa: Minister of Industry (cat. no. 89-503E)

– 1995c. *Earnings of Men and Women 1993*. Ottawa: Minister of Industry, Science and Technology (cat. no. 13-217)

– 1994a. *Women in the Labour Force, 1994*. Ottawa: Minister of Industry, Science and Technology (cat. no. 75-507E)

– 1994b. *Labour Force Annual Averages 1993*. Ottawa: Minister of Industry, Science and Technology (cat. no. 71-220)

– 1993. *91 Census*. Industry and Class of Worker. Ottawa: Minister of Industry, Science and Technology (cat. no. 93-326)

– 1992. *Canada's Women*. Ottawa: Minister of Industry, Science and Technology (cat. no. 71-205)

– 1990. *Women in Canada*, 2nd ed. Ottawa: Minister of Supply and Services Canada (cat. no. 89-503E)

– 1985. *Women in Canada*. Ottawa: Minister of Supply and Services Canada (cat. no. 89-503)

Stone, Leroy. 1994. *Dimensions of Job–Family Tension*. Ottawa: Minister of Industry, Science and Technology

Taylor, Malcolm. 1978. *Health Insurance and Canadian Public Policy*. Montreal: McGill-Queen's University Press

Walker, Gillian. 1990. *Family Violence and the Women's Movement*. Toronto: University of Toronto Press

White, Julie. 1980. *Women and Unions*. Ottawa: Supply and Services Canada for the Canadian Advisory Council on the Status of Women

Wilkinson, Derek. 1992. 'Change in Household Division of Labour Following Unemployment in Elliott Lake.' Paper presented at the Learned Societies Meeting, CSAA, Charlottetown, PEI

Yalnizyan, Armine. 1994. 'Creating Canadian Social Policy.' In Armine Yalnizyan, T. Ron Ide, and Arthur J. Cordell, *Shifting Time*. Toronto: Between the Lines, 17–72

3

A Little Sex Can Be a Dangerous Thing: Regulating Sexuality, Venereal Disease, and Reproduction in British Columbia, 1919–1945

DOROTHY E. CHUNN

Social Hygiene is at once more radical and more scientific than the old conception of social reform. It is the inevitable method by which at a certain stage civilization is compelled to continue its own course, and to preserve, perhaps to elevate the race.

Ellis (1912), 1–2

Contemporary feminist critiques have revealed the ideological resonance, historical malleability, and differential application of the concept of the public/private divide in Western liberal states (MacKinnon 1983; O'Donovan 1985; Pateman 1989). Although 'separate spheres' ideology – the belief that the marketplace and the family could and ought to be hived off from the political and the legal – reached a zenith in the nineteenth century minimalist *laissez-faire* state, it survived the era of so-called welfare states and has been rejuvenated with a vengeance in the current context of developing transnational states (Brodie 1995). Yet, as feminists and others have demonstrated, the public/private divide is a purely ideological one, because liberal states have always regulated the so-called 'private' sphere (Garland 1985; Pateman 1989).

Historically, then, it is not a matter of whether state intervention exists, but rather the form and extent of such intervention (Chunn 1992; Donzelot 1980; O'Donovan 1985; Sears 1995; Smart 1982). Thus, while the family can be a 'haven in a heartless world,' against racism (hooks 1991), for example, it has never been a completely privatized institution in liberal states. The fact that the nature and scope of state interventions into the domestic realm that came to characterize welfare states were both unprecedented and inconceivable in a *laissez-faire* state does not mean that families were wholly unregulated in the latter.

The variability and inconsistency of state interventions into the domestic realm reveal the malleability of the ideology of privacy. On the one hand, the historical reluctance of liberal states to address the intrafamilial violence of men against women and children is clearly and extensively documented (Dobash and Dobash 1979; Gordon 1988). On the other hand, the alacrity with which liberal states have moved to regulate biological and social reproduction over time is equally obvious and well researched (Arnup 1994; Arnup, Lévesque, and Pierson 1990; Boyd 1989b; Brodie, Gavigan, and Jenson 1992; Gordon 1977; McLaren 1990; McLaren and McLaren 1986). Moreover, the ways in which intertwined assumptions about gender, class, race, ethnicity, and sexual orientation either exacerbate or minimize state regulation of family life further illustrate the elasticity of the 'separate spheres' ideology. Generally speaking, the more closely men, women, and children adhere to the norms governing their respective roles in the white, middle class, nuclear family, the more freedom from state surveillance they will enjoy (Arnup 1994; Barrett and McIntosh 1982; Boyd 1989a; Chunn 1992; Donzelot 1980; Gavigan 1993; Roberts 1993).

The relative willingness of liberal states to regulate reproduction increased sharply during the late nineteenth and early twentieth centuries as industrialization, urbanization, immigration, and 'universal' suffrage[1] began to transform laissez-faire states into mass (welfare) societies. In the context of perceived social deconstruction, reformers increasingly linked 'sexual anarchy' to potential 'race suicide' and seized on the (white) nuclear family as the basis for the reconstruction and reintegration of society (Showalter 1990). A major ideological underpinning of the bourgeois family model is a repressive conceptualization of sex: sex is 'bad' unless stringently controlled via heterosexual marriage. Because the only legitimate sexual relations are implicitly intraracial ones between a wife and husband for the purpose of procreation, uncommitted sex for pleasure – pre- and extra-marital, homosexual – is deviant, dangerous, and must be prevented or contained to safeguard 'the family' and ensure social continuity (Foucault 1980; Showalter 1990; Weeks 1986, 1981; Young 1995).

Not surprisingly, reproducing the 'middle-class family' became a major focus of reform initiatives (Chunn 1992; Donzelot 1980; Finch 1993; Ursel 1992), and regulating sex became synonymous with the national interest in emergent welfare states such as Canada, the United States, and Britain (Bacchi 1983; Showalter 1990; Snitow, Stansell, and Thompson 1983;

Strange 1988, 1995; Valverde 1991; Weeks 1981). First wave feminists and other reformers of the late nineteenth and early twentieth centuries sought, and often received, state assistance in the form of legislation and policies designed to induce adherence to the norms governing the nuclear family and thereby guarantee the moral, mental, and physical fitness of the population. Women were particular targets of campaigns to confine sex to marriage, to monitor sexuality before and after marriage, and to oversee reproduction (Arnup 1994; Snell 1983; Snell and Abeele 1988).

Initiatives aimed at regulating sex and reproduction that were advocated or implemented from the 1880s to the 1940s reveal much about how Victorian *laissez-faire* states became Keynesian welfare states; or, more specifically, how different conceptualizations of the public/private divide emerge in different state formations. An analysis of shifting approaches to venereal disease (VD)[2] is particularly instructive in this regard. Over time the prevailing conceptualizations of sexually transmitted diseases became increasingly secular, professional, and institutional; the 'leprosies of lust' were reconstructed as a public health problem that could be solved only by experts, especially doctors, and with strong state support (Brandt 1985; Buckley and McGinnis 1982; Cassel 1987; McGinnis 1990, 1988; Weeks 1981). Therefore, proactive and expanded intervention in the private realm not only was necessary but also had a 'scientific' basis.

Far from disappearing, however, the discourses of overt religious moralism that informed pre–First World War discussions of VD meshed with and ultimately were submerged by the discourses of 'science.' Thus, the nineteenth-century distinction between the blameless and the blameworthy among the infected was not erased (Showalter 1990; Walkowitz 1992, 1980). Rather, it was obscured through a process of scientification whereby experts claimed a monopoly on the technical knowledge necessary to differentiate among, and tailor responses to, distinct categories of women (and of men): the potentially deviant who required protection from and education about the dangers of uncontrolled and unsafe sex; the deviant but salvageable who were 'deserving' of timely intervention that would help them to comply with bourgeois sexual norms; and the incorrigible, 'undeserving' deviants such as prostitutes who were the appropriate candidates for coercive state control (Brandt 1985; Cassel 1987; McGinnis 1988).

This chapter tracks the transformation of ideas and practices related to sex and reproduction in developing welfare states through an analysis of selected interwar efforts to eradicate sexually transmitted diseases in British Columbia, focusing primarily on the decade between 1935 and 1945.[3] Therefore, it does not attempt to provide a comprehensive account of anti-

VD initiatives in the province but, rather, to illustrate the reconceptualization of the public/private divide in an emergent state formation. The first
section is a brief overview of the growing secularization and scientification
of sex, VD, and reproduction from the 1880s to the 1940s in Canada and
elsewhere. Following this contextualization of the issues, a number of educational and legal initiatives that addressed the issue of sex, VD, and pregnancy among heterosexual women in British Columbia are examined: first,
legislation and policies that ostensibly were targeted at all women, but
which in practice were aimed at regulating sex and sexuality among
'deserving' middle- and working-class women; and, second, the explicitly
coercive measures that were directed at the containment and control of
'undeserving' or incorrigible women whose sexual deviance was considered
to be either wilful or untreatable. In conclusion, some implications of the
analysis for contemporary feminist struggles against the public/private
dichotomy are discussed.

Sex, Science, and Society

The regulation of the sex, sexuality, and reproduction (all private matters,
one would think) of women was on the political agenda of reformers
throughout the nineteenth century in Canada and other capitalist liberal
states. From the 1880s to the 1940s, especially during the period between
the two world wars, a rationalization occurred of the process through
which 'social problems' were defined, analysed, and treated. Positivism,
which reflected the explosion of the 'value-free' natural, physical, and
social sciences, provided the philosophical rationale for the emergent technocratic, interventionist state where social problems are stripped of their
political content and transformed into technical ones to be diagnosed and
resolved on an individualized basis using professional expertise. Thus, the
interwar years were marked by two interrelated developments: first, by the
decline of the overt moralism that had characterized prewar responses to
the deviant and the ascendancy of scientific approaches; and second, by a
blurring of the public/private distinction so central to *laissez-faire* ideology
(Chunn 1992; Rowbotham and Weeks 1977; Weeks 1981).

In regard to issues related to sex and sexuality, the medical doctor, the
sexologist, and, to a lesser extent, the social worker emerged as state-
sanctioned 'experts' who could disseminate authoritative knowledge on
such matters. Although the experts had not entirely displaced the moralists
by 1945, it is important to emphasize that in Canada generally, and British
Columbia specifically, they did gain considerable control over the defini-

tion, explanation, and response to 'sexual problems.' Especially interesting is how sex and sexuality came together in relation to 'scientific' pronouncements on VD and pregnancy during the 1920s and 1930s. The increasingly authoritative voices of doctors translated into a growing monopoly over pregnancy and birthing practices – evidenced by their control over pre- and post-natal care and hospital births – that coalesced around anti-VD campaigns from the First World War onward (Arnup, Lévesque, and Pierson 1990; Cassel 1987; Dickinson 1993).

Shifting perspectives on VD mirrored the more general reconceptualization of sex and sexuality in developing welfare states. Specifically, the mode and degree of state involvement in the regulation of sexually transmitted diseases were transformed. During the late nineteenth century in Canada and other liberal states, VD crystallized the fears about the decline of civilization that are 'typical of the fin de siècle' (Showalter 1990, 4). Syphilis became a graphic illustration of the consequences of 'sexual anarchy.' In the context of uncertainty generated by rapid social change, syphilis posed a triple threat to the moral, physical, and mental health of the nation. It also triggered a pervasive anxiety among the middle classes about sexual epidemics that intensified after the turn of the century, reaching a crescendo during the First World War and erupting periodically ever since (McGinnis 1990; Showalter 1990; Singer 1993).

After the turn of the century the primary definers of VD as a 'social' problem increasingly were secular professionals. Doctors and other experts achieved growing power to influence state intervention around reproduction through the disqualification of lay knowledge as 'quackery' and/or unscientific, uninformed moralism (Brandt 1985; Cassel 1987; Rowbotham and Weeks 1977; Weeks 1981). It is important to note, however, that they acquired this power only with support from the prewar reformers and their successors, who began to interweave the 'scientific' discourses of the experts with older religious, moral discourses. By 1945 the dominance of professionals (and the foundations of the welfare state) was secured.

The degree of state intervention with respect to VD also changed dramatically from the 1880s to the 1940s. While a focus on the (nuclear) family as the bulwark against social disintegration runs through the entire period, the state showed increasing willingness to regulate the most intimate aspect of social life – sexual relations – to combat VD. During and after the First World War, Ottawa and most provinces in Canada enacted legislation and policies and provided funding for initiatives aimed at eradicating the scourge of VD, including the creation of government venereal disease control units and public clinics, educational programs, the distribution of free drugs to private physicians, and so on (Cassel 1987, 145, 149). In addition, the growing emphasis on proactive rather than reactive approaches to sexually transmitted diseases, on prevention rather than treatment after the fact, greatly expanded the scope of anti-VD campaigns and activities. Now the entire population was potentially at risk, and VD became a question of public health like any other communicable disease and linked to protection of the general good. As a result, the public/private divide that characterized the *laissez-faire* state was rendered increasingly invisible over time, particularly during the interwar years (Buckley and McGinnis 1982; Cassel 1987).

Thus, the sin/disease model of venereal disease associated with a distinct group of women – street prostitutes – who infected foolish men, especially military men, was transformed into a scientific/medical model that targeted the civilian population more than the military (Walkowitz 1980). This model differentiated between women (prostitutes and 'casuals,' usually young, single women who engaged in casual sexual relations) who through wilfulness or negligence infected foolish men, and innocent victims (married and single working women) of foolish or predatory men who, in turn, constituted actual or potential threats to new life (fetuses). Consequently, all women were active, passive, or possible sources of danger to men, fetuses, and the race through the transmission of VD, especially syphilis. However, the criteria (i.e., race, ethnicity, class) for separating the guilty from the innocent, the deserving from the undeserving, remained consistent over time.

Redefining VD as a preventable plague that put entire nations at risk also entailed rethinking the traditional responses to it. In the nineteenth century when VD was identified with particular marginalized groups – prostitutes and homosexual men – the *laissez-faire* state relied on criminalization and on regulation of prostitutes through the Contagious Diseases Acts (enacted but never proclaimed in Canada) or private medical practitioners to stem the 'leprosies of lust' (Backhouse 1985; McGinnis 1990; Walkowitz 1980). Responses were privatized (individual or non-state) for most of the population, while public concern was focused on prostitutes and homosexuals and their hapless male 'victims.'

During the interwar years, state-sanctioned responses – government-operated VD divisions working in conjunction with non-government organizations concerned about VD – became more dominant. The emphasis shifted to mass, often sex-specific, education through the dissemination of advice literature, films, radio broadcasts, poster campaigns, and public lectures (Brandt 1985; Cassel 1987; Kuhn 1988) and to mass testing (premarital and prenatal) of the civilian population of 'deserving' women (and men)[4] under the direction of medical authorities and other experts. Publicly funded clinics were established to service the 'deserving' and 'undeserving' poor, while the more affluent continued to rely on private treatment by family physicians. Quasi-criminal legislation under the control of doctors allowed the expansion of the legal structures aimed at eradication of VD among the 'undeserving'; such statutes could be used in tandem with the criminal law to deal with infected prostitutes, but more importantly to regulate the wider population of so-called casuals who threatened public health through their indiscriminate sex lives. Deportation was a last resort for the incorrigible, non-citizen (Roberts 1988). Overall, the belief that VD could be eradicated through the 'magic bullet' (Brandt 1985) of scientific knowledge and technique provided the rationale for a greatly expanded state role in dealing with diseases.

Concern about VD always has centred on syphilis, presumably because it was more debilitating and therefore more feared than gonorrhea, although the latter disease was far more prevalent (Brandt 1985, 154; McGinnis 1988, 126). Thus, the detection and treatment of syphilis were the primary objectives of all attacks on sexually transmitted diseases, regardless of the target populations. The scientification of approaches to syphilis after the turn of the century that allowed its redefinition as a public health problem is easily tracked: the identification of the causal organism of syphilis – the spirochete – in 1905; the development of the Wassermann Test in 1906; the discovery of salvarsan or 606, an effective, albeit risky, treatment in 1909; the development of the Kahn Test in 1924 (used initially in Canada to corroborate results from the Wassermann Test, which was difficult to perform and unreliable, and ultimately replacing it); and, the introduction of penicillin during the Second World War (Brandt 1985; Cassel 1987; McGinnis 1988). It also is important to emphasize that public concern about syphilis (and VD in general) may have been exacerbated by, but was not simply a product of, wartime conditions. Interwar British Columbia is a case in point.

Combatting Venereal Disease in British Columbia

British Columbia emerged as a leader in the field of VD control, particularly over the decade from 1935 to 1945. Thus, while government and non-government agencies were influenced strongly by developments within and outside Canada, they were influential, innovative, and progressive forces in their own right in the battle against sexually transmitted diseases.[5] Around the mid-1930s, 'extraordinary things began to happen in British Columbia,' when the Liberal government of Premier Duff Pattullo attempted to intro-duce both province-wide medical insurance and a program to reduce VD. Concerted opposition from doctors pre-empted the medical scheme, but the anti-VD initiative 'fared much better' because of the government's per-ception that the incidence of disease was rising. In October 1936 the Divi-sion of Venereal Disease Control was created as a unit of the British Columbia Board of Health, analogous to the previously established Divi-sion of Tuberculosis (TB) Control,[6] and in 1937 the provincial government initiated a five-year plan that provided 'a substantial increase in the amounts allotted for VD control' (Cassel 1987, 200). Greater financial resources enabled the establishment of more public clinics for the testing, either voluntary or compulsory, of people without the means to consult a private physician. Vancouver and Victoria had long been the only urban centres with clinics, but by mid-1937 there were eight clinics in different areas (ibid., 177).

The reconceptualization of VD and the transformation of the mode and degree of state intervention in developing welfare states, as discussed above, were evident in the British Columbia context. VD was redefined as a communicable disease like TB that threatened public health and required vigilance and proactive, state-sanctioned interventions by experts who targeted the civilian population as much as, or more than, the military and prostitutes. By the mid-1930s medical authorities and other experts had assumed the leading role in British Columbia's battle against VD. However, they actively cultivated and mobilized support among long-established reform constituencies, including churches, women's organiza-tions, and social welfare agencies, as well as community groups concerned specifically with public health such as the Greater Vancouver Health League and the medical profession itself.

Women – and in particular the sex lives of single, young, female workers and of married, working-class women – were a major focus of anti-VD campaigns during the interwar years. In British Columbia, as elsewhere, initiatives tailored to the 'deserving' emphasized prevention through edu-cation and testing. At the same time the older association of VD with vice remained strong and underpinned both provincial legislation[7] that man-dated compulsory treatment for identified carriers and the federal criminal law provisions aimed at suppressing (as opposed to regulating) prostitution and other 'undeserving' women.[8]

The growing emphasis on distinguishing between 'deserving' and 'unde-serving' women in dealing with VD was clear in a 1936 evaluation report on the British Columbia situation. The report was prepared by Harry

Cassidy, director of social welfare, for the Division of Health and Welfare Services.[9] In his confidential assessment, Cassidy criticized the Vancouver Clinic for failing to adopt individualized approaches in diagnosing and treating VD:

Wholesale methods are employed at the clinic, with lack of segregation of different classes of patients (e.g., inadequate provision to keep respectable women apart from prostitutes), lack of consideration for the sensibilities of individuals, routine methods of dealing with all patients on exactly the same basis, etc. It is argued that such methods are bad socially and that they do not inspire confidence or cooperation in patients.[10]

This categorization of women and, more specifically, a concern with the sexual threat to health posed by young, working-class women, also are reflected in Cassidy's emphasis on the need for follow-up by the clinic: 'Women put under treatment often live in rooming houses and are a source of infection to other persons. Likewise, domestic servants who are infected may be living in homes where there are children and may constitute a menace to these children.'[11] Clearly, the attitude was that legislation and policies aimed at regulating sex and sexuality among 'deserving' women in British Columbia would not be suitable for the 'undeserving.'

Regulating Sex among 'Deserving' Women

Preliminary research suggests that in post-1918 British Columbia medical authorities, social workers, politicians, and reformers were equally concerned about the sex lives of married and single women because of their shared capability to reproduce the species. To guarantee the future of the (white) race, the reproductive health of certain women had to be protected against the dire consequences of disease. Like other jurisdictions during the interwar years, British Columbia emphasized two types of anti-VD initiatives, presumably universal in scope but in reality aimed at forestalling or counteracting sexual deviance among 'deserving' women who were deemed to be at risk through ignorance or abuse. The first was public education about congenital syphilis and the second was premarital and prenatal blood tests.

British Columbia thus followed the post–First World War trend in liberal democracies to make mass education the central focus of anti-VD programs. Indeed, by 1936 the government apparently had smuggled sex education into the schools.[12] However, a very public focus of educational work aimed at VD control was the prevention of congenital syphilis, which was a leading cause of blindness and death in many infants. In the late 1930s the provincial health officer, Dr Gordon Amyot, and the director of the VD control division, Dr Donald Williams, launched a concerted effort to link education with voluntary prenatal testing of pregnant women. Even the division stationery was used to publicize the issue: 'Prevent Prenatal Syphilis in Children – A Blood Test for Every Expectant Mother.'[13] Eventually, in January 1942, Amyot approached the provincial secretary, George Pearson, with a proposal for an organized six-month program that would require physicians to state on each Birth Notice Form 'whether the mother was examined for syphilis by a blood test.'[14]

The impetus for this educational initiative came from the provincial medical authorities responsible for controlling VD. However, the assumption that 'science' could easily prevent women from unwittingly causing harm to their babies was clearly one that resonated across a broad spectrum of individuals and organizations and garnered strong support for the campaign. Dr Amyot informed Pearson that the B.C. Medical Association's Committee on Maternal Welfare sent letters 'to every physician in British Columbia advising them of the importance of taking blood tests for syphilis in every expectant mother'; local health departments, public health nurses, and welfare workers were all participating through the provincial board of health; the National Council of Women of Canada, which included approximately 150 B.C. women's groups, 'endorsed and supported' the campaign; and the media (radio, newspapers and 'prominent store windows') were enlisted to publicize 'this important health problem.' To mark National Hygiene Day in Canada and the United States, a 'Prevention of Prenatal Syphilis Week,' 1–7 February 1942, was to be proclaimed by the mayors of Vancouver, New Westminster, and Victoria. Amyot felt that an endorsement from the lieutenant governor also 'would be highly advantageous.'[15]

In a letter that reveals a wholly uncritical acceptance of Amyot's definition of the problem, the provincial secretary apprised the lieutenant governor about the upcoming event and requested his endorsement. Pearson referred to the provincial board of health's concern over 'the preventable tragedy of children born in our Province with Syphilis' and emphasized that 'among health problems this one is most easily solved' by 'providing our citizens with knowledge regarding the simple fact that the discovery of infection in an expectant mother, followed by treatment, will give the new born baby an almost certain chance of being perfectly normal and healthy.'[16] The lieutenant governor was quick to oblige and his endorsement, as well as the mayoral proclamations, of the 'Prevention of Pre-Natal Syphilis Week' were virtual replicas of Pearson's letter: 'The heritage of health is the birthright of every child'; 'healthy children, the citizens of tomorrow, are our greatest civic asset'; 'modern medical science has one by one, removed the health hazards to our lives' and it can easily prevent syphilis which 'still robs some children of their heritage'; the efforts of the provincial board of health to co-ordinate the work of 'citizens, physicians and health departments' in British Columbia 'against this menace to our children ... deserve support.'[17]

The second type of initiative aimed at preventing or pre-empting the effects of sexual deviance among 'deserving' women (and men) was the implementation of legislation requiring premarital blood tests. Calls for statutes to compel VD testing before a marriage licence was issued predated the First World War, but the organized campaigns for such tests arose out of the more general movement to regulate heterosexual marriage and shore up the nuclear family during the interwar period (Arnup 1994; Chunn 1992; Snell and Abeele 1988). This movement increasingly was driven by a concern with eugenics or 'scientific breeding' that would encourage the 'fit' to reproduce and prevent the 'unfit' from doing so (Brandt 1985; McLaren 1990; Stephen 1995). During the 1920s and 1930s in British Columbia a perception that the spread of VD was threatening the reproductive health of the most valuable women (i.e., respectable middle- or working-class WASPs) fuelled recurrent demands by some political parties, churches, women's organizations, and doctors that the province's Marriage Act be amended to require compulsory premarital tests for venereal disease, mental defectiveness, and tuberculosis, as had been done in some American states (Brandt 1985).

Through the 1930s Liberal and Co-operative Commonwealth Federation (CCF) politicians in opposition attempted unsuccessfully to have mandatory premarital testing enacted in British Columbia.[18] Finally, in 1937 the governing Liberals pre-empted the latest attempt of Ernest Winch, leader of the CCF opposition, to introduce a bill mandating premarital testing. They established a committee, chaired by the provincial health officer and with broad representation, including women's organizations, ministerial associations, departmental officials, and Winch himself, to review the entire Marriage Act and make recommendations for change.[19] The committee reported in March 1938 and the Marriage Act was amended later that year (SBC 1938, c. 33) to require that a standard lab test for syphilis be performed in an approved facility; that the test be conducted by a medical practitioner twenty days before marriage; and that the result of the test be communicated to both parties to the intended marriage.[20]

The amended act did not follow American precedent by making positive test outcomes an absolute bar to marriage (Brandt 1985, 147–8). More importantly, the amendment was not proclaimed and remained unenforceable. Thus, the reform initiative may have been more a public relations exercise to appease the moralist pressure for action emanating from lay individuals and groups outside government than a serious attempt to compel 'deserving' women (and men) to undergo testing. Although medical authorities involved in VD control supported the idea of compulsory premarital blood tests, at least in principle, the medical profession itself apparently favoured voluntary compliance rather than compulsion for 'deserving' populations.[21]

Even wartime anxiety about VD did not persuade the then coalition government (Liberal–Conservative) to operationalize the 1938 Marriage Act amendment. Letters and resolutions urging the government to implement premarital VD testing – and in some cases prenatal blood tests – streamed into the premier's office from various organizations throughout the province, including women's groups, church associations, and social agencies, in what clearly was a coordinated campaign. Eight months after the educational initiative to encourage voluntary, prenatal blood tests, the Vancouver Local Council of Women raised the issue of compulsory prenatal testing for syphilis as part of the general wartime campaign against VD that had been launched under the auspices of the federal government. A resolution forwarded to Premier Hart in October 1942 urged the government to 'build the New Laboratories at the University which were planned sometime ago' because 'the present lab facilities are completely inadequate' to assist the campaign against VD 'which otherwise is likely to increase in Wartime.' The resolution then explicitly emphasized that 'one part of that Campaign is an effort to have pregnant women daignosed [sic] for venereal disease and treated if found infected so that congenital venereal disease may be checked.'[22]

On the subject of compulsory premarital blood tests, the Cobble Hill Women's Institute forwarded a 'typical' resolution to Premier Hart in December 1943, noting the 'grave prevalence' of social diseases in Canada and urging that any existing legislation 'and especially legislation requiring PreMarital Health Certificates be immediately [made operational and] enforced.'[23] Subsequently, Hart received almost identical letters from the women's institutes in other areas, as well as a follow-up from Cobble Hill.[24] Women's religious associations also joined the chorus of voices urging the government to proclaim and enforce the provincial legislation providing for premarital blood tests.[25]

By 1944 the Councils of Social Agencies (CSA) in Victoria and Vancouver also were pressuring the premier to put teeth in the Marriage Act. The CSA of Greater Victoria attributed the government's inaction to 'the scarcity of accomodation [sic] for laboratory tests,' but went on to argue 'that it would be in the best interests of all concerned for this act to be made effective and that the cost of providing lab service would be saved many times over and the future generation protected from congenital venereal disease.'[26] A month later the Vancouver CSA urged the government 'to consider at this time the advisability of proclaiming and enforcing the existing legislation in respect to blood tests for those contemplating marriage.'[27]

In the end the British Columbia government did not implement mandatory premarital and prenatal testing. After the provincial health officer, Dr Amyot, informed the premier that the existing laboratory facilities could not cope with 'this added burden,' but 'if and when suitable accommodation for the laboratory can be made available, we shall be pleased to undertake the examination of premarital blood specimens,'[28] the government was quick to use the rationalization of fiscal restraint for its own ends. Official responses to the letters and resolutions demanding compulsory blood tests stressed that it was 'impossible ... to get material and labour to have the [new] building erected.'[29] They added: 'Owing to the exigencies of war and the increased demand on our laboratory facilities, it has not been possible for the Government to consider the enforcement of the legislation it enacted in this respect. Until such time as the demands upon the laboratories relax, or we are in a position to obtain the necessary equipment, this matter will have to stand in abeyance.'[30] Political decisions to spend or not spend public monies always rest on a cost–benefit analysis, however. The fact that the wartime coalition government in British Columbia declined to provide funding to implement mandatory blood testing for VD may well have reflected an underlying unease about the idea of using coercion with 'deserving' women (and men)[31] and/or an assumption that the 'better' classes would meet their obligations to family and the nation without compulsion.

Regulating Sex among 'Undeserving' Women

In contrast to the velvet glove approach accorded 'deserving' women, political, medical, and legal authorities had no qualms about using direct legal coercion against 'undeserving' women who were identified as potential or actual carriers of venereal disease because they were viewed as inherently or irredeemably deviant. Again 'science,' often in the form of IQ and VD tests, was increasingly important in identifying these sources of contagion so that they could be segregated in the interests of social defence. However, legal strategies directed at the containment of women who were labelled by experts as incorrigibles must be viewed within the more general context of class and race-driven attempts during the interwar years, including the use of birth control and sterilization, to prevent 'defective' women from reproducing (Chapman 1977; McLaren 1990; Stephen 1995). In other words, many of the women who were identified 'scientifically' as likely sources of contagion also were women deemed to be potentially or demonstrably incapable of being 'good' mothers.

As discussed earlier, the major pieces of Canadian legislation used to contain 'undeserving' women who were suspected or known carriers of VD were the federal Criminal Code and the anti-VD statutes enacted by various provinces. The code was used almost exclusively against street prostitutes who were historically and wrongly perceived as a major repository of social diseases. The provincial laws were applied much more broadly to anyone suspected of having VD, including prostitutes. In British Columbia, from the 1920s to the 1940s, the Venereal Diseases Suppression Act (SBC 1919, c. 88) played a key role in the organized efforts to eradicate VD. Like most of the provinces British Columbia modeled its law after the pioneer Ontario statute (SO 1918, c. 42). Viewed retrospectively, the legislation is significant for two reasons. First, it contained extremely sweeping provisions that allowed extensive state-sanctioned intervention into people's private lives. Second, it created a medical and public health monopoly over the application of the Venereal Diseases Suppression Act (Cassel 1987, 161–4).

Among other things, the British Columbia legislation stipulated that any person incarcerated for a Criminal Code or provincial offence was to be tested for VD at the time of admission to the institution. Doctors and heads of public institutions were to keep a record of all infected persons under their care or supervision and report all cases to the provincial health officer. However, the Venereal Diseases Suppression Act did not specifically mandate the routine testing of all institutional admissions, nor did it mention young offenders incarcerated for status offences under the Juvenile Delinquents Act (SC 1929, c. 36). Nonetheless, the growing influence of the medical profession on the government response to VD during the 1930s was evident in 1937 when the director of venereal disease control, Dr S.C. Peterson, persuaded the provincial secretary that *all* persons admitted to *any* institution should be tested for syphilis. Letters were sent to the heads of the B.C. Gaol, the School for the Deaf and the Blind, the B.C. Mental Hospital, the B.C. Industrial Home for Girls, the B.C. Industrial School for Boys, and the B.C. Home for Incurables, with instructions 'to make a routine blood test for syphilis of all the patients under your care' and requesting that if the test already was a 'regular practice' that statistics should be submitted to the ministry.[32]

Responses revealed contradictory institutional practices. On the one hand, the Warden at the Oakalla Prison Farm for men, who ostensibly was required by law to test all new admissions for VD, reported that only those inmates suspected of having syphilis – either on admission or later – actually were tested and that to test the 420 inmates currently in the prison all at once 'would lead to misunderstanding and friction.'[33] On the other hand, the superintendent of the industrial home for girls said that it was 'a routine procedure for every girl upon admission to have a blood test' and reported only twelve positive cases for the eight-year period from 1929 to 1937.[34] In contrast, Matters (1984, 270) found that from one- to two-thirds of young women incarcerated in any given year between 1914 and 1936 were 'suffering from either syphilis or gonorrhea.' At the same time, she noted that while the vast majority of young women admitted to the home were convicted of 'status' (e.g., sexual immorality, incorrigibility) as opposed to criminal offences and had been sexually active prior to admission, many inmates had been 'sexually active only with a single partner,' 'several had asked permission to marry the men with whom they were involved,' and several 'were already married at the time of committal' (ibid.). Thus, it is difficult to avoid the conclusion that assumptions about the sexual threat posed by 'promiscuous' women and the need for social defence against this danger, which underpin the sexual double standard, were operating against young women committed to the industrial home.[35]

Authorities relied on IQ testing by the B.C. Child Guidance Clinic that consistently revealed the subnormal mental abilities of a large number of the inmates and confirmed links between low intelligence and sexual deviance. Ironically, the belief that so many incarcerated women were mentally subnormal justified training and placing the great majority of them in situations of high sexual risk as domestics (ibid., 272). As 'undeserving' women, they also were prime candidates for sterilization (McLaren 1990).

In 1938, following a recommendation from the British Columbia director of VD control to review the 'present efficacy' of the Venereal Diseases Suppression Act 'in light of recent changes in the VD problem,'[36] the legislation was amended (SBC 1938, c. 63) to further facilitate its use against the historical targets of anti-VD campaigns – street prostitutes. Initial control over the administration of the legislation shifted from local medical health officers to the provincial health officer, thereby centralizing state power in the hands of a doctor; and the provincial health officer was empowered to order VD testing of any person in police custody.[37] The revised statute, together with the Criminal Code, underpinned a sweeping drive against prostitution (and VD) that was launched in January 1939 and continued throughout the Second World War.[38]

The moral impetus for the suppression of prostitution campaign was unmistakable. Longstanding conceptions of prostitutes as 'undeserving' women, who infected unsuspecting men, clearly remained engrained in the public culture. Notwithstanding talk of medical science and public health, the British Columbia director of VD control, Dr Williams, sounded remarkably like the traditional moral reformers in his statements on the need to eradicate commercialized vice: 'The day has come when this illegal and unsavory provincial *business* can no longer be tolerated' (emphasis in original).[39]

Moreover, Dr Williams proactively and successfully recruited assistance for his anti-vice crusade from churches and other social reform constituencies; the media, the British Columbia Medical Association, and government ministers, including the provincial secretary.[40] As the latter explained to the mayor of Tacoma, Washington, in 1941: 'Despite all the insidious attacks that have been made upon Dr. Williams and myself ... we are ... actively committed to a policy of suppression ... and so long as I am actively charged with responsibility for administering the health services of the province I propose to continue the policy upon which we are now embarked.'[41] Social hygiene required the suppression of 'undeserving' women – 'Hitler's Girlfriends.'[42] This approach was the old moralism in technocratic guise.

Conclusions

Many people would ask what relevance the foregoing analysis has in today's world. From a feminist perspective looking at history is key to understanding the present. Virtually every contentious issue today, including sexual epidemic and safe sex and separating the 'fit' from the 'unfit,' also was the subject of debate during the late nineteenth and early twentieth centuries. The parallels and differences between the historical reaction to VD and the contemporary reaction to AIDS have been well documented (for example, Brandt 1985; McGinnis 1990; Showalter 1990). The point is not that history literally repeats itself, but rather, that feminists can learn from and build upon past struggles. Then, the antidote to social deconstruction and 'sexual anarchy' was a 'hands on' state and a blurring of the public/private line. Now, the emerging response to social fragmentation and 'sexual permissiveness' seems to be a decentralized state and the resurrection of a strict public/private divide. An historical analysis of anti-VD campaigns in British Columbia can help contemporary feminists to decipher the regulation of sex, sexuality, and reproduction in liberal democracies that are undergoing transformation and provide a basis for informed action. Therefore, I will conclude with a few comments on my main findings to date and their implications for feminist strategizing.

Among other things, the British Columbia study suggests that the form and degree of state regulation of the 'private' are never preordained. The structural/cultural context (e.g., historical specificities) sets the parameters of the possible options at a given moment, but it does not determine which of them will be pursued and/or implemented. Different approaches between (and within) countries are obvious. For instance, anti-VD initiatives in Canada were much more explicitly state funded than they were in the United States and Britain; mandatory premarital VD testing was enforced in many American states but not in British Columbia, and so on.

Moreover, the British Columbia case study shows that historical constructions of, and reactions to, 'social problems' are the outcome of struggle, resistance, negotiation, even chance, and that, when particular types of regulation are implemented, they do not automatically constitute a seamless system of social control. Competing ideologies and discourses underpin contradictory motivations and practices among and between the regulators as well as the regulated. During the interwar years in British Columbia, many lay reformers, doctors and other non-legal experts, legal agents, pharmaceutical companies, and government officials agreed that VD was 'bad' and ought to be eradicated, but there were intra- and intergroup conflicts related to the explanation of, and solution to, the problem. These disagreements obviously mitigated the impact of any measures that were implemented. For example, notwithstanding their legal obligation to do so, many doctors in private practice failed to report VD cases, perhaps out of a class-based desire to protect a clientele that could afford their services in a pre-Medicare era. The limits of state commitment to anti-VD initiatives also were demonstrated by a chronic underfunding of public clinics. In addition, the targets of VD regulation themselves – both public clinic and private patients – undermined enforcement efforts by using false names, lying about or not providing the names of their contacts, failing to return for follow-up treatment and/or resorting to 'quacks.'

The British Columbia study also illustrates the falseness of the persistent dichotomy between moralism and science in liberal states. Doctors (and other experts) who differentiated themselves so carefully from religious moralists during the interwar campaigns against VD often shared the same avoidance attitude towards sex. Ostensibly focused on the scientific tip of the iceberg above water, they foundered on the pervasive moralism that was submerged. They too harboured class, race, and gender-based assumptions about who was blameless and who blameworthy in the spread of VD. Respectable (white), working class, and affluent women deserved protection and assistance, not as individuals but as the reproductive insurance of the nation. All others were 'undeserving' and legitimate targets of coercion to protect society from their irresponsibility.

The enduring moralism that underpinned the scientification of sex, sexuality, and reproduction from the late nineteenth century onward helps to explain why VD was not eradicated in the same way as other communicable diseases such as tuberculosis and cholera. Regardless of 'scientific' pronouncements that VD should be treated like any other disease, it could not be divorced from sex. Attempts to inculcate the idea that people could catch VD from toilet seats and drinking fountains ultimately failed. Efforts to hide the sexual connotations of VD by taking the sex out of organizational names were similarly unsuccessful: 'social hygiene' still meant venereal disease and prostitution. Moreover, responses to VD reflected the moral conundrum confronted by eugenicists more generally: 'If we teach sex education in the schools and make condoms or washes widely available, will we not make it easier for people to engage in illicit sex and to spread disease?'

The historical analysis of anti-VD campaigns in British Columbia has several implications for contemporary feminists who are grappling with the public/private divide. First, in ongoing attempts to 'politicize the personal,' they need to recognize the class, race, and gender basis of 'the private' and to avoid making a blanket argument that privacy is 'bad' *per se*. At the same time, feminists should eschew the temptation to condemn all state intervention in the private, given the decimation of the 'social' that currently is under way in Canada and other liberal democracies. Second, feminists must analyse and exploit the contradictions, within and outside state institutions, which create spaces for struggle and change. The same lack of homogeneity that exists among women also characterizes those who make decisions about them, whether they be in government bureaucracies or non-government agencies, legal or non-legal experts. Finally, feminists must think beyond 'what is,' where the parameters of debate and struggle are the limits of liberalism. Disillusionment with the law, for instance, should lead to neither a privileging of the non-legal expert over the legal nor a failure to explore the feasibility of pursuing diverse strategies for achieving the equality of all women. As history tells us, what is dismissed as impossibly utopian today could be the status quo of tomorrow.

NOTES

The original version of this paper was presented at the Symposium, 'Women and the State,' University of Victoria, October 1993. Fiona Kay produced useful comments on an early draft and Bob Menzies provided much needed technical expertise. Special thanks to Susan Boyd for her excellent commentary and editing throughout the writing process. I also am grateful for the SSHRCC Postdoctoral Fellowship (1989–90) that enabled me to begin the research for this paper.

1 The racist basis of suffrage should be noted. In 1920 universal suffrage meant that most white, adult Canadians could vote in federal elections, but most aboriginal people and persons of colour could not (Bacchi 1983).

2 The 'classic' sexually transmitted diseases were chancroid, gonorrhea, and syphilis (Cassel 1987, 12).

3 In Canada, one of the first conditional federal grants to the provinces was for anti-VD initiatives and when Ottawa eliminated this funding during the 1930s Depression, most provinces continued their efforts at VD control 'despite serious financial difficulties' (Cassel 1987, 145, 199).

4 The gendered nature of anti-VD educational initiatives is clear. Educational materials for men focused mainly on the dire consequences *for them* of consorting with 'bad' women and medical quacks, whereas those directed at women centred largely on the threat *they* posed to biological and social reproduction if they contracted VD (Cassel 1987, chapter 9).

5 'British Columbia Leads in Venereal Disease Education,' *Vancouver News-Herald* (hereafter NH), 3 March 1942, p. 8.

6 United Church Archives (hereafter UCA), Dobson Papers, Box B13, File 8, 'The Record System as Set Up for the Division of VD Control,' *Bulletin of the British Columbia Board of Health*, vol. 7, no. 11, 1937 (Aug. Suppl.).

7 Like many provinces, British Columbia enacted anti-VD legislation after the First World War. See Venereal Diseases Suppression Act, SBC 1919, c. 88; Cassel 1987, 160–4.

8 Lacking any systematic data on the issue, I am assuming that in British Columbia the 'deserving' tended to be white, anglo, Protestant, middle or respectable working class, whereas the 'undeserving' included disproportionate numbers of working and dependent poor from ethnic (e.g., continental

European), racial (e.g., Asian and Aboriginal), and religious minorities (Barman 1991, 363).

9 Public Archives of British Columbia (hereafter PABC), Provincial Secretary, GR496 Box 37, File 20, H.M. Cassidy, *The Problem of VD Control in British Columbia: A Report With Recommendations*, 17 May 1936.

10 Ibid.

11 Ibid.

12 'Sex Education in BC Schools Accomplished Fact, Says Weir,' *Vancouver Province* (hereafter VP), 9 June 1939, p. 32.

13 PABC, Provincial Secretary, GR496 Box 37, File 20.

14 Ibid., Box 37, File 1, Amyot to Pearson, 27 Jan.1942.

15 Ibid., 'Syphilis Toll: Useless Tragedy,' NH, 2 Feb. 1942, p. 5.

16 Ibid., Pearson to Private Secretary, Lt Gov., 28 Jan. 1942.

17 Ibid., Pearson to Amyot 30 Jan. 1942; Endorsation 'Prevention of Prenatal Syphilis Week.' See also 'Drive Launched against Syphilis,' *Victoria Daily Times*, 2 Feb. 1942, p. 9.

18 For example, in 1930 a Liberal MLA, A.M. Manson, garnered support for a proposal that all people be required to obtain a medical bill of health before receiving a marriage licence, but the ruling Conservative party argued against hasty action in the interests of national uniformity of legislation. 'Seek Uniform Eugenic Laws,' VP, 22 Feb. 1930, p. 14; in 1936 Ernest Winch, leader of the CCF party, introduced the Marriage Act Amendment Act that would have required doctors to test all prospective brides and grooms for VD and inform them of the results. PABC, Provincial Secretary, GR496 Box 50, File 16.

19 Malcolm Baber, 'Weir Plans PreMarriage Health Certificate Probe to Sit During Year,' VP, 1 Dec. 1937.

20 Marriage Act Amendment Act, SBC 1938, c. 33. See also, PABC, Premier, GR1222 Box 154, File 4.

21 UCA, Dobson Papers, Box 13, File 9, BC Provincial Board of Health, Division of VD Control, *Monthly Bulletin*, vol. 2, no. 3, May 1938. The preference of the medical profession for voluntary compliance by the 'deserving' perhaps reflected a class-based reluctance to apply coercion to their own kind.

22 Premier, GR1222 Box 43, File 7, Gladys E. Simms, Hon. Corresp. Secty, VLCW to Premier John Hart, 7 Oct. 1942.

23 Ibid., Box 54, File 5, Mrs Elsie D. Hunt, Secty, Cobble Hill WI, to Hart, 22 Dec. 1943.

24 Ibid., Box 175, File 1, Mrs R. Miller, Pres., Somanos WI, to Hart 14 Jan. 1944; Mrs M.F. Maitland, Secty, Shawnigan Lake WI, to Hart, 17 Jan. 1944; Box 175, File 2, Edith M. Millward, Secty, Langford WI, to Hart, 28 Jan. 1944.

25 Ibid., Box 54, File 5, Mrs R.C. Weldon, Secty, Vancouver District WCTU, to Hart, 27 April 1944; Mrs E.D. Fletcher, Secty, Fairview Baptist Church Women's Auxiliary, to Hart, 12 May 1944; Mrs M. Reed, Secty, St Margaret's Women's Auxiliary (Vancouver), to Hart, 6 June 1944.

26 Ibid., Box 175, File 1, Frances Barr, Secretary, CSA, Greater Victoria to Hart, 6 March 1944.

27 Ibid., Box 54, File 5, Marjorie Bradford, Executive Director, VCSA, to Premier Hart, 4 April 1944.

28 Ibid., Amyot to Hart, 17 April 1944.

29 Ibid., Box 43, File 7, Provincial Secty Pearson to G.E. Simms, VLCW, 14 Oct. 1942.

30 Ibid., Box 54, File 5, Premier Hart to M. Bradford, VCSA, 18 April 1944.

31 To date, I have no data that directly support or refute this argument, but Pat Maitland, Conservative party leader and attorney general in British Columbia's wartime coalition government, had opposed unilateral implementation of such tests by the province. 'Seek Uniform Eugenic Laws,' VP, 22 Feb. 1930, p. 14.

32 PABC, Provincial Secretary, GR496 Box 41, File 18, P. Walker, Deputy PS, to Warden, Provincial Gaol, Oakalla; Principal, School for the Deaf and Blind, Vancouver; Medical Supt., Provincial Mental Hospital, Essondale; Supt., Prov. Industrial Home for Girls, Vancouver; Principal, Prov. Industrial School for Boys, Port Coquitlam; Medical Supt., Prov. Home for Incurables, Vancouver, 2 Mar. 1937.

33 Ibid., Gaol Surgeon to Warden, Oakalla Prison Farm, 24 March 1937; Warden, Oakalla, to J.H. McMullin, Inspector of Gaols, 24 March 1937; J.H. McMullin to attorney general, 25 March 1937.

34 Ibid., Annie Westman to P. Walker, Deputy PS, 8 Mar. 1937.

35 Matters (1984, 269–71) noted the class tilt of her sample (most of the 600 girls came from extremely poor families), but provided no information about their race or ethnicity except to say that she excluded 108 Doukhobor girls admitted in 1932 because they were not classed as delinquents.

36 UCA, Dobson Papers, Box B13, File 9, Prov. Board of Health, Division of VD Control, *Monthly Bulletin*, vol. 2, no. 3, May 1938.

37 PABC, Premier, GR1222 Box 154, File 4, 'Summary of Legislation, 1938.'

38 'Drastic Drive against VD Here,' *Vancouver Sun*, 13 Jan. 1939, p. 14; 'Vice Clean-Up Ordered in Vancouver, VD Situation Serious,' *Calgary Daily Herald*, 14 Jan. 1939, p. 3.

39 UCA, Dobson Papers, Box B13, File 10, D.E. Williams to Rev. Hugh Dobson, 10 June 1941.

40 Ibid., Box 13, File 9, BC Conference, United Church of Canada, Evangelism and Social Service Report, May 1941; Dobson to Williams, 2 Sept. 1943; 'Public

Information,' VH editorial, 14 June 1941; 'Editorial,' *Bulletin of the Vancouver Medical Assn.*, July 1941.
41 PABC, Provincial Secretary, GR496 Box 37, File 1, PS to Harry P. Cain, Mayor, City of Tacoma, 19 Aug. 1941.
42 This was the theme of anti-prostitution propaganda aimed at allied military personnel during the Second World War (Brandt 1985).

REFERENCES

Arnup, Katherine. 1994. *Education for Motherhood: Advice for Mothers in Twentieth-Century Canada.* Toronto: University of Toronto Press
– Andrée Lévesque, and Ruth Roach Pierson, eds. 1990. *Delivering Motherhood: Maternal Ideologies and Practices in the nineteenth and twentieth Centuries.* London: Routledge
Bacchi, Carol Lee. 1983. *Liberation Deferred? The Ideas of the English-Canadian Suffragists, 1877–1918.* Toronto: University of Toronto Press
Backhouse, Constance. 1985. 'Nineteenth-Century Canadian Prostitution Law.' *Histoire sociale / Social History* 18(36), 387–423
Barman, Jean. 1991. *The West beyond the West: A History of British Columbia.* Toronto: University of Toronto Press
Barrett, Michèle, and Mary McIntosh. 1982. *The Anti-Social Family.* London: Verso
Boyd, Susan B. 1989a. 'Child Custody, Ideologies and Employment.' *Canadian Journal of Women and the Law* 3(1), 111–33
– 1989b. 'From Gender-Specificity to Gender-Neutrality? Ideologies in Canadian Child Custody Law.' In Carol Smart and Selma Sevenhuijsen, eds., *Child Custody and the Politics of Gender.* London: Routledge, 126–57
Brandt, Allan M. 1985. *No Magic Bullet: A Social History of Venereal Disease in the United States since 1880.* Oxford: Oxford University Press
Brodie, Janine. 1995. *Politics on the Margins: Restructuring and the Canadian Women's Movement.* Halifax: Fernwood
– Shelley A.M. Gavigan, and Jane Jenson. 1992. *The Politics of Abortion.* Toronto: Oxford University Press
Buckley, Suzanne, and Janice Dickin McGinnis. 1982. 'Venereal Disease and Public Health Reform in Canada.' *Canadian Historical Review* 63(3), 337–54
Cassel, Jay. 1987. *The Secret Plague: Venereal Disease in Canada, 1838–1939.* Toronto: University of Toronto Press
Chapman, Terry. 1977. 'The Early Eugenics Movement in Western Canada.' *Alberta History* 25, 9–17
Chunn, Dorothy E. 1992. *From Punishment to Doing Good: Family Courts and Socialized Justice in Ontario, 1880–1940.* Toronto: University of Toronto Press

Dickinson, Harley D. 1993. 'Scientific Parenthood: The Mental Hygiene Movement and the Reform of Canadian Families, 1925–1950.' *Journal of Comparative Studies* 24(3), 387–402

Dobash, R. Emerson, and Russell P. Dobash. 1979. *Violence against Wives.* New York: Free Press

Donzelot, Jacques. 1980. *The Policing of Families.* New York: Pantheon

Ellis, Havelock. 1912. *The Task of Social Hygiene.* London: Constable

Finch, Lynette. 1993. *The Classing Gaze: Sexuality, Class and Surveillance.* Sydney: Allen and Unwin

Foucault, Michel. 1980. *The History of Sexuality,* vol. 1. New York: Vintage Books

Garland, David. 1985. *Punishment and Welfare: A History of Penal Strategies.* Aldershot: Gower

Gavigan, Shelley A.M. 1993. 'Paradise Lost, Paradox Revisited: The Implications of Familial Ideology for Feminist, Lesbian and Gay Engagement to Law.' *Osgoode Hall Law Journal* 31(3), 589–624

Gordon, Linda. 1988. *Heroes of Their Own Lives: The Politics and History of Family Violence.* Harmondsworth: Penguin

– 1977. *Woman's Body, Woman's Right: A Social History of Birth Control in America.* Harmondsworth: Penguin

hooks, bell. 1991. 'Homeplace: A Site of Resistance.' In *Yearning: Race, Gender, and Cultural Politics.* London: Turnaround; 41–9

Kuhn, Annette. 1988. *Cinema, Censorship and Sexuality, 1909–1925.* London: Routledge

MacKinnon, Catharine. 1983. 'The Male Ideology of Privacy.' *Radical America* 17(4), 23–35

Matters, Indiana. 1984. 'Sinners or Sinned Against?: Historical Aspects of Female Juvenile Delinquency in British Columbia.' In Barbara K. Latham and Roberta J. Pazdro, eds., *Not Just Pin Money: Selected Essays on the History of Women's Work in British Columbia.* Victoria: Camosun College, 265–77

McGinnis, Janice Dickin. 1990. 'Law and the Leprosies of Lust: Regulating Syphilis and AIDS.' *Ottawa Law Review* 22(1), 49–75

– 1988. 'From Salvarsan to Penicillin: Medical Science and VD Control in Canada.' In Wendy Mitchinson and Janice Dickin McGinnis, eds., *Essays in the History of Canadian Medicine.* Toronto: McClelland and Stewart, 126–47

McLaren, Angus. 1990. *Our Own Master Race: Eugenics in Canada, 1885–1945.* Toronto: McClelland and Stewart

– and Arlene Tigar McLaren. 1986. *The Bedroom and the State: The Changing Practices and Politics of Contraception and Abortion in Canada, 1880–1980.* Toronto: McClelland and Stewart

O'Donovan, Katherine. 1985. *Sexual Divisions in Law*. London: Weidenfeld and Nicolson

Pateman, Carole. 1989. 'Feminist Critiques of the Public/Private Dichotomy.' In C. Pateman, *The Disorder of Women: Democracy, Feminism and Political Theory.* Stanford: Stanford University Press

Roberts, Barbara. 1988. *Whence They Came: Deportation from Canada, 1900–1935.* Ottawa: University of Ottawa Press

Roberts, Dorothy E. 1993. 'Racism and Patriarchy in the Meaning of Motherhood.' *American University Journal of Gender and the Law* 1, 1–38

Rowbotham, Sheila, and Jeffrey Weeks. 1977. *Socialism and the New Life: The Personal and Sexual Politics of Edward Carpenter and Havelock Ellis*. London: Pluto Press

Sears, Alan. 1995. 'Before the Welfare State: Public Health and Social Policy.' *Canadian Review of Sociology and Anthropology* 32(2), 169–88

Showalter, Elaine. 1990. *Sexual Anarchy: Gender and Culture at the Fin de Siècle.* Harmondsworth: Penguin

Singer, Linda. 1993. *Erotic Welfare: Sexual Theory and Politics in the Age of Epidemic*. London: Routledge

Smart, Carol. 1982. 'Regulating Families or Legitimating Patriarchy? Family Law in Britain.' *International Journal of the Sociology of Law* 10, 129–47

Snell, James G. 1983. 'The White Life for Two: The Defence of Marriage and Sexual Morality in Canada, 1890–1914.' *Histoire sociale / Social History* 31, 111–29

– and Cynthia Comacchio Abeele. 1988. 'Regulating Nuptiality: Restricting Access to Marriage in Early Twentieth-Century English-Speaking Canada.' *Canadian Historical Review* 64(4), 466–89

Snitow, Ann, Christine Stansell, and S. Thompson, eds. 1983. *Powers of Desire: The Politics of Sexuality.* New York: Monthly Review Press

Stephen, Jennifer. 1995. 'The "Incorrigible," the "Bad" and the "Immoral": Toronto's "Factory Girls" and the Work of the Toronto Psychiatric Clinic.' In Louis A. Knafla and Susan W.S. Binnie, eds., *Law, Society and the State: Essays in Modern Legal History.* Toronto: University of Toronto Press, 405–39

Strange, Carolyn. 1995. *Toronto's Girl Problem: The Perils and Pleasures of the City, 1880–1930.* Toronto: University of Toronto Press

– 1988. 'From Modern Babylon to a City upon a Hill: The Toronto Social Survey Commission of 1915 and the Search for Sexual Order in the City.' In Roger Hall, William Westfall, and Laurel Sefton MacDowell, eds., *Patterns of the Past: Interpreting Ontario's History.* Toronto: Dundurn Press, 255–77

Ursel, Jane. 1992. *Private Lives, Public Policy: 100 Years of State Intervention in the Family.* Toronto: Women's Press

Valverde, Mariana. 1991. *The Age of Light, Soap, and Water: Moral Reform in English Canada, 1885–1925.* Toronto: McClelland and Stewart

Walkowitz, Judith. 1992. *City of Dreadful Delight: Narratives of Sexual Danger in Late-Victorian London.* Chicago: University of Chicago Press

– 1980. *Prostitution and Victorian Society: Women, Class, and the State.* Cambridge: Cambridge University Press

Weeks, Jeffrey. 1986. *Sexuality.* London: Tavistock

– 1981. *Sex, Politics and Society.* London: Longman

Young, Robert J.C. 1995. *Colonial Desire: Hybridity in Theory, Culture and Race.* London: Routledge

4

Sounds of Silence:
The Public/Private Dichotomy,
Violence, and Aboriginal Women

JENNIFER KOSHAN

A woman is beaten. She has a black eye, the left side of her chin and her left arm are a mass of green-yellow bruises. She has a cut on her forehead from where she hit the counter. Her forearm is scorched from the wood stove ...

The RCMP tell her that her husband has been picked up and will be charged, but they will have to let him go in about an hour. They suggest she and her two kids stay somewhere else. There is no shelter or transition home. She calls her sister, who reluctantly lets her in. The sister lives in a two-bedroom house and has three children of her own ...

The next day she goes to see the counsellor ... He tells her that she is eligible for social assistance and housing ..., but the fact is that there is no extra housing in town ... Three weeks have passed and life is very stressful. Everyone is quiet around her. Those who aren't quiet, lecture her ...

The preliminary trial date has arrived. A plane lands, and a judge, a clerk, a Crown Prosecutor, a court worker, and defence attorney get off and turn the community centre into a court room. Her husband is talking to his lawyer ... She is told that she doesn't need a lawyer because the Crown, who represents the country, will help her tell her story ... Her husband pleads not guilty, and a new court date is set ...

Six weeks pass. The court date arrives, the plane arrives and she goes to the community centre ... She tells her story. She cries a lot. She is nervous and upset and hasn't had much sleep for weeks. The judge says that her husband hit her without permission and fines him $200 and tells him he can't hit her for a year ...

She leaves the court alone because no one wants to be associated with a woman who breaks up a perfectly good family ... Her sister asks if she will be going home now. She says she has no choice. It was awful being hit and screamed at by one person, but by a town, it's much worse. And her husband doesn't work and hasn't for six months and so he won't be able to pay his fine. If he doesn't, he'll go to jail and then everyone will be even more upset with her ...

She packs her things and takes the kids and goes home. He cannot pay the fine, but she can ... She pulls out her sewing basket and some beads and starts to decorate the moccasins she has made. She will have to make a lot of moccasins to earn $200. But she has two months – she can do it – she's done it before.

Anonymous (1990). 'A Beaten Woman.' In Mary Crnkovich, ed., *'Gossip':*
A Spoken History of Women in the North, 163–5

Critiques of the public/private dichotomy have been very much in vogue in legal scholarship over the past decade and a half (Horwitz 1982). While no one discipline has a monopoly on such critiques, they have been particularly prevalent in, and some would say central to, feminist scholarship and activism (Pateman 1983; Rhode 1989). Within this set of discourses, the public/private dichotomy has engaged a wide spectrum of feminist perspectives in a wide variety of contexts. This chapter focuses on the ways in which male violence against women in intimate relationships has been examined through the prism of the public/private dichotomy.[1] Through this focus the chapter uncovers the history of state regulation of intimate violence against women, and the history of feminist theorizing and activism around intimate violence.

During the 1980s theorizing on the public/private dichotomy served as a backdrop for feminist efforts to reform the law and policy governing male violence against women in intimate relationships (Pahl 1985; Yllo and Bograd 1988). The literature in this context tended to focus on one aspect of the dichotomy – that between family and state. As a result, feminist law reform strategies in relation to male violence against women concentrated on bringing what were formerly treated as private family matters beyond the reach of the state into the public domain, most notably by lobbying for increased responsiveness of the criminal justice system.

I will argue that until quite recently feminist literature on the public/private dichotomy in the context of male violence against women has been reticent in addressing how the dichotomy functions in relation to diverse groups of women. While this omission is significant in relation to factors such as race (Cox 1990), class (Morley and Mullender 1992), disability (McPherson 1991), and sexual orientation (Faulkner 1991), this chapter concentrates on how one group of women – Aboriginal women[2] – has been left out of the analysis. The effects of this omission are twofold: the root causes and major sites of violence against Aboriginal women have been theorized too narrowly, and the solutions proposed and implemented, particularly police and prosecution policy directives, have not been responsive to the needs of Aboriginal women. Given the level of violence against Aboriginal women,[3] their inclusion in the analysis is particularly urgent.

At this point I should note that I am neither an Aboriginal woman nor a survivor of violence. I worked for three years prosecuting cases involving violence against women in the Northwest Territories and thus am familiar with some of the practical issues facing Aboriginal women in this context. The challenge facing me here is to accept responsibility for speaking out against racism, while being attentive to the fact that I should not and cannot speak for Aboriginal women, nor for survivors of intimate violence (Greschner 1992, 339; Kline 1989, 117–18; Monture 1991, 358). As is the case within many communities of women, Aboriginal women have diverse experiences and speak with a diversity of voices (Frank 1992, 2; Monture-Okanee 1992, 247; Turpel 1993, 179). In writing about 'Aboriginal women' at all, I risk homogenizing these voices and experiences. Wherever possible, I rely on the writings of Aboriginal women to ground my analysis, although I recognize that this may still exclude some Aboriginal women.[4]

Feminist Approaches to the Public/Private Dichotomy

Feminist Theorizing about Issues of Violence

Feminist scholarship on violence and the public/private dichotomy has often relied on Euro-Canadian legal history. Until the late nineteenth century violence by a husband against his wife was condoned by the law. According to Blackstone's *Commentaries on the Laws of England*: 'The husband also ... might give his wife moderate correction. For, as he is to answer for her misbehaviour, the law thought it reasonable to entrust him with this power of restraining her, by domestic chastisement, in the same moderation that a man is allowed to correct his apprentices or children' (Blackstone 1884, 444).

Although wife battering was not legally reproachable during this period, community intervention was not unheard of in serious cases (Backhouse 1991, 169; A. Clark 1992, 187; Doggett 1992, 30). The homes of friends, relatives, and neighbours served the same function as modern-day shelters, and family and community disapproval and sanctions served a peacekeeping function (Rhode 1989, 238). However, peace bonds were not readily available and did not authorize separation from an abusive spouse (Doggett 1992, 11–15). Restrictive divorce laws made it virtually impossible for a woman to leave her marriage (Backhouse 1991, 170).

Legal recognition of wife beating as a form of criminal assault finally came in the late nineteenth century.[5] This reform was made during a period of particular concern over violent crime, especially over intimate male violence, and particularly in relation to the working class (Doggett 1992). In Canada a specific offence of wife assault existed from 1909 to 1953 and was punishable by whipping.[6]

Despite these reforms, other legal impediments to the protection of women in the family sphere remained. Until 1983 in Canada a man could not, by definition, be convicted of raping his wife.[7] Moreover, even if a man's violent actions were defined as a crime, his wife was not always held to be a competent and compellable witness against him.[8] While it may have been possible to prove a charge of intimate assault other than through a wife's testimony, the enforcement of the law by the police, prosecution, and the courts was low level and erratic (Hilton 1989, 323; MacKinnon 1989, 239; O'Donovan 1985, 122). When police did respond to 'domestics,' they often attempted to reconcile the parties, and they rarely laid charges. Those charges that were laid were often withdrawn or stayed by the prosecution (Martin and Mosher 1995, 14). Such 'inaction' was justified ideologically by the state on the basis of preserving family unity and stability (Freeman 1989, 20; Hilton 1989; Rhode 1989, 120; Schneider 1994). Thus, the law has been implicated as playing a fundamental role in maintaining the boundary between public and private in the area of intimate violence against women (Polan 1982, 298; Taub and Schneider 1982, 123).

At the same time as feminists pointed to the state's inaction regarding intimate violence, they argued that the notion of state non-intervention in the family must be problematized. Given the state's role in the formation and functioning of families, the concept of non-intervention has been called a myth (Olsen 1985). To focus on the state's non-intervention in the private sphere ignores the mechanisms used by the state, including the law, to support male authority in this realm (O'Donovan 1985). Moreover, any inaction on the part of the state in the private sphere has been highly selective. For example, although courts have been reluctant to look behind the curtain in cases of spousal non-support and violence, they have delved into the details of domestic life in other contexts, such as divorce, child welfare, and, more recently, child sexual abuse (Rhode 1989, 27; Thornton 1991, 449). The extent of such state regulation of the family has often depended on factors such as race (Kline 1993), class (Chunn 1992; A. Clark 1992), and sexual orientation (Robson 1990), with those who challenged the normative model of family being more heavily regulated (Boyd this volume, chapter 1).

Feminist criticism of the public/private dichotomy and of the concept of state (non)intervention in the private sphere has taken a number of different modes (Gavison 1992; Olsen 1993). One mode of critique is exemplified by the radical feminist work of Catharine MacKinnon, who has queried the existence of any private realm for women. For MacKinnon, privacy 'is defined by everything that feminism reveals women have never been allowed to be or to have, and by everything that women have been equated with and defined in terms of men's ability to have' (1987, 99). It is thus a notion of male privacy that is said to have shielded matters such as intimate violence against women from public attention and redress. A second claim made by MacKinnon is that feminist theory views the family as the unit of male dominance, the location of male violence, and hence the primary site of women's oppression (1989, 61). MacKinnon's prescription is to explode the private and treat the personal as political.

Other feminists writing about male violence against women have criticized the social arrangements and structures that result in the vulnerability of women in the private, domestic sphere, and the resulting devaluation of that sphere (Gavison 1992, 35–6). Most have not, however, gone so far as to advocate the destruction of any sphere of privacy (Olsen 1993; Smart 1994). Violence has been identified as one aspect of the family sphere that should be displaced across the private/public dividing line, so that the otherwise private sphere becomes subject to state intervention in the case of intimate violence (Rhode 1989, 318; Schneider 1994). Despite differing levels of the critique of privacy, patriarchy is still construed as the major cause of male violence against women, and the family is seen as the main site of such violence (Dobash and Dobash 1979; Pateman 1983, 286; Schneider 1994).

Thus, during the 1980s much of the feminist scholarship on the public/private dichotomy in the context of male violence against women was unified in its identification of the primary source and site of women's oppression by male violence: the patriarchal family. A more nuanced analysis of the causes and sites of women's oppression has emerged from the work of socialist feminists (Chunn 1995; Gordon 1988), women of colour (Bhavani and Coulson 1986; Cox 1990), and lesbian scholars (Eaton 1994). These writers see the source of intimate violence as more complex than can be described by patriarchal gender relations, and they view the family as a site of contradiction. However, the more traditional formulation of the gendered public/private dichotomy has provided the major theoretical framework for feminist law reform efforts around the issue of violence against women. One of the main motivations behind such efforts has been to take violence out of the private realm and into the public (Comack 1993, 5; Currie 1990; Hilton 1989; Schneider 1994). While the strategies for accomplishing this goal have varied, many feminist legal activists have focused their attentions on the criminal justice aspect of the public domain.

Feminist Law Reform Efforts

Efforts to make wife abuse visible and a matter of public concern occupied the first stage of struggle for the battered women's movement in Canada in the late 1970s and early 1980s (Currie 1990; Walker 1990). This stage was characterized by lobbying for shelters and other support services for battered women. The second stage of struggle in the 1980s saw the strategic adoption of the 'wife assault' label in order to place the issue squarely within the realm of the criminal law (MacLeod 1980). Up to this point when cases of male violence against women were mounted, they were often dealt with by family courts rather than criminal courts, thereby perpetuating the 'privacy' of domestic violence (Fraser 1985; Hilton 1989, 328).

Reform efforts in the criminal justice realm of the 1980s were said to be justified on the basis of their potential to offer immediate protection to survivors and possibly more long-term protection by deterring future violence (MacLeod 1987, 79–86; McGillivray 1987, 37; Sheehy 1987, 11; Ursel 1990, 544). Some feminists argued that criminal justice reforms could serve to empower survivors by making them less susceptible to their batterers' threats (McGillivray 1987, 37) or by giving them the support and attention of police, lawyers, and the courts (Schneider 1994, 46). Criminal law was seen to have the potential to provide both symbolic and actual justice for women (Clark 1989–90, 428), and to increase public awareness of the issue of intimate violence (Currie 1990, 4–5). Reform efforts in this arena were complemented by lobbying for more and better services for battered women, including victim advocacy and support services (Ursel 1990, 530; Walker 1990).

In the early 1980s standing committees of the federal and Ontario governments were successfully lobbied for hearings on the issue of wife assault, and they were urged to adopt measures to emphasize and enforce its criminal nature (MacLeod 1987, 82; Walker 1990, 68–9). Feminist campaigns against wife assault advocated the creation of new offences, means to increase the number of arrests, charges, and convictions against batterers, as well as more severe levels of punishment (Currie 1990, 85).

One of the standing committees' recommendations was acted upon when police and prosecution policy directives were developed and implemented federally and in some provinces from 1982 to 1984 (Ursel 1990, 531–2). Before these policies were adopted, it was often incumbent on sur-vivors of intimate violence to request that charges be laid in a given case, unlike the charging practices in cases of assault between strangers, where no such request was required (Sheehy 1987, 15–16; Ursel 1990, 530). The policy directives were premised on the assumption that the dynamics in violent spousal relationships rendered the victim powerless to make deci-sions about involvement in the criminal justice system (Attorney General of B.C. 1993, 3–4). Thus, charges were to be laid by the investigating officer in cases of 'domestic violence' where supported by reasonable and proba-ble grounds to believe an offence had been committed, irrespective of the wishes of the complainant.[9] Arrests were to be made where a serious indictable offence had been committed as part of a domestic dispute, unless the officer had reasonable grounds to believe that the public interest could be satisfied without arresting the suspect.

The companion policy directive to federal Crown prosecutors provided that a decision to terminate a 'spousal assault' prosecution should be excep-tional, and it should be made by the Crown and not the victim.[10] This pol-icy was amended in 1993 to 'improve protection and assistance for victims' (Department of Justice 1993, V-7-2). In response to criticism of the earlier version of the policy (Snider 1994, 85), the amended policy notes that it is not 'intended to encourage the prosecution of spouses who defend them-selves during an attack.' Decisions to terminate prosecutions must now take into account, among other factors, any reliable evidence tending to suggest that the victim would be 'unduly traumatized' if required to testify. Still, Crown counsel are to 'make every effort to encourage reluctant vic-tims to testify, including putting them on the witness stand ... The more serious the offence, the more appropriate it will be to take all reasonable steps to compel testimony, including use of the adverse witness procedures' (Canada, Department of Justice 1993, V-7-7–V-7-8). Crown counsel are directed not to 'doubly victimize spousal assault victims by prosecuting them for failing to testify ... Crown counsel should not move to cite the victim for contempt except in compelling circumstances' (ibid., V-7-8).

As noted by Currie (1990), not all feminists claim the implementation of such policies as victories. Some feminist critiques have focused on the lack of structural change effected by criminal law reforms such as police and Crown policy directives (Currie 1990; Martin and Mosher 1995; Rhode 1989, 244; Snider 1990, 145). Others argue that reform efforts of the bat-tered women's movement were co-opted by the state (Hilton 1989, 327; Walker 1990, 172) and that they remove control of the process from survivors of intimate male violence (Snider 1994, 87–93). One result of such a loss of control has been the citing of some reluctant victim-witnesses for contempt of court.[11] The punitive 'law and order approach' of criminal law reforms has also been criticized, including the way in which such reforms are often enforced most stringently against non-middle class, non-white offenders (Snider 1994, 78; 1990, 145). Lastly, many critiques are based on the lack of conclusive evidence that the policies work.[12]

Insights such as these have rarely resulted in a rejection or even decentring of the criminal law as a site of reform, however. Arrest, charging, and prosecution policies remain in force across Canada, causing forced engagement with the public realm. There has been little movement in reforming the criminal arena itself to provide greater control to survivors of violence or to answer the other criticisms noted above.[13] Indeed, some feminists have asserted that the 'private' interests of individual victims must give way to those of the state in controlling violence (McGillivray 1987), and others note that civil remedies and criminal injuries compensation schemes exist to speak to such private interests (West 1992; Wiegers 1994). Critiques of the public/private dichotomy, and the law reform efforts grounded in such critiques, have been largely silent on the difficulties caused by the separation of the legal system itself into public and private realms.

Moreover, feminist legal scholarship has only recently begun to account for the ways in which the experiences of women other than the white middle-class 'norm' may complicate the theoretical backdrop for law reforms and how such women may be adversely affected by reforms in practice (Dobash and Dobash 1992; Schneider 1992). In particular, scant attention has been paid to the ways in which police and prosecution policies on male violence against women in intimate relationships affect diverse groups of women.[14]

An Intersectional Analysis of the Public/Private Dichotomy and Feminist Law Reform Efforts

The Exclusion of Aboriginal Women from Feminist Theorizing about Violence

Much of the feminist literature on male violence against women has tended to assume that patriarchy is the primary cause of women's oppression. The focus has been on how gendered power relations are the main contributing factor to violence. When Aboriginal women write about these issues, however, they often begin by noting how violence against women was not prevalent or accepted in their traditional communities. Rather, violence by Aboriginal men against Aboriginal women[15] is described as resulting in large part from the process of colonization (Frank 1992, 2–3; Monture-Okanee 1992, 260; Nahanee 1992, 11–15; Ontario Native Women's Association 1989, 7–9). According to one Aboriginal woman, the term 'domestic violence' itself conjures up images of state violence against First Nations people in addition to male violence against women (Turpel 1993, 183).

The view that violence against women was not acceptable in traditional Aboriginal communities is not universal, however. A recent study on traditional justice among the Dene found that intimate male violence against women may have been accepted to some extent (Ryan 1993, 106). The work of some Aboriginal women maintains that gender relations differed among various Aboriginal cultures (Midnight Sun 1988, 45) and may have included violence against women (La Rocque 1994, 75). Moreover, many Aboriginal women note that even if traditional communities were relatively violence free, some Aboriginal men have internalized the Western de-valuation of women (Courchene 1990, 20; La Rocque 1994, 75; Monture-Okanee 1992, 250), resulting in higher levels of violence. It would be overly simplistic to put gender oppression at the root of male violence in this context – racism and cultural and economic oppression must be recognized as contributing to a complex and intersecting set of oppressions.[16]

The dominant feminist conceptualization of the 'family' as patriarchal and as a key source of women's oppression is also problematic. Aboriginal writers often note that women were traditionally at the centre of the family in their communities (Courchene 1990, 16–19; Turpel 1993, 180). Although there may have been separate spheres for men and women, these were not exclusive, nor were they necessarily ordered in a hierarchical fashion. Gender roles were flexible, and women could and often did participate in both political and productive 'public' life (Johnson, Stevenson, and Greschner 1993, 166; Turpel 1993, 180). There was also a recognized and valued place in many traditional communities for gay and lesbian, or 'two-spirited,' people (Burns 1988).

Moreover, there was no clear demarcation between families and the state in traditional Aboriginal communities. Families were not nuclear or linear entities, and they were at the centre of society in terms of structure and governance (Frank 1992, 7–8; Monture 1991, 356; Ontario Native Women's Association 1989, 8). Cases of violence, for example, were dealt with by families and communities using methods of healing, reconciliation, compensation, and shaming (Courchene 1990, 18). Arguably, therefore, the public/private dichotomy does not accurately depict the relationships between gender, family, and the state in traditional Aboriginal communities (Monture-Okanee and Turpel 1992, 258).

Dominant Euro-Canadian notions of family and state continue to be problematic in many contemporary Aboriginal communities. First, the Canadian state itself is not necessarily accepted as a legitimate entity, as evidenced by the struggle of Aboriginal peoples for self-determination (Turpel 1993, 176). Although the Indian Act[17] regime of band councils has imposed the structures and ideologies of the Canadian state on many Aboriginal communities, families often continue to be the basic organizational and governing units of Aboriginal communities, even in urban centres (Ontario Native Women's Association 1989, 8). If the experiences of women of colour (Bhavani and Coulson 1986, 88; Cox 1990, 244; Ruttenberg 1994, 186) and lesbians (Eaton 1994) are any indication, families are important sites of resistance against the dominant culture as well as sites of violence. Not only is it overly simplistic to say that the family is necessarily a site of oppression for women, it is also inaccurate to identify the family as the *primary* sphere of such oppression for Aboriginal women. The legacy of residential schools is only one example of how Aboriginal women have been subjected to violence outside the private family sphere (Das Gupta 1995, 148; Nahanee 1992, 13).

A related difficulty with the application of a public/private analysis to contemporary Aboriginal communities is the feminist critique of state nonintervention in the private sphere. Although feminists have shown this conceptualization to be inaccurate, they have generally not noted the ways in which different families may be more or less immune to state intervention.[18] Aboriginal families have been particularly susceptible to state intervention in the child welfare arena (Kline 1993; Monture 1989), for example. Conversely, the state has often been all too willing to avoid intervening where housing and other social services are required by Aboriginal peoples. This contradiction emphasizes the highly selective nature of action/inaction on the part of the state.

Aboriginal women do not allow traditional gender and family relations, and the impact of colonization thereon, to justify or excuse male violence against women in contemporary Aboriginal communities (La Rocque 1994; Nahanee 1992). There may be community pressure on Aboriginal women to avoid perpetuating racist stereotypes about Aboriginal men and violence, or to support their families and not expose them to criticism. This pressure, however, does not necessarily render them silent. The salient point is that the dominant theoretical framework that has been used by feminists and their strategies for responding to violence should not be assumed to be the same as those of Aboriginal women, or equally relevant to them (Monture-Okanee 1992, 256). Nor are solutions conceived of in a singular fashion by Aboriginal women (Frank 1992, 17). Factors of poverty, age, disability, and sexual orientation may be germane to how different Aboriginal women experience violence and in the construction of solutions that respond appropriately to their diverse needs (Canadian Panel on Violence Against Women 1993, 160–3). There tended to be silence on these diverse needs and concerns at the level of earlier feminist law reform efforts around intimate male violence.

The Exclusion of Aboriginal Women from Feminist Law Reform Efforts

The perception of some Aboriginal (Ontario Native Women's Association 1989) and other 'minority women' (Kohli 1991) is that the battered women's movement in Canada was neither diverse nor attuned to the needs of all women at the time when it lobbied for charging and prosecution policy directives (Currie 1990, 90). Recent studies on violence against women have perhaps been more sensitive to the need to hear the voices of all women. For example, recent reports on family violence at the federal and provincial levels have included parallel studies on violence against Aboriginal women.[19] Nevertheless, it is instructive to examine how one concrete reform that emanated from early feminist lobbying efforts in the public realm – namely, charging and prosecution policies – has had, and continues to have, an adverse impact on Aboriginal women.

No empirical studies have been published to date on how such policies affect different women in practice in Canada,[20] but the reports on violence against Aboriginal women and their engagement with the criminal justice system make it possible to hypothesize the effects of such policies on them. A review of these reports suggests that both traditional values and contemporary realities may play a role in how Aboriginal women experience the policy directives at different stages of the criminal process.

The preceding discussion of the concept of family in Aboriginal communities is relevant in this regard. The desire to maintain domestic relationships because of their importance to Aboriginal women and their communities has been identified as a factor that may discourage Aboriginal women from reporting cases of violence or from wanting to proceed with charges or prosecution (Courchene 1990; Native Women's Association of Canada 1991; Ontario Native Women's Association 1989). Aboriginal women often say that what they want is a healing process to end the violence, not an adversarial, punitive process to end their families. This refrain echoes throughout other communities of women as well (Martin and Mosher 1995, 4–6).

Many Aboriginal women also articulate a fear of pressure and potential ostracism from family members and their community if they speak out about violence (La Rocque 1994, 77; Ontario Native Women's Association 1989, 18; Peterson 1992, 61). These factors may also come into play in the case of non-Aboriginal women survivors of male violence. In particular, immigrant and refugee women, lesbians, women living in rural areas, and women with disabilities may experience contradictory notions of family and community (Canadian Panel on Violence Against Women 1993; Law Reform Commission of Nova Scotia 1995).

Another critical factor is the well-documented racism and lack of cultural sensitivity of the Euro-Canadian criminal justice system towards Aboriginal peoples (Alberta 1991; Jackson 1989; Law Reform Commission of Canada 1991; Manitoba 1991; Nova Scotia 1989; Royal Commission on Aboriginal Peoples 1996). Aboriginal women may be unwilling to subject their partners to a system that has resulted in the significant overrepresentation and incarceration of Aboriginal men (Frank 1992, 16). Moreover, Aboriginal women reportedly lack confidence in the justice system and its ability to stop violence, and they may be unwilling to subject themselves to the victim blaming that occurs at different levels of the criminal arena (Frank 1992, 16; Native Women's Association of Canada 1989; Peterson 1992, 64). Again, these factors may also be relevant in other contexts. In particular, women of colour and immigrant women often express a reluctance to subject themselves or their partners to a racist justice system (Crenshaw 1990; Martin and Mosher 1995, 27–31; Law Reform Commission of Nova Scotia 1995, 18–19). On the other hand, some Aboriginal women decry as racist the lenient sentencing of Aboriginal men convicted of crimes of violence, including the use of sentencing circles. They maintain that the criminal justice system should be applied in full force pending the implementation of self-government and the creation of separate Aboriginal justice systems (La Rocque 1994, 83–4; Nahanee 1992, 4–5; Pauktuutit 1995).

Other facets of the Euro-Canadian criminal justice system have also been identified as problematic. Delays in hearing cases of intimate violence against women, especially in small and isolated communities, may create a disruption to any healing that has taken place and may affect whether a complainant wishes to testify (Courchene 1990, 99–103; Peterson 1992, 58, 68). In addition, charging and prosecution policies removed what little control survivors of intimate violence had retained over the criminal justice process (Peterson 1992, 57). Although these problems may face all survivors of intimate male violence, Aboriginal women are particularly affected in that this lack of control does not accord with traditional justice processes in Aboriginal communities (Monture-Okanee and Turpel 1992, 258). This discordance creates an even more foreign 'justice experience' for Aboriginal women.

Another difficulty lies in the lack of support services and shortage of housing for Aboriginal women who experience male violence (Turpel 1991). Again, this concern is particularly significant in small and isolated communities (La Rocque 1994, 81–2; Manitoba 1991, 484–5; Peterson 1992, 49). Even for Aboriginal women living in urban settings, who may have better access to shelters, counselling, and advocacy services, support services are rarely culturally appropriate (Courchene 1990, 28–32; Frank 1992, 10–15). Aboriginal women may also lack information about such services, depriving them of the ability to make informed decisions about their involvement with the criminal justice system (Native Women's Association of Canada 1991, 8; Ontario Native Women's Association 1989, 27–8). Given the high incidence of poverty confronting many Aboriginal women, and their lack of employment opportunities, they may be forced to maintain their financial dependence on an abusive partner (Native Women's Association of Canada 1991, 4; Peterson 1992, 62). Similarly, lack of resources and services may affect the experience of non-Aboriginal women with the criminal justice system (Martin and Mosher 1995).

The cumulative effect of these factors renders Aboriginal women's engagement with the criminal justice system very problematic. Where such engagement is forced by way of charging and prosecution policies, the opportunities for injustice are magnified. An Aboriginal woman would have to weigh, if she even knew such a choice existed, the option of calling the police at the risk of having to proceed through the full criminal process against the risks involved in not reporting an incident of violence (Peterson 1992, 19). Worse still, the policies may remove a woman's control over violence itself by failing to recognize that some women choose not to pursue charges, and to remain with abusive partners as a matter of survival (Mahoney 1991). Alternatively, if a woman chose to call the police for assistance, but later decided she did not want to proceed to trial for any of the myriad reasons discussed above, she would risk being revictimized by a policy that calls for rigorous prosecution or by being cited in contempt of court. According to some sources, the problem of intimate violence has been driven underground in many Aboriginal communities as a result (Billson 1990, 56–8). Two reports dealing with Aboriginal women, violence, and the criminal justice system therefore recommended that the prosecution policy directives be abrogated in the case of Aboriginal women (Ontario Native Women's Association 1989, 44; Peterson 1992, 50).

Conclusion

The public/private dichotomy may be a useful starting point for feminist theorizing around issues of male violence against women, as it describes the historical treatment of such violence by the Euro-Canadian state. The analysis breaks down, however, where it leads to assumptions about the causes and sites of violence against women that ignore factors such as racialization, class, disability, and sexual orientation. Feminist critiques must be broadened to recognize that public/private analysis may be of limited utility in some cases. For example, theorizing violence against Aboriginal women involves very different conceptions of gender relations, family, and the state than those that may operate in a non-Aboriginal setting. To assume that patriarchal gender relations are the primary cause and to locate the family as the primary site of women's oppression, does not accord with the analysis of these issues by Aboriginal women, or indeed, by many non-Aboriginal women.

When the public/private dichotomy becomes the framework for feminist law reform efforts in the context of male violence against women, as it did in the early 1980s, these difficulties may be further entrenched. It is overly simplistic, and perhaps harmful, to equate 'public' with a response that results in survivors' forced engagement with the criminal justice system via police and prosecution policy directives. Whereas initially it was thought that these policies may be useful as both symbols of and vehicles for state action around issues of intimate violence, time has shown that any such initiatives must be more responsive to the needs and concerns of survivors of violence, in all their diversity.

For Aboriginal women, the fact that self-government and the creation of separate Aboriginal justice systems have wide support (Courchene 1990, 99; Monture-Okanee and Turpel 1992; Nahanee 1992, 2; Ontario Native Women's Association 1989, 89–90) magnifies the injustice of their forced engagement with the Euro-Canadian criminal process. Aboriginal justice initiatives often collapse the divide between civil and criminal realms, focusing on more holistic approaches to healing in which the accused, survivor, and community all play central roles (Monture-Okanee and Turpel 1992). If coalitions could be built around issues of intimate violence,

Aboriginal women would have much knowledge and experience to share with other women.

Silence has surrounded the treatment of violence against Aboriginal women for too long, both within the feminist community and elsewhere.[21] Just as the concept of state non-intervention has been exposed as action in disguise, so must these silences be recognized as sounds. The voices of Aboriginal women must be heard within their own communities, the feminist community,[22] and the larger society if their own ideas about, and solutions to, violence are to become a reality.

NOTES

The title is taken from a song by Simon and Garfunkel, 'The Sounds of Silence,' 1964, *Wednesday Morning 3 a.m.* Columbia Records. I would like to thank Susan B. Boyd and the contributors to this collection for their insightful comments on this piece. The views expressed are my own and do not represent the views of West Coast LEAF.

1 Battering also occurs in some lesbian relationships. This phenomenon poses a particular challenge to the conception of violence against women as rooted exclusively in patriarchy. See Robson (1990) and Faulkner (1991). See also Eaton (1994), who examines feminist theories of domestic violence in the context of lesbian difference.

2 I use the term 'Aboriginal women' to refer to women who are of Indian, Inuit, and Métis ancestry, regardless of their legal status. While the term 'First Nations' is often used today to emphasize historical and political status, it may connote only the inclusion of 'status Indians,' and it does not normally include Inuit or Métis peoples. See Johnson, Stevenson, and Greschner (1993), Turpel (1993).

3 The figures range from a 33 per cent incidence rate (i.e., 33 per cent of women are survivors of violence) cited in the *Report of the Aboriginal Justice Inquiry of Manitoba* (Manitoba 1991) to a rate of 80 per cent reported by Ontario Native Women's Association (1989). See also Courchene (1990), reporting a rate of 53 per cent for women responding to the survey conducted by the Indigenous Women's Collective for the Manitoba Aboriginal Justice Inquiry. According to a review of three Canadian Centre for Justice Statistics studies in Moyer (1992), 60.6 per cent of violent acts against Aboriginal women are committed by family members, usually spouses. Aboriginal women are particularly likely to be beaten to death.

4 Little is written by or about Aboriginal women who also identify themselves

according to factors of age, disability, poverty, and sexual orientation. These factors will be relevant to how individual Aboriginal women experience violence.

5 The legal right to batter was finally removed in England, at least in the formal sense, in the case of *R. v Jackson*, [1891] 1 QB 671 at 682 (CA). See Doggett 1992, 5–8.

6 Criminal Code of Canada, RSC 1927, c. 36, s. 292; replaced by SC 1953–4, c. 51, s. 231.

7 The exemption that permitted men to rape their wives was repealed when the offence of rape was replaced with a gender-neutral scheme of 'sexual assault' provisions in the Criminal Code, by SC 1980–81–82, c. 125, ss. 6, 19.

8 At common law, one spouse was a competent witness for the Crown where an offence against her person, liberty, or health was committed by the other spouse, but this did not necessarily mean she was a compellable witness. See *R. v Singh and Amar*, [1970] 1 CCC 299 (BCCA). Spouses became both competent and compellable witnesses against each other in cases involving interpersonal offences in 1983. See SC 1980–81–82, c. 125, s. 29.

9 See, e.g., the *Recommended Police Directive – Spousal Assault* (Solicitor General 1983). This directive also obliged police to provide protection and assistance to victims by acquainting them with community resources such as emergency shelters, legal aid, counselling facilities, and welfare services, and assisting them in contacting these resources.

10 See the *Recommended Directive to Prosecutors – Spousal Assault* (Attorney General of Canada 1983). The factors to be included in such a decision included any history of prior assault, the safety of the victim and other family members, and any threats of intimidation.

11 Even if it is not Crown policy to pursue contempt proceedings, it remains open to the presiding judge to do so. See *R. v Moore*, [1987] NWTR 47 (TC). See also Adelberg 1984. Another risk is that victim-witnesses who are forced to testify and then deny or minimize an assault could be criminally liable for perjury. See Criminal Code, RSC 1985, c. C-46, s. 132.

12 See Snider (1990, 145), Buzawa and Buzawa (1992), Ruttenberg (1994, 191–4). An early study in the United States suggested that arrest was a better deterrent than providing informal mediation or a short separation in cases of intimate male violence against women (Sherman and Berk 1984). The results of this study have been widely criticized, and despite several efforts, have not been replicated (Martin and Mosher 1995, 33). Also, the replication experiments that found that the offender's racial and employment status affected the question of whether arrest deters future violence have been criticized as fundamentally flawed (see Zorza 1994).

13 While several provinces have recently enacted victims of crime legislation, these initiatives focus on the provision of information and services rather than resulting in any meaningful shift in the role of victims in the criminal justice system. See, e.g., Victims of Crime Act, SBC 1995, c. 47.

14 Some authors, see, e.g., Forell (1991), Morley and Mullender (1992), Peterson (1992), Ruttenberg (1994), Martin and Mosher (1995), have dealt with the differing effects of police and prosecution policies on diverse groups of women. Only Peterson and Martin and Mosher deal with the Canadian context.

15 I will focus on intraracial heterosexual violence because it raises unique issues as to how Aboriginal concepts of family, gender, and the state are left out of mainstream feminist analysis. Of course, interracial family violence is also perpetrated against Aboriginal women. An emphasis on racism and cultural oppression may be even more pertinent in these situations. See Stevenson in Johnson, Stevenson, and Greschner (1993). Violence against lesbians (or 'two-spirited women' in Aboriginal culture) may also occur; however, there is little evidence of the incidence of such violence between lesbians. See Canadian Panel on Violence Against Women 1993. As a practical matter, intraracial heterosexual violence is most pervasive against Aboriginal women. See Moyer (1992).

16 The same point has been made by women of colour writing about issues of oppression. See Cox (1990), Harris (1990), Kohli (1991). I do recognize the need not to overgeneralize how racialization and culturalization may play out in the context of violence against different groups of women (Monture-Okanee 1992, 247); nevertheless, it is useful to look at a broad range of work with a view to identifying the difficulties with some feminist theorizing and the breadth of its impact.

17 RSC 1985, c. I-5.

18 For exceptions where authors have discussed the ways in which different families may be more or less immune to state intervention, see Boyd (1995), who notes that the state was not unwilling to intervene in 'deviant families' such as poor, immigrant, or First Nations families. See also Chunn (1992, 36–44), and A. Clark (1992).

19 A recent study of intimate violence against women in British Columbia included a parallel report of the situation in Aboriginal communities. See Frank (1992). An Aboriginal Women's Circle was added to the Canadian Panel on Violence Against Women after it sustained some criticism that it did not sufficiently represent diverse groups of women (1993).

20 Canadian studies on the efficacy of such policies have been conducted by Jaffe et al. (1991) and Ursel (1990). Neither study analysed data on the basis of race, although this limitation was recognized by Jaffe et al. Generally speaking, both studies found the policies resulted in a higher percentage of charges being laid,

an increased level of victim satisfaction and cooperation, and a decrease in recidivism. In contrast, a recent study by the B.C. Institute on Family Violence found that despite a prosecution policy, almost 30·per cent of domestic violence charges were withdrawn or stayed by the Crown in 1993. See British Columbia Institute on Family Violence 1995. Similar results were obtained by the Law Reform Commission of Nova Scotia in its study of domestic violence policies in that province (1995).

21 Of the many reports dealing with Aboriginal justice issues, only the Manitoba Aboriginal Justice Inquiry (1991) and the Royal Commission on Aboriginal People's Report on Criminal Justice (1996) speak to the needs of Aboriginal women survivors of violence.

22 Aboriginal women have, in the past, expressed ambivalence about the utility of 'feminism' in their struggles, largely because of their perceived exclusion from the feminist mandate. Feminism is said to be only one tool in their fight against multiple forms of oppression (Monture-Okanee 1992, 251–6; Stevenson in Johnson, Stevenson, and Greschner 1993, 159, 167).

REFERENCES

Adelberg, Ellen. 1984. 'When the Victim Goes to Jail: The Law on Contempt of Court.' *Status of Women News* 9(3), 8–10
Alberta. 1991. *Justice on Trial: Report of the Task Force on the Criminal Justice System and Its impact on the Indian and Métis People of Alberta*. Edmonton: Solicitor General
Anonymous. 1990. 'A Beaten Woman.' In Mary Crnkovich, ed., *'Gossip': A Spoken History of Women in the North*. Ottawa: Canadian Arctic Resource Committee, 163–5
Attorney General of BC. 1993. *Violence against Women in Relationships Policy*. Victoria: Ministry of the Attorney General
Attorney General of Canada. 1983. *Recommended Directive to Prosecutors – Spousal Assault*. Ottawa: Department of Justice
Backhouse, Constance. 1991. *Petticoats and Prejudice: Women and Law in Nineteenth Century Canada*. Toronto: Women's Press
Bhavani, Kum-Kum, and Margaret Coulson. 1986. 'Transforming Socialist Feminism: The Challenge of Racism.' *Feminist Review* 23, 81–92
Billson, Janet M. 1990. 'Violence toward Women and Children.' In M. Crnkovich, ed., *'Gossip': A Spoken History of Women in the North*. Ottawa: Canadian Arctic Resource Committee, 151–62
Blackstone, Sir W. 1884. *Commentaries on the Laws of England*, 3rd ed. Chicago: Callaghan

Boyd, Susan B. 1995. 'Can Law Challenge the Public/Private Divide? Women, Work and Family.' *Windsor Yearbook of Access to Justice* 15, 161–88

British Columbia Institute on Family Violence. 1995. *Family Violence in British Columbia: A Brief Overview*. Vancouver: BCIFV

Burns, Randy. 1988. 'Preface.' In Will Roscoe, ed., *Living the Spirit: A Gay American Indian Anthology*. New York: St Martin's Press, 1–2

Buzawa, Carl, and Eva Buzawa, eds. 1992. *Domestic Violence: The Changing Criminal Justice Response*. Westport, Conn: Auburn House

Canadian Panel on Violence Against Women. 1993. *Changing the Landscape: Ending Violence – Achieving Equality*. Ottawa: Minister of Supply and Services

Chunn, Dorothy E. 1995. 'Feminism, Law and Public Policy: Politicizing the Personal.' In Nancy Mandell and Ann Duffy, eds., *Canadian Families: Diversity, Conflict and Change*. Toronto: Harcourt Brace, 177–210

– 1992. *From Punishment to Doing Good: Family Courts and Socialized Justice in Ontario, 1880–1940*. Toronto: University of Toronto Press

Clark, Anna. 1992. 'Humanity or Justice? Wifebeating and the Law in the Eighteenth and Nineteenth Centuries.' In Carol Smart, ed., *Regulating Womanhood: Historical Essays on Marriage, Motherhood and Sexuality*. London: Routledge, 187–206

Clark, Lorenne. 1989–90. 'Feminist Perspectives on Violence against Women and Children: Psychological, Social Service and Criminal Justice Concerns.' *Canadian Journal of Women and the Law* 3, 420–31

Comack, Elizabeth. 1993. *Feminist Engagement with the Law: The Legal Recognition of the Battered Women's Syndrome*. Ottawa: Canadian Research Institute for the Advancement of Women

Cox, Cherise. 1990. 'Anything Less Is Not Feminism.' *Law and Critique* 1, 237–48

Courchene, E.J. 1990. *Aboriginal Women's Perspective of the Justice System in Manitoba*. Manitoba: Aboriginal Justice Inquiry

Crenshaw, Kimberle. 1990. 'Mapping the Margins: Intersectionality, Identity Politics and Violence against Women of Colour.' *Stanford Law Review* 43, 1241–99

Currie, Dawn H. 1990. 'Battered Women and the State: From the Failure of a Theory to a Theory of Failure.' *Journal of Human Justice* 2, 77–96

Das Gupta, Tania. 1995. 'Families of Native Peoples, Immigrants and People of Colour.' In Nancy Mandell and Ann Duffy, eds., *Canadian Families: Diversity, Conflict and Change*. Toronto: Harcourt Brace, 141–74

Department of Justice, Canada. 1993. *Spousal Assault Prosecutions*. Ottawa

Dobash, Rebecca E., and Russell P. Dobash. 1992. *Women, Violence and Social Change*. London: Routledge

– 1979. *Violence against Wives*. New York: Free Press

Doggett, Maeve. 1992. *Marriage, Wife-Beating and the Law in Victorian England*. London: Weidenfeld and Nicolson

Eaton, Mary. 1994. 'Abuse by Any Other Name: Feminism, Difference and Intralesbian Violence.' In Martha Fineman and Roxanne Mykitiuk, eds., *The Public Nature of Private Violence*. New York: Routledge, 195–223

Faulkner, Ellen. 1991. 'Lesbian Abuse: The Social and Legal Realities.' *Queen's Law Journal* 16, 261–86

Forell, Caroline. 1991. 'Stopping the Violence: Mandatory Arrest and Police Tort Liability for Failure to Assist Battered Women.' *Berkeley Women's Law Journal* 6, 215–62

Frank, Sharlene. 1992. *Family Violence in Aboriginal Communities: A First Nations Report*. British Columbia: Ministry of Women's Equality

Fraser, Gwen. 1985. 'Taking Spousal Assault Seriously: A Philosophical View of Legal Contradiction.' *Windsor Yearbook of Access to Justice* 5, 368–80

Freeman, M.D.A. 1989. 'Domestic Violence: The Limits of Effective Legal Action.' *Cambrian Law Review* 20, 17–37

Gavison, Ruth. 1992. 'Feminism and the Public/Private Distinction.' *Stanford Law Review* 45, 1–45

Gordon, Linda. 1988. *Heroes of Their Own Lives: The Politics and History of Family Violence*. New York: Viking

Greschner, Donna. 1992. 'Aboriginal Women, the Constitution and Criminal Justice.' *University of British Columbia Law Review*, special ed., 338–59

Harris, Angela P. 1990. 'Race and Essentialism in Feminist Legal Theory.' *Stanford Law Review* 42, 581–616

Hilton, N. Zoe. 1989. 'One in Ten: The Struggle and Disempowerment of the Battered Women's Movement.' *Canadian Journal of Family Law* 7, 313–35

Horwitz, Morton J. 1982. 'The History of the Public/Private Distinction.' *University of Pennsylvania Law Review* 130, 1423–8

Jackson, Michael. 1989. 'Locking Up Natives in Canada.' *University of British Columbia Law Review* 23, 205–300

Jaffe, Peter et al. 1991. *Wife Assault as a Crime – The Perspectives of Victims and Police Officers on a Charging Policy in London, Ontario from 1980–1990*. Ottawa: Department of Justice Research and Development Directorate

Johnson, Rhonda, Winona Stevenson, and Donna Greschner. 1993. 'Peekiskwetan.' *Canadian Journal of Women and the Law* 6(1), 153–71

Kline, Marlee. 1993. 'Complicating the Ideology of Motherhood: Child Welfare and First Nations Women.' *Queen's Law Journal* 18, 306–42

– 1989. 'Race, Racism and Feminist Legal Theory.' *Harvard Women's Law Journal* 12, 115–50

Kohli, Rita. 1991. 'Violence against Women: Race, Class and Gender Issues.' *Canadian Woman Studies* 11(4), 13–14

La Rocque, Emma. 1994. *Violence in Aboriginal Communities*. Ottawa: National Clearinghouse on Family Violence

Law Reform Commission of Canada. 1991. *Aboriginal Peoples and Criminal Justice*, Report no. 34 (Minister's Reference). Ottawa

Law Reform Commission of Nova Scotia. 1995. *From Rhetoric to Reality: Ending Domestic Violence in Nova Scotia*. Halifax

MacLeod, Linda. 1987. *Battered but Not Beaten ... Preventing Wife Battering in Canada*. Ottawa: Canadian Advisory Council on the Status of Women

– 1980. *Wife Battering in Canada: The Vicious Circle*. Ottawa: Canadian Advisory Council on the Status of Women

MacKinnon, Catharine. 1989. *Toward a Feminist Theory of the State*. Cambridge: Harvard University Press

– 1987. *Feminism Unmodified: Discourses on Life and Law*. Cambridge: Harvard University Press

Mahoney, Martha. 1991. 'Legal Images of Battered Women: Redefining the Issue of Separation.' *Michigan Law Review* 90, 1–94

Manitoba. 1991. *Report of the Aboriginal Justice Inquiry of Manitoba*. Winnipeg

Martin, Dianne L., and Janet E. Mosher. 1995. 'Unkept Promises: Experiences of Immigrant Women with the Neo-Criminalization of Wife Abuse.' *Canadian Journal of Women and the Law* 8, 3–44

McGillivray, Anne. 1987. 'Battered Women: Definitions, Models and Prosecution Policies.' *Canadian Journal of Family Law* 6, 15–45

McPherson, C. 1991. 'Violence against Women with Disabilities: Out of Sight, Out of Mind.' *Canadian Woman Studies* 11(4), 49–50

Midnight Sun. 1988. 'Sex/Gender Systems in Native North America.' In Will Roscoe, ed., *Living the Spirit: A Gay American Indian Anthology*. New York: St Martin's Press, 32–47

Monture, Patricia A. 1991. 'Reflecting on Flint Woman.' In Richard F. Devlin, ed., *Canadian Perspectives on Legal Theory*. Toronto: Emond Montgomery, 351–66

– 1989. 'A Vicious Circle: Child Welfare and the First Nations.' *Canadian Journal of Women and the Law* 3, 1–17

Monture-Okanee, Patricia A. 1992. 'The Role and Responsibilities of Aboriginal Women: Reclaiming Justice.' *Saskatchewan Law Review* 56, 237–66

– and Mary Ellen Turpel. 1992. 'Aboriginal Peoples and Canadian Criminal Law: Rethinking Justice.' *University of British Columbia Law Review*, special ed., 239–77

Morley, R., and A. Mullender. 1992. 'Hype or Hope? The Importation of Pro-Arrest Policies and Batterers' Programmes for North America to Britain as Key

Measures for Preventing Violence against Women in the Home.' *International Journal of Law and Family* 6, 265–88

Moyer, Sharon. 1992. 'Race, Gender and Homicide: Comparisons between Aboriginals and Other Canadians.' *Canadian Journal of Criminology* 34, 387–402

Nahanee, Teressa. 1992. *Dancing with a Gorilla: Aboriginal Women, Justice and the Charter.* Ottawa: Royal Commission on Aboriginal Peoples

Native Women's Association of Canada. 1991. *Voices of Aboriginal Women: Speak Out about Violence.* Ottawa

Nova Scotia. 1989. *Findings and Recommendations* of the Royal Commission on the Donald Marshall, Jr Prosecution. Halifax

O'Donovan, Katherine. 1985. *Sexual Divisions in Law.* London: Weidenfeld and Nicolson

Olsen, Frances. 1993. 'Constitutional Law: Feminist Critiques of the Public/Private Distinction.' *Constitutional Commentary* 10, 319–27

– 1985. 'The Myth of State Intervention in the Family.' *Michigan Journal of Law Reform* 18, 835–64

Ontario Native Women's Association. 1989. *Breaking Free: Report on Aboriginal Family Violence.* Thunder Bay

Pahl, Jan, ed. 1985. *Private Violence and Public Policy: The Needs of Battered Women and the Response of the Public Services.* London: Routledge and Kegan Paul

Pateman, Carol. 1983. 'Feminist Critiques of the Public/Private Dichotomy.' In S. Benn and G.F. Gaus, eds., *Public and Private in Social Life.* London: Croom Helm, 281–303

Pauktuutit. 1995. *Setting Standards First: Community Based Justice and Correctional Services in Inuit Communities.* Ottawa

Peterson, Katherine. 1992. *The Justice House: Report of the Special Advisor on Gender Equality.* Yellowknife: Minister of Justice

Polan, Dianne. 1982. 'Toward a Theory of Law and Patriarchy.' In David Kairys, ed., *The Politics of Law.* New York: Pantheon

Rhode, Deborah L. 1989. *Justice and Gender: Sex Discrimination and the Law.* Cambridge: Harvard University Press

Robson, Ruthann. 1990. 'Lavender Bruises: Intra-Lesbian Violence, Law and Lesbian Legal Theory.' *Golden Gate University Law Review* 20, 567–91

Royal Commission on Aboriginal Peoples. 1996. *Bridging the Cultural Divide: A Report on Aboriginal People and Criminal Justice in Canada.* Ottawa

Ruttenberg, Miriam. 1994. 'A Feminist Critique of Mandatory Arrest: An Analysis of Race and Gender in Domestic Violence Policy.' *American University Journal of Gender and the Law* 2, 171–99

Ryan, Joan. 1993. *Traditional Dene Justice Project: Final Report.* Lac La Martre, NWT

Schneider, Elizabeth. 1994. 'The Violence of Privacy.' In Martha Fineman and
  Roxanne Mykitiuk, eds., *The Public Nature of Private Violence*. New York: Routledge, 36–53
– 1992. 'Particularity and Generality.' *New York University Law Review* 67,
  520–68
Sheehy, Elizabeth. 1987. *Personal Autonomy and the Criminal Law: Emerging
  Issues for Women*. Ottawa: Canadian Advisory Council on the Status of Women
Sherman, Lawrence W., and Richard A. Berk. 1984. 'The Specific Deterrent Effects
  of Arrest for Domestic Violence.' *American Sociological Review* 49(2), 261–72
Smart, Carol. 1994. 'Law, Feminism and Sexuality: From Essence to Ethics.' *Cana-
  dian Journal of Law and Society* 9(1), 15–38
Snider, Laureen. 1994. 'Feminism, Punishment and the Potential for Empower-
  ment.' *Canadian Journal of Law and Society* 9, 75–104
– 1990. 'The Potential of the Criminal Justice System to Promote Feminist Con-
  cerns.' *Studies in Law, Politics and Society* 10, 143–72
Solicitor General of Canada. 1983. *Recommended Police Directive – Spousal
  Assault*. Ottawa
Taub, Nadine, and Elizabeth M. Schneider. 1982. 'Perspectives on Women's
  Subordination and the Role of Law.' In David Kairys, ed., *The Politics of Law: A
  Progressive Critique*. New York: Pantheon, 117–39
Thornton, Margaret. 1991. 'The Public/Private Dichotomy: Gendered and Dis-
  criminatory.' *Journal of Law and Society* 18, 448–63
Turpel, Mary Ellen. 1993. 'Patriarchy and Paternalism: The Legacy of the Canadian
  State for First Nations Women.' *Canadian Journal of Women and the Law* 6,
  174–92
– 1991. 'Home/Land.' *Canadian Journal of Family Law* 10,17–40
Ursel, E. Jane. 1990. 'Examining Systemic Change in the Criminal Justice System:
  The Example of Wife Abuse Policies in Manitoba.' *Manitoba Law Journal* 19,
  529–48
Walker, Gillian. 1990. *Family Violence and the Women's Movement: The Concep-
  tual Politics of Struggle*. Toronto: University of Toronto Press
West, Nora. 1992. 'Rape in the Criminal Law and the Victim's Tort Alternative: A
  Feminist Analysis.' *University of Toronto Faculty of Law Review* 50, 96–118
Wiegers, Wanda A. 1994. 'Compensation for Wife Abuse: Empowering Victims?'
  University of British Columbia Law Review 28, 247–307
Yllo, Kersti, and Michelle Bograd, eds. 1988. *Feminist Perspectives on Wife Abuse*.
  Newbury Park, Calif: Sage
Zorza, Joan. 1994. 'Must We Stop Arresting Batterers?: Analysis and Policy Impli-
  cations of New Police Domestic Violence Studies.' *New England Law Review*
  28, 929–90

PART 2
FAMILY, HOME, AND WORK

5

Who Pays for Caring for Children? Public Policy and the Devaluation of Women's Work

KATHERINE TEGHTSOONIAN

A large fraction of women [in Sweden] work in the public sector to take care of the children of other women who work in the public sector to take care of the parents of the women who are looking after their children.[1]

This observation is presented in an article in the *Economist* that criticizes the growth of the public sector in Sweden, and suggests that it is responsible for many of the country's recent economic woes. If only, the author seems to suggest, these Swedish women would return home to care for the dependent members of their *own* families, life would be simpler and government finances much healthier. The passage conveys both a sense that women's employment outside the home is something less than legitimate, and that women's caregiving work is not particularly worthy of financial compensation.

In this chapter I argue that neoconservative attitudes similar to those implicit in this discussion of Sweden have informed Canadian child care policies.[2] These attitudes have served to limit the extent of government support for child care services in general and for adequate compensation of child care providers in particular. As a result, Canadian women who care for children – as mothers and as child care providers – continue to pay a high price for the belief that child care should be primarily a private responsibility rather than a universally available service supported by generous government funding. Rhetorical flourishes to the contrary, women's caregiving work in both private and public spheres remains devalued.

Federal Child Care Policy: A Failure to Act

During the past ten years in Canada, new federal child care legislation has been much discussed, but little of substance has been accomplished. The litany of consultative exercises that have been carried out, committee reports written, and promises made and broken is by now both familiar and discouraging. The Task Force appointed by the soon-to-be-defeated Liberal government in 1984 conducted extensive consultations and, in its 1986 report, recommended the development of a fully funded child care system (Task Force on Child Care 1986). Meanwhile, the Conservative government elected in 1984 appointed its own Special Committee on Child Care in November 1985; it too held hearings, received submissions from the public, and issued a report (Special Committee on Child Care 1987). The child care proposals introduced by the Conservatives fell far short of the original Task Force's proposals. Based, instead, on the Special Committee's recommendations, they included expanded funding for tax measures, as well as a new federal spending program intended to replace the provisions for funding child care services on a shared-cost basis with the provinces under the Canada Assistance Plan (Friendly 1994, 171–8; Government of Canada 1987; Hum 1989; Phillips 1989).[3]

Both the high level of funding devoted to tax measures and the specifics of Bill C-144 (the legislation outlining the proposed new spending program) were sharply criticized by child care advocates, women's groups, labour organizations, and representatives of First Nations, immigrant, and ethnic communities.[4] Despite this strong opposition to the government's approach, and evidence that its proposals were inconsistent with the preferences expressed to the Special Committee by members of the public (Friendly, Mathien, and Willis 1987), the Mulroney government proceeded with its plans. Increases to the amount of the tax deduction for child care expenses and a new supplement to the refundable Child Tax Credit (to be made available to parents without receipts for child care expenses) were implemented. Bill C-144 was hurriedly passed by the House of Commons, but died when the 1988 election was called before it had received Senate approval. Although they had promised to reintroduce child care legislation if re-elected, the Conservatives increasingly distanced themselves from such action. Eventually, in the 1992 budget, the government formally abandoned pursuit of a new federal child care program, citing economic constraints.

This decision was widely criticized,[5] and the federal Liberal Party promised that it would act on child care if returned to office in the 1993 election.

The party's actual campaign commitment was to provide federal funding for the creation of 50,000 new child care spaces in each of three years to a maximum of 150,000 spaces and $720 million but *only* if there had been a minimum of 3 per cent economic growth in the preceding year.[6] Although couched in contingent terms, this promise did offer some hope of positive developments at the federal level. Following the Liberals' 1993 election victory, advocacy groups were further encouraged by the new government's initial framing of child care as central to the country's economic well-being (Friendly and Oloman 1995, 7–8).

Hope has been replaced by disappointment, however, as the Liberals' track record on child care policy while in office federally has echoed that of the Conservatives before them: lots of talk, but no action. Child care was much discussed during the Axworthy Social Security Review conducted during 1994; many of those presenting briefs to the Standing Committee considering the Axworthy proposals reiterated the importance of a new federal spending program on child care. Their views seemed to be reflected in the official documents emerging from this consultative exercise, which did provide rhetorical acknowledgment of the need for improved child care (Government of Canada 1994a, 1994b; House of Commons 1995). However, this round of public consultation has been as fruitless, in terms of child care policy development, as those that preceded it: the promised new spending program had vanished from the government's agenda by mid-1996.[7]

Neither are prospects for positive developments at the provincial level bright. Child care advocates have noted that by the mid-1990s many provinces had begun significantly reducing their financial commitment to child care services, taking their cue from the lack of interest and funding at the federal level (Friendly 1995). This trend will only be aggravated by the transformation of federal social transfer payments into the block grant Canada Health and Social Transfer (CHST) which has opened the door to *reduced* spending on child care by giving provincial governments greater latitude to determine their spending priorities.[8] Improvement in the availability and affordability of child care services is unlikely to result from new departures in federal policy, at least in the foreseeable future.

This failure to adopt new federal child care legislation during the past decade has been accompanied by the persistence of low wages, minimal benefits, and difficult working conditions for child care providers.[9] Background research conducted for the Task Force on Child Care in the mid-1980s revealed the extent of the problem: in 1984, the average wage of child care providers working full-time in a licensed centre was $7.29 per hour;

the average net annual income of licensed family day care providers was estimated to be $5,288, or $2.26 per hour, reflecting both the low pay and long hours of those offering this service (Task Force on Child Care 1986, 114–16).[10] There has been little improvement since. The Canada-wide *Caring for a Living* study indicated that in 1991 the average hourly wage of a child care provider working in a licensed centre had risen to only $9.60, or $18,870 per year. Adjusted for inflation, this represents a 4.5 per cent *decrease* in wages between 1984 and 1991 (Karyo Communications 1992, 23). Indeed, the 1991 census revealed that child care is the lowest paid occupation in Canada. Those working full-time, full-year in child care jobs earned on average only $13,518, less than half the average annual earnings for all full-time working Canadians in 1990 ($33,714), and only slightly more than half of the average annual earnings of all full-time working women ($26,033).[11]

In addition to low wages, child care occupations are often characterized by poor working conditions and the absence of work-related benefits. Studies in both Canada and the United States have shown that many child care providers do not enjoy paid vacations, paid overtime, regular breaks during the work day, health and dental benefits, or regular access to opportunities for professional development (Child Care Connection–NS 1990; Hartmann and Pearce 1989; Karyo Communications 1992; LaGrange and Read 1990; Schom-Moffatt 1984; Strober, Gerlach-Downie, and Yeager 1995; Whitebook, Howes, and Phillips 1989). Both the lack of benefits and the low wage levels characteristic of the field are even more problematic in light of the above-average educational and training qualifications that child care workers bring to their work. As the author of *Caring for a Living* noted: 'Almost seven out of 10 staff working in early childhood education have a post-secondary certificate, diploma, or degree; in the Canadian employed labour force, only four out of 10 workers have this level of education' (Karyo Communications 1992, xvii).

One reflection of the poor wages and benefits and the often trying working conditions that characterize the field is the high rate of staff turnover in both Canada and the United States (Doherty 1991). Consistency of caregivers has been identified as a key component of quality care, and thus high turnover has troubling implications for children's well-being (Karyo Communications 1992). In addition, many child care providers indicate that they love their chosen profession but cannot afford to continue to pursue it, which reflects a tremendous waste of their training, talent, and commitment to the next generation (ibid. 93; Nelson 1990, 196–216).

Efforts to address these problems at the provincial level have been uneven and limited by a lack of federal leadership and funding. Consequently, there has been only a patchwork of policy support for improvements in child care providers' wages and working conditions across the country, and insufficient resources to address the problem adequately (Childcare Resource and Research Unit, CRRU 1994, 94). Rather than developing a national policy framework within which these problems could be addressed, the federal government has largely abandoned the field to those provincial governments inclined to tackle the issues and to parents and providers in the private spheres of market and family to cope with their own resources as best they can.

How can we understand these failures of public policy, both with respect to a new federal child care program and with respect to the persistent sorry state of child care providers' wages and working conditions? In this chapter I identify a number of ideological and material factors that have shaped policy in this area:

1 The ideological construction of caring for children as primarily a private responsibility. This conceptualization has been significantly reinforced in recent times by the tenets of social and economic conservatism as these have been expressed in Canadian public life.
2 Prevailing assumptions about the nature of women's caregiving work, which diminish it and legitimize its translation into low-wage occupations with limited benefits. These include (a) a conceptualization of caregiving as an inherently gendered activity and as a spontaneously occurring expression of 'women's nature'; (b) a resistance to understanding caregiving as 'work' which should be paid; and (c) a belief that nurturing attitudes are undermined by, or cannot coexist with, financial compensation.
3 The conflict between child care providers' need for a living wage and parents' need for affordable fees in which, absent supportive government intervention, the gains of one group inevitably come at the expense of the other.

Public Versus Private: The Role of Mothers, Market, and State in Caring for Children

In Canada caring for children is an activity that appears to be firmly anchored on the 'private' side of the ideological division between 'public' and 'private.' To clarify this assertion and to elaborate the role that neoconservative ideology has played in constructing child care as appropriately 'private,' it is useful to delineate more fully how 'public' and 'private' are understood in the dominant discourse. Three relevant realms of activity can be identified: state, market, and household (Olsen 1983; Pateman 1989):

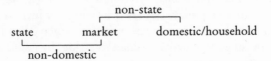

We can thus think of public versus private as meaning state versus non-state, with the latter including both the market (extra-household) and domestic (household) spheres. Or we can juxtapose the public, that is, non-domestic (state and market) realm against the domestic (household) sphere. The ideological precept that the care of children should be a private responsibility thus can mean either that it should be carried out in the domestic context or, if it is to take place in a non-domestic context, that it is best accomplished in the market (rather than state) arena. These two prescriptions for the private provision of child care have been expressed through two different strands of neo-conservative ideology in Canada – social conservatism and economic conservatism – each of which emphasizes one of these domains of the private (non-state) realm as the appropriate site of child care provision.

Social Conservatism: The Solution Is Mothers at Home

By 'social conservatism' I mean the ideological position that stakes out a defence of 'traditional moral values,' including a commitment to public policies supportive of 'The Family' (understood to be composed of a breadwinning husband and full-time, economically dependent wife and mother, and their children). During the late 1980s and early 1990s these views were expressed on the federal level through the 'Family Caucus' of the Conservative Party, the Reform Party, and groups such as REAL Women and Kids First.[12] Although social conservatism has not singlehandedly prevented the adoption of federal child care legislation, it has played an important role in contributing to, and legitimizing, a failure to act on this issue.

This ideological position was expressed in a number of contexts while Bill C-144 was being debated during 1987 and 1988. In the committee hearings held on the bill, it was articulated primarily by representatives of Kids First, an organization that lobbies for public policies supportive of full-time parenting. The following statement from their testimony captures a number of the elements of a social conservative position: the idea that government support for child care services will inappropriately encourage mothers' labour force participation, the negative depiction of such participation, and the notion that this choice by women is selfish and harmful:

It is indeed obvious that there is going to be an increase in women going back to the labour force. But a great deal of that increase will be a consequence of this bill, which encourages women to get into the workforce. We think someone should recognize the critical importance in a child's development – especially from birth to three years – of a woman's presence in the home ... Instead of saying 10 years down the road that we have a problem because there are no mothers at home and every child is in day care, and having to say, like many of the European countries, that maybe it is a positive thing that some mothers want to stay home, Canada could be a leader and say, here is equality; you choose what you want. You ask high-school kids what they are going to do if they have children, and they say, put them in day care. It is a given. There is no emphasis on what is good for children. It is what is good for the parents.[13]

A similar rhetorical position was staked out by a Conservative MP from Alberta in defending his government's decision to abandon plans for a new national child care program in 1992. He argued that during the 1988 election campaign:

I knocked on door after door and was greeted by a great cross-section of people, in terms of income, in my riding. I was astonished to hear people rejecting the idea of universal day care. It was a ground swell, and one that I felt could not be ignored. There were young mothers, many of them professionals or otherwise, who had chosen to take up to four or five years out of their careers in order to nurture and bond with their children. They said it was great if the two income families chose to both continue working and using day care, but what about mothers at home? They made a choice they felt was necessary for their children ... They believed staying at home was very, very important to the nurturing and upbringing of their children and they were given no recognition for that through the tax system.[14]

Here again, 'the problem' is framed as one of how to support the laudable decision of women to care for their own children at home, full-time. Government support for child care services is presented as not needed, essentially irrelevant.

It is important to note that the social conservative commitment to providing policy support for full-time motherhood tends to falter at the boundaries of the economically privileged heterosexual nuclear family. Families structured on a different basis – for example, those formed by gay men or lesbians – are not generally viewed as appropriate beneficiaries of public policy (Reform Party 1995a, 4). In addition, implicit in the arguments of many social conservatives is the view that mothers in low-income families or receiving income assistance should be in paid employment rather than caring for their children at home full-time.[15] In this view, full-time motherhood is desirable, and should be supported by public policy, only in the context of the 'traditional' family; non-familial child care is a second-best solution which should be supported only as a service to families that are dysfunctional or 'in need.'

Such views have played an important role in Canadian policy debates, but their influence is not often acknowledged. Instead, the absence of greater government support for child care services is explained solely in the language of economic conservatism: additional spending is deemed impossible because 'we can't afford it.' But decisions about whether we can afford policy X or policy Y are never about the *absolute* availability of resources; instead, they reflect priorities: we can't afford policy X because we have decided that the money needs to be spent instead on policies A, B, and C. And policy decisions that are being made about child care, and related areas of social policy, can be understood fully only if we also attend to the role that *social* conservatism plays in this arena. The views comprising this ideology, including a preference for full-time mother care in the context of a 'traditional family' and a hostility to mothers' participation in the paid labour force except where dictated by economic circumstance, facilitate the argument that supporting a diverse child care system as a universal service to families should not be a priority for government.

I stress this point because there is a tendency to identify social conservatism as a phenomenon associated primarily with the religious right in the United States, and as being not much of an influence on policy in Canada. It *is* true that the arguments of social conservatism did not appear as frequently, nor were they always voiced as vigorously, in the Canadian child care policy debates of the late 1980s as they were in the comparable American debates taking place at about the same time. However, not only did they play a role at that time, they have arguably moved closer to centre-stage in the years since.

One expression of this trend has been the emergence of the Reform Party as a significant presence in the Canadian House of Commons, winning fifty-two seats in the 1993 federal election. In its policy statements the Reform Party has indicated clearly that it favours the transfer of a number of responsibilities from the public to the private sphere. Rather than 'universal social programs run by bureaucrats,' Reform has indicated that it 'would actively encourage families, communities, non-governmental organizations, and the private sector to reassume their duties and responsibilities in social service areas' (Reform Party 1995a, 4). The party's 1995 Taxpayers' Budget also argues the need to 'move responsibility for social security away from big, distant, expensive governments' in part by 'building on the Canadian tradition of self-reliance and recognizing the family as the primary care-giver in society' (Reform Party 1995b, 2). Although not couched in gender-specific terms, this vision rests on an implicit assumption that it is *women* in 'the family' and in volunteer organizations who will provide these services on an unpaid basis. Thus, one of the consequences of Reform's commitment to cutting back state services would be the transformation of many women from salaried public employees into unpaid caregivers in the private sphere (see also Kline, this volume).

Testimony presented to the Standing Committee considering the Axworthy Social Security Review in 1994 provided another indication that proponents of social conservatism are alive and well, and eager to shape public policy in accordance with their vision of appropriate family life and gender roles. Representatives of a number of groups argued that the federal government should focus its energies on developing policies that would encourage and support parents who choose to care for their children at home. They expressed dismay at the prospect of increased government spending on non-parental child care services.[16] The final report of the Standing Committee did not give much explicit weight to such views in its analysis or recommendations (House of Commons 1995), but it is important not to dismiss them as irrelevant. They contribute to the ideological construction of child care as appropriately consigned to the private, domestic realm and help to legitimate the failure to adopt legislation supporting child care as a universal service to families with children.

Economic Conservatism: The Market Knows Best

I use the term 'economic conservatism' to refer to those elements in conservative ideology that stress the importance of decreasing government spending, enhancing the role of the market in service provision, and, more generally, reducing the role of the state (Mishra 1990; Teghtsoonian 1995, 1993). Those committed to these goals thus share both the antipathy of

social conservatives towards an expanded role for government in supporting the provision of child care, and their preference that this issue be
addressed in the private sphere. However, many key goals of economic
conservatism conflict with social conservatism's vision of women located in
the domestic arena. These include a desire to encourage women receiving
social assistance to secure paid employment in order to reduce government
spending on welfare, and a belief that women's participation in the paid
labour force (as low-wage earners, although this point is generally not
acknowledged) contributes to the improvement of economic productivity
and international competitiveness. From this perspective, policies supportive of full-time motherhood are not entirely helpful. Instead, economic
conservatives reconcile their distaste for government spending on child
care with their desire to facilitate women's labour force participation by
advocating policies that maximize the role of the market in allocating the
provision of child care services and minimize the role of the state.

To the extent that government directly funds child care, conservatives
argue that it should not do so on a universal basis, but rather provide
targeted assistance delivered only to those in need. In addition, economic
conservatives have argued the merits of relying on the tax system as a
mechanism for delivering assistance to families with children. This policy
preference has been defended through repeated arguments that tax benefits
permit the free exercise of 'parental choice' with respect to child care
options and that it is desirable to allow 'the market' to respond to parental
choices regarding such care (Teghtsoonian 1996).

Relying on tax measures is problematic in that it reflects and reinforces
the construction of child care provision and purchase as a set of private
arrangements to be negotiated by individuals. It provides government
financial support for the purchase of care at abysmally low rates of remuneration and, especially for domestic workers living in their employers'
homes, in contexts in which care providers are vulnerable to abuse and
exploitation (Arat-Koç 1990; Macklin 1992; Young 1994, 563–4). Tax measures create no opportunity for public authority to shape the quality, availability, or affordability of child care services; instead, it is assumed that 'the
market' will ensure an adequate supply. Furthermore, tax benefits that are
delivered in the form of a deduction from taxable income rather than a
refundable credit (amounting to over $300 million in foregone revenue in
1991) provide the greatest benefit to the wealthy, and none at all to those
who are the least well-off (Young 1994, and this volume).

Neither do tax measures offer a vehicle through which government
might systematically address the issue of child care providers' wages and

working conditions (Friendly 1994, 196–7). As a consequence, provider. and parents must negotiate privately their conflicting economic interests in a highly constrained and unpromising context: 'Costs associated with wages and benefits can constitute 70% to 90% of a centre's total budget. As such, day care workers' wages are closely tied to fees, debts and enroll-ments. The centres paying the most reasonable wage are generally those charging the highest fees. The consequence is that, in the day care system, salaries remain low to allow fees to remain reasonable. Day care workers subsidize parents' fees through their low wages' (Schom-Moffatt 1984, 90; see also Nelson 1990). Those interested in reducing government spending have a vested interest in keeping providers' wages down, since lower wages help to minimize the child care expenses incurred by single mothers seek-ing to leave social assistance for paid employment. This calculus also helps to explain the enthusiasm demonstrated by conservatives for the (un- or under-paid) caregiving of relatives or neighbours as the preferred child care solution.

Low Cost Child Care: The Devaluation of Women's Caregiving

The desire of economic conservatives to limit government spending consti-tutes part of the explanation for the reluctance to expand federal support for child care services, or to address the issue of child care workers' wages and working conditions through public policy. In this section I argue that this resistance is *also* rooted in the ways in which women's domestic responsibilities in general, and the activity of caring for children in particu-lar, are conceptualized. I develop the argument, advanced by a number of feminist scholars, that the distinction between public and private can obscure the ways in which the two realms are tightly interlinked, both con-ceptually and in the everyday lives of women (Baines, Evans, and Ney-smith 1991a; Saraceno 1984; Tom 1992–3; Ungerson 1990). My goal is to explore these linkages by suggesting the ways in which assumptions about, and understandings of, women's work in the private, family context have been reflected in perceptions and beliefs that have limited federal policy support for child care services and child care providers (see also Ferguson 1991).

There is significant resistance to considering women's responsibilities in the private, domestic sphere as 'work' at all. Often rendered invisible and unrecognized, the difficulty and complexity of domestic labour are dimin-ished by the perception that such activities flow more or less spontaneously from 'women's nature.' In addition, it is considered inappropriate and

ɔmpensate women's domestic activities financially. Unlike
:h is seen to be motivated by pragmatic considerations and
s caregiving in the family context is perceived to be moti-
:ional attachment and is understood to create its own
rewaɪᴜᴢ.

This conception of women's caregiving in the domestic context also
informs prevailing views about such work in the world of paid employment, thereby legitimizing its low status and poor pay. Just as women's
domestic labours are frequently invisible, research on women in a variety
of caregiving occupations (such as social work and nursing) indicates that
much of the actual work women do in these jobs goes unacknowledged –
sometimes even by women themselves – and unrepresented in the internal
record-keeping systems of organizations (Callahan and Attridge 1990; Diamond 1990; Nelson 1990; Waring 1988). And, just as women are *un*paid in
the domestic sphere, women are starkly *under*paid for the caring and nurturing work they do in the public sphere, both in comparison to similarly
skilled occupations numerically dominated by men and in comparison to
men employed in 'women's jobs' (Armstrong and Armstrong 1994; Baines,
Evans, and Neysmith 1991; Statistics Canada 1994). Arlene Daniels has
suggested that the higher pay received by men for caregiving work in the
public sphere reflects, at least in part, the view that such 'female' activities
do not come to men 'naturally.' Men's caregiving work is assumed to reflect
effort, rather than the expression of natural impulse, and hence to deserve
greater compensation than the 'natural' (and therefore relatively effortless)
performance of such duties by their female co-workers (1987, 409–10).

This naturalization of the gendered division of talent and responsibility
for caregiving has come to be superimposed on 'common-sense' understandings of the division between public and private spheres. An example
was provided by Barbara McDougall, a minister in the Conservative government during the late 1980s. In explaining why the federal government
was moving at that particular time to provide support for child care services, she argued: 'The structures that have existed from the beginning of
time where men work outside the home and women work inside the home
are changing, and they are changing fast because of economic needs.'[18] This
presentation of the gendered public/private divide as universal and (until
now) eternal serves, however inadvertently, to suggest that the structure of
the 'traditional' nuclear family with its gendered division of labour is 'natural,' as is women's responsibility for child care within the family unit.

A number of unwarranted implications flow from these problematic
assumptions, inhibiting the development of federal support for child care

as a universally available service to families. First, the framing of mother-care in the nuclear family as 'natural' suggests that federal government policies supportive of non-parental child care are aligned with parenting practices and family arrangements that are 'unnatural,' and therefore second best. These views were reflected in the testimony presented by a representative of Kids First during the Axworthy Social Security Review. She argued against defining the problem as one of how to increase the availability of child care services: 'As a society we appear to be ignoring what history has taught us: that children are best cared for in a home setting ... Kids First believes that children deserve more than second best and that families should have more than second choice. We want to know why government is so adamant in pursuing a second-best solution to the child care problem. ... Quality day care does not exist. It is a myth – a fantasy. You can never pay someone enough to do what a mother does for free' (*Minutes of Proceedings* 1994, 9:145,147). Such views support efforts to frame non-parental child care as an option of last resort, at most a welfare service to low-income parents or to those identified as unable to care adequately for their own children.

Second, these arguments suggest that even where mother-care is not possible, intrafamilial, private solutions are better than public solutions. For example, during the debates on Bill C-144 in 1987 and 1988 some Conservative MPs argued the virtues of care by grandparents, or shared between two parents trading off child care responsibilities by working different shifts. And, during the 1994 Social Security Review, representatives of REAL Women, Kids First, and Westcoast Women for Family Life, argued that government should explore ways to support care by relatives as a superior alternative to formal child care that is preferred by parents.[19] The potential drawbacks of these arrangements go unremarked in such arguments: the different shift/shared child care scenario affords little opportunity for partners, or the family as a whole, to enjoy time together (and, of course, is irrelevant for single parents); mothers and grandmothers may disagree about appropriate approaches to child-rearing; and, of course, many aunts and grandmothers are themselves in paid employment and unavailable to provide the (generally unpaid) caregiving services on which this scenario rests (Presser 1992; Skold 1988). Yet the depiction of intrafamilial caregiving arrangements as unarguably superior to care by non-family members is mobilized against claims that it is desirable for the federal government to expand its support for non-familial child care services.

Prevailing attitudes about women's work in the home have also served to undermine the efforts of child care providers to improve their wages and working conditions. Important in this regard is the tendency to take this work for granted, that is, its 'invisible' nature. This invisibility is due partly to the context within which it is performed – in private homes, out of the public eye – and partly to its nature: cleaning, cooking, and providing emotional support are all tasks that have no definite conclusion or 'final product' that can be displayed to attest to the performance of the work (Armstrong and Armstrong 1994; Graham 1983). In addition to being unacknowledged or unobserved, much of women's domestic work is invisible in a more fundamental sense. In Marjorie DeVault's analysis of the work women do in planning, preparing, and serving meals to their families, she argued: '[These tasks] are also literally invisible: much of the time, they cannot be seen. Planning is largely mental work, spread over time and mixed in with other activities. In addition, these tasks can look like other activities: managing a meal looks like simply enjoying the companionship of one's family – and of course, is partly so – and learning about food prices can look like reading the newspaper. The work is noticeable when it is not completed (when the milk is all gone, for example, or when the meal is not ready on time), but cannot be seen when it is done well' (DeVault 1991, 56–7). As a consequence, DeVault argued, the effort involved in domestic work is not visible and the activities appear as 'what comes naturally.'

The work of caring for children also involves the performance of many simultaneous tasks and the investment of a great deal of (unobservable) mental energy in emotional support and caretaking. As Arlene Daniels suggested: 'The aspect of [women's] activities most difficult for everyone to conceptualize as work involves the warm and caring aspects of the construction and maintenance of interpersonal relations' (1987, 409). Rather than being understood as the product of learned skills and constant effort, the work required to care for children appears to emerge spontaneously from instinct and/or innate knowledge that women possess by virtue of their sex and which they implement more or less without difficulty. These perceptions contribute to an underestimation of the effort and skill of those who are employed as child care providers and the value of the training that they bring to their positions. In turn, this devaluation of the work of caring for children makes the low wages of child care providers appear less inappropriate than they otherwise might.

The perception that at-home mothers care for their own children 'for free' also helps to legitimize the low pay of child care providers, especially those in family day care homes where the work environment resembles so closely the context in which care is provided on an unpaid basis (Nelson

1990). However, these understandings of full-time mother-care as something that is provided 'for free' do not take into account the opportunity costs to the mother herself of choosing to provide such care, for example in terms of foregone income, expected lifetime earnings, and educational opportunities (Spalter-Roth and Hartmann 1991). Just as the work of caring for children is invisible, so too are the costs of doing so, for mothers and for child care providers.

One of the consequences of the invisibility of these costs is a tendency to ignore them in assessing the need for a national child care program. For example, in his *Globe and Mail* business column, Terence Corcoran airily dismissed the Liberal government's tentative commitment to make available $720 million federal dollars over three years towards the creation of 150,000 new child care spaces. In identifying this commitment as a prime target for elimination in the interests of deficit reduction, Corcoran argued that 'this is a new program and no money is being spent at the moment, so why start?'[20] Mothers scrambling for affordable quality child care, and poorly paid child care providers struggling to make ends meet, could probably provide a number of reasons; however, the invisibility of their caregiving work – and of the price that they pay for the *absence* of an adequate national child care system – facilitates Corcoran's, and federal policy makers', disregard.

In the context of a general unwillingness to acknowledge and support the value of women's caregiving work, it is worth considering the position of groups like REAL Women, Kids First, and Westcoast Women for Family Life. Their representatives have repeatedly emphasized the tremendous value of the work that women do in their homes, raising and nurturing their families, and the need for public policy to acknowledge and support this work. How compatible are these views with the emerging feminist commitment to ensuring that women's caregiving work is properly valued?

While some elements in the positions staked out by these socially conservative groups are valuable, as an overall package their policy prescriptions leave much to be desired. They do articulate an important truth about society's failure to acknowledge the value of women's domestic work and the lack of policy supports for it. However, their assumption that mothers in paid employment enjoy both moral and policy support for their decision to combine motherhood and labour force participation is contradicted by the evidence,[21] and their dismissal of the need for better policies to support women making this choice is troubling. The emphatic testimony presented by Gwendolyn Landolt (REAL Women) during the Social Security Review is telling: 'We would object strongly – I can't begin to tell you how much we'd object – to a national day care program' (*Minutes of Proceedings* 1994, 8: 104). Although child care advocates have argued that governments must *both* expand support for child care services *and* benefits for parents choosing to care for their children at home (Beach 1992; Task Force 1986), social conservative organizations such as REAL Women and Kids First endorse only the latter. It is thus difficult to credit their claim that they are supportive of 'choices for families.'

In addition to confronting many of the attitudes outlined above, child care providers who have tried to improve their wages and working conditions have also had to contend with the prevalent belief that money and love cannot, and/or should not, coexist in a caregiving relationship. In this view, caregiving relationships within families are ideal (and idealized) because they are understood to be motivated by a loving, altruistic commitment to the well-being of the person receiving the care, whose interests and needs are not subordinated to the self-interest (pecuniary or otherwise) of the care provider. When the need for money supplements altruistic commitment as a motivation for providing the care, as is the case for those who care for a living, the quality of that care is called into question. The implicit concern underlying this logic is that economic need may come to displace 'true caring' entirely, erasing any interest on the part of the care provider in the well-being of the care receiver. The receipt of money for the work of caregiving is seen to jeopardize its quality, to render it less affectionate or caring than if it were provided solely 'for love.'[22] Caregivers who seek better wages for themselves run the risk of being accused of selfishness, of not caring enough about their clients (Baines, Evans, and Neysmith 1991).

These assumptions and beliefs were reflected in the comments of one Conservative MP, as he sarcastically presented his rendition of the New Democratic Party's position on federal minimum standards during the 1988 child care debates: 'Let us have a standard that fits the cities. It may not fit the children but it fits workers because you can control the supply and raise the wages of those who are lucky enough to be inside the system.' He concluded by suggesting: 'In the next election you can vote for the Party who cares about their child care workers and their union bosses [the NDP], or you can vote for the Party who cares about children and parental choice [the Conservatives].'[23] Child care workers emerge, in his description, as greedy, 'lucky' individuals; the possibility that they might genuinely care about children is depicted as entirely incompatible with their efforts to secure their personal economic well-being.[24]

Who Pays for Caring for Children?

Child care providers' efforts to improve their low wages are further confounded by the labour-intensive nature of the service they provide. Unlike many economic goods, the cost of child care cannot be reduced by pursuing economies of scale without seriously jeopardizing the quality of the care provided and placing children at risk. The resulting relationship between providers' wages and parental fees is outlined in the following illustration: 'In Ontario, 1 staff person takes care of 5 toddlers. Each family pays 1/5 of the staff person's annual salary of $17,500 so each family's fees will be $3,500. An additional 20% for food, supplies, equipment, building maintenance, benefits and administration must be added to each family's fees, for a total annual cost of $4,200 per child' (Canadian Day Care Advocacy Association, CDCAA, Fact Sheet #4, 1985). Parental fees could be sharply reduced if the one staff person in this example were to take care of ten toddlers instead of only five. Or, her salary could be raised to $20,000 per year by increasing the annual fee for each of the five children by $500. Either one of these scenarios is highly problematic. Together they illustrate a crucial point: without direct government assistance (via ongoing operating or salary enhancement grants, or a fully funded system), there is a direct trade-off between parent fees and providers' wages. As a result, when governments fail to subsidize adequately the costs of care, child care providers all too often provide the subsidy instead, through their low wages (Nelson 1990; Zinsser 1986).

Some provinces have adopted policies intended to address this issue. For example, under the NDP government in British Columbia, the Ministry of Women's Equality has attempted to respond to the twin challenges of affordability and wages through its infant/toddler incentive grant program, and through a wage supplement initiative. Infant and toddler care is particularly expensive because the maximum number of children for which an individual caregiver can be responsible is lower for this age group than for older children. The caregiver's salary must thus be covered by the fees of fewer parents, and hence the cost to parents is increased. The British Columbia Infant/Toddler Incentive Grant Program addresses this problem by providing grants of $5 per day per occupied space in licensed centres offering care to children less than 3 years of age, on the understanding that 85 per cent of the grant will be directed to the wages and benefits of staff who are caring for children. The program also provides a grant of $3 per day per child under the age of 2 (to a maximum of two) being cared for by a licensed family day care provider. In both contexts, it reduces the costs associated with the care of very young children with a view to increasing its general availability and affordability while supporting providers' wages (Ministry of Women's Equality 1993, 4).

The British Columbia Child Care Wage Supplement Initiative is an additional policy response by the NDP government to the problem of child care providers' low wages. Launched in early 1994, this program initially allocated $5 million to enhance the wages of approximately 3,000 child care providers employed by licensed, non-profit centres for the hours that they had worked between 1 October 1993 and 31 March 1994. It was expanded in 1995 to cover a full one-year period (1 April 1994 to 31 March 1995) and to include approximately 1,500 providers working in the private sector.[25] Like the infant/toddler incentive grant, it provides a vehicle through which child care providers' wages can be improved (by an average of 9 per cent during 1994–5) without imposing an additional financial burden on parents (Ministry of Women's Equality 1995a, 5 and 1995b, 5).

Yet, even in the political climate that has supported such initiatives, there is continuing resistance to the idea that the costs of caring for children should be borne by society (the public) rather than by individual women. One context in which these attitudes were expressed was a discussion on CBC Radio's 'Almanac' of the decision taken in March 1995 by British Columbia's then Minister of Labour, Dan Miller, to exclude babysitters[26] working for a given family for more than 15 hours a week from the increases to the province's minimum wage scheduled for March and October 1995.[27]

Although babysitters employed under such circumstances were included in the government's original plan to increase the minimum wage, this fact was apparently not raised as an issue during the public hearings held on this and other proposed changes to the Employment Standards Act during 1994. Nevertheless, Miller indicated that he had received strong representations concerning the financial difficulties that this provision would have created for low-income parents when its implementation was pending in March 1995. He acknowledged repeatedly the legitimacy of child care providers' need for a living wage and the difficult 'conundrum' that resulted from parents' inability to pay wages generous enough to ensure this wage, and expressed particular concern about the 'working poor': 'We do have subsidies for the working poor, [and] there is a wage supplement program for those who work in day care because, quite frankly, people who work in the day care business are not highly paid, and yet they have a very, very important job: taking care of our children. There is no single answer I sus-

pect ... but we do not want to impair the ability of working people – particularly, as I say, those people who are in low-wage jobs – from maintaining
those jobs. I think people in this province want to have an opportunity to
be employed, to participate in our economy, and it was never our intention – it is not our intention – to impair their ability to do just that' (Dan
Miller, CBC Radio, 'Almanac,' 22 March 1995). From the three possible
sources – babysitters working more than 15 hours a week for a given family, working-poor parents, and government subsidy – Miller decided that it
was best to allow babysitters to continue to absorb the cost of the provision of care by failing to guarantee them the minimum wage in this context.
He rejected the notion that government is necessarily the appropriate place
to look: 'The issue is still out there, quite frankly, and I'll admit freely that I
don't have ... and I think that's fair. Governments don't have the answer to
every single problem in our society. We're working to try to make it better,
to provide more day care ... maybe this debate has been good for British
Columbia. Maybe it will spark some innovations, some new ideas, about
how we can care for what really are our most precious resource, and that's
our children' (ibid.). At the end of the day, a public solution to this particular problem was rejected and the conflict between babysitters' economic
needs and parents' limited economic resources was deflected into the realm
of private negotiation.

The difficulties created by this privatization of the issue for child care
providers seeking to improve their wages are aggravated by the deeply
ingrained tendency in our society to understand child care costs as being
paid for by the mother's income. This assumption is reflected in the frequently articulated view that it is 'not worth it,' and to some degree not
legitimate, for mothers in two-parent families to take on paid employment
if the costs of child care services absorb a significant portion of their take-
home pay (Abel and Nelson 1990a; Nelson 1990; Skold 1988). One caller
to the radio program on which Miller was being interviewed expressed this
point of view: 'My wife ... takes home roughly around $11.00 an hour.
Now [if] we go and take six-plus off on top of that ... well, you can see our
point of view. It almost gets to the point of 'what's the use of working
then?' Might as well just have her stay at home, and take my wife and
deduct her completely for income tax deductions' (CBC Radio, 'Almanac,'
22 March 1995). As Kathy Modigliani has noted, from this perspective 'the
idea that the father's earnings are equally dependent upon paid child care is
not recognized' (1988, 14). And, in our society, these views all too rarely
lead to a more general critique of women's low wages relative to men's as
the source of this particular problem. Instead, the solutions that more

readily move to centre-stage are ones that exact a price from women: mothers forego opportunities for paid employment because 'it isn't worth it'; child care providers endure low wages and limited benefits.

A significant proportion of the low-wage 'parents' whose ability to secure employment Dan Miller wanted to protect by limiting their child care costs are poorly paid women in poorly paid 'women's jobs.' In this context, increases to the minimum wage such as those adopted in British Columbia are one step in the right direction. However, there is something amiss when women's opportunities for employment continue to depend on low wages for the women who care for their children.

Conclusion

This chapter has suggested that the issues at stake in child care policy debates, and the passions they evoke, can best be understood by emphasizing the interconnectedness of the public and private spheres rather than by accentuating their separateness. The current profile of federal child care policy has imposed significant costs on women in their private roles as mothers, as labour force participants in general, and as child care providers in particular. At the same time, public policy in this area has reflected conservative ideological conceptions about how the private realm of family should be structured, and about the appropriate balance between market and state. There are similar interrelationships between the devaluation of women's work in the domestic sphere, women's generally low earnings as paid employees, and the assumption that women rather than men will be primary caregivers for their children. Disagreements about Canadian child care policy have thus reflected far more than competing views about appropriate policy instruments. They have also engaged deeply held beliefs about motherhood, women's roles, and the nature of families and caregiving. Understanding these connections between public and private helps to illuminate the sources of resistance to redistributing the costs of caring for children away from individual women and into the public sphere.

NOTES

My thanks to Susan Boyd, Nitya Iyer, and Claire Young for helpful comments on earlier drafts of this chapter. Thanks also to Beverly Boisseau, Gillian Calder, Michelle Gieselman, and Lenore Kennedy for research assistance. The financial support for this research provided by the Social Sciences and Humanities Research

Council of Canada under its Women and Change strategic theme is also gratefully acknowledged.

1 American economist Sherwin Rosen, quoted in 'Judgment day,' *Economist*, 18 Feb. 1995, 51.
2 I draw on a variety of empirical sources, including House of Commons debate and legislative committee hearings concerning the Conservative government's child care proposals (1987 and 1988); House of Commons debate on the 1992 budget; the discussion papers that formed the basis of the Axworthy Social Security Review; testimony presented to the Standing Committee on Human Resources considering the Axworthy proposals during 1994, and the Committee's final report (House of Commons 1995); ongoing coverage of, and commentary on, these developments in the media, particularly the *Globe and Mail*; and the transcript of a 1995 discussion with then B.C. Labour Minister Dan Miller on CBC radio concerning his decision to exclude babysitters working less than 15 hours a week for a given family from the province's new minimum wage provisions.
3 Child care falls under provincial jurisdiction in Canada. However, the federal government has participated in this policy arena through the exercise of its spending power. Between 1966 and 1996, Ottawa contributed to the cost of child care services for social assistance recipients under the Canada Assistance Plan (CAP). This arrangement vanished with the demise of CAP and its replacement by the Canada Health and Social Transfer (CHST) on 1 April 1996. See Margaret Philp, 'Last Shared Cost Program Scrapped,' *Globe and Mail*, 30 March 1996, A5.
4 See National Council of Welfare 1988; Canadian Day Care Advocacy Association 1988, 'National Groups Criticize Federal Child Care Strategy,' *Vision* 7, 1–3; and the testimony and briefs presented to the legislative committee that held hearings on Bill C-144, in *Minutes of Proceedings* 1988.
5 See Donn Downey and Geoffrey York, '$500-million Aimed at Child Poverty: Move a Publicity Ploy after Day-care Pullout, Critics Charge,' *Globe and Mail*, 5 May 1992, A5; Geoffrey York, 'Day Care Decision Called Shameful: Critics Vow to Keep Fighting for Program,' *Globe and Mail*, 28 Feb. 1992, A5.
6 Federal funds were intended to cover 40 per cent of the cost of creating these spaces; they would only be made available if provinces provided a matching 40 per cent. The remaining 20 per cent would be covered by parent fees (Liberal Party of Canada 1993, 40).
7 The marginalization of child care as a policy concern for the federal Liberals has been gradual, but steady. In 1994 the $720 million commitment described above was included in the federal budget, but was not referred to in either the Speech

from the Throne or the budget speech. The 1995 budget made no provision at
all for new spending on child care. It is true that in late 1995 then-Human
Resources Development Minister Lloyd Axworthy announced that $720 mil-
lion in federal money would be made available if enough provinces agreed to
participate in a new program. However, by early 1996 (following the replacement of Axworthy by Doug Young as Minister of Human Resources Development) these plans appeared to be crumbling. The 1996 budget again lacked any
provision for a new child care program. In addition, there were reports that officials had been asked to develop an 'exit strategy' to extract Ottawa from
Axworthy's 1995 proposal. Although initially downplayed by Young's office,
these reports gained credibility with subsequent indications by Young that federal plans concerning child care needed to be reworked and that he was not prepared to indicate whether or when a new proposal would be announced, or
what it might look like. In June 1996 the federal government was reportedly
willing to commit only $250 million over three years, aimed at 'getting parents
back to work' rather than creating new spaces. See Alan Freeman, 'Ottawa Qui-
etly Restates Liberal Day-care Promise,' *Globe and Mail*, 12 March 1994, A4;
Margaret Philp, 'National Child Care Back on the Shelf: Budget Ignores $360-
million Pledge,' *Globe and Mail*, 1 March 1995, A5; Margaret Philp, 'Axworthy
Offers Child-care Funding: $720-million Plan Met with Caution,' *Globe and
Mail*, 14 Dec. 1995, A1 and A19; 'Federal Child-care Plan Reported Doomed:
Ottawa Suggests Provinces Weren't Keen but Most Had Expressed Interest,'
Globe and Mail, 16 Feb. 1996, A1 and A7; Jane Gadd, 'Child-care Plan Still
Being Discussed: Human Resources Minister only Halfway through Provincial
Visits, Spokeswoman Says,' *Globe and Mail*, 17 Feb. 1996, A3; 'Child-care Pro-
gram to Be Reassessed,' *Globe and Mail*, 21 Feb. 1996, A4; Michael Valpy, 'The
End of a Promise,' *Globe and Mail*, 8 March 1996, A21; 'Funds for Grit Child-
care Promise Gone,' *Globe and Mail*, 10 June 1996, A4.

8 Now that federal funds for child care under CAP have been amalgamated into
the CHST, provincial governments can reduce the number of provincial dollars
spent on child care services without losing corresponding federal dollars. It will
also be easier to direct provincial funding to for-profit providers. The cuts in
funding for fee subsidies, operating grants, transfers to municipalities, and child
care research being pursued by the Harris government in Ontario offer a grim
indication of what may lie ahead. See Margaret Philp, 'Day-care Subsidies
Expected to Suffer: Reduced Flow of Cash to Municipalities Likely to Shut
Centres, Cut Ontario Jobs,' *Globe and Mail*, 1 Dec. 1995, A7; Margaret Philp,
'Review May Sap Day-care Quality: Ontario Proposals Sign of Future,' *Globe
and Mail*, 8 April 1996, A1 and A5.

9 Non-parental child care is provided in a number of different contexts in Can-

ada. These include care (paid or unpaid) by relatives or neighbours; by paid but unregulated family day care providers (who care for a small number of children in their own home); by nannies or other domestic workers who live in their employers' homes; by regulated family day care providers; in nursery schools; and in licensed day care centres. These latter may be run either on a non-profit basis, or as commercial, profit-making businesses. Advocates have insisted that a national system of child care must include, and support, many different types of care in order to ensure that parents have access to arrangements with which they are comfortable and which suit their needs (CCAAC 1995; Friendly 1994). They have also argued that higher quality care is associated with regulated, non-profit contexts, and that domestic workers who reside in their employers' homes are vulnerable to economic and personal exploitation, especially if they do not hold Canadian citizenship (Arat-Koç 1990; Friendly 1986). In this chapter I focus mainly on care provided in family day care homes and child care centres.

10 By comparison, the average hourly rate for all women working full-time in 1984 was $9.00; for men working full-time, it was $12.10 (Avebury Research 1986, 106).

11 In child care occupations, as in each of the other ten lowest paying occupations, women earned on average less than men. Thus, although the average annual earnings for those in child care occupations were $13,518, the average annual earnings for men in this category were $20,987 compared with $13,252 for women (Statistics Canada 1994, 86).

12 See, e.g., Geoffrey York, 'Tory Politicians Form Family Compact,' *Globe and Mail*, 3 June 1992, A1 and A4; testimony presented by representatives of Kids First in *Minutes of Proceedings* (1988) 4:41–4:55 and 4A:1–22 and *Minutes of Proceedings* (1994) 9:142–53 and 39:57–66; of REAL Women in *Minutes of Proceedings* (1994) 8:103–9 and 51:21–9, and of Westcoast Women for Family Life in *Minutes of Proceedings* (1994) 39:40–8. The Reform Party has carefully avoided statements prescribing full-time motherhood, but a number of its policy positions assume or explicitly endorse 'traditional' family arrangements. See the discussion below.

13 Brenda Ringdahl (President, Kids First), *Minutes of Proceedings* (1988) 4:53–5. Similar views were voiced in the parliamentary arena, during legislative debate on Bill C-144. For example, one Conservative MP (Alex Kindy) stated his view that 'the main objective of a social policy aimed at children must be to keep them with their families. There are exceptional cases where parents must work outside the home. The Government has a responsibility to help them, and that is where a federal public day care policy is required.' House of Commons, *Debates*, 17 Aug. 1988, 18452 (hereinafter *Debates*).

14 Jim Edwards (PC), *Debates*, 10 March 1992, 7912. There is an important truth
being voiced by the women Edwards spoke with about the devaluation of the
work they do in their homes, raising their children. I explore the implications of
the deployment of this truth within a social conservative framework below.

15 I have developed this point at greater length elsewhere. See Teghtsoonian 1996
and 1995. See also Iyer, this volume, for a discussion of the class and race biases
structured into existing policy supports for full-time motherhood. Note that
one prominent social conservative group, REAL Women, does endorse policies
that would provide financial support to low-income women, as well as to those
who are well-off, who wish to care for their children full-time. For example, in
testimony presented during the Social Security Review, Gwendolyn Landolt
(National Vice President, REAL Women) argued that 'under the CAP regulations at present, money is extended to single mothers only to entitle them to
look for work or to take job upgrading skills. We would like to see CAP used to
give increased financial assistance for mothers to remain at home with the children at least while they're of pre-school age. It seems to me there should be
more choice for the single-parent family.' *Minutes of Proceedings* (1994) 51:26.
REAL Women's policy positions are explored further below.

16 See the testimony presented in *Minutes of Proceedings* (1994) by representatives
of Kids First (9:142–53 and 39:57–66) REAL Women (8:103–9 and 51:21–9); and
Westcoast Women for Family Life (39:40–8).

17 A number of these views were reflected in the arguments advanced by William
Beblow's lawyers in trying to persuade the Supreme Court of Canada that
Beblow's former common-law partner, Catherine Peter, should *not* be awarded
an equal share of their assets in recognition of her contribution in running the
household and raising the couple's six children during the twelve years of the
relationship. Beblow's lawyers took the position that Ms Peter had carried out
her household and child-rearing tasks out of 'natural love and affection,' and
that 'Mr Beblow had not been unjustly enriched by her work,' despite the fact
that after she moved in he stopped employing a housekeeper at $350 a month,
and 'was able to pay off his mortgage and buy a van and a houseboat.' The
Supreme Court ruled that Ms Peter was entitled to 'an equal share of the assets
from the relationship.' Alanna Mitchell, 'Household Work Gets Top-Court
Nod: Common-law Spouse Shares Assets,' *Globe and Mail*, 26 March 1993, A1
and A4. A recent Statistics Canada report has estimated the value of unpaid
household work in 1992 as falling between $234 billion and $374 billion,
roughly the equivalent of between 1/3 and 1/2 of the GDP. The report also estimated that if the time spent on unpaid work were to be translated into paid
employment it would add 13 million jobs to the Canadian economy. Margaret
Philp, 'Unpaid Work Worth at Least $234-billion: Women Continue to Perform

Majority of Household Chores, Statscan Study Finds,' *Globe and Mail*, 21 Dec. 1995, A5.

18 *Debates* 23 Aug. 1988, 18713.

19 For examples from the debates on Bill C-144, see Shirley Martin (PC), *Debates*, 11 Aug. 1988, 18219, and Rob Nicholson (PC), *Debates*, 26 Sept. 1988, 19610. For examples from the Social Security Review, see the citations in note 16. Spokeswomen for these groups frequently invoked public opinion data to support their argument that government spending on child care services is misguided because parents prefer that their children be cared for by relatives. In this context, it is worth noting that a Decima poll concluded (1) that the preference for care by relatives was strongest among 'people who have not yet or will never use child care'; (2) that less than 30 per cent of those using licensed child care would prefer relative care; and (3) 'that while people like the idea of using relatives for child care purposes, they also feel that it is very difficult in practice to set up a workable arrangement with a relative' (Decima Research 1991, 8).

20 'How to Find $10-billion in Axworthy Paper,' *Globe and Mail*, 8 Oct. 1994, B2.

21 The work full-time mothers do is *not* appropriately valued in our society, but it does not logically follow that women choosing otherwise receive support for their decision. In a 1991 *Globe and Mail*–CBC News Poll, 76 per cent of respondents agreed that 'children's well-being is being sacrificed these days because both parents have to work.' Alanna Mitchell, 'Working Parents Spark Concern: Canadians Worry the Well-being of the Nation's Children Is Being Sacrificed,' *Globe and Mail*, 5 Nov. 1991, A4. A Gallup Poll survey conducted in 1993 found that 53 per cent of respondents (54 per cent of men and 51 per cent of women) believed that married women with families being 'in the working world' had a harmful effect on family life. Lorne Bozinoff and André Turcotte, 'Canadians Split over Effects of Working Moms,' *Gallup Report*, 24 Jan. 1993, 2. The assumption that employed mothers enjoy general approbation also seems untenable in light of the persistent flow in the mainstream media of articles about the guilt that employed mothers suffer at 'leaving' their children, and concern about the potential damage this causes to the healthy development of kids. My point here is not to argue that mothers in paid employment do not experience guilt, but to suggest that perhaps part of the reason that they do is precisely this ongoing commentary in the media, combined with policy 'supports' that are inadequate to the task of easing their double burden. For examples of media commentary on employed mothers' guilt, see Marlene Habib, 'Motherhood: Guilt Trip Impedes Return to Work,' *Victoria Times-Colonist*, 13 Aug. 1991, C1 and C3; Alanna Mitchell, 'June Cleaver-style Moms Back in Fashion,' *Globe and Mail*, 20 April 1992, A1 and A5; Alanna Mitchell, 'Guilt

and the Working Mother,' *Globe and Mail*, 21 April 1992, A3; Jane Litchfield, 'For Mothers Today, Freedom and Angst,' *Globe and Mail*, 25 May 1995, A22; Suanne Kelman, 'What Is It about Women and Guilt?' *Chatelaine*, April 1993, 55–7 and 159–60.

22 Some child care providers share this view. Margaret Nelson has reported that some of the unlicensed family day care providers in Vermont that she interviewed were critical of their licensed counterparts for 'being in it for the money,' i.e., motivated more by a desire for personal gain than by a commitment to the well-being of the children in their care. Ironically, some of the licensed providers expressed exactly the same critical sentiment about those who were unlicensed. Nelson (1990, 162–70). See also Enarson (1990, 239).

23 Jim Hawkes (PC), *Debates*, 23 Aug. 1988, 18767–8.

24 There is a related aspect of the love–money nexus that helps to legitimate child care providers' low wages. This is the argument that the poor pay in these occupations can be explained, in part, by the fact that the women doing this work love the children, and hence their jobs, so much that the intrinsic satisfaction of the work compensates for the low pay (Barnett 1993, 86). The fact that the intrinsic rewards of many high-paying jobs dominated by men – the thrill of closing the deal, the elation of scoring a goal – do not exert a similar downward pressure on the salaries attached to them generally goes unremarked in such commentary. See the argument in Folbre and Hartmann (1988). My thanks to Nitya Iyer for drawing my attention to this point.

25 The initial program had been criticized by the child care community for excluding providers working in the private, for-profit sector. See Alicia Priest, 'Subsidy of $5 Million for Child-care Workers Receives Mixed Reviews,' *Vancouver Sun*, 29 Jan. 1994, B10, and 'Press Release: ECEBC [Early Childhood Educators of British Columbia] Responds to Wage Supplement Initiative,' *Early Childhood Educator* 9(2) (March/April 1994), 2. The program was continued in 1995–6 and 1996–7 (Ministry of Women's Equality 1996, 8).

26 The term 'babysitter' evokes images of teenagers trying to earn money for new clothes or movies – 'pin money' – whereas many of those providing this service for more than 15 hours a week may well depend on the income in order to support themselves and their families.

27 See Denise Helm, 'Reform Raps Wage Hike for Babysitters' *Victoria Times-Colonist*, 18 March 1995, A3, and 'Province Backtracks on Benefits for Sitters,' *Victoria Times-Colonist* 23 March 1995, B3. The minimum wage was raised from $6.00 per hour to $6.50 in March 1995, and to $7.00 in Oct. 1995. Family day care providers working in their own homes are considered to be self-employed; hence they are not covered by minimum wage legislation.

REFERENCES

Abel, Emily K., and Margaret K. Nelson. 1990a. 'Circles of Care: An Introductory
  Essay.' In Emily K. Abel and Margaret K. Nelson, eds., *Circles of Care: Work
  and Identity in Women's Lives*. Albany, NY: State University of New York Press,
  4–34
'Almanac' hosted by Cecilia Walters on CBC Radio (AM 690), 22 March 1995, with
  guest Hon. Dan Miller (B.C. Minister of Labour)
Arat-Koç, Sedef. 1990. 'Importing Housewives: Non-Citizen Domestic Workers
  and the Crisis of the Domestic Sphere in Canada.' In Meg Luxton, Harriet
  Rosenberg, and Sedef Arat-Koç, eds., *Through the Kitchen Window: The Politics
  of Home and Family*, 2nd ed. Toronto: Garamond Press, 81–103
Armstrong, Pat, and Hugh Armstrong. 1994. *The Double Ghetto: Canadian
  Women and Their Segregated Work*, 3rd ed. Toronto: McClelland and Stewart
Avebury Research and Consulting Limited. 1986. *Decade of Promise: An Assess-
  ment of Canadian Women's Status in Education, Training and Employment,
  1976–1985*. Toronto: Canadian Congress for Learning Opportunities for Women
Baines, Carol T., Patricia M. Evans, and Sheila M. Neysmith. 1991. 'Caring: Its
  Impact on the Lives of Women.' In Carol T. Baines, Patricia M. Evans, and Sheila
  M. Neysmith, eds., *Women's Caring: Feminist Perspectives on Social Welfare*.
  Toronto: McClelland and Stewart, 11–35
Barnett, W. Steven. 1993. 'An Introduction to the Economics of Family Home
  Day Care.' In Donald L. Peters and Alan R. Pence, eds., *Family Day Care:
  Current Research for Informed Public Policy*. Toronto: Canadian Scholars' Press,
  72–91
Beach, Jane. 1992. 'A Comprehensive System of Child Care.' Paper prepared for
  the Canadian Day Care Advocacy Association national conference, Ottawa, Oct.
  1992
Callahan, Marilyn, and Carolyn Attridge. 1990. *Women in Women's Work: Social
  Workers Talk about Their Work in Child Welfare*. Victoria: University of Victoria
Canadian Day Care Advocacy Association (CDCAA). 1988. 'National Groups
  Criticize Federal Child Care Strategy.' *Vision* 7, 1–3
– 1985. 'Fact Sheet #4: CDCAA Proposes Direct Government Funding for Child
  Care.' Ottawa: Canadian Day Care Advocacy Association
Child Care Advocacy Association of Canada (CCAAC). 1995. *Taking the First
  Steps – Child Care: An Investment in Canada's Future*. Executive Summary,
  Report on Child Care. Ottawa: Child Care Advocacy Association of Canada
Child Care Connection–NS. 1990. *Where We Work: Nova Scotia Child Care Cen-
  tres as Workplaces*. Halifax

Childcare Resource and Research Unit (CRRU). 1994. *Child Care in Canada: Provinces and Territories 1993*. Toronto

Daniels, Arlene Kaplan. 1987. 'Invisible Work.' *Social Problems* 34(5), 403–15

Decima Research. 1991. *Canadian Attitudes towards Child Day Care*. Ottawa: Decima Research

DeVault, Marjorie L. 1991. *Feeding the Family: The Social Organization of Caring as Gendered Work*. Chicago: University of Chicago Press

Diamond, Timothy. 1990. 'Nursing Homes as Trouble.' In Emily K. Abel and Margaret K. Nelson, eds., *Circles of Care: Work and Identity in Women's Lives*. Albany, NY: State University of New York Press, 173–87

Enarson, Elaine. 1990. 'Experts and Caregivers: Perspectives on Underground Day Care.' In Emily K. Abel and Margaret K. Nelson, eds., *Circles of Care: Work and Identity in Women's Lives*. Albany, NY: State University of New York Press, 233–45

Ferguson, Evelyn. 1991. 'The Child-Care Crisis: Realities of Women's Caring.' In Carol T. Baines, Patricia M. Evans, and Sheila M. Neysmith, eds., *Women's Caring: Feminist Perspectives on Social Welfare*. Toronto: McClelland and Stewart, 73–105

Folbre, Nancy, and Heidi Hartmann. 1988. 'The Rhetoric of Self-interest: Ideology and Gender in Economic Theory.' In Arjo Klamer, Donald N. McCloskey, and Robert M. Solow, eds., *The Consequences of Economic Rhetoric*. Cambridge: Cambridge University Press, 184–203

Friendly, Martha. 1995. 'So You Say You Want a Devolution ...? Child Care and the Federal Budget of 1995.' Presentation to the House of Commons Finance Committee Hearings on Bill C-76. Toronto: Childcare Resource and Research Unit

– 1994. *Child Care Policy in Canada: Putting the Pieces Together*. Don Mills: Addison-Wesley

– 1986. 'Daycare-For-Profit: Where Does the Money Go?' Brief presented to the Special Committee on Child Care. Toronto: Daycare Resource and Research Unit

– and Mab Oloman. 1995. 'Child Care at the Centre: Child Care on the Social, Economic and Political Agenda in the 1990s.' Paper presented at the Seventh National Social Welfare Policy Conference, Vancouver, 25–8 June

Friendly, Martha, Julie Mathien, and Tricia Willis. 1987. *Child Care – What the Public Said*. Ottawa: Canadian Day Care Advocacy Association

Government of Canada. 1994a. *Agenda: Jobs and Growth. Improving Social Security in Canada: A Discussion Paper*. Ottawa: Human Resources Development Canada

– 1994b. *Improving Social Security in Canada: Child Care and Development: A Supplementary Paper*. Ottawa: Human Resources Development Canada

- 1987. *Sharing the Responsibility: Federal Response to the Report of the Special Committee on Child Care*. Ottawa: Health and Welfare Canada

Graham, Hilary. 1983. 'Caring: A Labour of Love.' In Janet Finch and Dulcie Groves, eds., *A Labour of Love: Women, Work and Caring*. London: Routledge and Kegan Paul, 13–30

Hartmann, Heidi I., and Diana M. Pearce. 1989. *High Skill and Low Pay: The Economics of Child Care Work,* rev. ed. Washington: Institute for Women's Policy Research

House of Commons. 1995. Standing Committee on Human Resources Development. *Security, Opportunities and Fairness: Canadians Renewing their Social Programs. Report of the Standing Committee on Human Resources Development*. Ottawa: Queen's Printer

Hum, Derek P.J. 1989. 'Compromise and Delay: The Federal Strategy on Child Care.' In Ronald L. Watts and Douglas M. Brown, eds., *Canada: The State of the Federation 1989*. Kingston: Institute of Intergovernmental Relations, 151–65

Karyo Communications. 1992. *Caring for a Living: Final Report*. Ottawa: Canadian Child Day Care Federation and Canadian Day Care Advocacy Association

LaGrange, Annette, and Malcolm Read. 1990. *Those Who Care: A Report on Child Caregivers in Alberta Daycare Centres*. Red Deer, Alberta: Child Care Matters

Liberal Party of Canada. 1993. *Creating Opportunity: The Liberal Plan for Canada*. Ottawa

Macklin, Audrey. 1992. '*Symes* v *M.N.R.*: Where Sex Meets Class.' *Canadian Journal of Women and the Law* 5(2), 498–517

Ministry of Women's Equality. Province of British Columbia. 1996. 'Update: Wage Supplement Initiative.' *Child Care Information Update* 5(1), 8

- 1995a. 'Wage Supplement Is Making a Difference.' *Child Care Information Update* 4(1), 4–5

- 1995b. 'Wage Supplement: The Next Step.' *Child Care Information Update* 4(2), 5

- 1994. 'An Overview – Child Care: Choices at Work.' *Child Care Information Update* 3(1), 2–3, 8

- 1993. 'Infant/Toddler Incentive Grant Program.' *Child Care Information Update* 2(1), 4

Minutes of Proceedings and Evidence of the Legislative Committee on Bill C-144. 1988. 2nd Session of the 33rd Parliament, 1986–87–88. Ottawa: Queen's Printer

Minutes of Proceedings and Evidence of the Standing Committee on Human Resources Development. 1994. 1st Session of the 35th Parliament, 1994. Ottawa: Queen's Printer

Mishra, Ramesh. 1990. *The Welfare State in Capitalist Society: Policies of Retrench-*

ment and Maintenance in Europe, North America and Australia. Toronto: University of Toronto Press

Modigliani, Kathy. 1988. 'Twelve Reasons for the Low Wages in Child Care.' *Young Children* 43(3), 14–15

National Council of Welfare. 1988. *Child Care: A Better Alternative.* Ottawa

Nelson, Margaret K. 1990. *Negotiated Care: The Experience of Family Day Care Providers.* Philadelphia: Temple University Press

Olsen, Frances E. 1983. 'The Family and the Market: A Study of Ideology and Legal Reform.' *Harvard Law Review* 96(7), 1497–1578

Pateman, Carole. 1989. 'Feminist Critiques of the Public/Private Dichotomy.' In Carole Pateman, *The Disorder of Women: Democracy, Feminism and Political Theory.* Stanford: Stanford University Press, 118–40

Phillips, Susan D. 1989. 'Rock-a-Bye, Brian: The National Strategy on Child Care.' In Katherine A. Graham, ed., *How Ottawa Spends 1989–90: The Buck Stops Where?* Ottawa: Carleton University Press, 165–208

Presser, Harriet B. 1992. 'Child-Care Supply and Demand: What Do We Really Know?' In Alan Booth, ed., *Child Care in the 1990s: Trends and Consequences.* Hillsdale, NJ: Erlbaum, 26–32

Reform Party of Canada. 1995a. *Blue Sheet: Principles – Policies.* Calgary
– 1995b. *The Taxpayers' Budget.* Calgary

Saraceno, Chiara. 1984. 'Shifts in Public and Private Boundaries: Women as Mothers and Service Workers in Italian Daycare.' *Feminist Studies* 10(1), 7–29

Schom-Moffatt, Patti. 1984. *The Bottom Line: Wages and Working Conditions of Workers in the Formal Day Care Market. Background Paper Prepared for the Task Force on Child Care.* Ottawa: Status of Women Canada

Skold, Karen. 1988. 'The Interests of Feminists and Children in Child Care.' In Sanford M. Dornbusch and Myra H. Strober, eds., *Feminism, Children, and the New Families.* New York: Guilford Press, 113–36

Spalter-Roth, Roberta M., and Heidi I. Hartmann. 1991. 'Science and Politics and the "Dual Vision" of Feminist Policy Research: The Example of Family and Medical Leave.' In Janet Shibley Hyde and Marilyn J. Essex, eds., *Parental Leave and Child Care: Setting a Research and Policy Agenda.* Philadelphia: Temple University Press, 41–65

Special Committee on Child Care. 1987. *Sharing the Responsibility: Report of the Special Committee on Child Care.* Ottawa

Statistics Canada. 1994. 'The Daily, April 13 1993: Income.' In *1991 Census Highlights.* Ottawa: Statistics Canada, 80–6

Strober, Myra H., Suzanne Gerlach-Downie, and Kenneth E. Yeager. 1995. 'Child Care Centers as Workplaces.' *Feminist Economics* 1(1), 93–119

Task Force on Child Care. 1986. *Report.* Ottawa: Status of Women Canada

Teghtsoonian, Katherine. 1996. 'Promises, Promises: "Choices for Women" in Canadian and American Child Care Policy Debates.' *Feminist Studies* 22(1), 119–46

– 1995. 'Work and/or Motherhood: The Ideological Construction of Women's Options in Canadian Child Care Policy Debates.' *Canadian Journal of Women and the Law* 8(2), 411–39

– 1993. 'Neo-Conservative Ideology and Opposition to Federal Regulation of Child Care Services in the United States and Canada.' *Canadian Journal of Political Science* 26(1), 97–121

Tom, Allison. 1992–3. 'The Messy Work of Child Care: Addressing Feminists' Neglect of Child Care Workers.' *Atlantis* 18(1 and 2), 70–81

Ungerson, Clare. 1990. 'The Language of Care: Crossing the Boundaries.' In Clare Ungerson, ed., *Gender and Caring: Work and Welfare in Britain and Scandinavia*. New York: Harvester/Wheatsheaf, 8–33

Waring, Marilyn. 1988. *If Women Counted: A New Feminist Economics*. San Francisco: HarperCollins

Whitebook, Marcy, Carollee Howes, and Deborah Phillips. 1989. *Who Cares? Child Care Teachers and the Quality of Care in America: Executive Summary, National Child Care Staffing Study*. Oakland, Calif: Child Care Employee Project

Young, Claire F.L. 1994. 'Child Care – A Taxing Issue?' *McGill Law Journal* 39(3), 539–67

Zinsser, Caroline. 1986. *Day Care's Unfair Burden: How Low Wages Subsidize a Public Service*. New York: Center for Public Advocacy Research

6

Across the Home/Work Divide: Homework in Garment Manufacture and the Failure of Employment Regulation

AMANDA ARABA OCRAN

When Zhu, an industrial homeworker, wished to separate her working day from her domestic day, she left home by the front door and, a minute later, re-entered by the back door. This ritual act of leaving home to go to work enabled Zhu, at least for brief intervals, to assert her role as paid worker apart from her position as unpaid caregiver and homemaker. She said: 'When I say now I go to work, the children wave goodbye, neighbours see me leave ... with everyone knowing that I really am working, I get more respect like in a real job out in public.' Although, as Zhu suggested, homework is devalued by its location in the domestic domain, in her East Vancouver neighbourhood, and elsewhere in Canada, home-based employment is becoming commonplace (Public Service Alliance of Canada, PSAC 1992; Statistics Canada 1991c). Zhu's ritual demonstrates that this devaluation is largely ideological, but her last comment illustrates how notions of private and public are bound up with the spatial separation of home and work.

The division between homeplace and workplace as separate sites of social life originated during the early nineteenth-century period of industrialization, when the factory system invented the *workplace* as something outside of the familial household. This division supplanted, but never eliminated, the industrial practice known as 'cottage industry' or industrial homework. The survival of industrial homework into the late twentieth century, and its revival as a feminized and racialized form of labour in contemporary economic restructuring, has prompted re-examinations of the gendered relationship between home and work, the discourses that shape it, and the wider political economy in which it is embedded (Boris 1994; Boris and Prügl 1996; Leach 1993; Pennington and Westover 1989; Phizacklea and Wolkowitz 1995).

In this chapter I explore the practice of home-based employment (industrial homework)[1] in the garment industry and its positioning within the regulatory framework of employment standards. By relocating the labour process to the home, employers are able to evade regulatory provisions, such as employment standards, and are participating in a wider political shift towards privatizing social and economic relations. The increased use of homework, as feminized labour, is one dimension of economic restructuring that is achieved through exploiting gender-related public/private distinctions between home and work.

The privatization of production also embraces inequalities other than gender. An examination of homework shows that the dualist model of privatization, as primarily shifting relations between state and market, is complicated by gendered, class-based, and racialized counterpoints of experience. The complexity of relations among state, market, and home defy attempts either to reduce the private and public to two spheres of experience (see Fraser 1989), or to treat the home and market, in contrast to the state, as part of a one-dimensional private domain.

Home and Work: A Contradictory Relationship?

In identifying the gendered dichotomy between home and work, analysts have pointed to the ideological structure of women's subordinate place *inside* a domestic domain and men's dominance *outside* of it in the 'world of work' (Boris 1994, 1–5). The oppositional spatial/legal referents of workplace and homeplace tend to reify the public/private distinction. However, the notion of work or employment as part of a public sphere of activities is itself a contradictory construct within the liberal ideology of public and private and the legal discourses that support it (see Pateman 1988, 12–13). The law, for example, typically locates employment relations in the private sphere ('private enterprise') by codifying the workplace on the basis of employer's property rights where employees 'are no longer entitled to the protection afforded them as members of the public – as "citizens"' (Blomley and Bakan 1992, 635). As citizens, workers are entitled to the minimum protections afforded by the state in setting employment standards; but not all workers are constructed equally as citizens, and not all employees leave home to go to work.

The public/private dichotomy between state and market positions the state as the universal (public) agent of intervention in antagonisms between ideology and economy (see Moss 1994, 81; Young 1987, 58–9). This dualism conceals the historical role of the market in provoking the gendered public/private divide that gave rise to oppositional, exploitative relations between home and work. The home/household, for example, has been identified, mainly by Marxist feminist scholars, as a significant site of women's oppression where the reproduction of labour power and labourers takes place (Barrett 1980; Folbre 1982). This perspective provides a method of connecting women's subordination in the private, domestic sphere to capitalist relations of production in the market (Fox 1980; Seccombe 1973).

However, redefining the home as a workplace and advocating making it public (Blumenfeld and Mann 1980) did not necessarily threaten the integrity of ideologically inscribed gender subordination (see Hartmann 1981, 9–10). Instead, it encouraged the idea that integrating the home into the market (wages for housework) or, as in liberal approaches, integrating women into the paid workforce (the feminization of labour?) would resolve gender inequality. For many women, integration into the paid workforce is not a liberating experience (Boulding 1981, 17–19). The integration approach negates the experiences of groups of working-class women, and 'women of colour'[2] who have been historically and racially configured in terms of their labour power for the market *and* for middle-class households (Giles and Arat-Koç 1994, 1–12; Jones 1985, 36–69; Mohanty 1991, 28–9; Valenze 1995, 172–7), rather than recognized as members of their own families. Likewise, a particular feminist history – 'white,' European, and middle class – underlay the idea that wages are the answer to public/private gender inequality (Mohanty 1991, 20; Nicholson 1986, 203–7).

The need to restructure relations between the public and private is clearly an appropriate direction for feminist thinking. Nevertheless, there are dangers inherent in efforts either to abolish the distinction between public and private or to essentialize women's embodied reproductive activities in an attempt to make them central to notions of the public (Mouffe 1992, 74). Both moves, understood within the paradigm of state power, imperil prospects for self-determination (see Young 1987, 59). Still, the construction of a private sphere as separate, or safe, from state (or market) interventions has been available only to the most privileged of women (and men) (Mohanty 1991, 9).

In this vein, some analysts view the re-emergence of homework in terms of global economic changes in which women's cheaper, more disposable (flexible) labour has once again become more central to capitalism and therefore more exploited as a compromise form of employment (Beneria and Roldan 1987, 73; Boris and Daniels 1989, 1; Boris and Prügl 1996, 4–6).

Others suggest that the changes in economic and social life associated with new opportunities for paid work at home permit a significant renegotiation of the home/work split to the advantage of women (Christensen 1988, 167–9; Hakim 1991, 109–14). Homework, however, is not a *new* form of labour. Far from being a panacea for women seeking to integrate reproductive and productive work in a liberating way, its history is deeply implicated in the very structures of marginalization that it might be thought to ameliorate.

Homework: From 'Cottage Industry' to the 'Feminization of Labour'

Industrial homework, also known as 'putting-out' or 'outsourcing,' originated with the textile and garment industry in the late seventeenth century (Bythell 1978, 29). During the industrial revolution in Britain, outsourcing in these 'sweated trades' relied on pools of disenfranchised labour: the rural poor, Jewish immigrants, Irish migrants, married women, and children (ibid. 269; Morris 1986, 12). In the transition from an agricultural to industrial economy, economic and technological transformations in the market changed the gendered composition of households as productive units. By the 1900s Western European and North American gender ideologies were structured by the capitalist class relations of industrial society (Boris 1996, 24; Valenze 1995): 'The separation of productive work from the home was making it harder for women to combine domestic responsibilities with the newly dominant form of productive work. Single women still worked in shops or factories and in domestic service, but married women were ... employed as home workers. Pushed out of the industrial labour force, they turned to ... taking in boarders and laundry, or doing factory outwork, often in tenement sweatshops' (Bose 1987, 274). As men's paid work in the market became alienated from the home, women's labour in the home was disassociated from paid work. This ideological divorce was reinforced by the socially desirable confinement of middle-class women to the home. There, women were seen to be consumers rather than producers.

Changing perceptions of gendered contributions within the household also tended to strengthen class divisions. Working-class women were caught between the need to earn a living and unattainable middle-class standards of domestication. Their turn to commodified work in the home, or within a 'family' enterprise (belonging to the male 'head of the family'), further reduced the social visibility of women's work. Although male and female spheres were never completely separate, most historical accounts have assumed the model of wage-earning patriarchs and dependent housewives (Bose 1987, 282; Davis 1983, 229; Valenze 1995, 185).

Three important aspects of the *'invisibility'*[3] of contemporary homework relate to the historically gendered nature of homework labour markets in Canada. First, the disassociation of the home from the market, as a site of production, reduces the social visibility (and significance) of all labour within it (Boris 1994, 2; Christensen 1988, xii–4; Davis 1983, 222–9; Luxton 1980). Second, the marginal position of industrial homeworkers is structured by class, ethnic, and racial distinctions: many are immigrant women (Johnson and Johnson 1982, 60, 95; Phizacklea 1988). Third, historically fuelled by the middle-class 'cult of domesticity,' state, employer, and union policies have reinforced the inequalities of women's labour in the home *and* in the market by constructing women as dependants of male wage-earners and therefore as secondary, disposable workers (Creese 1992, 366–74; Peck 1989, 130–1; Pennington and Westover 1989, 2–7). This configuration justifies lower wages paid to women, fewer employment benefits, and their segregation in jobs associated with the home (Armstrong and Armstrong 1978; Fox and Fox 1987; Walby 1988). At present, most women's labour is disproportionately regulated by the minimal protections of employment standards legislation (with weak enforcement mechanisms) rather than by more comprehensive and closely monitored collective agreements (Fudge 1990).[4]

The resurgence of homework in contemporary production strategies is connected to the historically less protected and subordinate status of most women's work (Valenze 1995, 184). The growth of casualized, contingent, or flexible labour, including homework, is part of an international phenomenon referred to as 'the feminization of labour' (McDonald 1991; McDowell 1991; Standing 1989; Walby 1989). The term 'feminized labour' alludes both to large increases in women's labour force participation rates and to the increased casualization of employment associated with women's jobs (part-time, temporary, and non-union) that, in recent years, is being experienced by women and men alike (Phizacklea and Wolkowitz 1995, 5; Standing 1989, 1077).

Although greater attention is being paid to the gendered nature of economic life, and women's inequality in it, the home as the final frontier in restructuring economic relations through shifts between public and private goes unrecognized. Regulatory provisions for even minimal protection of employees often do not apply to home-based workers (Ruiz 1992). Where they do apply, the putative neutrality of labour law with respect to the home as a workplace tends to operate in a manner that excludes homeworkers from protection. This exclusion opens the door to employers seeking vulnerable labour for low-wage production strategies.

Economic Restructuring in the Garment Industry:
Home, Market, and Employment Standards

In British Columbia, and elsewhere in Canada, the decline of the manufacturing sector since the 1970s, part of the trend towards de-industrialization and the rise of a service-based economy, has been accompanied by the restructuring of labour and production processes. Significant aspects of economic restructuring revolve around the idea of increased production flexibility entailing different forms of work and work organization (Pollert 1991; Walby 1989). Restructuring in the garment and textile industry centres on production strategies that reduce labour costs without significantly replacing labour. Reducing labour costs while maintaining the same level of labour inputs translates into an increased demand for low-waged, non-unionized workers. By the early 1980s the homework, or domestic subcontracting, system had expanded on a multinational basis as the garment industry's major response to the search for low-cost, vulnerable (i.e., non-regulated and disposable) labour (Mytelka 1991, 127). The expansion of homework in the local context of restructuring is recognized as part of these wider changes in the nature and location of work nationally and internationally (Das Gupta 1996, 41–2; Seward 1990, 4).

Canada has approximately 100,000 industrial homeworkers, with up to 3,000 in British Columbia, most of whom are garment workers (Thompson 1994, 35). Although fewer workers are on the shop floor, increasing numbers of homesewers perform jobs that are relocated from the factory to the home (Das Gupta 1996, 43–6; Leach 1993, 70). Thus, the increased use of home-based workers, attributed to requirements for flexible labour, has contributed to both the rising rate of non-unionized garment workers and the relatively small size of individual clothing manufacturers (INTER-CEDE 1993, 16–17; Leach 1993, 71).

More specifically, accessing vulnerable labour in the garment industry depends on side-stepping regulatory frameworks such as labour laws. This tactic hinges on adapting production strategies to exploit social inequalities among workers based on gender, citizenship, and ethnicity (Beneria and Roldan 1987; Leach 1993; Phizacklea 1988; Phizacklea and Wolkowitz 1995). Free Trade Zones (FTZs) are one method of ducking both organized labour and state regulatory frameworks in internationalized production (Beneria and Roldan 1987, 32–9; Boris and Prügl 1996, 5–6; Mitter 1986), as is the localized strategy of 'sacking all the workers or ... closing down the firm and re-opening under a new name with a new [non-union] workforce' (Phizacklea 1988, 52). Wherever organized labour or state regulatory frameworks effectively oversee the employment contract, flexible labour markets are more likely to be constituted on the basis of pre-existing social inequalities among workers that enhance the invisibility and vulnerability of the worker. The relocation of work to the home provides employers with just such an opportunity for procuring unprotected labour while obscuring the employee–employer relationship.

The identification of an employee–employer relationship is pivotal for regulatory intervention in labour relations (Ruiz 1992). Labour law uses the concept of a worker's *subordination* to the employer as a key criterion of employee status. This doctrine is encoded in regulatory frameworks in terms of the *supervision and control* of workers in a managed workplace (ibid. 201). These terms are difficult to apply to homework because it is done independently of direct supervision, and contact with the employer is minimal or even non-existent (Prügl 1996, 207). Relations of subordination are characteristic of homework but in different ways that are at once manipulated by employers and ignored by employment standards.

Whereas employers who use homeworkers bring the home to the market, production strategies that depend upon homework also move aspects of the market, such as paid labour and the workplace, to the home. In this sense, the home becomes a market factor both as a place of employment and a site of production. One might expect that regulatory frameworks such as employment standards could be adjusted accordingly (Ruiz 1992, 197). Yet this 'marketization' of the home is negated by its treatment in employment standards as a place of work no different than that of locations provided or designated by the employer.

The Employment Standards Act (hereafter 'the Act')[5] is the primary legislative instrument in British Columbia for providing a minimum standard for wages, conditions of work, and employment benefits for the non-unionized two-thirds of the working population (Province of British Columbia 1991). Comparable provisions exist in all of the provinces (Labour Canada 1991). The Act categorically excludes certain professions and occupations from its mandate. For other types of work not specifically addressed in the Act, the Employment Standards Branch (hereafter ESB) serves as a policy interpretation body that determines the scope of the Act. Homework is not explicitly excluded by the text of the Act. Employees working in private residences (the home) are recognized in Part 3 of the Employment Standards Regulation (hereafter ESR)[6] and in section 15 of the Act. In fact, homeworkers in the garment industry are given special mention in an occupational designation based on the location of their work in the home: '"textile worker" means a person employed to make fabrics, or fabric articles, including clothing, in a private residence.'[7]

Curiously, while the Act always has treated the 'private residence' or home as a distinctive location of work requiring separate definition,[8] as a matter of policy interpretation, the location of work in the home is irrelevant. When questioned as to how the Act is actually applied to industrial homeworkers, a senior policy interpreter for the ESB asserted that 'whether or not someone is working from the home it makes no difference to us ... we look at the employee–employer relationship the same way' (interview ESB, February 1993). The interpretation that employer–employee relations in work performed in the home are no different from work performed elsewhere, treats the homeworker as formally equal to a factory or office worker regardless of their differences. Despite assertions that the Act is 'driven by the market,'[9] the increased use of the home as a workplace is not considered to create an impetus for a more appropriate policy interpretation.

Without suggesting that minimum standards are enjoyed equally by all other workers, the putative neutrality of the Act is potentially exclusionary and contradictory in its application to homework. It effectively excludes homework by not recognizing that regulatory principles, such as the supervision and control of employees and employer accountability, are based on characteristics of the centralized (public) workplace – the factory or office – that are not present in the homework system (see Prügl 1996, 206). The lack of recognition of the differences inherent in homework permits the obfuscation of homework employee–employer relationships under the guise of impartiality.

The paradox lies in the assertion of an impossible neutrality. Employment standards were established to regulate labour relations in the market as a public place based on the spatial separation of work and home in public/private thinking (see Luxton 1980, 11; Pennington and Westover 1989, 102–14). This separation is reflected in the Act where public/private distinctions give rise to a separate category for 'employees working in private residences' (see the Act, s. 15), although ESB policy holds that location makes no difference. Meanwhile, employers resort to homework expressly because of its effective exclusion from 'controls exercised over employment in ... factories and workshops' (Pennington and Westover 1989, 106). Ironically, the survival of homework is ensured by the regulatory frameworks that once heralded its demise through codifying the separation of home from work.

The false neutrality of employment standards allows employers to sidestep labour regulation by relocating production processes to the domestic, 'private,' and effectively unregulated (insofar as the performance of labour is concerned) sphere. As well, in the garment industry, homework is predominantly carried out by particular groups of women whose access to public entitlements as workers has been attenuated in different ways. One labour advocate stated: 'The coincidence between the need for cheap, unprotected labour and an industrial homework labour market made up of 97 per cent visible minority women should be considered in assessing ... obstacles to minimum standards of employment for homeworkers' (Interview, ACTWU, March 1993). The portrayal of homework labour markets as made up largely of 'visible minorities' marks a difference in the way workers are ideologically represented and inserted into production processes as unprotected labour. Employment standards not only negate the home as a different place of employment from the market, but also obscure how other discourses and practices, such as racialization and immigrant status, promote vulnerability.

Neither Citizen Nor Employee:
Racialized and Gendered Discourses on Homeworkers

The formation of Canadian garment industry labour markets, both in the factory and in the home, has traditionally relied on various flows of immigrant women workers. Indeed, the contemporary clothing industry in industrialized countries is uniquely dependent upon immigrant women's labour (Davidson 1984, xvii; Johnson and Johnson 1982, 60; Leach 1993; Peck 1992). Immigrant women are also among the most vulnerable and least protected labour force participants, particularly in recent Canadian restructuring strategies (Ecumenical Coalition 1992, 2; INTERCEDE 1993, 3–5). Although previous groups of immigrant women from European countries were regarded as having 'passed through' the experience of low-waged, casual employment with the acquisition of local job skills, this pattern has changed. Immigrant women from 'non-traditional' source countries (i.e., non-European) increasingly remain occupationally segregated in declining and low-waged sectors of the economy such as garment manufacturing (Seward and Tremblay 1989, x).

Added to this dynamic is the resurgence of racialized images[10] of the suitability of immigrant women and 'women of colour' for homework and servitude (Committee for Domestic Workers and Caregivers Rights, CDWCR 1993; Giles and Arat-Koç 1994; INTERCEDE 1993; Silvera 1989). In British Columbia racialized notions of skill also have a geographic aspect. Places where industrial homework is widespread, such as East Vancouver, are commonly identified by ethnocultural attributes in which a foreign or immigrant status is associated with notions of race, for example, 'China Town' and 'India Town' (interviews with homeworker, ILGWU, Shah, March 1993; see Anderson 1987). Thus, in the Vancouver area, garment industry homework is closely associated with ethnic communities identified as Chinese, Asian, or Indian.

Labour history in British Columbia is replete with illustrations of the ties between the location of particular groups of workers in the labour force and ethnic or racial characteristics (Adilman 1984, 53–78; Creese 1991, 109–24). Some groups of workers continue to be excluded from better paying jobs on the basis of actual or attributed immigrant status or ethnicity, regardless of length of time spent in the labour force and comparative educational attainments (Li 1992). The status of many workers, particularly those identified as visible minorities in the eyes of the larger society, is that of 'permanent foreigner' (Creese 1991). Those who are seen as 'visible minority' are often assumed to have immigrant status in public life. Such assumptions are part of contemporary racial discourses in the Vancouver area and correspond to the findings of wider studies on immigrant women's experience in the Canadian labour force (Ng 1988; Das Gupta 1996, 55). Such studies show that immigrant women fare worse than immigrant men in accessing mainstream jobs and educational resources. The devaluing of non-Canadian (read European) work experience or education is also frequently cited in the local context as a constraint to immigrant women's employment outside the home (interviews with homeworkers, March and April 1993; February and March 1994). Allophone women are even more likely to be pushed into industrial homework.[11] These dynamics promote an insidious tautology. With homework considered to be *the option* for allophone immigrant and 'visible minority' women unable to access mainstream jobs, homework itself becomes associated with a lack of skills or qualifications.[12]

After several years of homework taken as a temporary income-earning strategy, many homeworkers find themselves trapped outside of the formal labour market. Access to training after years of homeworking is negligible, since homeworkers will no longer qualify for settlement services from immigrant service societies, nor are they eligible for government programs administered on the basis of formal unemployment status (interview, OASIS, February 1993; ILGWU April 1994).

Interviews with immigrant service societies revealed a widespread concern about inadequate settlement and training program even for recently arrived immigrants (interviews, OASIS and MOSAIC, February, March 1993). With the introduction of unemployment insurance registration as the central criterion for eligible applications to training programs, language and job training have become even less accessible. Consequently, immigrant homeworkers can be twice excluded from eligibility for training or other government services that rest on either formal unemployment or a 'new' immigrant status.

Industrial homeworkers, who tend to be immigrant women for whom restricted access to well-paying jobs has been well documented, often cite child care and domestic responsibilities – combined with the need for paid work – as foremost among their reasons for taking homework (INTER-CEDE 1993, 15; Phizacklea 1988, 53; Weiner and Green 1984, 286–7). A range of contemporary homework studies in Canada, the United States, Mexico, and Britain found that reproductive and caregiving responsibilities are cited as the primary motivation for women to take home-based employment regardless of their class position or ethnic identity (Beneria and Roldan 1987; Christensen 1988; Fernandez-Kelly and Garcia 1989; Johnson and Johnson 1982; Phizacklea and Wolkowitz 1995). Women are more likely than men to take on homework in order to provide domestic services for their family/household at the same time.

For immigrant women and their families, homework remains an important economic survival tactic, as it was in the nineteenth century. It allows them to undertake both reproductive roles and employment within the space of the home. Reformers who ignore this agency while advocating the abolition of homework are resisted by homeworkers (Boris 1994, 107). However, the homework strategy of economic survival is often misconstrued or justified solely as women's choice. Homeworkers frequently related, with a sense of despair, the view that 'most people [homeworkers] do not like working at home, but many have no choice' (interview with homeworker, March 1993). The image of choice where 'good' mothers combine child care and paid work by undertaking homework is used as a recurring justification for encouraging women to do homework (Beneria and Roldan 1987, 74; Phizacklea and Wolkowitz 1995, 12).

In fact, women face overt pressures in the workplace to take the homework 'option.' Factory workers who become homeworkers are often offered homework as either an alternative or a supplement to inadequate maternity leave benefits (see Iyer this volume), part-time work, or as a 'favour' to help them during domestic crises (Fernandez-Kelly and Garcia 1989, 174). This strategy targets (but is not limited to) women with young children (Johnson and Johnson 1982) and is common to the homework system in the Vancouver area, where it is consistently reported as part of management's labour-procuring policies (interview, OASIS, March 1993; interviews with homeworkers, March and April 1993; February and March 1994). Despite these 'favours,' once an employee 'goes home' her identity as a worker is radically transformed, often starting with her immediate exclusion from employment-related benefits.

Homeworkers in this study invariably made unfavourable comparisons of their homework employment to their shop-floor experiences even when citing the advantage of combining child care with paid work. They reported isolation and loss of worker identity or formal employment status as a primary reason for preferring factory work (or any non-home-based work for that matter) to homework (interviews with homeworkers, February, March, April 1993). For both employers and homeworkers, homework is often not considered to be a 'real job,' but a compromise form of employment. Factory work has a higher status because of its recognition as 'real' work without the associations with domestic and unskilled labour that devalue homework.

The convergence of family responsibilities, industrial labour demands, and exclusion from the mainstream labour market engender an informal, *invisible*, industrial homework labour force made up of mostly allophone, immigrant women who, ironically, are often identified as *visible minority*. Outside the home, immigrant or visible minority status positions industrial homeworkers as foreigners in the public sphere of the citizen.

In the context of public policy trends towards privatizing the costs of unemployment (Seward 1990, 1) and immigrant settlement (Seward and Tremblay 1989, x–xi), public disentitlements are borne heavily by industrial homeworkers whose experiences as mothers, workers, and immigrants share the same marginalized space in home, market, and state. Neither as citizens nor as employees are homeworkers included in the public domain. The next section elaborates how these exclusions create relations of subordination between homeworkers and employers that enable the latter to procure and control home-based labour without the need for formal contracts or direct supervision.

Homework Employment Relations: Procuring Labour and Avoiding Disputes in the Public/Private Seam

Homework in the garment industry is usually found at the bottom of a pyramid of labour-procuring relationships, a system of subcontracting common to the garment industry that can extend from the level of retail and factories down through contractors to homeworkers (Leach 1993; Ruiz 1992). The farther away from the retail level that a worker is positioned in this pyramid, the lower the piece-rate wage and the more precarious the employee–employer relationship.

The tenuous nature of the employee–employer relationship is both ideological and concrete. Industrial homework is widely perceived to be at the bottom of the occupational hierarchy. It is commonly viewed as unskilled immigrants' work and devalued by association with gendered and increasingly racialized perceptions of domestic labour. Employer and managerial attitudes towards 'immigrant' women workers and homework reveal contradictory valuations of new labour strategies in flexible production. On the one hand, homeworkers are sought and valued as cost-efficient, 'just-in-time' labour. Managers and contractors might go to great lengths to procure groups of homeworkers. On the other hand, homeworkers are often viewed as interlopers, 'scab' labour; a necessary evil. One manager wished that he did not have to use the 'inferior' labour of 'immigrant women' (interview with factory manager, March 1994). Another complained that 'all we have here are sewing jobs for unskilled workers like the Asians ... and women' (interview with factory manager, February 1993).

Ethnocultural and racialized discourses surrounding garment work are normalized in the labour-procuring strategies of employers as well as by management attitudes. With 'word of mouth' reported as the primary means of labour procurement, the formation of industrial homework labour markets is particularly dependent on contacts within local linguistic groups and existing garment factory labour markets. The residential clustering of garment factory workers near the factories where they work (in Vancouver these are generally also areas of lower cost housing) facilitates the building of local networks of homeworkers (Vancouver Planning Department 1994). Some firms use shop supervisors to contact employees in the factory to do extra work at home in order to avoid paying overtime wages. Outside contractors or 'jobbers' in the industry often rely on experienced homeworkers to recruit other women in their families and neighbourhoods to take up homework.

Particular linguistic or ethnic characteristics often coincide with specific types of homework that are occupationally differentiated (Christensen 1988, 2–5; Phizacklea and Wolkowitz 1995). Notably, the significance of ethnic ties for homeworkers is often a manipulated one. Contractors who share some ethnic commonality, such as language or family ties, that gives them access to homeworkers, might use the link to oblige them to work at even lower rates of pay than otherwise could be expected and to control homeworkers' contact with agents of authority (interviews with Coyne, February 1993; Shah, March 1993; homeworker, April 1993; see Weiner and Green 1984, 287–8).

Fears about becoming 'troublemakers' are often related by homeworkers asked to talk about their work (Johnson and Johnson 1982, 11). With homework frequently perceived to be an illegal activity, homeworkers are often reluctant to draw attention to themselves or to relate information about their employment to 'outsiders' (such as academic researchers and government agents) that might endanger relationships with contractors or solicit government surveillance (Phizacklea 1988, 53; Weiner and Green 1984, 282). Immigration status, which is frequently male-dependent for married women, was also cited by Vancouver-area homeworkers as a key factor in their distrust of dealing with agents of authority (interviews with homeworkers, March and February 1993). As one advocate stated: 'The situation of immigrant women is charged with fear!' (interview with Shah, March 1993).

In addition to the vulnerable and therefore tractable status of homeworkers, the devaluing of homework as low-skilled work makes it more attractive to employers. Its ideological marginalization is realized in the production process as disposable, contingent labour, where employers use homeworkers to supply labour strictly in accord with demand for production. Unlike factory workers, for homeworkers, employment is tied to the supply of work in the most immediate sense. Downturns in demand mean that homeworkers are out of work. Peak seasons in the fashion industry and rapid product change that intensify labour inputs and shorten turnover times, create stressful, hazardous conditions of work.[13] Long hours and insufficient time for rest when work is available are doubly difficult when combined with caregiver obligations. Homeworkers accept tight deadlines so that, regarded as 'good workers,' they will receive more work (interviews with homeworker, March 1993). Pressures to meet short deadlines by extending the work day or week could not be imposed on non-homeworkers without overtime pay or other compensation.

The elasticity of a homeworker's employment relation extends to the use of her skills. While factory machine operators are able to specialize in a few elements and are able to access the help of other operators and of supervisors, homeworkers often sew entire garments and plan sewing operations in the most efficient way by themselves. Although the same garments can be fabricated on the same machines – industrial sewing machines and sergers usually purchased secondhand – this necessary independence in the labour process creates a sense of autonomy and isolation from the larger production operation. Homeworkers are a vital part of this process but contact with the employer, supervisors, or other employees might never occur. For employers, not only labour costs are lowered, but also overhead such as lighting, space, and investments in machinery are eliminated.

The piece-work form of wage payment in garment manufacture also contributes to the attenuation of the employee–employer relationship. Paying by the piece rather than the time it takes to complete the work is the primary form of wage payment in garment manufacture in and out of the factory (Gannage 1986, 120). Industry standards for piece rates usually do not apply to home-based piece-workers since they are not members of either a shop-floor or union local (ibid. 120–31). Unions negotiate base, or minimum rates, equivalent to the minimum wage under contracts with manufacturers on behalf of factory workers. Homeworkers are paid at lower rates with no guarantee of a minimum wage for the time required to complete their work.

Employers of homeworkers keep records of units produced for quality and speed control, but they do not keep a record of the time spent by homeworkers constructing the units of clothing. Without a record of time, there is no record of employment recognizable to the regulatory frameworks in place which, with few exceptions, predicate minimum wage on an hourly rate.[14] As one labour advocate stated, 'Employment Standards ignores the most fundamental nature of homework which is that homework is not time work, it is piece work' (interview with Coyne, March 1993). By ignoring the method of wage payment in homework, the ESB allows employers to evade minimum wage requirements.

Not only the different nature of the wage payment system but also the different nature of subordination between the employer and employee in industrial homework is ignored by the ESB regulatory framework: 'The biggest problem with homeworkers is that employers do not keep a record of hours worked and if no records are kept there is no way to enforce minimum wage. The employer is required to keep a record. If they don't, the onus shifts to the employee to provide evidence of providing services to the employer' (interview, ESB, February 1993). Shifting the burden of proof onto homeworkers is far more problematic than for factory workers. Contact with the 'real' employer, as already mentioned, might never occur in a pyramid of labour procuring relationships with subcontractors. Besides which, a homeworker who generally works alone, perhaps with young children present, is unable to evidence the terms of supervision and control that indicate an employment relationship. Most significantly the 'private' space of the home as a workplace precludes co-workers as witnesses. Also, labour advocates report that employers exploit the tendency of government authorities to find allophone immigrant women less credible witnesses (interviews with Coyne, Shah, and Gunaratna, March 1993). Consequently, the most commonly reported defence used by employers, when complaints to the ESB arise from homeworkers, is simply to deny that the employer–employee relationship ever existed, thus avoiding disputes (interview with Howells, 1993). As a result, employers rarely apply minimum provisions, such as the minimum wage, overtime, vacation, or sick pay to homeworkers.

The lack of basic entitlements is the norm in the Canadian homework system (Johnson and Johnson 1982, 101–17) where even the minimum wage guarantee is effectively withheld from a homeworker with an inadequate piece rate for the design of garment or the quality of material to be sewn (Leach 1993, 71). In turn, homeworkers perceive little advantage to be gained from broadcasting problems with employers or laying formal complaints. An advocate/translator who assisted in employment disputes said: 'After you make a grievance ... your family will condemn you for stirring up trouble. Your so-called employer will blacklist you ... and after a couple of years they [the ESB] might decide that somebody should give you eighty dollars, but you never really get the money. So you go through all that for a principle' (interview with Shah, March 1993). The relocation of the labour process to the home operates to the advantage of employers searching for the cheapest labour possible. By taking work out of the factory, the system of wage payment and employer accountability is detached from the wider context of the labour process in which homeworkers are engaged.

Relations of subordination based on 'race and ethnicity, citizenship, and gender' (Leach 1993, 66) allow employers to procure, keep, and control homeworkers without the need for a formal employment contract or direct supervision. The putative neutrality of employment standards fails to address the employment practices embedded in the homework system that are masked by the 'privacy' of the home as a site of work.

Conclusion: Restructuring the Separation of Work and Home

The historical alienation of work and home, as economically separate and gendered spheres, is bound up with the development of public/private domains. Hence, the social significance of work in the home is different and marginal compared with other work locations. Yet, regulatory frameworks do not acknowledge the difference between the social relations of homework and of work in the factory. If there were no differences between the two locations, domestic subcontracting would not have become such a notable low-waged, racialized, and feminized production strategy. The re-emergence of industrial homework points to the significance of both racial-ized and gendered discourses in the manifestation of vulnerable (flexible) labour markets.

From the perspective of dualist notions about the relationship between public and private, the home as workplace presents a gaping hole in the regulatory net (Zhu's back door) through which employers reprivatize the labour process in economic restructuring. The assumed neutrality of employment standards provides an opportunity for employers to privatize the employee–employer relationship when that relationship is conducted in the ideological and concrete space of the home. However, the dualist view of the state as the primary agent behind shifts in the public/private divide offers only a partial explanation of the gendered and racial construc-tion of homework. Homework is shaped also by particular production strategies that manipulate public/private distinctions between home and work.

Attempts to restructure the ways in which public/private distinctions operate to exclude the home from regulation as a place of work must account for the complexity of the home as a sphere of marginalization for women, which in turn attenuates their access to public entitlements. More-over, the home and the market must be distinguished as 'private' spheres in radically different ways that invoke multiple discourses of privatization in the subordination of some workers to others.

Easy solutions to this complex problem are unlikely. The ideological space of the home as a 'private' domain that marginalizes women's labour cannot be altered simply by asserting that regulatory frameworks apply within it.[15] The nexus of social and economic relations that position some women in a multiply 'privatized' sphere as immigrants, mothers, and workers needs to be both ideologically and materially challenged as part of wider, intensified privatization trends.

NOTES

I owe many debts of gratitude to Susan Boyd for several insightful editorial reviews that furnished myriad improvements. Much appreciation also goes to Trevor Barnes, Nitya Iyer, and Ulrich Rauch for timely and helpful reviews. I credit Trevor Barnes, Daniel Hiebert, and Geraldine Pratt of the Geography Department, Uni-versity of British Columbia, for providing funds from a Social Sciences and

Humanities Research Council Canada grant at a critical moment. Not least, I grate-fully acknowledge the women who are the true experts on industrial home work. While wishing to remain anonymous here, they generously met with me for lengthy and sometimes tedious interviews.

1 Homework is paid work done in the private residence of the employee. The industrial aspect identifies the sectoral character of home work. Both service and manufacturing sector jobs are increasingly relocated to the home (Clarke 1993). In this trend, home-based business and home-based employment must be distinguished. The former involves self-employment which is independent of an employee–employer relationship.

2 My liberal use of quotation marks is the result of my distress at having to engage in the very discourses of racialization, e.g., the essentialist, determinist, coloniz-ing belief in the notion of 'race,' that I reject, but must assert as a powerful con-struction of difference and subordination.

3 Constructions of *(in)visibility* are integral to subordination in the public sphere but with different outcomes shaped by (but not limited to) ethnicity, class, sexu-ality, and gender. Notions of *visibility* can be used to marginalize by marking bodies racially, for example, 'visible minority.' Also, *invisibility* can entail con-flicting experiences of privilege and oppression (see Caron 1994, 273–7).

4 In British Columbia, 65 per cent of employed women are non-unionized (Prov-ince of British Columbia 1991), and 70 per cent of all part-time workers are women (Statistics Canada 1993, B42). In Canada over 50 per cent of women work in the lowest paid occupations: clerical, sales, service, assembly, fabricat-ing, and agriculture (Statistics Canada 1991b, 34–5).

5 Employment Standards Act, SBC 1995, c. 38 (hereafter 'The Act'), in force 1 November 1995.

6 Employment Standards Regulation, British Columbia 396/95, 1995 (hereafter ESR).

7 Ibid. s.1(1). Section 15 of the new Act requires employers to register textile homeworkers. It is doubtful that employers will comply unless the ESB takes proactive enforcement measures. At present, such measures are described as 'out of the question' (telephone interview with Kayhill, Jan. 1996).

8 The Act has always identified homework based primarily on its location in the home: "'Homeworker' means a person who (i) provides labour in the perfor-mance of work in his [*sic*] own home' (SBC 1980, c. 10, s. 105(2)(d)). The new Act replaced the term 'home' with 'private residence.' Most employment stan-dards legislation refers to location as a distinguishing feature of homework (see Ruiz 1992).

9 Interview, ESB, Feb. 1993. The senior policy interpreter repeatedly asserted

that 'our act is driven by the market place.' This also was the underlying rationale for the review of employment standards as described in the Thompson
Report, *Rights and Responsibilities in a Changing Workplace* (Thompson
1994, 25–7).
10 Such images are not restricted to Canada. Commentators on homework in Britain also observe that gendered and racialized constructions of unskilled work
often serve to segregate women identified as 'ethnic' or 'visible minority' in
low-paid jobs in cheap labour strategies (Phizacklea 1988, 49).
11 The experience of being allophone, which often means speaking English or
French with a 'foreign accent,' further devalues the immigrant worker. The
effects of allophone status on occupational mobility and income are dramatic.
Allophone women not only work at the least well-paid jobs even when participating in the formal labour market but are documented as having the highest
rates of downward occupational mobility in Canada (see Statistics Canada
1991a, 52).
12 Distinctions between 'skilled' and 'unskilled' work are often ideologically
based. Recent research has pointed to the gendered nature of skill (e.g., Boyd,
Mulvihill, and Myles, 1991) and I suggest that immigrant or visible minority status is also ideologically connected to notions of skill.
13 The ITGLWF (1991, 29) reports that while fatalities in the industry are rare,
'years of exposure to hazards such as cotton dust, dyes and other chemicals'
cause chronic health disorders 'ranging from musculoskeletal stress to hearing
loss.'
14 The few exceptions are for farmworkers harvesting fruit or vegetables: ESR,
supra note 6, s. 18(1).
15 See, e.g., the recommendation of the B.C. Employment Standards Review
(1993–4) that attempts to reinforce the recognition of home work as paid work
subject to the minimum provisions of the Act: 'that the definition of "work" in
the Act state clearly that it includes home work' (Thompson 1994, 35).

REFERENCES

Personal Interviews

Counsellor, Multilingual Orientation Services for Immigrants Association for
   Immigrant Communities (MOSAIC), Vancouver (Feb., March 1993)
Coyne, Pauline, Business Agent, Amalgamated Textile and Clothing Workers'
   Union (ATCWU), Vancouver (Feb., March 1993)
Factory Manager, Vancouver Garment Factory (March 1994)
Factory Manager, Vancouver Garment Factory (Feb. 1993)

Gunaratna, Vas, Business Agent, International Ladies Garment Worker's Union (ILGWU), Vancouver (March 1993, April 1994)
Homeworker, Vancouver (Feb. 1993)
Homeworker, New Westminster (March 1993)
Homeworker, Surrey (April 1993)
Homeworker, Vancouver (Feb. 1994)
Homeworker, Vancouver (March 1994)
Howells, Mary, Senior Policy Interpreter, Employment Standards Branch (ESB), Burnaby (Feb. 1993)
Shah, Priti, Director, Employment Programs, Orientation and Adjustment Services for Immigrants Society (OASIS), Vancouver (Feb., March 1993)

Telephone Interviews

Kayhill, Dan, Regional Director, Employment Standards Branch (ESB), Burnaby (25 Jan. 1996)

Books and Journal Articles

Adilman, Tamara. 1984. 'A Preliminary Sketch of Chinese Women and Work in British Columbia.' In Barbara K. Latham and Roberta J. Pazdro, eds., *Not Just Pin Money*. Victoria: Camosun College, 53–78
Anderson, K.J. 1987. 'The Idea of Chinatown: The Power of Place and Institutional Practice in the Making of a Racial Category.' *Annals of the Association of American Geography* 77, 580–98
Armstrong Pat, and Hugh Armstrong. 1978. *The Double Ghetto: Canadian Women And Their Segregated Work*. Toronto: McClelland and Stewart
Barrett, Michèle. 1980. *Women's Oppression Today: Problems in Marxist Feminist Analysis*. London: Verso
Beneria, Lourdes, and Martha Roldan. 1987. *The Crossroads of Class and Gender*. Chicago: University of Chicago Press
Blomley, N.K., and Joel C. Bakan. 1992. 'Spatial Categories, Legal Boundaries, and the Judicial Mapping of the Worker.' *Environment and Planning*. A24, 629–44
Blumenfeld, Emily, and Susan Mann. 1980. 'Domestic Labour and the Reproduction of Labour Power: Towards an Analysis of Women, the Family and Class.' In Bonnie Fox, ed., *Hidden in the Household: Women's Domestic Labour Under Capitalism*. Toronto: Women's Press, 267–308
Boris, Eileen. 1996. 'Sexual Divisions, Gender Constructions.' In Eileen Boris and Elisabeth Prügl, eds., *Homeworkers in Global Perspective*. New York: Routledge, 19–37

- 1994. *Home to Work*. Cambridge: Cambridge University Press
- and Cynthia R. Daniels, eds. 1989. 'Introduction.' In *Homework*. Chicago: University of Illinois Press, 1–9
Boris Eileen, and Elisabeth Prügl. 1996. 'Introduction.' In Eileen Boris and Elisabeth Prügl, eds. *Homeworkers in Global Perspective*. New York: Routledge, 3–17
Bose, Christine. 1987. 'Dual Spheres.' In Beth B. Hess and Myra Marx Ferree, eds., *Analyzing Gender*. London: Sage, 267–85
Boyd, Monica, Maryanne Mulvihill, and John Myles. 1991. 'Gender, Power and Post-industrialism.' *Canadian Review of Sociology and Anthropology* 28(4), 407–36
Boulding, Elise. 1981. 'Integration into What?' In Rosalyn Dauber and Melinda L. Cain, eds., *Women and Technological Change in Developing Countries*. Boulder: Westview, 1–33
Bythell, Duncan. 1978. *The Sweated Trades*. London: Batsford Academic
Caron, Michèle. 1994. 'Variations sur le thème de l'invisibilisation.' *Canadian Journal of Women and the Law* 7(2), 271–85
Christensen, Kathleen. 1988. *Women and Home-Based Work*. New York: Henry Holt
Committee for Domestic Workers and Caregivers' Rights (CDWCR). 1993. 'Recommended Changes to B.C. Employment Standards Legislation.' Vancouver
Creese, Gillian. 1992. 'The Politics of Dependence: Women, Work and Unemployment in the Vancouver Labour Movement before World War II.' In Gillian Creese and Veronica Strong-Boag, eds., *British Columbia Reconsidered; Essays on Women*. Vancouver: Press Gang, 364–90
- 1991. 'Exclusion or Solidarity? Vancouver Workers Confront the "Oriental Problem."' In Neil Guppy and Kenneth Stoddart, eds., *Sociological Insights*. Vancouver: University of British Columbia Press, 10–34
Das Gupta, Tania. 1996. *Racism in Paid Work*. Toronto: Garamond
Davidson, Sue. 1984. 'Introduction.' In Joan M. Jensen and Sue Davidson, eds., *A Needle, a Bobbin, a Strike: Women Needleworkers in America*. Philadelphia: Temple University Press, xi–xxii
Davis, Angela Y. 1983. *Women, Race and Class*. New York: Vintage
Ecumenical Coalition for Economic Justice 1992. *Economic Justice Report* 3(4). Toronto, 11 Madison Ave
Fernandez-Kelly, Patricia M., and Anna M. Garcia. 1989. 'Hispanic Women and Homework: Women in the Informal Economy of Miami and Los Angeles.' In Eileen Boris and Cynthia Daniels, eds., *Homework*. Chicago: University of Illinois Press, 165–82

Folbre, Nancy. 1982. 'Exploitation Comes Home: A Critique of the Marxian Theory of Family Labour.' *Cambridge Journal of Economics* 6, 317–29

Fox, Bonnie, ed. 1980. *Hidden in the Household: Women's Domestic Labour under
Capitalism.* Toronto: Women's Press

Fox, Bonnie J., and John Fox. 1987. 'Occupational Gender Segregation of the Canadian Labour Force.' *Canadian Review of Sociology and Anthropology* 24(3),
376–94

Fraser, Nancy. 1989. *Unruly Practices, Power, Discourse and Gender in Contemporary Social Theory.* Minneappolis: University of Minnesota Press

Fudge, Judy. 1990. 'Labour Law's Little Sister: The Employment Standards Act and
the Feminization of Labour.' Ottawa: Canadian Centre for Policy Alternatives

Gannage, Charlene. 1986. *Double Day, Double Bind.* Toronto: Women's Press

Giles, Wennona, and Sedef Arat-Koç. 1994. *Maid in the Market.* Halifax: Fernwood

Hakim, Catherine. 1991. 'Grateful Slaves and Self-made Women: Fact and Fantasy
in Women's Work Orientations.' *European Sociological Review* 7(2), 101–20

Hartmann, Heidi. 1981. 'The Unhappy Marriage of Marxism and Feminism:
Toward a More Progressive Union.' In Lydia Sargent, ed., *Women and Revolution.* Boston: South End Press, 18

INTERCEDE. 1993. 'Meeting the Needs of Vulnerable Workers: Proposals for
Improved Employment Legislation and Access to Collective Bargaining for
Domestic and Industrial Homeworkers.' Toronto Organization for Domestic
Worker's Rights (INTERCEDE) and the Ontario District Council of the Inter-
national Ladies' Garment Workers' Union (ILGWU). Toronto, 33 Cecil St.

International Textile, Garment and Leather Workers' Federation (ITGLWF). 1991.
'Informations – News – Nachrichten.' 2, 1–29, Oct. Brussels: ITGLF

Johnson, L., and R.E. Johnson. 1982. *The Seam Allowance.* Toronto: Women's
Press

Jones, Jacqueline. 1985. *Labor of Love, Labor of Sorrow: Black Women, Work, and
the Family from Slavery to the Present.* New York: Basic Books

Labour Canada. 1991. *Employment Standards Legislation in Canada.* Ottawa: Ministry of Supply and Services Canada

Leach, Belinda. 1993. '"Flexible" Work, Precarious Future: Some Lessons from the
Canadian Clothing Industry.' *Canadian Review of Sociology and Anthropology*
30(1), 64–82

Li, Peter S. 1992. 'Race and Gender as Bases of Class Fractions and Their Effects on
Earnings.' *The Canadian Review of Sociology and Anthropology* 29(4), 488–510

Luxton, Meg. 1980. *More Than a Labour of Love.* Toronto: Women's Press

McDonald, Martha. 1991. 'Post-Fordism and the Flexibility Debate.' *Studies in
Political Economy* 36, 177–201

McDowell, L. 1991. 'Life without Father Ford.' *Transactions of the British Geographers* 16, 400–19

Mitter, S. 1986. *Common Fate, Common Bond.* London: Pluto Press

Mohanty, Chandra T. 1991. 'Introduction.' In Chandra Mohanty, Ann Russo, and Lourdes Torres, eds., *Third World Women and the Politics of Feminism.* Bloomington: University of Indiana Press, 1–47

Morris, J. 1986. *Women Workers and the Sweated Trades.* Brookfield: Gower

Moss, Pamela. 1994. 'Spatially Differentiated Conceptions of Gender in the Workplace.' *Studies in Political Economy* 43, 79–116

Mouffe, Chantal. 1992. 'Feminism and Radical Politics.' In Chantal Mouffe, ed., *Dimensions of Radical Democracy: Pluralism, Citizenship, Community.* New York: Verso

Mytelka, Krieger Lynn. 1991. 'Technological Change and the Relocation of Production in Textiles and Clothing.' *Studies in Political Economy* 36, 109–44

Ng, Roxanna. 1988. *The Politics of Community Services: Women, Class and the State.* Toronto: Garamond

Nicholson, Linda. 1986. *Gender and History: The Limits of Social Theory in the Age of the Family.* New York: Columbia University Press

Pateman, Carol. 1988. *The Sexual Contract.* Stanford: Stanford University Press

Peck, Jamie. 1992. ' "Invisible Threads": Homeworking, Labour-market Relations, and Industrial Restructuring in the Australian Clothing Trade.' *Environment and Planning D: Society and Space* 10(6), 671–90

– 1989. 'Labour Market Segmentation Theory.' *Labour and Industry* 2(1), 119–44

Pennington, Shelley, and Belinda Westover. 1989. *A Hidden Workforce.* London: Macmillan

Phizacklea, Annie. 1988. 'Gender, Racism and Occupational Segregation.' In Silvia Walby, ed., *Gender Segregation at Work.* Philadelphia: Open University Press, 43–54

– and Carol Wolkowitz. 1995. *Homeworking Women: Gender, Racism and Class at Work.* London: Sage

Pollert, Anna. 1991. 'The Orthodoxy of Flexibility.' In Anna Pollert, ed., *Farewell to Flexibility?* Oxford: Basil Blackwell, 3–31

Prügl, Elisabeth. 1996. 'Biases in Labour Law.' In Eileen Boris and Elisabeth Prügl, eds., *Homeworkers in Global Perspective.* New York: Routledge, 203–17

Province of British Columbia. 1991. *B.C. Labour Directory.* Victoria: Ministry of Labour and Consumer Services

Public Service Alliance of Canada (PSAC). 1992. 'Homeworking (Telework) for Federal Public Workers.' Toronto, Conference on Homeworking Kit

Ruiz, Luz Vega 1992. 'Home Work; Towards a New Regulatory Framework?' *International Labour Review* 131(2), 197–216

Seccombe, Wally. 1973. 'The Housewife and Her Labour Under Capitalism.' *New Left Review* 83, 3–24

Seward, Shirley. 1990. 'Challenges of Labour Adjustment: The Case of Immigrant Women in the Clothing Industry.' Discussion Paper 90.B1, *Studies in Social Policy*. Ottawa: Institute for Research on Public Policy

– and Marc Tremblay. 1989. 'Immigrants in the Canadian Labour Force: Their Role in Structural Change.' Discussion Paper 89.B2, Studies in Social Policy. Ottawa: Institute for Research on Public Policy

Silvera, Makeda. 1989. *Silenced.* Toronto: Sister Vision Press

Standing, Guy. 1989. 'Global Feminization through Flexible Labour.' *World Development* 17(7), 1077–95

Statistics Canada. 1993. *The Labour Force.* Ottawa (cat. no. 72–002)

– 1991a. *Ups and Downs on the Ladder of Success: Social Mobility in Canada.* General Social Survey Analysis Series, Gillian Creese, Neil Guppy, and Martin Meissner. Ottawa: Minister of Industry and Technology (cat. no. 11–612E), 5

– 1991b. *Earnings of Men and Women.* Ottawa (cat. no. 13–217)

– 1991c. 'Where Vancouver's Residents Work, by Occupation – 1991.' Census, BST Q9102, Vancouver: Planning Department

Thompson, Mark. 1994. *Rights and Responsibilities in a Changing Workplace: A Review of Employment Standards in British Columbia.* Victoria: Ministry of Skills, Training, and Labour

Valenze, Deborah 1995. *The First Industrial Woman.* Oxford: Oxford University Press

Vancouver Planning Department. 1994. 'Residential Survey of Vancouver Garment Workers.' Vancouver: City Planning Office

Walby, Sylvia, ed. 1988. *Gender Segregation at Work.* Philadelphia: Open University Press

– 1989. 'Flexibility and the Sexual Division of Labour.' In Steven Wood, ed., *The Transformation of Work?* London: Unwin and Hyman, 127–40

Weiner, Elizabeth, and Hardy Green. 1984. 'A Stitch in Our Time: New York's Hispanic Garment Workers in the 1980s.' In Joan M. Jensen and Sue Davidson, eds., *A Needle, a Bobbin, a Strike.* Philadelphia: Temple University Press, 278–96

Young, Marion Iris. 1987. 'Impartiality and the Civic Public.' In Seyla Benhabib and Drucilla Cornell, eds., *Feminism as Critique.* Minneapolis: University of Minnesota Press, 56–76

7

Some Mothers Are Better Than Others: A Re-examination of Maternity Benefits

NITYA IYER

As women have entered the paid labour force in greater and greater numbers, the question of how to reconcile having babies with continuing to work for money has become pressing both individually, for each woman who confronts this dilemma, and collectively, for Canadian society. Demographers have identified trends that may well reflect women's responses to the inhospitability of the workplace to reproduction: as female labour force participation has increased, there has been a marked decline in the birth rate (Phillips and Phillips 1993, 44). Women are having fewer children: the average number of children per family is now 1.8, down from 2.3 in the 1970s and 3.9 in 1960 (Lero and Johnson 1994, 11; Statistics Canada 1993a). We are also postponing childbirth: a mother's median age at the birth of her first child is now 26.4 compared with 22.8 in 1971 (MacBride-King 1990, 1–2; Statistics Canada 1993a). Public concern has been expressed, both about these trends, and about the various measures to 'encourage' women to have children that have been proposed. These range from the controversial, such as Quebec's baby bonus, a lump sum payment that increases with the birth of each subsequent child (Jenson 1986; Maroney 1992), to the rhetorical, such as the much vaunted but never-implemented national child care policy (Teghtsoonian 1995).

Against this background, the maternity/parental leave benefits provided until recently in the federal Unemployment Insurance Act,[1] and retained in the Employment Insurance Act,[2] are particularly interesting. The provision of a temporary leave with financial compensation around the time of birth was the result of feminist advocacy that presented it as a way to promote sex equality in the workplace (Bird 1970; Canadian Advisory Council on the Status of Women, CACSW 1989, 15–17; Dowd 1993; Townson 1984).

This kind of measure seems to be the only mechanism through which our western industrialized society has conceived of addressing birth and the workplace. From its first inception in provincial legislation in 1921, as a twelve-week period of unpaid leave with job security,[3] through its current incarnation in the federal legislation as a seventeen-week period of leave with some compensation for birth mothers coupled with a ten-week, partly compensated leave for any 'parent,' much feminist analysis has focused on the need to increase the length of leave and to elevate compensation levels. Other than concerns about the dangers of 'special treatment' and 'backlash' that continue to plague U.S. feminists (Minow 1990), there is little critical analysis of whether the benefit is actually effective as a sex equality-enhancing reform. The maternity benefit has been advocated as a means by which to support the child-bearing activity of female workers, while gender-neutral parental leave benefits are considered to encourage changes in the sexual division of labour within the family because they allow both men and women to take time off work in order to parent. It seems to have been assumed that proclaiming a liberal egalitarian vision of work, family, and gender through legislation in the public sphere will assist in realizing a liberal egalitarian organization of work, family, and gender in the private sphere (Evans and Pupo 1993). The assumption persists despite the considerable feminist literature on the public/private divide suggesting that feminist reform of family and market cannot be accomplished by change on only one side of the divide (Armstrong and Armstrong 1990; Gavison 1992; Olsen 1983; Ursel, 1986).

In this chapter I examine the maternity/parental leave benefit in the former Unemployment Insurance Act (and continued in the Employment Insurance Act) as a *feminist* reform.[4] I take seriously its claim to assist women to become mothers without being penalized in their capacity as paid workers, and I find the benefit to be gravely deficient in this regard. I show that the structure of the benefit is premised on damaging assumptions about women as mothers. These assumptions correspond to an ideological division of women into 'good' mothers or 'bad' mothers. Women in the first group have access to the benefit and are its intended beneficiaries. Access to the benefit, however, entails an attenuation of the 'good' mother's ties to the workplace and pressure to adopt a traditional female role within the family. Women considered to be 'bad' mothers within the ideology of motherhood are disproportionately represented in the group of women who lack access to the maternity/parental leave benefit and are thereby denied public recognition of their reproductive work. Thus, one goal of this analysis is to question the ability of such a public scheme to transform rather than reproduce such a fundamental social order as the gendered division of labour.

My analysis also illustrates the complex interaction of the public and private spheres of state, market, and family. Through a public policy instrument (the maternity/parental leave benefit), pregnant workers are divided into two groups that are allocated different positions within the 'private' domains of market and family. Those excluded from the benefit are assigned to a market niche; their maternal status is privatized, rendering their familial labour invisible. Recipients of the benefit, by contrast, are escorted by this state policy into the recesses of the public ideal of the private family, where social approval for their maternal status is expected to subsume any need or desire in these women for a market presence.

Before turning to the maternity/parental leave benefit, it is important to outline the criteria by which I judge a 'feminist' or 'sex equality-enhancing' reform. At a minimum, a sex equality-enhancing measure must attempt to reduce inequality between men and women in a way that is respectful of and attentive to differences among women. Given the complex hierarchies of oppression in our society, any reform will have a differential impact across groups of women divided by class, racialization, disability, sexual orientation, and so on. Clearly, it would be impossible to stipulate that a feminist reform be equally beneficial to all women, regardless of their differing situations; it is also impossible to require that a feminist reform not benefit some women at the expense of others. However, I suggest that it is possible to insist that feminist reforms not exacerbate existing avenues of oppression, thereby contributing to the entrenchment of patterns of domination in the larger society. For example, a publicly funded pregnancy-related benefit will obviously assist only women who become pregnant and may mean that these women are subsidized in part by women who do not have children. A problem only arises if the recipients of the benefit can be distinguished from non-recipients by group characteristics that are associated with existing oppressions, *and* the effect of the distinction is to magnify those particular oppressions. If the maternity benefit is available disproportionately to economically privileged pregnant women while it is disproportionately paid for by poorer women, the benefit would exacerbate economic oppression and could not be said to be a feminist reform. Similarly, if the benefit is available to heterosexual women and denied to lesbians, it would exacerbate the oppression of the latter group because it would reinforce the existing stigmatization of lesbians as mothers. Yet both of these distinctions would be acceptable if the characteristics of included and excluded groups were reversed: a maternity benefit disproportionately received by poorer women and paid for by wealthier women, or one received by lesbians to the exclusion of heterosexual women would still meet my criteria for a sex equality-enhancing reform.

Some Mothers Are Better Than Others

Following from my definition of a feminist reform, the first avenue for examination of the maternity benefit[5] requires an analysis of the social characteristics of those who receive it compared with those who do not. Although it is commonly understood as a 'universal' benefit, the maternity benefit provision actually reflects a disturbing pattern of exclusion, in terms of both its formal and its actual availability to pregnant women with differing social characteristics. Simply put, the benefit is effectively available only to (because it is only affordable for) middle- and upper-class female employees or female employees who are in relationships with partners who bring in most of the family income. When factors such as age, fertility pattern, occupational category, relationship status, income, and ethnicity are considered, the profile of the typical recipient of the benefit emerges as a white, middle-class, female employee, over 25, with either a higher than average income or, more likely, partnered with someone else who is the primary income earner.

The maternity benefit is available to birth mothers regardless of sexual orientation. However, the parental leave benefit is available only to 'parents.' This provision excludes a birth mother's female partner (or a gay male parent's partner) because adoption laws do not permit lesbians or gay men to adopt their partner's children.[6] Thus, on this basis, the parental leave component of the benefit is inadequate as a feminist reform.

To be eligible for the maternity benefit, a pregnant woman must qualify as a 'major attachment claimant.' Under the Unemployment Insurance Act this meant that she had at least twenty weeks of insurable earnings (i.e., she had paid at least twenty weeks of unemployment insurance premiums) in the past fifty-two weeks or since her last claim for unemployment insurance. A week of insurable earnings was a week in which she worked for at least fifteen hours or earned at least 20 per cent of the maximum weekly insurable earnings ($163.00 at the 1995 rate). This requirement was absolute: there was no reduced maternity benefit available to women who did not meet the minimum. From 1 January 1997 eligibility is based on hours of work rather than weeks of work. A mother or parent must have worked for 700 hours within the past fifty-two weeks or since the last claim. This is equivalent to twenty 35-hour weeks or approximately forty-eight 15-hour weeks. Thus, for women who work less than 35 hours per week, the eligibility requirements are significantly more onerous under the new legislation.

The benefit is payable for a maximum of fifteen weeks between the eighth week before the week the baby is due or is born, whichever is earlier, and seventeen weeks after the expected or actual week of birth, whichever is later. There is a two-week mandatory 'waiting period' between the last day of employment and the first day of benefits entitlement, which means that for two weeks the woman will receive no money at all (unless her employer has a 'SUB plan,' as discussed below). There may be a further delay before she actually receives her first cheque. The amount of the benefit is 55 per cent of the average weekly insurable earnings to a fixed maximum. The maximum weekly benefit as of March 1995 was $448.00.[7] To receive this amount, a woman would have to earn at least $815.00 per week. Unlike regular unemployment insurance benefits that permit a claimant to earn up to 25 per cent of the amount of the benefit in part-time work before earnings are deducted, *any* money earned by a maternity benefit claimant is deducted from her benefit. The legislation does permit employers to augment unemployment insurance payments through the supplementary unemployment insurance benefit plan (hereafter 'SUB plan') which allows employers to top up the basic payment to a maximum of 95 per cent of the employee's earnings and to pay 95 per cent of salary during the two-week waiting period. However, these plans are very rare. They tend to be instituted only by large employers, in organized workplaces, and available only to more highly paid employees.[8] For over three-quarters of women receiving any paid maternity leave in 1991, the basic benefit of 55 per cent percent of weekly earnings was their only compensation (La Novara 1993, 25; see also Evans and Pupo 1993, 410).

From this benefit structure, it is possible to develop a partial picture of women who are precluded from claiming the maternity benefit. With respect to the formal criteria, the most obvious exclusion is the restriction of the benefit to employees; self-employed women and women who are not in the paid labour force receive nothing. This pattern of exclusion is a consequence of housing maternity benefits within (un)employment[9] insurance legislation.[10]

The legislation contains two other important exclusions, namely, the lengthy qualifying period and the part-time cut-off. Under the Unemployment Insurance Act, the qualification period was twenty weeks. Under the Employment Insurance Act, it is now 700 hours (which means twenty 35-hour weeks, or longer for women who work fewer than 35 hours per week). Under the former Act, women working fewer than 15 hours per week were formally disentitled from claiming benefits. Under the new Act, there is no part-time cut-off on the face of the statute. However, a woman who works less than 14 hours per week cannot accumulate 700 hours within fifty-two weeks, as required, because it would take forty-eight 14-hour work weeks to accumulate 700 hours. Thus, the only positive change is that the part-time cut-off is lower by one hour per week – and this is more than offset by the significantly greater qualifying period imposed on part-time workers. Formerly, all women working between 15 and 34 hours per week qualified for benefits after twenty weeks. Now the same women must work between 20.5 and 46.6 weeks in order to accumulate the required number of hours.

Most women who work in temporary, seasonal, and/or unstable employment situations, which are increasingly prevalent as economic restructuring occurs, cannot satisfy these requirements. Women of colour, particularly immigrant women and Aboriginal women, tend to work in these situations. Because they are heavily overrepresented in the lowest wage sectors, Aboriginal women (Gerber 1990), women of colour (Employment and Immigration Canada 1993; Seward and Tremblay 1989), and women with disabilities (Harvey and Tepperman 1990) comprise a 'marginal' labour force that is especially vulnerable to work reduction and lay-off as employers respond to changes in the economy. Foreign domestic workers, who are also disproportionately immigrant women of colour, are in an especially precarious situation in that they cannot claim maternity benefits without risking deportation.[11]

Even if a woman formally qualifies for the maternity benefit, the amount of the benefit operates as a significant exclusionary factor. Many women simply cannot afford a 45 per cent drop in their income, particularly when they have just given birth to a dependant, unless they can look to someone else for financial support.[12] The need for sufficient financial resources to subsist with a new baby on *no* income at all for two weeks also excludes many women. According to Statistics Canada's low income cut-offs, the poverty line income for a single wage earner with one dependant living in a city of 500,000 or more was $402.79 per week in 1993 (National Council of Welfare 1995, 3). The poverty line income for a single wage earner with two dependants was $512.00 per week, a figure that already substantially exceeded the maximum weekly maternity benefit for that year of $425.00.[13] To receive a mere poverty line income from maternity benefits, a new mother would have to have been earning a weekly wage of $665 (or $16.63 per hour based on a 40-hour work week). By comparison, the minimum wage in British Columbia was $6.50 per hour or $260 per week in March 1995 (Ministry of Skills, Training, and Labour 1994). In fact, the average amount of maternity benefit received by women in 1993 was $276 per week which is just *under* 70 per cent of the one-dependant poverty line income for that year. For most single wage-earning mothers this means that the maternity benefit scheme drives them well below the poverty line for the duration of the benefit period. Unless they can rely on another source of income, then, most women simply cannot afford to stop working and claim the maternity benefit.

Although for almost all women the amount of the maternity benefit is insufficient to permit financial independence, it is least affordable for those who have the lowest incomes. Who is likely to work in an occupation that yields an unaffordably low maternity benefit? The lowest paid group by job classification of maternity benefit recipients is sales and services, an occupational category that includes sales clerks, food services, and cleaners (Statistics Canada 1994, 8–15). The lowest paid occupations for women generally are agriculture, service, material handling, and sales (Statistics Canada 1991, 53, 54), and it is in these occupations that most women work (Statistics Canada 1992, B35–B36). Part-time workers, who are over-whelmingly female (Phillips and Phillips 1993, 47), are paid disproportion-ately less than full-time workers (Lero and Johnson 1994, 5). Further, for white women, at least, age and education level are directly related to income in that higher education levels attract higher earnings, and older employees earn more than younger ones (Creese, Guppy, and Meissner 1991).

Immigrant women of colour, Aboriginal women, and women with disabilities are disproportionately likely to earn incomes that yield extremely low levels of maternity benefits. Immigrant women of colour have the greatest downward occupational mobility (Seward and Tremblay 1989) and are overrepresented in the lowest paid job categories (Employment and Immigration Canada 1993, 45). Since 1971, for example, 25 per cent of employed immigrant women are found in sales and services, processing, and manufacturing – they work as garment makers, cleaners, and domestic workers (Christofides and Swidinsky 1994). Increased educational levels do not necessarily lead to higher-paying jobs for these women. Despite the fact that they have higher educational attainments than the general popula-tion, their credentials often are not recognized or rewarded in the Canadian labour market (ibid.; Creese, Guppy, and Meissner 1991, 87).

Aboriginal women are also occupationally segregated in poorly remu-nerated jobs to a greater degree than other women. Statistics for 1992 indicate that the majority of full-time employed Aboriginal women, 68 per cent, are clerical workers. They are also more likely than other women to work in blue collar positions, as manual workers and technicians. Their wages reflect these occupational patterns: 'The estimated average full-time salary for aboriginal women was $29,412, or 88.66% of that for all women under the Act' (Employment and Immigration Canada 1993, 33). Further, Aboriginal women are overrepresented in the very lowest salary ranges: almost 5 per cent of Aboriginal women earn less than $15,000 per year compared with less than 1 per cent of the total female population (ibid.). Aboriginal women are more than four times as likely to have less than Grade 9 education than non-Aboriginal women, a factor that contributes to low remuneration levels (Gerber 1990).

Women with disabilities are much less likely to be employed than women without disabilities. Only about half of women with disabilities between the ages of 15 and 54 are employed (compared with 66 per cent of non-disabled women aged 15 to 34 and 74 per cent of non-disabled women aged 35 to 54), which means that half of the women in this group are formally barred from claiming the maternity benefit (Statistics Canada 1995, 165). Those who are employed earn less as a group than non-disabled women and men with and without disabilities (ibid., 166). About two-thirds work in the poorly remunerated clerical sector (Employment and Immigration Canada 1993, 38). Further, women with disabilities have lower levels of educational attainment than non-disabled women, which would tend to restrict their access to the high paying jobs that make maternity benefits more affordable. For example, women with disabilities are only about half as likely as non-disabled women to have a university degree and much more likely than non-disabled women to have less than a Grade 9 education (Statistics Canada 1995, 165).

Women's fertility patterns are highly relevant in assessing the availability and value of the maternity benefit. Aboriginal women and women of colour from certain ethnocultural groups have fertility patterns that clearly disadvantage them with respect to claiming maternity benefits. Caribbean and African women, Indo-Canadian women, and Chinese-Canadian women (including Canton, China, Hong Kong, Macau, Singapore, Taiwan, Tibet, and Vietnam), and Aboriginal women all tend to have children at younger ages than white women (British Columbia Division of Vital Statistics 1994). Fertility is also linked to class and education level: middle-class women and women with more years of education tend to have children when they are older (Jenson 1986). Young mothers across all occupational categories claim much lower levels of maternity benefit. For example, the average claim for mothers under 24 working in sales and services in 1993 was $151 per week, in contrast to the average $247 per week claimed by mothers over 35 in the same occupational category (Statistics Canada 1993b).

From a feminist perspective, the reality of exclusion obscured by a state benefit that is presented as universal is troubling for two reasons. First, the provision of the benefit exacerbates the economic oppression of poorer women. The benefit ties the amount received to an individual's earnings so that women who earn more get a greater maternity benefit than women who earn less, and women who do not earn 'enough' receive no benefit at all. It is true that women who receive a higher maternity benefit have paid greater premiums, a fact that may allay concern for some. (Alternatively, it may highlight the inappropriateness of (un)employment insurance as a vehicle for a socialized maternity benefit, a point discussed further below.) Moreover, the structure of the benefit contemplates a group of pregnant women who pay (un)employment insurance premiums but are disqualified from claiming the maternity benefit, either because they cannot satisfy the qualifying conditions or because they cannot afford the drop in earnings that taking the benefit entails. These women are less economically privileged than the group of women who claim the benefit, yet their premiums, in part, subsidize the reproductive activities of more economically privileged women. The woman in a minimum wage job who cannot afford to take time off work to be with her new baby is legally required to contribute 3 per cent of her meagre earnings into a public scheme to help support a better-paid woman to stay at home with her new baby.[14] Although even a relatively economically privileged woman may require a socialized maternity benefit in order to address her situation relative to male workers, less economically privileged women should not have to pay for it. In this way, the (un)employment insurance maternity benefit exacerbates the economic oppression of poor women and is unsatisfactory as a feminist reform.

The second way in which the benefit fails as a feminist reform is that it exacerbates the oppression experienced by Aboriginal women, women of colour, women with disabilities, women who are single parents, and lesbians (with respect to the parental leave component of the benefit[15]) as *mothers*. As I have demonstrated, the maternity benefit is disproportionately unavailable to these women because the structure of the benefit is not tailored to their patterns of labour force participation or fertility. In fact, the maternity benefit is most available to women with partners who earn enough to support two (or more) dependants, women in higher-paying occupations (particularly those working for employers with SUB plans), women over 25, and those with more years of education. In short, the primary beneficiaries of the maternity benefit are disproportionately white, middle- and upper-class, able-bodied, high school (or post-secondarily) educated women in their late 20s (or older) living in heterosexual relationships with men possessing similar characteristics. A socialized maternity benefit should recognize and support the mothering activity of all female workers. The pattern of exclusion inherent in the benefit's current structure, however, ensures that some women workers are recognized (and subsidized) by the public sphere as bearers of and carers for children, while the maternal work of other women workers remains privatized and invisible.

The social characteristics determining which pregnant women are deserving mothers and which are not, according to the (un)employment insurance scheme, closely correspond to the oppressive 'good mother / bad mother' division within the prevailing ideology of motherhood. Feminist analysis of the ideology of motherhood has revealed that some women are perceived as 'good mothers' on the basis of their social characteristics, and are socially encouraged and supported to become mothers and to raise children. Other women are labelled as 'bad mothers,' again on the basis of their social identity, and are discouraged from bearing and raising children (Arnup 1994; Fineman 1991; Kline 1993; Mosoff 1995; Roberts 1994). A number of feminist writers have demonstrated that various legal regimes concerning mothering reinforce this good mother / bad mother dichotomy. In certain areas, the discouraging function of the law with respect to women labelled 'bad mothers' is coercive in the extreme: by divesting them of legal status as mothers, the law makes them 'non-mothers.' Court-ordered interventions in pregnancy and birth to 'protect' fetuses from pregnant women are inflicted primarily upon poor women, women of colour, and immigrant women (Hanigsberg 1991; Ikemoto 1992; Oberman 1992). The operation of child welfare laws disproportionately strips Aboriginal mothers (Hamilton and Sinclair 1991; Kline 1992), mothers with disabilities (Goundry 1994, 49–69; Mosoff 1995), women on social assistance, and mothers from religious and cultural minorities (Van Praagh 1993, 238) of their children. Child custody law effectively regards lesbian mothers, low-income mothers, mothers of colour, and mothers with disabilities, among others, as 'suspect' mothers, who are especially likely to lose custody of their children (CACSW 1994). Most glaringly, lesbian mothers who are not biologically related to their children are often denied legal recognition (Arnup and Boyd 1995).

The (un)employment insurance maternity benefit conveys the same message about motherhood, albeit in more subtle form. The groups of women I have identified as unlikely to be able to claim the maternity benefit – women with low incomes, women of colour, particularly immigrant women of colour, Aboriginal women, women with disabilities, women who cannot rely on another (usually a male partner) for financial support, women under 25, less formally educated women, and, with respect to parental leave, lesbian mothers who are not birth mothers – all have characteristics that exclude them from the dominant conception of the 'good mother' and therefore experience social stigmatization as mothers. Denying the maternity benefit to these women is one way in which they are denied public recognition and support as mothers. This denial exacerbates their gender oppression because it withholds recognition of an important aspect of their identity as women. In a deeply sexist society, in which the ultimate in feminine achievement is motherhood, a refusal to recognize some women as mothers is to relegate them to the margins of their gender. Refusing to recognize some mothers as mothers is reminiscent of the imperialist strategy that has been used against African-American and Third World women of 'defeminizing' racialized women in order to better exploit them as workers (Bell Scott 1982; Mohanty 1991; see also Glenn 1985).

Some Mothers Had Better Be Mothers

Thus far I have addressed the situation of women who are unable to claim maternity benefits under the (un)employment insurance regime. I have argued that the scheme fails as a feminist reform because of the undesirable consequences that flow from its pattern of exclusion. First, it exacerbates the economic oppression of low-income women who must divert some portion of their earnings, through the payment of (un)employment insurance premiums, to support the mothering of the more economically privileged women who are more likely to be able to claim the benefit. Second, because its benefits are disproportionately unavailable to low-income, young, non-white, single, and/or disabled pregnant women, that is, women who correspond to the image of the 'bad' mother within the prevailing ideology of motherhood, the scheme affirms the oppressive good mother / bad mother dichotomy. In this section I take up the other side of this dichotomy. I argue that recipients of the benefit, who disproportionately correspond to the image of the 'good' mother, are effectively encouraged to conform to that image by weakening their ties to the paid labour force. A 'working mother' (a mother who works for pay) is not a truly 'good' mother according to the ideology of motherhood (S. Boyd this volume; see also M. Boyd 1984, 11, 12). The (un)employment insurance scheme accordingly encourages women whose social characteristics otherwise identify them as candidates for 'good motherhood' to leave the workforce entirely (at least for their children's early years) or reduce the amount of time that they spend there by moving to part-time work, casual work, self-employment, or working out of the home.

The most striking feature of the operation of the maternity leave benefit, from the perspective of a recipient,[16] is that it is intended to remove her completely from her workplace for the duration of the benefit period, thereby creating a traditional gendered division of labour within her family. Any income she earns during the benefit period is deducted from the amount of her benefit, in sharp contrast to the 25 per cent of the benefit amount that may be earned without penalty in the regular benefits stream. This deduction sends a strong message that maternity benefit recipients should stay out of the paid labour force: they are paid *not* to work. Altering the dynamic of a dual-earner heterosexual family in this way, at what is already a critical moment, namely, the birth of a child, contributes significantly to a set of pressures that operate along at least three intersecting axes to impel the mother to remain at home beyond the expiration of her maternity leave. The pressure on the woman to be at home full-time is particularly acute at two instances: immediately following the birth of the child and four to six months later when she is about to return to paid work. At each of these times, pressures along emotional, occupational, and economic axes combine to produce a compelling set of constraints that encourage her to remain out of the market and within the (publicly approved) family.

Childbirth is an intensely emotional experience for most women. The impact of the birth, with its consequential, ideologically laden change in status from non-mother to mother or from mother to 'real' mother,[17] is exacerbated when it occurs in tandem with the abrupt and total dissociation from the workplace that the maternity benefit scheme requires. The mother of a new baby experiences a complete break from her former pattern of life and social identification as an employee in the paid labour force. Her workplace friends and acquaintances will be relatively inaccessible to her as she struggles with internal and external expectations bound up with her new maternal image (Glenn, Chang, and Forcey 1994). The message from a mandatory full-time leave provision amplifies the social belief that mothering an infant is a full-time job and a full-time identity (Duffy, Mandell, and Pupo 1989). The mother of a new baby is expected (and internalizes these expectations) to be as much of an 'expert' at mothering as she was at her previous occupation (Arnup 1994; for examples, see Eisenberg, Murkoff, and Hathaway 1989; Leach 1993). Indeed, the more deeply a woman's sense of her identity was bound up in her work and workplace, the more necessary she may find it to develop and proclaim her expertise as a mother.

The period of early infancy also creates pressure to be in the home full-time in the occupational dimension: babies create a lot of work. Particularly in a culture in which ties to extended family are greatly attenuated as a result of the ideological prominence of the nuclear family, and dominant social expectations for home and child care are high (Hartmann 1981; Luxton, Rosenberg, and Arat-Koç 1990; Maroney and Luxton 1987), a mother of a new baby has an enormous amount of work to do. Further, the nature of domestic work is such that it rapidly expands to fill and overfill the time available: there is always more that could be cleaned or cooked, always more that can be done with or for the baby. Thus, being at home necessarily becomes a full-time occupation, affirming the message implicit in the maternity benefit scheme.

Finally, in the economic realm, the maternity benefit greatly widens the gap between the parents' earnings. The sharp drop in a mother's earnings (a reduction of *at least* 45 per cent, absent any SUB plan) strains family finances at a time when both parents are probably concerned about financial security. However, within a cultural context in which 'good mothering' requires a woman to care for her baby full-time, at least during its infancy (Boyd 1984, 11–12; Maynard 1988, 85), the pressure to increase and intensify identification with the paid labour force will not be experienced in a gender-neutral way. Both mother and father are likely to consider ways in which *he* could earn more, if needed, to compensate for the loss of her earnings. The maternity benefit cushions the impact of her loss of earnings to some extent, but it also encourages parents to think of him as the primary breadwinner.

The emotional, occupational, and economic pressures that encourage the woman (as well as her partner and others) to regard her maternal status as necessitating a complete absence from the paid labour force intensify again when, several months later, the maternity/parental leave benefits are about to expire. Emotionally, leaving her full-time preoccupation with home and baby as abruptly as she left the workplace may be very difficult.[18] The prevailing ideology of motherhood, with its assumption of 'primary caregiver' bonding (Swiggart 1991),[19] its conviction that substitute care is a poor second best to full-time care by a baby's 'natural' mother, and its strong disapproval of any mother who would *prefer* paid work to parenting her children full-time,[20] is a powerful influence against immediate return to full-time work. The maternity benefit, by requiring that the woman's formation of her identity as a mother be that of a full-time mother, works with rather than against this ideological current.

Intertwined with an emotional impulse against return to full-time paid work are the more pragmatic occupational and economic constraints. Because of the maternity benefit, reallocation of responsibility for domestic labour in the post-birth family has been established in the context of a traditional, sexual division of labour. If the woman returns to paid work, this allocation will be strained (Duffy, Mandell, and Pupo 1989, 59–61). Statistically, her responsibility for doing the lion's share of the household and child care work is not likely to change much once she returns to work (Marshall 1990). However, it will certainly be much harder for her to do this work in addition to her full-time job (Hessing 1992; 1991), and her return to work will therefore also have some adverse impact on her partner (Lero and Johnson 1994, 8). Further, at the point in time when the parents are contemplating her return to full-time work, the prospect of adding a 40-hour week in the paid labour force to a body of work in the home that has been occupying the woman day (and night) for the past few months is daunting indeed. During the maternity leave her occupation has been 'mother'; returning to the paid labour force is like taking on two full-time jobs.

Economic pressures to augment the family's financial resources would appear to favour the mother's return to paid work, but leaving the home for the workplace can be expensive. The cost of high-quality substitute care for their children is considerable (Khosla 1993), particularly where lack of availability may require complicated transportation routines to get children to care and parents to work on time. When these and other work-related costs are calculated against the woman's income, especially in light of the fact that the family has already learned how to survive on roughly half her former income, remaining out of the paid workforce (or shifting to casual or part-time employment) begins to look both attractive and affordable (La Novara 1993, 23). Further, the serious shortage of adequate substitute care may take the decision out of some mother's hands, forcing them to give up their jobs because there is no one else to look after the children.

In summary, the combined effect of pressures along all three axes is a strong admonition to mothers against returning to full-time paid work following the expiration of the benefit. The message conveyed through the operation of the ideology of motherhood along the emotional axis is that full-time paid work is undesirable for a mother of a baby; along the occupational axis full-time paid work is portrayed as overwhelming; and along the economic axis staying at home is presented as affordable. The maternity benefit, as currently structured, intensifies all three pressures. Emotionally, it permits the woman's identity as a mother to be developed outside of paid work; occupationally, it teaches parents that the work of mothering is a full-time job; and, in the economic realm, it shows the family that her income may not be required to support it. Thus, this public benefit operates to attenuate the 'good' mother's connection to the market and ensconce her in the private realm of family. Interestingly, it is precisely those characteristics that made her a 'good' worker (race, age, educational attainment, dis/ability, and so on) who could attract sufficient earnings to afford the benefit that now qualify her as a 'good' mother who should not return to work.[21]

Fathers Are Not Mothers

Having reviewed the maternity benefit, the sex equality-enhancing potential of the ten-week gender-neutral parental leave provisions deserves brief consideration. The current provision was originally enacted in response to the decision in the *Schachter* case.[22] The trial court in *Schachter* portrayed gender-neutral parental leave as a means to combat the 'sexual stereotyping of the respective roles of the mother and the father' (*Schachter* 1988, 539) and as a way to achieve 'equality between parents with respect to responsibility, and opportunity, for care of a newborn child,' which it considered to be a value of 'contemporary Canadian society' (ibid. 541). The court explicitly stated that a gender-neutral parental leave coupled with a gender-specific maternity benefit would recognize the particular needs of the 'natural' mother for some time away from work and *give her the option* of returning to work while the 'natural' father stayed at home (ibid. 539).

The trial court's efforts to articulate a non-sexist organization of birth, parenting in early infancy, and participation in the paid labour force should be commended. However, the reality of providing a combined maternity and parental leave through (un)employment insurance legislation not only misses the goal of sexual equality in the parenting of babies, but also contains serious impediments to attaining equality. The parental leave provision is only facially gender neutral, and formal neutrality cannot overcome the material conditions of sexual inequality within family and market. Failure to recognize these features turns parental leave into a justification for the continued exploitation of women's productive and reproductive labour rather than a way to combat it.

The text of the parental leave provision is gender neutral only in the most superficial sense. In the vast majority of cases in which parental leave is available and financially feasible (the exception being the situation of adoptive parents), the parents are not similarly situated when the time comes to claim the leave: if the father takes it, there will be a major disruption in the household as he comes home and the mother goes out to work; if she takes it, the status quo simply continues. Exacerbating this unequal positioning and further undermining the gender neutral text of the legislation, the federal government amended the unemployment insurance regulations in November 1990 to 'streamline' maternity/parental benefit claims by permitting women to apply simultaneously for maternity and parental leave benefits.[23] The effect of the change was to eliminate the 'interruption of benefits' (i.e., two weeks of no income at all) that would otherwise precede receipt of parental leave benefits. If someone other than the maternity benefit recipient claims the parental leave benefit, the two-week waiting period is still imposed. This discrepancy is continued under the new legislation. Further, for the small minority of employees who do have access to SUB plans, nothing in the regulations requires that they be provided on a gender-neutral basis. Employers may thus top up benefits for women claiming parental leave immediately after a maternity leave but refuse to top up parental leave benefits claimed by the other parent.[24]

Even if the problems outlined above were corrected, parental leave would still not provide the equality of opportunity for gender-neutral parenting described in *Schachter* in any real sense. A formally gender-neutral parental benefit proclaimed in the public sphere will never produce gender-neutral parenting in the private sphere because it does not take account of actual sexual inequalities in the family and the market (Dowd 1993; Evans and Pupo 1993). It assumes the existence of the very conditions it is supposed to help achieve. As long as the father continues to earn significantly more than the mother, reducing his income by 45 per cent or more will be a much greater loss than hers. As long as prevailing social attitudes, informed by the ideology of motherhood, promote the belief that mothers (not fathers or anyone else) are superior caregivers for babies, it will be far harder for him to leave his job than for her to postpone her return to employment by ten more weeks.[25] Evans and Pupo summarized the multiple constraints that ensure that in the vast majority of cases, mothers – not fathers – will 'choose' to take parental leave: 'This is not a free detached decision about whose best interest would be met with time off for parental caregiving. Rather, the decision is influenced by the ideology of motherhood, the pressure to breastfeed for extensive periods, women's relative powerlessness in the family, and the joy and fulfilment of mothering, as well as by women's disadvantaged position in the labour market, financial circumstances, the nature and structure of the specific form of employment, the workplace culture, the support of the labour movement, cultural practices, and other structural considerations' (1993, 417).

Parental leave is emphatically not gender-neutral: it just looks like it is. Therein lies the danger. By presenting who stays home as a simple matter of individual choice regardless of gender, a gender-neutral leave provision implies that if more women than men take it, this phenomenon merely reflects 'private' (gender based) preference, not a 'public' (gender discrimination) problem.[26] The detrimental consequences of a gendered pattern of actual use of the leave, including the continued perception that women are 'less committed' to the workplace that justifies the persistent wage gap, are legitimated by the veneer of formal equality provided by the parental leave provision. By assuming a non-existent sex equality, the provision supports the perception that any continued sexual inequality in the market is not an issue requiring public response; it is merely a function of legitimate, 'private' choice.

Conclusion

This chapter has shown that the maternity/parental leave benefit provided in the Unemployment Insurance Act, and continued in the Employment Insurance Act, contributes to a good mother / bad mother dichotomy whereby access to the benefit is largely restricted to women who conform to the ideological image of the 'good mother.' Further, because a truly 'good' mother (at least of a baby) does not work for pay outside the home, the scheme is structured so as to remove benefit recipients from the workplace entirely during the benefit period and also to encourage them to postpone returning to work for some time afterwards. The operation of these benefits illustrates the complex interaction of public and private in the realm of family and family policy – and stands as a testament to the power of familial ideology and the limits of law to change it. Here, a public scheme effectively denies public recognition of the mothering work of 'bad' mothers, ensuring that their mothering remains invisible in the private realm. Non-recognition of their maternal status makes these mothers into 'workers,' placing them firmly in the market (see also Teghtsoonian 1995). By contrast, precisely by according limited public support for benefits recipients as mothers, the scheme encourages these women to move themselves entirely into the private realm of family in order to continue to fulfil social expectations of (and receive social approbation for) good mothering. Privatization of the costs of biological and social reproduction is neatly accomplished for both women who do and those who do not receive the benefit.

The maternity/parental leave scheme does not challenge the public/private divide with respect to work and family. Rather, it affirms and supports it. It sends a strong message, both to those who cannot claim the benefit and to those who can, that family is a private responsibility. Because it does so through the vehicle of a public instrument that appears to be sensitive to the sex equality aspirations of feminists, its damaging effects are masked by its seductive appeal to feminist dreams of a society in which such a benefit could operate in a sex equality-enhancing fashion. Such a society is not ours, however, and the danger of the benefit lies in its tendency to convey the impression that it is.

The argument advanced in this chapter is not intended to justify termination of the benefit. That result would simply extend to all mothers the many hardships confronted by those currently excluded from the benefit scheme and reprivatize the tiny portion of the costs of reproduction that now is publicly subsidized. Women want greater access to maternity benefits as well as longer periods of leave and higher compensation levels (CACSW 1989; Conway 1990; Kay this volume; Schroeder 1989). As the first section of this chapter demonstrates, however, the principle of equality among women demands substantial reform of the benefit. The (un)employment insurance regime is clearly inappropriate for a socialized maternity benefit. If the purpose of the benefit really is to encourage women to maintain their connections to the labour force while they have children, neither the age at which a women has a child nor the amount she earns should be relevant. By tying the amount of the benefit to the amount a woman earns while pregnant, the scheme rewards higher earnings and delayed childbearing. But how much a woman earns is not relevant to the object of the benefit; it is the amount of her labour force participation that is important. Yet groups with the highest labour force participation – women of colour – are among those with the least effective access to the benefit. A policy promoting delayed childbearing is of dubious benefit to women, both physiologically (Maranto 1995) and with respect to adjusting to the realities of the work/family divide. Having children earlier in one's working life might be easier for some women than having to revise one's work/family pattern radically when one becomes a mother in 'mid-career.' In any event, women should not be penalized for the decisions they make about when to have children: a public maternity benefit ought to provide an array of choices that allow for different kinds of workforce participation and for different fertility patterns. Enacting independent legislation that provided the benefit at a flat rate to everyone for a specified period regardless of their employment status and permitted earnings up to some percentage of former income without penalty, would be a way to begin correcting the inequities outlined in the first section of the chapter. Providing a financial incentive to resume at least part-time work would encourage continuing links to the workplace and also allow some of the women who cannot now afford the benefit greater access to it.

I have suggested how the benefit could be improved with respect to its pattern of exclusion. It is important to provide a universal benefit of this kind because it is what most mothers of young children want and need to help ease the reality of negotiating the contradictions of paid work and family as these institutions are currently structured. But, as the second section of this chapter argues, it is imperative to resist the notion that a maternity/parental leave benefit, no matter how extensive, has much potential as a sex equality-enhancing reform. As experience in the Scandinavian countries over the past two decades amply demonstrates, even the most 'generous' benefits imaginable – lengthy and flexible full- and part-time periods of leave for either parent at virtually full compensation – have done little to alter the gendered division of labour. Far more women than men take such leaves, moving into the private realm either fully or partially to care for their families (Dowd 1989; Leira 1992). Scandinavian feminists complain about the ghettoization of women in the part-time labour force (Evans and Pupo 1993, 45), a phenomenon also present in Canada (Lero and Johnson 1994, 4).

The Scandinavian experience demonstrates that even removing all financial pressures militating in favour of mothers rather than fathers taking child-related leave (not a very likely prospect in the current climate of privatization: Kline this volume) is insufficient to reform the gendered allocation of family responsibilities that pervades the private realms of family and market. While it is essential that feminists advocate for reforms to make the benefit truly accessible to all mothers, instead of only socially approved ones, it is equally imperative that we not be deluded into thinking that such a relatively simple and inexpensive public benefit will 'solve' the intransigent and complex inequality of women in family and market. In my view, the *best* a maternity/parental leave benefit can be is a survival tool for individual women in negotiating the work/family conflict. It is not and should not be considered to be a mark of sexual equality in the private sphere.

NOTES

I would like to acknowledge the financial support of the Social Sciences and Humanities Research Council, and to thank Amanda Ocran, Susan Boyd, Fiona Kay, Jennifer Koshan, and Kathy Teghtsoonian for their insights and assistance.

1 RSC 1985, c. U-1, as amended.
2 As of 1 July 1996 the Unemployment Insurance Act was replaced by the Employment Insurance Act, SC 1996, c. 23. However, the provisions with respect to maternity and parental leave benefits are virtually unchanged in the new statute.
3 Maternity Protection Act, SBC 1921, c. 37.
4 Although my analysis focuses on the operation of the now repealed provisions, about which much more is known, any relevant differences under the new statutory regime must be noted. The most significant change is that the basis of eligibility for all benefits is no longer calculated from the number of *weeks* of insurable earnings, but from the number of *hours* worked. To the extent that this change affects the arguments presented in this chapter, it strengthens the claim that this benefit is inadequate as a feminist reform.
5 In this part of my argument I focus on the 17-week maternity leave benefit and treat parental leave merely as a 10-week extension of the maternity leave benefit period, which is the way it is most commonly used. The reasons for this pattern of use together with a consideration of the appropriateness of a gender-neutral provision are the subject of the third section of the chapter.
6 There are encouraging signs of change in this area, both in the legislative and judicial spheres: *Re K.*, (1995) 15 RFL (4th) 129; 'Adoption Laws to Be Overhauled; Gay and Lesbian Couples Can Apply; Access to Information to Be Expanded,' *Vancouver Sun*, 21 June 1995, A1.
7 Telephone call to Unemployment Insurance Inquiry line, 9 March 1995. Under the Employment Insurance Act, the period of leave remains at 17 weeks with the same 2-week 'waiting period.' The amount of the benefit is also unchanged, at approximately 55% of average insured earnings. However, the maximum cap has been lowered to $413.00 per week, an amount which is fixed through the year 2000 (Human Resources Development Canada, *Employment Insurance: Maternity, Parental and Sickness Benefits*; 1996 Brochure IN-201–06–96; Human Resources Development Canada, *Employment Insurance: The New Employment Insurance System*; 1996 Brochure IN-AH068–07–96E).
8 For example, at the University of British Columbia, a SUB plan is available to female faculty for 27 weeks, but to female staff for only 17 weeks. A SUB plan

has recently been negotiated for instructors, but teaching and research assistants, cafeteria workers, cleaners, and clerks do not have a SUB plan.

9 I use the designation '(un)employment insurance legislation' for convenience in referring to both statutes and to underscore the primarily semantic nature of the difference between them.

10 The maternity benefit was likely put in the Unemployment Insurance Act of 1971 on the recommendation of the Royal Commission on the Status of Women in Canada which tabled its report in 1970. The Commission conceptualized the problem as a 'need for employment protection during and immediately after pregnancy,' recommending that federal, provincial, and territorial employment standards legislation include entitlement to unpaid leave and job security (Bird 1970, 84–7). Provision of a public maternity benefit was discussed as a consequence of the unpaid leave: 'Being entitled to maternity leave may relieve a woman's anxiety [about losing her job] but it will not help her financially unless some pay is provided' (ibid. 87). Since the context of the discussion was already restricted to employees, the Unemployment Insurance Act seemed an obvious place to house the benefit. As the Commission stated: 'Both unemployment insurance and paid maternity leave are intended to provide compensation for temporary loss of earnings, and the unemployment insurance plan already has a system for drawing contributions from the same sources that would be contributing to paid maternity leave' (ibid. 87–8). Although there was some recognition that the scheme would not assist 'non-working' women who might also need financial support (ibid. 88), there was no mention of self-employed women or women in the labour force who would not meet the eligibility criteria in the Unemployment Insurance Act.

11 To be able to claim the unemployment insurance maternity benefit, a woman must have ceased work. However, if a domestic worker is without an employer for two weeks, she becomes liable to be deported under the special immigration rules governing the 'Live-In Caregiver Program.' Telephone call to Cenen Bagon, Coordinator, Committee for Domestic Workers' and Caregivers' Rights, 27 April 1995.

12 Over 60 per cent of single mothers in Canada live in poverty: Canadian Council on Social Development 1993.

13 The weekly figures were determined by dividing the annual figures provided in the National Council of Welfare Report by 52 weeks. The figure cited for the maximum weekly maternity benefit was provided by telephone, 14 Feb. 1996, by a service representative at Unemployment Insurance, in Vancouver, B.C.

14 Employees pay premiums of $2.95 on every 100 dollars of earnings through 30 June 1997. New rates may be set thereafter (Human Resources Development

Canada, *Employment Insurance: The New Employment Insurance System*; 1996 Brochure IN-AH068–07–96E).

15 Other than the glaring discrimination evident in the parental leave provision discussed above, I have not been able to determine whether lesbian mothers are disproportionately unable to claim maternity benefits.

16 For the purposes of this portion of my argument, I assume that recipients of the maternity benefit are white, able-bodied, middle to upper income women with average or above average educational training, over 25 years of age, and living in heterosexual relationships with men who are able to substantially support them and their children. By demonstrating that the unemployment insurance scheme channels the 'ideal' recipients of its benefits into a traditional, sexist model of good mothering and the 'good family,' I want to show that the scheme oppresses 'good' as well as 'bad' mothers.

17 My argument applies to subsequent as well as first births. While it is widely acknowledged that the birth of one's first child is emotionally intense and ideologically significant, many mothers describe the birth of a second or third child as signalling an equally important change in status. In informal exchanges with a number of women, I have heard comments such as 'now I feel like a real mother' or 'now we are really a family.' The increased difficulty in finding and affording substitute care consequent upon the birth of a subsequent child escalates pressure on the mother of multiple children to leave the labour force.

18 This is only true for some mothers – others, who have felt trapped at home during their maternity leave, may feel relief at seeing the benefit period expire, facilitating a return to the paid workplace. However, pressures along the other two axes, in addition to ideologically driven feelings of guilt about 'leaving the baby,' remain a powerful influence to remain out of the paid labour force.

19 A 6-month-old baby is also adorable! (In other words, many mothers experience a strong positive emotional attachment to their babies.) Most babies of this age are also at a developmental stage where the mother is likely to feel that her mothering work is beginning to generate some emotional 'return' to her in terms of the baby's responsiveness, making it hard to leave.

20 A number of women I have spoken to said that they felt guilty about 'admitting' that they wanted to return to paid work, particularly when their babies were less than a year old. See also Jane Litchfield, 'For Mothers Today Freedom and Angst,' *Globe and Mail*, 25 May 1995, A22.

21 The one exception is the characteristic of being partnered to the father of the child which is an essential qualification for good motherhood but is not necessary to be a good female worker. Being married and fathering children has long been regarded as a positive attribute for male workers, however.

22 *R. v Schachter* (1989), 52 DLR (4th) 525 (TD) aff'd (1990), 66 DLR (4th) 635

(FCA) aff'd [1992] 2 SCR 679. Page references are to the decision of the trial court since judgments on appeal were confined to other issues.

23 SOR/90–756, 1990, *Canada Gazette*.

24 For example, this is the situation at the University of British Columbia. When asked why female employees otherwise eligible for the SUB plan receive a top-up for the period of parental leave while their male counterparts do not, the administrator of UBC's maternity/parental leave benefits replied that 'no men ask for parental leave at UBC' and 'only women need parental leave as part of a maternity benefit to help them as employees.' Telephone call to Department of Financial Services, University of British Columbia, 18 August 1995.

25 Statistics attest to the gendered nature of parental leave: in 1991 men took 4.3 per cent of parental leaves; by 1994 this percentage had dropped to 3.8 per cent. 'Few Men Take Advantage of Parental Leave,' *Vancouver Sun*, 14 Sept. 1996, F2.

26 The recasting of discrimination against women in the workplace as a legitimate 'private,' albeit gender-based, preference is well illustrated in the American case, *EEOC* v *Sears* in which Sears argued (and the court accepted) that gender disparity in sales positions for 'big ticket' appliances was a matter of private individual choice and not the product of sex discrimination (Frug 1992; Scott 1988).

REFERENCES

Armstrong, Pat, and Hugh Armstrong. 1990. *Theorizing Women's Work*. Toronto: Garamond

Arnup, Katherine. 1994. *Education for Motherhood: Advice for Mothers in Twentieth-Century Canada*. Toronto: University of Toronto Press

– and Susan Boyd. 1995. 'Familial Disputes? Sperm Donors, Lesbian Mothers, and Legal Parenthood.' In Didi Herman and Carl Stychin, eds., *Legal Inversions: Lesbians, Gay Men, and the Politics of Law*. Philadelphia: Temple University Press, 77–101

Bell Scott, Patricia. 1982. 'Debunking Sapphire: Toward a Non-Racist and Non-Sexist Social Science.' In Gloria T. Hull, Patricia Bell Scott, and Barbara Smith, eds., *All the Women Are White, All the Blacks Are Men, But Some of Us Are Brave*. New York: Feminist Press, 85–92

Bird, Florence. 1970. *Report of the Royal Commission on the Status of Women in Canada*. Ottawa: Information Canada

Boyd, Monica. 1984. *Canadian Attitudes towards Women: Thirty Years of Change*. Ottawa: Minister of Supply and Services (Cat. no. L24–1248/84B)

British Colombia Division of Vital Statistics. 1994. 'Birth Outcome Indicators.' *Quarterly Digest* 4, 93

Canadian Advisory Council on the Status of Women (CACSW). 1994. *Child Custody and Access Policy: A Brief to the Federal/Provincial/Territorial Family Law Committee.* Ottawa: CACSW
– 1989. *Submission by the Canadian Advisory Council on the Status of Women to the Legislative Commitee on Bill C-21, An Act to Amend the Unemployment Insurance Act.* Ottawa: CACSW, 15–17
Christofides, L.N., and Swidinsky, R. 1994. 'Wage Determination by Gender and Visible Minority Status: Evidence from the 1989 LMAS.' *Canadian Public Policy* 20, 34–51
Conway, John F. 1990. *The Canadian Family in Crisis.* Toronto: Lorimer
Creese, Gillian, N. Guppy, and M. Meissner. 1991. *Ups and Downs on the Ladder of Success: Social Mobility in Canada.* General Social Survey Analysis Series, Ottawa (cat. no. 11–612E, no. 5)
Dowd, Nancy. 1993. 'Family Values and Valuing Family: A Blueprint for Family Leave.' *Harvard Women's Law Journal* 30, 335–65
– 1989. 'Envisioning Work and Family: A Critical Perspective on International Models.' *Harvard Journal on Legislation* 26, 311–47
Duffy, Ann, Nancy Mandell, and Norene Pupo. 1989. *Few Choices: Women, Work and Family.* Toronto: Garamond
Eisenberg, Arlene, Heidi E. Murkoff, and Sandee E. Hathaway. 1989. *What to Expect in the First Year.* New York: Workman Publishing
Employment and Immigration Canada. 1993. *Employment Equity Act, Annual Report 1993.* Ottawa: Human Resources Development Canada, 32–3, 38–9
Evans, Patricia, and Norene Pupo. 1993. 'Parental Leave: Assessing Women's Interests.' *Canadian Journal of Women and the Law* 6(2), 402–18
Fineman, Martha. 1991. 'Images of Mothers in Poverty Discourses.' *Duke Law Journal*, 274–95
Frug, Mary Joe. 1992. 'Sexual Equality and Sexual Difference in American Law.' *New England Law Review* 26, 665–82
Gavison, Ruth. 1992. 'Feminism and the Public/Private Distinction.' *Stanford Law Review* 45, 1–45
Gerber, Linda M. 1990. 'Multiple Jeopardy: A Socio-Economic Comparison of Men and Women among Indian, Métis and Inuit Peoples of Canada.' *Canadian Ethnic Studies* 22, 69–84
Glenn, Evelyn Nakano. 1985. 'Racial Ethnic Women's Labour: the Intersection of Race, Gender and Class Oppression.' *Review of Radical Political Economy* 7(3), 86–108
– Crace Chang, and Linda Rennie Forcey. 1994. *Mothering Ideology, Experience, and Agency.* New York and London: Routledge.
Goundry, Sandra. 1994. *Women, Disability and the Law: Identifying Barriers to*

Equality in the Law of Non-Consensual Sterilization, Child Welfare and Sexual Assault. Winnipeg: Canadian Disability Rights Council

Hamilton, A.C., and C.M. Sinclair, Commisioners. 1991. 'Report of the Aboriginal Justice Inquiry of Manitoba by the Public Inquiry into the Administration of Justice and Aboriginal People.' Winnipeg: Public Inquiry Into the Administration of Justice and Aboriginal People

Hanigsberg, Julia E. 1991. 'Power and Procreation: State Interference in Pregnancy.' *Ottawa Law Review* 23(1), 35–70

Hartmann, Heidi. 1981. 'The Family as the Locus of Gender, Class and Political Struggle: The Example of Housework.' *Signs* 6(3), 377–86

Harvey, Edward B., and Lorne Tepperman. 1990. *Selected Socio-economic Consequences of Disability for Women.* Ottawa: Statistics Canada

Hessing, Melody. 1992. 'Mothers' Management of their Combined Workloads: Clerical Work and Household Needs.' *Canadian Review of Sociology and Anthropology* 30, 37–63

– 1991. 'Talking Shopping: Office Conversations and Women's Dual Labour.' *Canadian Journal of Sociology* 16, 23–50

Ikemoto, Lisa. 1992. 'The Code of Perfect Pregnancy: At the Intersection of the Ideology of Motherhood, the Practice of Defaulting to Science, and the Interventionist Mindset of the Law.' *Ohio State Law Journal* 53, 1205–1306

Jenson, Jane. 1986. 'Gender and Reproduction or Babies and the State.' *Studies in Political Economy* 20, 9–46

Khosla, Punam. 1993. *Review of the Situation of Women.* Ottawa: National Action Committee on the Status of Women

Kline, Marlee. 1993. 'Complicating the Ideology of Motherhood: Child Welfare Law and First Nation Women.' *Queen's Law Journal* 18, 306–42

– 1992. 'Child Welfare Law, "Best Interest of the Child" Ideology, and First Nations.' *Osgoode Hall Law Journal* 30, 375–425

La Novara, Pina. 1993. *A Portrait of Families in Canada.* Ottawa: Statistics Canada (cat. no. 89–523E)

Leach, Penelope. 1993. *Your Baby and Child from Birth to Age Five.* New York: Knopf

Leira, Arnlaug. 1992. *Welfare States and Working Mothers: The Scandinavian Experience.* Cambridge and New York: Cambridge University Press

Lero, Donna S. and Karen L. Johnson. 1994. *110 Canadian Statistics on Work and Family.* Ottawa: Canadian Advisory Council on the Staus of Women

Luxton, Meg, Harriet Rosenberg, and Sedef Arat-Koç. 1990. *Through the Kitchen Window: The Politics of Home and Family.* Toronto: Garamond

MacBride-King, Judith. 1990. *Work and Family: Employment Challenges of the '90s.* Ottawa: Conference Board of Canada

Maranto, Gina. 1995. 'Delayed Childbearing.' *Atlantic Monthly* 275(6), 55–66

Maroney, H.J. 1992. '"Who Has the Baby?" Nationalism, Pronatalism and the Construction of a Demographic Crisis in Quebec, 1960–1988.' *Studies in Political Economy* 39, 7–36

– and Meg Luxton. 1987. *Feminism and Political Economy: Women's Work and Women's Struggles.* Toronto: Methuen

Marshall, Katherine. 1990. 'Household Chores.' *Canadian Social Trends* 16, 18–19

Maynard, Rona. 1988. 'The Changing Canadian Woman.' *Chatelaine* 61(3), 81–93

Ministry of Skills, Training, and Labour. 1994. *News Release*, 21 Nov. 1994, ref. no. 11-135-94

Minow, Martha. 1990. 'Adjudicating Differences: Conflicts among Feminist Lawyers.' In Marianne Hirsch and Evelyn Fox Keller, eds., *Conflicts in Feminism.* New York: Routledge, 149–63

Mohanty, Chandra. 1991. 'Under Western Eyes: Feminist Scholarship and Colonial Discourses.' In Chandra Talpade Mohanty, Ann Russo, and Lourdes Torres, eds., *Third World Women and the Politics of Feminism.* Bloomington: Indiana University Press, 51–80

Mosoff, Judith. 1995. 'Motherhood, Madness, and Law.' *University of Toronto Law Journal* 45, 107–142

National Council of Welfare. 1995. *Poverty Profile 1993: A Report by the National Council of Welfare.* Ottawa: Minister of Supply and Services Canada

Oberman, Michelle. 1992. 'The Control of Pregnancy and the Criminalization of Femaleness.' *Berkeley Women's Law Journal* 7, 1–12

Olsen, Frances E. 1983. 'The Family and the Market: A Study of Ideology and Legal Reform.' *Harvard Law Review* 96, 1497–1578

Phillips, Paul, and Erin Phillips. 1993. *Women and Work: Inequality in the Canadian Labour Market.* Toronto: Lorimer

Roberts, Dorothy. 1994. 'The Value of Black Mothers' Work.' *Connecticut Law Review* 26, 871–8

Schroeder, Patricia. 1989. 'Is There a Role for the Federal Government in Work and the Family?' *Harvard Journal on Legislation* 26, 299–309

Scott, Joan. 1988. 'Deconstructing Equality-Versus-Difference: Or, the Uses of Poststructuralist Theory for Feminism.' *Feminist Studies* 14, 33–50

Seward Shirley B., and Marc Tremblay. 1989. *Immigrants in the Canadian Labour Force: Their Role in Structural Change.* Discussion Paper 89.B.2, Studies in Social Policy, Ottawa

Statistics Canada. 1995. *Women in Canada,* 3rd ed. Ottawa: Minister of Industry

– 1994. Labour Division. *Maternity Benefits by Age and Occupation.* Ottawa: Minister of Supply and Services (cat. no. 13:17–20)

- 1993a. *Selected Birth and Fertility Statistics, Canada 1921-1990*. Ottawa: Minister of Supply and Services (cat. no. 82-553)
- 1993b. Labour Division. *Maternity Benefits by Age and Occupational Group*. Ottawa: Minister of Supply and Services
- 1992. *Labour Force Annual Averages*. Ottawa: Minister of Supply and Services (cat. no. 71-220)
- 1991. *Earnings Groups and Occupation, Female Workers*. Ottawa: Minister of Supply and Services (cat. no. 13-217)
Swiggart, Jane. 1991. *Myth of the Bad Mother: Parenting without Guilt*. New York: Avon
Teghtsoonian, Katherine. 1995. 'Work and/or Motherhood: The Ideological Construction of Women's Options in Canadian Child Care Policy Debates.' *Canadian Journal of Women and the Law* 8(2), 411-39
Townson, Monica. 1984. 'A National System for Parental Leave.' In Economic Council of Canada. *Towards Equity: Proceedings of a Colloquium on the Economic Status of Women in the Labour Market, November 1984*. Ottawa: Supply and Services, 21-30
Ursel, Jane. 1986. 'The State and the Maintenance of Patriarchy: A Case Study of Family, Labour and Welfare Legislation in Canada.' In James Dickinson and Bob Russell, eds., *Family, Economy and State: The Social Reproduction Process under Capitalism*. Toronto: Garamond, 150-91
Van Praagh, Shauna. 1993. 'Religion and Culture in Canadian Family Law (Book Review).' *McGill Law Journal* 38, 232-50

8

Balancing Acts: Career and Family among Lawyers

FIONA M. KAY

I'm happy with my professional life now, but I'm afraid that when I have children in the near future my career will conflict with my family obligations and goals. Law is unforgiving and unwelcoming to mothers.

During the past decade the dilemma of balancing paid work and family responsibilities has emerged as a pressing concern within the profession of law. Recently, a Canadian Bar Association task force published a controversial report on gender equality in the legal profession (1993). Titled *Touchstones for Change*, the report describes a legal profession that regularly discriminates against women through restricted professional opportunities and a failure to accommodate the special needs of women with children, resulting in further reductions of career opportunities and loss of income. The report argues that client development activities, evaluation methods, law firm culture, billable hour targets, and inflexible working arrangements act to exclude women with child-rearing responsibilities. These findings echo a familiar debate over a traditionally male-dominated profession and its inflexibility to accommodate the needs of a diversified membership, including women with significant family responsibilities (see also Boston Bar Association 1991).

As the number of women in law reaches a sizeable proportion, at present close to one-third of the profession, scholars are beginning to ask the question: will women change the organization and structure of law practice? Unfortunately, only a few researchers have explored this 'transformative potential' of women's entry to elite professions such as law (see Brockman, Evans, and Reid 1992; Menkel-Meadow 1989, 1987; Mossman 1994a, 1994b, 1993; Rhode 1994). Rather, those examining the growth of the profession and its changing membership have expressed concern about a perceived prospect of dampening of earnings with the large number of entrants (Sander and Williams 1989; Stager and Foot 1988). Others have expressed concern over the 'flood' of lawyers on the market that may be contributing to a propensity for legal conflict (Abel 1986; Kidder 1983). In these debates, little mention is made of the potential contribution of a growing diversity within the profession, including the possibility of a more humane and integrated profession with a broader array of work arrangements (Hagan and Kay 1995, 6). How have large numbers of women in the profession changed the immediate concerns of the profession? How are women influenced by the profession they have entered? In this regard, Menkel-Meadow asked, 'Will women who enter the profession conform to a 'male' model of what it means to be a legal professional, or will the profession innovate and adapt to previously excluded entrants, who may have different perspectives on how to practice law' (1989, 197)? As individuals with heightened family responsibilities, will women introduce important changes in the workplace such as alternative work schedules (Mossman 1994b; Rhode 1994) or different styles of practice (Brockman 1995; Menkel-Meadow 1989)?

New challenges and potential transformations within the profession are beginning to emerge. This chapter focuses on the recent entry of women in critical numbers to the legal profession and the challenges women face in attempting to balance the demands of legal work and family responsibilities. Three questions are central to this chapter: (1) How is the 'public/private' divide intrinsically connected to the problem of the 'glass ceiling' of earnings and occupational segregation within the legal profession? (2) What strategies have women adopted in their efforts to balance responsibilities in the home (private sphere) and demands in law practice (public sphere)? (3) What are the consequences for women striving to meet multiple role obligations within a traditionally 'male' model of how legal work and career patterns are structured? First, however, I consider dimensions of the changing representation of women across several traditionally male-dominated professions. These professions provide interesting possibilities for comparison and offer a context for assessing women's growing representation in the legal profession.

Demographic Changes in the Professions

Women's labour force participation in Canada has been on the rise throughout the latter half of the twentieth century. In 1951 women represented 22 per cent of the Canadian labour force, 34 per cent in 1971, and by 1991 women were approximately 45 per cent of the labour force (Dominion Bureau of Statistics 1953; Statistics Canada 1993, 1974). However, women's rising representation in the labour force has been concentrated primarily in traditionally 'female' occupations (Armstrong and Armstrong 1994, 28; Reskin and Padavic 1994, 43). The legal profession is one of the traditionally male-dominated professions that has changed significantly in its gender composition. Over the past two decades women's representation has increased from 5 per cent of lawyers in 1971, to 15 per cent in 1981, to 29 per cent in 1991. Among judges and magistrates, women's representation grew from 6 per cent in 1971 to 20 per cent in 1991 (see Table 8.1). Women also made steady gains during this period in professions such as medicine, dentistry, architecture, and financial management. The percentage of physicians who were women rose from 10 per cent in 1971 to 27 per cent in 1991, while the figure among dentists rose from 5 per cent to 15 per cent over the same twenty-year period. There were also increases from 8 per cent to 43 per cent for financial managers and 3 per cent to 19 per cent for architects. In sharp contrast are the very slow growth rates among women in the physical sciences and engineering.

The doors to many of these professions opened to women only very recently. Entry to the 'learned' professions, including law and medicine, was prohibited by law in many countries well into the twentieth century (Menkel-Meadow 1989, 199). Access to the professions was restricted through dominant social conceptions of men and women as naturally occupying separate spheres, with women's primary obligations being to the private sphere of the family. The professions were deemed unsuitable for women as a result of their assumed biological and psychological differences from men, particularly their reproductive and nurturing capacities (Armstrong and Armstrong 1994; Reskin and Padavic 1994). Medicine and teaching opened their doors to women earlier than did law because the occupational roles more closely approximated stereotyped conceptions of women as maternal and nurturing. In contrast, women were excluded from law because they were considered to be unsuited to the harsh adversarial system (Brockman 1995; Morello 1986; Mossman 1988).

In an early study of women in the law, James White (1967) argued that, while other women had followed the first women to practise law, 'this dribble of women has grown to a persistent and continuous trickle in the twentieth century, but it shows no signs of becoming a flood' (1051). As Table 8.1 reveals, White's prediction was proven inaccurate in the twenty-five years to follow. The recent entry of women to law in sizeable numbers

TABLE 8.1
Number of Women and Men in Selected Professions (1971–91)

Selected Professions	1971[a]			1981[b]			1991[c]		
	Women	Men	%F	Women	Men	%F	Women	Men	%F
Law professionals									
Judges & magistrates	70	1190	5.6	—	1785	—	530	2125	20.0
Lawyers & notaries	780	15535	4.8	5175	29030	15.1	15610	37965	29.0
Physical Sciences									
Chemists	795	5340	11.1	1805	7365	19.7	3345	8005	29.5
Geologists	140	4550	3.0	760	6740	10.1	915	6900	11.7
Physicists	40	740	5.1	—	1240	—	175	1215	12.6
Meteorologists	40	760	5.0	—	865	—	150	945	13.7
Engineering									
Electrical	180	14715	1.2	945	25660	3.6	3260	34100	8.7
Civil	220	21225	1.0	865	30360	2.8	3080	37930	7.5
Chemical	55	3410	1.6	330	5225	5.9	745	5270	12.4
Mechanical	80	12760	0.6	380	18680	2.0	1370	24205	5.4
Health Professions									
Physicians & surgeons	2890	25695	10.1	6965	33655	17.1	14535	39975	26.7
Dentists	310	6120	4.8	820	9515	7.9	1980	10845	15.4
Osteopaths & chiropractors	80	990	7.5	295	1895	13.5	1050	3005	25.9
Pharmacists	2170	7240	23.1	5710	7935	41.9	11175	8895	55.7
Managers									
Financial management	635	7075	8.2	13960	45550	53.4	39765	52300	43.2
Personnel & industrial relations	445	3610	11.0	7200	18805	27.7	18565	25440	42.2

TABLE 8.1 (concluded).

Selected Professions	1971[a]			1981[b]			1991[c]		
	Women	Men	%F	Women	Men	%F	Women	Men	%F
Other Professions									
Mathematicians, statisticians, & actuaries	775	2885	21.2	1795	3840	31.9	3050	4710	39.3
System analysts & computer programmers	3235	19245	14.4	17320	43355	28.5	45190	10470	30.1
Architects	115	3925	2.8	645	6965	8.5	2260	9555	19.1
Accountants, auditors, & other financial officers	15655	87360	15.2	47175	104505	31.1	107970	121760	47.0

— Indicates that figures are not appropriate or applicable for selected year.
%F Represents the percentage of women in the profession.

[a]Statistics Canada. 1974. *Occupations: Occupations by Sex for Canada and Provinces*. Ottawa: Minister of Industry, Trade, and Commerce. 1971 Census of Canada. Catalogue number 94-717, vol. 3, Part 2 (Bulletin 3.2-3) at pp. 2-1, 2-3, and 2-5.

[b]Statistics Canada. 1984. *Population*. Ottawa: Minister of Supply and Services Canada. 1981 Census of Canada. Catalogue number 92-919 (vol. 1, National Series) at pp. 1-1 to 1-6.

[c]Statistics Canada. 1993. *Occupation*. Ottawa: Industry, Science, and Technology Canada. 1991 Census of Canada. Catalogue number 93-327 at pp. 6-10.

has been described as 'nothing short of revolutionary' (Abel 1988b, 202) and the trend towards increased participation of women in law promises to continue with the rise in female law school entrants. Currently, women constitute close to 50 per cent of all law school students in Canada (Donovan 1990, 37). Although the gender composition of the legal profession has been altered dramatically in recent years, the same cannot be said of social class, race, and ethnicity. The majority of women and men entering law are from upper-class backgrounds (Abel 1989, 83) and ethnic and racial minorities remain vastly underrepresented in the profession (Greer and Samson 1993; Harrington 1995; Neallani 1992).

The entry of women to the legal profession has taken place against a backdrop of exclusion followed by decades in which few women entered the profession. The number of women entering law in Canada remained relatively small until the 1970s (Mossman 1994a, 63–4). The very recent entry of women to law in sizeable numbers has shaped the demographic profile of women lawyers today. In comparison with men, who are distributed across different stages of the life cycle, women are disproportionately young, and many are approaching the years in the life span when family responsibilities are most demanding (ibid., 65). These different demographic profiles create unique pressures for the Canadian legal profession in the 1990s.

In exploring the challenge of balancing legal work and family responsibilities, it is important to examine assumptions about appropriate gender roles and current arrangements for legal work associated with public and private lives. The existing organization of law practice fundamentally reflects the ways in which economic interests are entrenched in the gendered structure of legal work that has been facilitated by women's unpaid labour in the private sphere of the home. These assumptions are connected to the problem of the 'glass ceiling' of earnings and occupational segregation within the profession. In spite of the changes to the demographics of the legal profession, the profession itself has changed little and is still based on an unaccommodating 'male' model of work. In fact, considerable structural resistance to women entering the public sphere of the legal profession exists. Women, particularly women with children, face sometimes irreconcilable competing demands when they attempt to enter the public sphere of the legal profession in the face of their traditional responsibilities in the private sphere of the family.

In the next section I provide a brief overview of research into patterns of segregation in the legal profession and problems of 'glass ceiling' effects for women lawyers. Particularly relevant to this discussion are the constraints of inflexible work structures that shape the 'choices' available to women lawyers with family responsibilities.

'Glass Ceiling Effects'[1] in the Practice of Law

In Canada and the United States research reveals that women are consistently located towards the base of the legal profession's hierarchy. Abel (1988a) observed that women have gravitated towards employee over self-employed status and the public sector over the private practice of law. As a consequence, they remain severely underrepresented in the more prestigious and financially rewarding forms of practice (ibid. 36, 43; Thorner 1991, 94). Hagan, Huxter, and Parker (1988) found in their analysis of Toronto lawyers that women are more highly represented among positions of lower authority, lower supervisory powers, and lower prestige. In private practice women are overrepresented in large firms and in solo practice or small firms and underrepresented in medium-sized firms; there is a curvilinear relationship between degree of formal organization and the proportional representation of women (Arthurs, Weisman, and Zemans 1987; Curran 1986). Menkel-Meadow suggested that 'this may reflect [women's] perception that large firms are more bureaucratic, adhering to universalistic standards, and small firms offer close personal relationships, whereas medium-sized firms permit the greatest scope for discrimination' (1989, 213). Women are also disproportionately represented among the unemployed, those employed on a part-time basis, and the underemployed (Kay, 1992; Liefland 1986). A smaller proportion of women law graduates enter practice, and a higher proportion of those who enter leave during the first few years (Abel 1988b; Brockman 1992a; Chambers 1989). Research suggests that pressures of work and family tend to push women out of the practice of law (Brockman 1992c, 150).

Recent studies also demonstrate that women have not yet become partners at a rate proportionate to that of their male counterparts (Meier 1990, 169).[2] A study of men and women who started in private practice after graduating from Harvard Law School in 1974 (and were still in private practice in 1982) found that 63 per cent of the women had become partners compared with 73 per cent of the men (Abramson and Franklin 1986). Canadian research reveals that regardless of years of experience, fields of specialization, size of law firm, or the numbers of women in the legal profession, men continue to have a consistently higher probability of attaining partnership than women (Kay and Hagan 1994, 450). One impediment to women becoming partners is the expectation of 'rainmaking': the generation of new clients for the firm. Donovan (1990, 148) pointed to the lack of access to an 'old boy network' as a source of women's reduced ability to generate clients. It has also been suggested that some women lawyers are assigned less desirable and less lucrative clients because firms assume that they will not be available in the long term because of their family responsibilities; for similar reasons they may be retained as 'permanent associates' or salaried partners rather than promoted to full partnership (Kingston 1988; Menkel-Meadow 1989). The recent growth in the profession has resulted in smaller proportions of associates becoming partners (Galanter and Palay 1991), and women have fared worse than men in these declining shares of opportunity (Kay and Hagan 1994). These inequities are even more extreme for women of colour. Neallani (1992) pointed out that there are virtually no women of colour who are partners in the large prestigious firms in Canada, very few are in partnership-track positions, or even in articling positions at these firms (ibid., 151).

A consequence of women's overrepresentation in those segments of the profession that traditionally have received the lowest status is that women also tend to receive lower earnings than men (Abel 1989; Adam and Baer 1984; Vogt 1986). That many women are new entrants to the profession and possess fewer years of experience does not fully account for the observed income differences. Nor is the gender disparity in earnings explained by the different distribution of women and men across settings of legal work. Kay and Hagan's study of Ontario lawyers (1995) showed that women lawyers earn on average $59,302 (1990 dollars), while their male counterparts average $93,223. Their analysis revealed that a sizeable differential (61 per cent) was attributed to different *rates* of remuneration for men and women for similar employment positions and qualifications. That is to say, women and men of similar experience, working in equivalent positions, are differentially rewarded for their hours of legal work (see also Hagan 1990; Stager and Foot 1988).[3] Most concerning is the finding that there appears to be an amplification of the earnings differential for women as they ascend mobility ladders within the profession (Kay and Hagan 1995, 279).

A final aspect of research into women and the legal profession has examined job satisfaction among lawyers. A common pattern revealed in these studies is that women are more likely than men to mention the relationship of family life to work life in evaluating their employment (Chambers 1989). For example, an American study found that both men and women law students continue to expect women to perform primary child-rearing responsibilities and that women, but not men, consider an employer's policy on maternity and child-rearing leave in selecting a job (Stanford Law Project 1988). Recent Canadian research found that for both women and men, high satisfaction exists for the substance of practising law, while lower levels of satisfaction are reported regarding balance with personal life and benefits. For instance, Brockman's study of lawyers in British Columbia revealed that the second most frequent category of discrimination against women was a 'lack of accommodation for family commitments' (1992c, 119). This finding reflects women's struggle to balance their work in the public sphere with their responsibilities in the private sphere of the family.

This review of the research literature offers considerable evidence that women continue to occupy lower positions in the power hierarchy of the profession: they are overrepresented in government employment and underrepresented in the private practice of law; within private practice women experience lower chances for partnership; women also earn less and are more dissatisfied with their conditions of work. However, little is known about how these differences relate to family commitments at different stages in lawyers' careers or about the relevance of workplace supports. To establish these interconnections it is necessary to further conceptualize the association between career and family commitments and the structure of law practice.

Sociological Approaches to Balancing Career and Family

Sociological research has emphasized constraints imposed on women lawyers' career trajectories; in particular, that of their different role demands. Traditionally, women have borne primary responsibility in the private sphere, including housekeeping and child care duties, and these responsibilities do not diminish significantly for women who enter the public sphere by working in the professions (Pollock and Ramirez 1995, 87; Reskin and Padavic 1994, 150). As several authors in this book demonstrate (Iyer, Teghtsoonian, Young), inadequacies in policies involving parental leave, flexible work hours, and child care contribute greatly to women's struggles in accommodating paid work (public sphere) and family (private sphere) commitments. Women are subject to a potential role conflict between career and family (Katz 1988, 96) principally because the practice of law is structured with the assumption that there is no need for the (traditionally male) lawyer to attend to child care responsibilities. This model of structuring work does not operate well for women who are unlikely to have a spouse at home tending to domestic and family responsibilities (Lennon and Rosenfield 1994).

Difficulties in balancing career and family responsibilities are often attributed to role overload and conflict (Houseknecht, Vaughan, and Macke 1984). Role overload is defined as having an excess of role demands and insufficient time to fulfil them (Baruch, Biener, and Barnett 1985). Role conflict refers to 'the extent to which a person experiences pressures within one role that are incompatible with the pressures that arise within another role' (Kopelman, Greenhaus, and Connolly 1983, 201). Role overload is likely to lead to role conflict when there is no alternative mechanism to help individuals fulfil the demands of various roles (Coverman 1989; Silver and Goldscheider 1994). For example, a woman lawyer who experiences unstable child care arrangements is more likely to experience role conflict than a woman lawyer employed in an organization that provides adequate child care facilities.

Studies of the legal profession lend support to theories of role overload and conflict. Liefland (1986) remarked that the traditional legal career path affords lawyers little time for activities that involve a substantial commitment of time and energy outside the office or courtroom. As Fox and Hesse-Biber (1984, 139) observed, professional work demands a 'rapid and relentless pace – and performance is measured against time.' This observation is particularly salient in the legal profession where increasing competitiveness has driven billable hour requirements to unprecedented levels (Rhode 1994, 62). This conflict of role demands is accentuated by the fact that women's peak child-bearing and child-rearing years coincide with the critical years of career establishment (Liefland 1986, 613–14). In this respect, Taber and colleagues noted: 'Torn by family pressures, it is often difficult for women to maintain the appearance of total dedication to their careers that is necessary to compete in settings such as law firms' (1988, 1228). Williams (1990) argued more forcefully that 'the crushing strain of inconsistent demands is grinding down women's sense that they can control their lives and meet their responsibilities to others' (355). The result of these role conflicts is that women lawyers must decide between career rewards and a decent family life at least during part of their working lives, a constraint which men, argued Epstein (1981), experience only rarely.

Some researchers have offered an alternative view of combining career and family roles: that of role enhancement. According to this theory, multiple roles bring privileges, resources, and self-enhancement. Conflict and overload arising from the possession of multiple roles may be overshadowed or compensated for by rewards resulting from the diversity of roles. These researchers find that despite demanding schedules, women often respond to multiple diverse roles and their associated demands with satisfaction rather than despair (Chambers 1989; Nieva 1985). Taylor and Spencer (1988) suggested that as a result of strong commitments to numerous diverse involvements, women may enjoy 'fuller, though more hectic lives.' Moreover, Rosenberg, Perlstadt, and Williams (1990) argued that women's political orientation, particularly feminist dispositions, may have important effects on female lawyers' role orientations and career patterns. New norms and expectations may have lowered role conflicts experienced by women.

Nonetheless, concerted efforts to minimize role conflict and achieve greater role enhancement require flexibility to manage competing demands. Overwhelmingly, women have been the ones to make these sorts of accommodations in their careers, while organizational structures in law practice have conceded few options by way of flexible or reduced hours or workplace family supports. Mossman (1994b, 173) observed that the creation of different working patterns to accommodate family life is most frequently a matter of individual negotiation and decision making. For example, Brockman found in her study of the legal profession in Alberta that child care responsibilities had significantly greater effects on women's career decisions regarding jobs, specialties, cases, and the hours they worked than on men's (1992b, 761). Therefore, women often pursue law practices that satisfy at least two important criteria: first, the hours of work must be predictable and not unexpectedly extended so that family responsibilities are not complicated; and, second, interruptions (for maternity leave or child care responsibilities) will be relatively non-disruptive to their career progress (Halliday 1986, 75). Typically, these work settings are the least prestigious within law practice and offer lower remuneration. Thus, those women lawyers who succeed in achieving a satisfactory balance in their public and private lives may also find themselves eventually thwarted by the 'glass ceiling' (Mossman 1994b, 171).

A third approach to the study of career and family emphasizes the multidimensional aspects of role commitments and directs attention to temporal changes in transitions among these roles. A life-course dynamics approach considers multiple life domains simultaneously and examines how, over time, changes in one domain affect, and are affected by, those in other domains (Elder 1985). This approach emphasizes the interconnections between public and private spheres and a synchrony among the range of roles. This perspective also avoids the assumption of uniform stages over the life course or necessarily 'progressive' and linear career development. Rather, a life-course dynamics approach alerts us to the relevance of the diversity of timing and order of career and family transitions (Rindfuss,

Swicegood, and Rosenfeld 1987, 785). This appreciation of the multiple role commitments and the synchronization of timing among these roles is particularly well suited to an understanding of women's careers, which research shows to be characterized by greater diversity than men's (Jones, Marsden, and Tepperman 1990).

A life-course dynamics approach also emphasizes the organizational context in forming individual status and opportunities as well as the wider cultural systems in which individuals and transitions are embedded (Meyer 1988, 50). Clearly, a consideration of organizational structures is essential to our understanding of career mobility. As Skvortez argued: 'Substantively, the workplace structure determines the generation of movement opportunities while the individual attributes differentially situate persons with respect to taking advantage of or being given these opportunities' (1984, 201). To the extent that law firms and other organizations that employ lawyers adhere to a fixed bureaucratic form (see Ferguson 1984), with little flexibility in work routine, hours, and with few workplace supports, women with family responsibilities are likely to experience few options in adapting to pressures of role conflict as well as reduced opportunities for career advancement (Rhode 1994, 61). As Menkel-Meadow observed: 'Occupational segregation is the result of complex forces that push or keep women out of particular jobs and locations and simultaneously pull them into others that are more compatible with family responsibilities, less attractive to men, or preferred by women because of their work structure, style, or substantive content. Indeed, the one factor that may be said to unify women as an analytic category is their common experience of exclusion and domination' (1989, 238).

Each of these approaches, role conflict, role enhancement, and life-course dynamics, make particular assumptions about role obligations, flexibility to balance (or more appropriately, juggle) roles, and the consequences of competing or asynchronous role demands in the public and private spheres of work and family. The three approaches are in some respects complementary to each other. However, the life-course dynamics approach offers the more complex appreciation of the importance of timing in the intersection of heavy demands of career and family and the impact of workplace structures on the 'choices' available to women and men lawyers managing these periods in their lives. In the next section, on the basis of a survey of lawyers, I examine more closely the relationship among family responsibilities, workplace supports and schedules, and job transitions. This survey reveals the sacrifices that women regularly make in order to strike a balance between their public (career) and private (family) lives.

Strategies in the Balancing Act

The analysis to follow is based on a survey conducted in 1990 of lawyers who entered the legal profession in Ontario during the period 1975 to 1990. This random sample was stratified to include equal representation of women and men, and it also includes respondents who left the practice of law during this period. The sample consists of 1,583 lawyers (68 per cent response rate).[4]

Like women in other occupations, women lawyers continue to assume primary responsibility for the care of their children while managing full-time employment (Brockman 1992b, 761). Table 8.2 sets out time investment and responsibility for child care as reported by lawyers working full-time.[5] Clearly, women lawyers reported on average a greater proportion of the responsibility for child care as their own. Women reported the proportion of responsibility borne by themselves to average 49 per cent, compared with 26 per cent reported by male lawyers. Women lawyers were also more likely to report a lower proportion of responsibility for child care to be borne by the person with whom they live: women reported that the person they lived with averaged 21 per cent of the child care responsibility, while male lawyers reported that the person they lived with assumed close to 61 per cent of the responsibility.[6] As well, women lawyers were more likely to report the presence of a paid child care worker: paid child care workers assumed on average 26 per cent of the responsibility. In contrast, male lawyers were more likely to report that their spouse assumed most of this responsibility, with approximately 10 per cent assumed by a paid child care worker. In terms of hours spent each week on child care, women lawyers invested considerably more time than men: women with children averaged the equivalent of a second full-time job, spending on average 48 hours per week on child care; while men with children averaged 21 hours.

Women are also the ones who are expected to assign priority to family demands over paid work when unexpected problems and small emergencies arise (Blau and Ferber 1985, 30; Hessing 1993, 24). I therefore asked lawyers to describe who leaves the place of paid work most often when the children are in need of assistance.[7] Answers to this question lend further insight into the division of child care responsibilities within the home. Women are more likely to leave work to attend to their children's activities than the person they live with and their male colleagues. Fifty-two per cent of female lawyers, compared with only 8 per cent of male lawyers said that they leave work most often. Similarly, a greater proportion of male lawyers

TABLE 8.2
Division of Child Care and Housework between Women and Men

Task	Men		Women	
Proportion of responsibility for child care	Mean	SD	Mean	SD
You	25.9	13.9	48.8	24.4
Person with whom you live	60.8	24.0	21.4	17.6
Child's other parent (if not living with you)	3.2	15.3	3.3	13.3
Paid child care worker	9.5	18.9	25.6	24.6
Other	0.8	4.7	1.0	5.2
Hours of child care per week	21.3	16.9	47.7	34.4
N	559		157	

Departure from work most often when children are at home	%	%
You	7.7	52.3
Person with whom you live	39.3	7.0
Child's other parent (if not living with you)	2.6	1.2
Equal division	10.2	13.6
One of us already works in the home	28.9	6.2
Someone else in the home (relative or paid employee)	11.2	19.6
Total	100.0	100.0
N	557	155

Chi-square value = 213.20, df = 5, $p < .001$

Distribution of Housework	%	%
I do most of it	3.6	39.3
We share it half/half	36.2	48.9
Person I live with does most of it	57.6	4.5
Most of it is done by someone else	2.6	7.3
Total	100.0	100.0
N	750	276

Chi-square value = 345.9, df = 3, $p < .001$

reported that the person with whom they live leaves work most often (39 per cent), whereas only 7 per cent of female lawyers said that the person with whom they live leaves work most often. A greater proportion of male lawyers reported that one parent already stays at home to provide child care (29 per cent) compared with the proportion of female lawyers reporting that one parent is at home during the day (6 per cent). Finally, female lawyers were more likely than their male counterparts to say that there was someone else in the home (relative or paid employee) who provided child care (20 per cent and 12 per cent, respectively).

Women lawyers are also more likely to assume primary responsibility for housework.[8] A far greater proportion of male than female respondents reported that the person they lived with did most of the housework (58 per cent and 5 per cent, respectively). Women lawyers were more likely than their male colleagues to report an even distribution of housework between themselves and the person they lived with (49 per cent and 36 per cent, respectively) and slightly more likely than their male counterparts to report someone else (i.e., relative or paid employee) fulfilled most of the housework demands (7 per cent and 3 per cent, respectively).

Research discussed earlier in this chapter found that women lawyers often delay marriage and childbearing until they have passed their major career hurdles. As a result of repeated delays, many women lawyers may forgo parenting roles altogether (Cooney and Uhlenberg 1989, 757). Almost two-thirds of the men (61 per cent) compared with about one-third of the women (38 per cent) in the sample had become parents. Although women in this sample are still relatively young, a pattern of delay was apparent. Numerous women described work histories in which they delayed having children until their career was established; others described strategies for timing childbearing so as to reduce conflict with the demanding schedule of the early years of career development; still others decided not to have children at all.

The sorts of tensions and struggles involved in attempting to coordinate career and family plans are evident in the following woman's assessment of the balancing act and her decision to delay childbearing: 'Having no children is partly due to anticipated problems with care arrangements and managing household chores, as well as a perception that part-time lawyers who are mothers, even if such positions are available, are perceived as having assigned a higher priority to home and children than to work. In other words, I would continue to work full-time even with children, but expect this would be draining, so I haven't had any.'

Another woman lawyer's decision to leave Toronto and avoid the large firm settings reveals one path taken in an attempt to better accommodate family demands: 'I left Toronto because I did not feel it was possible to find a job as a lawyer where I would not have to "sell my soul" to the firm and leave my children to be raised by babysitters. My current job enables me to be a mother and a lawyer, but of course my salary is much lower than it would be if I were in Toronto or working for a firm where billable hours was the most important factor. Generally, I'm very satisfied with my current lifestyle and work pattern.'

Workplace Supports

The intersection of female lawyers' public and private responsibilities demands consideration of the supports offered in the workplace to aid them in balancing career and family. To examine flexibility in work arrangements and availability of employee benefits, lawyers were asked to identify supports offered by their firm or employer. A total of nine types of arrangements were identified for consideration, including disability insurance, part-time work, flexible hours (full-time), job sharing, maternity leave, paternity leave, part-time partnerships, child care, and leave of absence or sabbatical. Overall, the findings were discouraging and point to continued dissonance for women struggling with heavy family and professional responsibilities.

The most widely offered benefits included disability insurance (64 per cent) and maternity leave (60 per cent). In contrast, only 7 per cent reported that their firm or office offered paternity leave benefits, reinforcing the expectation that the care of newborn children should rest with the woman. Also, the majority of employers and firms did not offer any child care arrangements to their lawyer-employees (98 per cent). Twenty-four per cent of lawyers reported that part-time work arrangements were available at their firm or office. Flexible hours (on a full-time basis) were reported to be offered at firms and offices by 39 per cent of respondents. However, only 7 per cent reported that job-sharing arrangements were offered by their firm or employer. Also rare were part-time partnerships, reported to be offered through law firms by only 8 per cent of the lawyers. Nor were leave arrangements widespread: only 31 per cent of respondents indicated that their firm or employer provided such benefits as leaves of absence or sabbaticals.

Interestingly, different employment settings offered varying degrees of workplace supports. Table 8.3 presents an overview of these variations. Government and private industry offered improved benefits on almost all

TABLE 8.3
Workplace Supports Available to Lawyers

| | No. of Lawyers at Workplace | | | | All Workplace Settings | | | | | |
| | | | | | Type of Workplace Setting | | | | Overall across Workplace Settings | P< |
Type of Support	<10	10–49	50+	P<	Law Firms	Government[a]	Private Industry[b]	Other[c]		
Disability insurance	41.5	70	91.7	.001	63.9	90.1	92.3	28.6	64.3	.001
Part-time work	10.7	25.7	39.5	.001	23.5	36.6	22.7	11.3	23.5	.001
Flexible working hours (full-time)	51.6	38.2	28.7	.001	41.3	43.5	44	22.4	39	.001
Job sharing	6.1	6.7	1.8	.01	4.8	24.8	3.3	2.8	7.3	.001
Maternity leave	32.2	67.4	95.4	.001	60.6	90	78.6	21.4	60.4	.001
Paternity leave	3.4	0.9	0.7	.05	1.9	24	16.9	6.2	6.9	.001
Part-time partnership	0.5	5.4	19.9	.001	7.9	—	—	—	5.5	.001
Child care	1	0.3	0.2	NS	0.6	5.1	4.6	1.4	1.7	.001
Leave of absence/Sabbatical	13.7	24.1	57.3	.001	30.1	60	25.2	8.2	30.9	.001
N	377	194	261		833	192	94	193	1312	

[a]Includes employees of government and those employed with Legal Aid or law clinic.
[b]Includes employees of corporations and those employed in private industry.
[c]Includes sole practitioners and those defining their practice as 'other work settings.' The majority of lawyers in this category are sole practitioners (82%).

types of workplace supports compared with the private practice of law. Part-time work, flexible working hours (on a full-time basis), job sharing, and leaves of absence are all more readily available in government employment than private practice. Ninety per cent of lawyers in government reported maternity leaves were available and an additional 24 per cent noted that paternity leaves were also available. In sharp contrast, 53 per cent of lawyers in private practice reported that their firm offered maternity leaves, and only 2 per cent said paternity leave options existed. Child care provisions were rare across all work settings, and rarer still in private law firms. Within private firm settings, larger law firms (over 50 lawyers) offered greater flexibility for part-time work (40 per cent), maternity leaves (95 per cent), part-time partnerships (20 per cent), and leaves of absence or sabbaticals (57 per cent). However, small- and mid-sized firms (fewer than ten lawyers and ten to forty-nine lawyers, respectively) offered greater opportunities for flexible work hours on a full-time basis (52 per cent and 38 per cent, respectively) compared with the large law firms (29 per cent). Job sharing and paternity leaves, although extremely uncommon, were slightly less rare in smaller law firms.

The lack of flexible work arrangements also surfaced in the comments of lawyers: 'Every women lawyer with children with whom I have discussed the matter has advised that it is very difficult to cope with child-rearing responsibilities with the demands of full-time practice. Quality of life seems to be more and more of an issue for men and women, and sometimes members of a firm who have made sacrifices in giving up family and recreational time and other activities are reluctant to allow others the flexibility of part-time, at-home or other alternative work style, even if compensation is adjusted accordingly. This can place a strain on working relationships. I think that it is vital that firms be prepared to try new approaches and flexible working arrangements.'

Another lawyer described the deficiencies of maternity leave plans as follows: 'I feel that one issue which is not addressed at all by the legal profession is providing flexibility for parents of young children, especially female parents, who end up with most of the responsibility. Maternity leave policies at most firms are ridiculous and draconian. Leaves based on numbers of years of service discriminate against the very people who are most likely to require leave – women of child-bearing years. When a woman is in the early years of practice, she is also in her prime child-bearing years. She should not be forced to postpone child-bearing in order to qualify for a reasonable length of maternity leave (6 months). If law firms would begin to support their employees in this area, they would find that they had grateful and loyal employees in the years after child-bearing. After all, a woman's productive years of lawyering number far more than her productive years of child-bearing.'

In a study of alternative work schedules, Mossman (1994b, 167) found that such opportunities have been available to women lawyers infrequently and that they have been even less available in private practice, especially in large law firms. Even when law firms and organizations provide maternity (and more broadly, parental) leaves or allow part-time work and job sharing, women who avail themselves of such innovations may discover they are perceived to be less committed as lawyers (Abramson and Franklin 1986; Pollock and Ramirez 1995). These options frequently are not actively encouraged and supported by the employer; rather they are viewed as a decision to divest from the organization, a decision that holds serious penalties in earnings and status (Hertz 1986, 122).

One woman lawyer in this study summarized the consequences for women with children: 'As a woman in private practice I do not see my career goals as being compatible with my hopes to have a family. I find the profession to be very male dominated despite the increasing number of women. My firm is predominantly male and no associate to my knowledge has ever had a child. The general issue is that in order to advance, make sure you don't have children. (This has actually been said by one of our partners to an associate engaged to be married.) Although it is certain that the male associates will become partners, I honestly believe that women who choose to have a family will become permanent associates.'

Career Transitions

The outcome of the balancing act between career and family is at times the decision to make changes in one's career, such as a transition to alternative forms of law practice that offer greater flexibility in work arrangements and improved benefits. In some cases, women may decide to leave law entirely. One woman who successfully negotiated a part-time partnership explained: 'While this decision to work part-time was approved by the partners, I believe that very little thought is given by the firm to the incredible stress imposed on the working mother who works full-time ... Hopefully with increasing numbers of women practising law, part-time work and flex hours will become more common. Most of the women I attended law school with and others whom I know practising law have left full-time practice in a private firm because of the inflexibility, i.e., balancing family and career obligations.'

Table 8.4 provides a descriptive picture of the early career moves traced in the survey of lawyers. Several aspects of the work histories are examined: the number of positions occupied, the type of employment pursued, and the level of employment at each position (full-time versus part-time, not in practice). I consider the first four professional positions because the sample is restricted to the first fifteen years of practice.

Nearly three-quarters of the lawyers in this sample had experienced some movement beyond their first professional position, with women having a slightly, but nonetheless significantly, higher average number of positions than men (2.35 and 2.27, respectively). Although the great majority of both men and women initially worked on a full-time basis, a slightly greater proportion of women compared with men began their first professional position on a part-time basis. As well, the proportion of women working part-time increased substantially with shifts in positions across careers. For example, about 3, 5, and 11 per cent of women respectively worked part-time in their first, second, and third positions. The figures for men are 0.9, 1.3, and 0.6 per cent (positions first through third, respectively). Most striking is the proportion of men and women who are not practising law. The difference peaks by the fourth position when 22 per cent of women are not practising, compared with 12 per cent of men.

Distributions of women and men across types of employment are also detailed by position in Table 8.4. The largest proportion of Ontario lawyers, close to 60 per cent of men and women, started their careers as associates. The percentage of lawyers working as associates declines in later positions, partly because of their success or failure in becoming partners. Twelve per cent of male lawyers, but less than 4 per cent of female lawyers, began their careers as partners. Men also moved towards partnership in fewer positions: nearly three times the proportion of men (29.4 per cent), compared with women (9.9 per cent) became partners within three moves from call to the bar.

Outside the private practice of law women are more likely to begin their careers as government employees, and at each successive position they are more likely than their male counterparts to find employment with government. About 11 per cent of women compared with 7 per cent of men started in government positions. In their second position, nearly 16 per cent of women compared with 10 per cent of men were employed in government. By their fourth position, the comparison peaks at about 25 per cent and 12 per cent, respectively. It is important to recall that government is more receptive to women lawyers with family responsibilities, offering improved maternity leaves and more flexible work schedules. Yet lawyers

TABLE 8.4
Characteristics of Lawyers' Work Histories by Gender

Employment Characteristics	Position	Male Lawyers				Female Lawyers			
		1	2	3	4	1	2	3	4
Level of Employment (%)									
Full-time		96.2	92.9	93.5	87.9	93.0	86.0	73.0	61.3
Part-time		0.9	1.3	0.6	0.0	2.6	5.1	11.3	16.4
Not practising		2.9	5.8	5.9	12.1	4.5	8.9	15.7	22.3
Type of Employment (%)									
Government		7.3	10.1	14.8	11.8	10.8	15.8	17.5	24.5
Corporation		3.5	5.5	8.5	11.3	3.9	7.8	8.6	4.8
Legal Aid/Law clinic		1.2	1.7	2.8	5.3	3.0	4.6	3.8	1.6
Private industry		0.4	0.7	0.5	0.0	0.2	1.7	1.3	1.5
Associate		60.0	28.9	22.6	24.0	58.4	32.4	20.6	16.2
Partner		12.1	26.3	29.4	24.3	3.5	12.7	9.9	10.2
Sole practitioner		8.6	15.2	12.0	7.5	7.2	8.2	12.6	10.4
Other		4.0	5.8	3.5	3.7	8.5	7.9	10.1	8.1
Not practising		2.9	5.8	5.9	12.1	4.5	8.9	15.7	22.3
No. of lawyers		1,110	785	388	149	467	329	173	77

in government undertake similar types of work to lawyers in private practice, including litigation, drafting, and negotiating agreements among multiple parties (Mossman 1994a, 69). Differences in the 'culture' of the work (i.e., a preoccupation with hours and billings) rather than the substantive content of the work may therefore make government employment more attractive to women. However, these transitions are not without their associated costs. One lawyer remarked: 'Many governmental lawyers (Legal Aid, municipal, etc.) are capable, hard working, and responsible. They have made career choices to leave time for family and other interests and are prepared to sacrifice advancement and financial achievement for these goals. Yet they are often significantly underpaid and have low status (largely undeserved).'

Conclusion

The research discussed in this chapter indicates that women lawyers experience role overload and conflict in attempting to balance their public (career) and private (family) lives. Many of them seek alternative positions to reduce this conflict, or leave the practice of law entirely. Interestingly, the public realm of law practice in government, rather than private practice, appears to be a more hospitable environment to women with significant family responsibilities. These gendered outcomes are not simply the product of individual choices among a range of possible career options. Rather, they reflect organizational constraints that limit the available options to women striving to manage demanding law practices and family commitments. As Brockman observed, 'Impediments systematically block access by women to certain positions, but they often appear to be, or are interpreted as, personal choices' (1992a, 51). The gender stratification of the legal profession also limits opportunities for men to participate more fully in family life. Conversely, women with families are often limited by their disproportionate familial responsibilities from contributing fully to their legal practice. For women, this conflict between their public and private sphere activities can be virtually intransigent (Hagan and Kay 1995, 117–18).

The effects of privatized home and child care responsibilities encourage women to maximize employment characteristics other than professional status or remuneration (e.g., more flexible working hours, improved workplace benefits) (Halliday 1986). The 'push' factors involved in leaving private practice and the 'pull' factors involved in attracting lawyers to non-private practice can be seen in the following quote: 'I do not enjoy private practice because of the stress level and the antagonism and competition that exists between the members of the private bar. Government is ideal for me because I find the work interesting, relations with co-workers and other lawyers more congenial, lower stress level, good benefits and the opportunity (admittedly rare) to work part-time. It is unfortunate that there are not more part-time job opportunities for lawyers both in government and private practice. I feel that I am lucky to have obtained a part-time position, although if I wish to change positions or advance within the government, I will have to return in all likelihood to working full-time.'

This chapter contributes to our understanding of gender inequities in professions by emphasizing the importance of workplace structures and processes in generating divergent gendered patterns. Women's strategies for arriving at a satisfactory balance between career and family (and hence role enhancement) are understood as attempts to reduce role conflicts resulting from the intersection of heavy family responsibilities and a culture of law practice that offers little flexibility in the organization of law practice. As one lawyer in the study commented: 'Most law firms do not accommodate lawyers who are not willing to commit to long hours of work, the "all or nothing" principle.' This 'all or nothing' principle is apparent in the lack of alternative work schedules available in many law firms. The availability of various forms of leaves and alternative schedules as well as their consequences for subsequent career advancement demand further examination. Future research should examine the career trajectories of men and women lawyers, with particular attention to the timing of childbearing, the sequencing of work and family demands, and the effects on job transitions. Scholars need to move beyond debates that focus attention on women's experiences of role conflict versus role enhancement, to a more complex appreciation of individuals' varying role commitments across the life course and the constraints of organizational structures in determining the range of options available to both men and women in the profession of law.

NOTES

I would like to acknowledge the support of the Social Sciences and Humanities Research Council of Canada, and the research assistance of Rachel Edgar and Kim Brooks.

1 Various structural and social factors often conspire to confine female lawyers to the less prestigious and financially rewarding forms of practice, a phenomenon known as the 'glass ceiling.'

2 A lawyer employed in a medium or large law firm generally works for about five to seven years as an associate before being invited into the partnership. During the period as an associate, the junior lawyer receives a salary from the firm, while gaining significant experience and legal skills under the supervision of senior lawyers of the firm. At the end of the 'untenured' period as associate, the lawyer is considered for partnership, a position that usually involves a sizeable increase in earnings, prestige, and authority, as well as a share in the profit of the firm (Galanter and Palay 1991). The once dominant 'up-or-out system,' by which associates were either invited to partnership or fired, is no longer as common, and many firms can no longer be described as a simple two-tier structure of partners and associates. Increasingly, many young associates find that they are neither promoted to partner nor 'let go' from the firm; rather, they find themselves in new categories of lawyer-employees, as permanent associates, staff lawyers, special counsel, or non-equity partners (Gilson and Mnookin 1989, 567).

3 Furthermore, Hagan and Kay (1995) found that differences in direct measures of family involvements, for example, hours spent on child care, do not mediate effects of gender on hours billed or earnings in the ways that may be expected. Rather, men gain billable hours as a result of hierarchical positions in firms and greater involvement in the decision making of the firm. These findings suggest differences in earnings and billings have more to do with social context within firms than competitive demands or comparative disadvantages that involve family demands (Hagan and Kay 1995, 152).

4 The sample criteria and survey design are described in detail elsewhere (Kay 1992, 1991).

5 Respondents were asked two questions. The first question asked: 'If you have children who require care (including feeding, supervision, attendance at sporting and school events): What proportion of responsibility for that care is borne by each of the following?' Response categories included the following: 'you, the person you live with, child's other parent (if not living with you), paid child care worker, or other.' Second, respondents were asked: 'How many hours per week do you spend on this care?'

6 The survey instrument was designed to address both heterosexual and same-sex relationships. Questionnaire items refer to the 'person you live with' and 'partner' rather than 'spouse,' the legal term that usually excludes same-sex relationships. All lawyers working full-time in the practice of law in the relevant period were included in the analysis of responsibilities for child care. In the subsequent analysis of the division of housework only lawyers who reported themselves to be 'married (including cohabitation)' were included in the analysis.

7 Individuals practising law were asked: 'When the children are at home (for med-

ical reasons, P.D. days or require transportation to activities) who leaves work most often?' Six response categories were provided: 'you, the person you live with, child's other parent (if not living with you), the person you live with and yourself leave work equally, one of us already works in the home, and there is someone else in the home (relative or paid employee).'

8 Lawyers currently practising law and either married or cohabiting were asked two questions with regard to housework. The first question was: 'Thinking about the jobs that need to be done to keep a home running (such as shopping, cooking, cleaning and planning, but excluding child care), how much of the work is shared between you and your partner?' The question provided six response categories: 'I do it all, I do most of it, we share it half and half, my partner does most of it, my partner does it all, and most of it is done by someone else (e.g., relative or paid employee).' The second question was: 'Do you feel the amount of housework your partner does is...' Four response categories were provided, including: 'too much, about right, not enough, and not applicable.'

REFERENCES

Abel, Richard L. 1989. 'Comparative Sociology of Legal Professions.' In Richard L. Abel and Philip S.C. Lewis, eds., *Lawyers in Society: Comparative Theories*, vol. 3. Berkeley: University of California Press, 80–153
– 1988a. 'Lawyers in the Civil Law World.' In Richard L. Abel and Philip S.C. Lewis, eds., *Lawyers in Society: The Civil Law World*, vol. 2. Berkeley: University of California Press, 1–53
– 1988b. 'United States: The Contradictions of Professionalism.' In Richard L. Abel and Philip S.C. Lewis, eds., *Lawyers in Society: The Common Law World*, vol. 1. Berkeley: University of California Press, 186–243
– 1986. 'The Transformation of the American Legal Profession.' *Law and Society Review* 20(1), 6–17
Abramson, Jill, and Barbara Franklin. 1986. *Where Are They Now: The Story of the Women of Harvard Law*. New York: Doubleday
Adam, Barry D., and Douglas E. Baer. 1984. 'The Social Mobility of Women and Men in the Ontario Legal Profession.' *Canadian Review of Sociology and Anthropology* 21(1), 21–45
Armstrong, Pat, and Hugh Armstrong. 1994. *The Double Ghetto: Canadian Women and Their Segregated Work*, 3rd ed. Toronto: McClelland and Stewart
Arthurs, Harry W., R. Weisman, and F.H. Zemans. 1987. 'The Canadian Legal Profession.' *American Bar Foundation Research Journal* 3, 447–519
Baruch, Grace K., Lois Biener, and Rosalind C. Barnett. 1985. 'Women and Gender

220 Fiona M. Kay

in Research on Stress.' Working Paper no. 152. Wellesley, Mass: Wellesley College, Center for Research on Women

Blau, Francine D., and Marianne A. Ferber. 1985. 'Women in the Labor Market: The Last Twenty Years.' *Women and Work: An Annual Review* 1, 19–49

Boston Bar Association. 1991. *Parenting and the Legal Profession: A Model for the Nineties*. A Report of the Boston Bar Association Task Force on Parenting and the Legal Profession. Boston: Boston Bar Association

Brockman, Joan. 1995. '"Exclusionary Tactics": The History of Women and Visible Minorities in the Legal Profession in British Columbia.' In Hamar Foster and John McLaren eds., *Essays in the History of Canadian Law, Vol. 6, British Columbia and the Yukon.* Toronto: University of Toronto Press for The Osgoode Society for Canadian Legal History, 508–61

– 1992a. '"Resistance by the Club" to the Feminization of the Legal Profession.' *Canadian Journal of Law and Society* 7(2), 47–92

– 1992b. 'Bias in the Legal Profession: Perceptions and Experiences.' *Alberta Law Review* 30(3), 747–808

– 1992c. 'Leaving the Practice of Law: The Wherefores and the Whys.' *Alberta Law Review* 32, 116–80

– Denise Evans, and Kerri Reid. 1992. 'Feminist Perspectives for the Study of Gender Bias in the Legal Profession.' *Canadian Journal of Women and the Law* 5, 37–62

Canadian Bar Association. 1993. *Touchstones for Change: Equality, Diversity and Accountability.* Ottawa: Canadian Bar Association Task Force Report

Chambers, David L. 1989. 'Accommodation and Satisfaction: Women and Men Lawyers and the Balance of Work and Family.' *Law and Social Inquiry* 14, 251–87

Cooney, Teresa M., and Peter Uhlenberg. 1989. 'Family-Building Patterns of Professional Women: A Comparison of Lawyers, Physicians, and Postsecondary Teachers.' *Journal of Marriage and the Family* 51, 749–58

Coverman, Shelley. 1989. 'Role Overload, Role Conflict, and Stress: Addressing Consequences of Multiple Role Demands.' *Social Forces* 67(4), 965–82

Curran, Barbara A. 1986. 'American Lawyers in the 1980s: A Profession in Transition.' *Law and Society Review* 20(1), 19–51

Dominion Bureau of Statistics. 1963. *Labour Force: Occupations by Sex, Canada and Provinces.* Ottawa: 1961 Census of Canada (vol. 3, part 1) Table 6 at 6-2 (cat. no. 94-717)

– 1953. *Labour Force: Occupations and Industries.* Ottawa: Minister of Trade and Commerce, Ninth Census of Canada (vol. 4)

Donovan, Kathleen. 1990. 'Women Associates' Advancement to Partner Status In Private Law Firms.' *Georgetown Journal of Legal Ethics* 4, 135–52

Elder, Glen H., Jr. 1985. 'Perspectives on the Life Course.' In Glen Elder, Jr, ed., *Life Course Dynamics: Trajectories and Transitions, 1968–1980*. Ithaca: Cornell University Press, 23–49

Epstein, Cynthia Fuchs. 1981. *Women in Law*. New York: Basic Books

Epstein, Scarlett. 1986. 'Time Management at Work and at Home.' In T.S. Epstein, K. Crehan, A. Gerzer, and J. Sass, eds., *Women, Work and Family in Britain and Germany*. London: Coom Helm, 3–22

Fox, Mary, and Sharlene Hesse-Biber. 1984. *Women at Work*. Boston: Mayfield

Galanter, Marc, and Thomas Palay. 1991. *The Tournament of Lawyers*. Chicago: University of Chicago Press

Gilson, Ronald J., and Robert H. Mnookin. 1989. 'Coming of Age in a Corporate Law Firm: The Economics of Associate Career Patterns.' *Stanford Law Review* 41(3), 567–95

Greer, Steven, and Colin Samson. 1993. 'Ethnic Minorities in the Legal Profession – A Case Study of the San Francisco Bar.' *Anglo-American Law Review* 22, 321–36

Hagan, John. 1990. 'The Gender Stratification of Income Inequality among Lawyers.' *Social Forces* 68(3), 835–55

– and Fiona Kay. 1995. *Gender in Practice: A Study of Lawyers' Lives*. New York: Oxford University Press

Hagan, John, Marie Huxter, and Patricia Parker. 1988. 'Class Structure and Legal Practice: Inequality and Mobility among Toronto Lawyers.' *Law and Society Review* 22(1), 501–50

Halliday, Terence C. 1986. 'Six Score Years and Ten: Demographic Transitions in the American Legal Profession, 1850–1980.' *Law and Society Review* 20(1), 54–76

Harrington, Mona. 1995. *Women Lawyers: Rewriting the Rules*. New York: Plume

Hertz, Rosanna. 1986. *More Equal than Others: Women and Men in Dual-Career Marriages*. Berkeley: University of California Press

Hessing, Melody. 1993. 'Mothers' Management of Their Combined Workloads: Clerical Work and Household Needs.' *Canadian Review of Sociology and Anthropology* 30(1), 37–63

Houseknecht, Sharon K., Suzanne Vaughan, and Anne S. Macke. 1984. 'Marital Disruption among Professional Women: The Timing of Career and Family Events.' *Social Problems* 31, 273–84

Jones, Charles, Lorna Marsden, and Lorne Tepperman. 1990. *Lives of Their Own: The Individualization of Women's Lives*. Toronto: Oxford University Press

Katz, Marsha. 1988. 'Have Women's Career and Family Values Changed?' In S. Rose and L. Larwood, eds., *Women's Careers: Pathways and Pitfalls*. New York: Praeger, 95–104

Kay, Fiona M. 1992. *A Profession in Transition: Gender and Career Mobility in Law.* Doctoral dissertation, University of Toronto

– 1991. *Transitions in the Ontario Legal Profession: A Survey of the Past Fifteen Years of Bar Admissions.* Report Submitted to the Law Society of Upper Canada, Toronto

– and John Hagan. 1995. 'The Persistent Glass Ceiling: Gendered Inequalities in the Earnings of Lawyers.' *British Journal of Sociology* 46(2), 179–310

– 1994. 'Changing Opportunities for Partnership for Men and Women Lawyers during the Transformation of the Modern Law Firm.' *Osgoode Hall Law Journal* 32(3), 413–56

Kidder, Robert L. 1983. *Connecting Law and Society: Introduction to Research and Theory.* Englewood Cliffs, NJ: Prentice-Hall

Kingston, Jennifer. 1988. 'Women in Law: The Glass Ceiling.' *American Bar Association Journal*, special issue, 1 June 49–75

Kopelman, R.E., J.H. Greenhaus, and T.F. Connolly. 1983. 'A Model of Work, Family, and Interrole Conflict: A Construct Validation Study.' *Organizational Behavior and Human Performance* 32, 198–215

Lennon, Mary Claire, and Sarah Rosenfield. 1994. 'Relative Fairness and the Division of Housework: The Importance of Options.' *American Journal of Sociology* 100(2), 506–31

Liefland, Linda. 1986. 'Career Patterns of Male and Female Lawyers.' *Buffalo Law Review* 35(2), 601–19

Meier, Jody. 1990. 'Sexual Harassment in Law Firms: Should Attorneys be Disciplined Under the Lawyer Codes?' *Georgetown Journal of Legal Ethics* 4, 169–88

Menkel-Meadow, Carrie. 1989. 'Feminization of the Legal Profession: The Comparative Sociology of Women Lawyers.' In Richard L. Abel and Philip S.C. Lewis, eds., *Lawyers in Society: Comparative Theories*, vol. 3. Berkeley: University of California Press, 196–255

– 1987. 'Excluded Voices: New Voices in the Legal Profession Making New Voices in Law.' *University of Miami Law Review* 42(7), 29–53

Meyer, John W. 1988. 'Levels of Analysis: The Life Course as a Cultural Construction.' In Matilda White Riley, ed., *Social Structures and Human Lives*. Newbury Park: Sage, 49–62

Morello, Karen Berger. 1986. *The Invisible Bar: The Woman Lawyer in America, 1638 to the Present.* New York: Random House

Mossman, Mary Jane. 1994a. 'Lawyers and Family Life: New Directions for the 1990's (Part One).' *Feminist Legal Studies* 2(1), 61–82

– 1994b. 'Lawyers and Family Life: New Directions for the 1990's (Part Two).' *Feminist Legal Studies* 2(2), 159–82

– 1993. 'Gender Bias and the Legal Profession: Challenges and Choices.' In Joan Brockman and Dorothy E. Chunn, eds., *Investigating Gender Bias in the Law*. Toronto: Thompson, 147–68

– 1988. '"Invisible" Constraints on Lawyering and Leadership: The Case of Women Lawyers.' *Ottawa Law Review* 20(3), 567–600

Neallani, Shelina. 1992. 'Women of Colour in the Legal Profession: Facing the Familiar Barriers of Race and Sex.' *Canadian Journal of Women and the Law* 5(1), 148–65

Nieva, Veronica. 1985. 'Work and Family Linkages.' *Women and Work* 1, 162–90

Pollock, Joycelyn M., and Barbara Ramirez. 1995. 'Women in the Legal Profession.' In Alida V. Merlo and Joycelyn M. Pollock, eds., *Women, Law, and Social Control*. Boston: Allyn and Bacon, 79–95

Reskin, Barbara, and Irene Padavic. 1994. *Women and Men at Work*. Thousand Oaks: Pine Forge Press

Rhode, Deborah L. 1994. 'Gender and Professional Roles.' *Fordham Law Review* 63, 39–72

Rindfuss, Ronald R., C. Gray Swicegood, and Rachel A. Rosenfeld. 1987. 'Disorder in the Life Course: How Common and Does It Matter?' *American Sociological Review* 52, 785–801

Rosenberg, Janet, Harry Perlstadt, and William R.F. Phillips. 1990. 'Politics, Feminism and Women's Professional Orientations: A Case Study of Women Lawyers.' *Women and Politics* 10(4), 19–47

Sander, Richard H., and E. Douglass Williams. 1989. 'Why Are There so Many Lawyers? Perspectives on a Turbulent Market.' *Law and Social Inquiry* 14(3), 431–79

Silver, Hilary, and Frances Goldscheider. 1994. 'Flexible Work and Housework: Work and Family Constraints on Women's Domestic Labor.' *Social Forces* 72(4), 1103–19

Skvoretz, John. 1984. 'Career Mobility as a Poisson Process: An Application to the Career Dynamics of Men and Women in the U.S. Office of the Comptroller of the Currency from the Civil War to World War II.' *Social Science Research* 13, 198–220

Stager, David A.A., and David K. Foot. 1988. 'Changes in Lawyers' Earnings: The Impact of Differentiation and Growth in the Canadian Legal Profession.' *Law and Social Inquiry* 13(1), 71–85

Statistics Canada. 1974. *Occupations by Sex for Canada and Provinces*. Ottawa: Minister of Industry, Trade and Commerce. 1971 Census of Canada (cat. no. 94-717, Vol. 3, Part 2, pp. 2-1, 2-3, and 2-5

Statistics Canada. 1993. *Occupation*. Ottawa: Industry, Science, and Technology Canada. 1991 Census of Canada (cat. no. 93-327), Table 1 at 6

Taber, Janet, Marguerite T. Grant, Mary T. Huser, Risë B. Norman, James R. Sutton, Clarence C. Wong, Louise E. Parker, and Claire Picard. 1988. 'Gender, Legal Education, and the Legal Profession: An Empirical Study of Stanford Law Students and Graduates.' *Stanford Law Review* 40, 1209–97

Taylor, Jan Cooper, and Barbara A. Spencer. 1988. 'Lifestyle Patterns of University Women: Implications for Family/Career Decision Modeling.' In Elizabeth B. Goldsmith, ed., *Work and Family: Theory, Research and Applications*, special issue of the *Journal of Social Behavior and Personality* 3(4), 265–78

Thorner, Abbie Willard. 1991. 'Gender and the Profession: The Search for Equal Access.' *Georgetown Journal of Legal Ethics* 4, 81–114

Vogt, Leona M. 1986. *Career Paths Study.* Cambridge, Mass.: Harvard University Law School

White, James J. 1967. 'Women in the Law. *Michigan Law Review* 65, 1051–1122

Williams, Joan C. 1990. 'Sameness Feminism and the Work/Family Conflict.' *New York Law School Law Review* 35, 347–60

PART 3
LEGAL REGULATION OF MOTHERHOOD:
CHILD CUSTODY AND CHILD WELFARE

9

'A Jury Dressed in Medical White and Judicial Black': Mothers with Mental Health Histories in Child Welfare and Custody

JUDITH MOSOFF

All those experts lined up in a jury dressed in medical white and judicial black – social workers, caseworkers, child guidance counsellors, psychiatrists, doctors, nurses, clinical psychologists, probation officers – all those cool knowing faces had caught her and bound her in their nets of jargon hung all with tiny barbed hooks that stuck in her flesh and leaked a slow weakening poison. She was marked with the bleeding stigmata of shame.

Piercy 1976, 60

Over the past two decades feminists have demonstrated how idealized conceptions of motherhood and family pervade the legal standard of 'the best interests of the child' in child custody and child welfare law (e.g., Arnup 1989; Boyd 1989; Fineman 1990; Kline 1993, 1992). As essentialist views of women's experience and forms of oppression were increasingly rejected (Butler 1989; Riley 1988; Spelman 1988), the analytical focus shifted to how the state and law operate in varying ways for different groups of women (Boyd 1994). At the forefront of discussions of the ways in which diversity matters are the 'differences' of class, race, and sexual identity, but the place of disability in this scholarship is much less developed (Begum 1992; Goundry 1994; Morris 1991). To consider what it means to be a mother with a disability, especially a psychiatric disability, is an important facet to an understanding of motherhood and family. This chapter outlines the ideas that dominate legal thinking in child welfare and child custody decisions where mothers have a psychiatric label. In particular I look at the ways in which the ideology of motherhood (Kline 1993; Oakley 1979;

Wearing 1984) influences psychiatric discourse, which in turn affects the application of the 'best interests of the child' standard in both child welfare and child custody law.

Legal decisions about children are characterized by a perceived distinction between the private nature of the family and the public nature of the state. In a formalistic sense, child welfare law represents a 'public' contest between parent and state when the private world of the family is seen as problematic for children. The child is the subject of the hearing and parents are portrayed only as interested legal actors with substantially fewer rights than a criminal accused (Thompson 1989; Toope 1991; Zybelberg 1992). The task of the court is to oversee an inquiry and discharge its responsibility to protect children. In this role, the state questions outright a woman's fitness, and psychiatric discourse operates directly to assist the state in proving that a child is 'at risk' and ought to be removed from a mother who has a psychiatric disorder.[1] Child welfare matters illustrate how, increasingly, the state controls people through administrative regulation (Chunn 1988; Rose 1987), especially where marginalized populations are concerned. Central to any successful administrative inquiry about entitlements and breaches of law are the actors cast by the state to engineer the regulatory systems, that is, social workers, unemployment counsellors, and financial aid workers. Mental health workers are pivotal in regulating people through the mental health system.

In contrast, child custody is constructed as a 'private' contest between parents in which adults are unable to agree on who should have custody of the children when the private world of the family is in disarray. Here the 'fitness' of a parent is not usually the issue that initiates proceedings, but it often quickly becomes the central question. The job of the court is to determine which of two private actors, usually a father and a mother, is the better parent to assume custody after separation in the 'best interests of the child.'[2] Despite current trends towards shared parenting and alternative dispute resolution, custody proceedings are explicitly adversarial and psychiatric evidence becomes a 'battle of the experts.' Within the context of a custody decision, the role of mother is perceived through a woman's more global status defined by her mental health label. Adjudicating who is a better parent often means that what a woman says or does is selectively rolled into her psychiatric label and an expert's mental health category or diagnosis becomes a ready vessel for a gendered interpretation of parenting.

In this chapter I argue that the separation between the public and private in legal decisions about children is ephemeral, especially when looking at the role of psychiatric discourse which operates in a similar way in both child welfare and child custody law. Psychiatric services are understood to be confidential, private therapeutic relationships usually dispensed by a publicly funded health system. Although therapy may be initiated in an effort to maintain the family, it may later be used by the state to remove children from the family or from one parent. Alternatively, psychiatric services may be purchased by the party with the greater private means, usually the father. Despite any apparent differences in the format of legal proceedings, judicial pronouncements about children clearly are made in the public sphere. Probably the most tenuous line between public and private contests is when women with mental health labels are involved in custody disputes. Because a mother's 'fitness' often becomes the focus, psychiatric evidence is usually the major aspect of the inquiry, much as it is in child welfare. Although child welfare proceedings are characterized by a more direct reach of the state into the lives of women, whereas custody proceedings unfold in a more obviously gendered way, psychiatric discourse works to buttress the ideology of motherhood in both arenas.

Since the nineteenth century psychiatry has evolved as an expert discourse and has pervaded Western culture in the realms of intimate relationships, work, family, and social policy. The disciplines of psychiatry and psychology[3] have become especially important in most child custody (Fineman 1988) and child welfare (Mosoff 1995) matters, but their power is clearly augmented when mothers are defined as mentally ill. Not only do psychiatrists and psychologists claim specialized scientific knowledge about child development, they are also the diagnosticians of pathological mental functioning in general. Therefore, it is roughly the same voice of authority that pronounces a woman as mentally disordered and that forecasts the risk for her child's well-being. Mental health experts are now powerful influences on the courts, particularly in areas central to women's lives. In addition to custody and child welfare, legal decisions in child abuse or 'false memory syndrome' cases are made on the basis of expert evidence arising from a psychiatric paradigm. In part, this chapter offers a critique of the apparent ease with which the courts accept psychiatric expert opinion. However, I do not suggest that all mothers should retain custody of their children regardless of their behaviour, but rather that judges should look to the equality rights of women with disabilities and examine the evidence of mental health experts with the same critical tools that courts use in other areas.

In this chapter I first outline important assumptions of psychiatric discourse that infuse the best interests test in both child welfare and child custody. Second, I describe two judicial decisions as case studies to illustrate the interpretive themes. Third, I discuss the power of psychiatric evidence in legal decisions about children, including two significant tensions: the paradox between motherhood and patienthood, and the relationship of psychiatry to the gendered dynamics of custody. Finally, I discuss the implications of the feminist strategy of the primary caregiver presumption for women with disabilities.

Psychiatric Discourse

Certain fundamental tenets of psychiatric discourse account for its powerful influence on the best interests test: the objectivity of science, the emphasis on the individual, techniques of assessment and typologies, the ability to predict, and hidden meanings of human behaviour. First, psychiatry and psychology position themselves in the realm of science and medicine. The roots of this knowledge evoke both the 'truth' of science and the 'compassion' of healing, a combination that is extremely persuasive in making decisions about children. Although many writers from a variety of disciplines have pointed out the difficulties of applying orthodox conceptions of science to the realm of human behaviour (Durkheim 1938; Harding 1991; Ingleby 1982; Prilleltensky 1989; Sarason 1981), the apparent truth that these disciplines offer depends on their image of objectivity.

Second, psychology and psychiatry use the individual rational person as the unit of analysis, an approach that makes psychiatric and psychological knowledge compatible with legal knowledge (Smart 1989, 17–20). Even when there is some recognition that social factors are relevant, typically the focus remains on personal weaknesses or defects. The individual is held responsible for not altering whatever social factors or systems would improve the particular situation, a form of reasoning that is common in child welfare cases (Kline 1993).

Third, although the type and formality of measurement varies widely and may include physiological measurements, interviews, or psychological tests, the psychiatric paradigm is organized around techniques of assessment as the critical starting point to understanding a person. Regardless of the procedure, the objective of an assessment is to categorize the individual according to a predefined taxonomy that is seen by the professionals to categorize or type people in a useful way. The taxonomy provides a means of saying whether a person is in the 'normal range' or the 'pathological range,' according to the framework. Particularly important is whether the person who falls in the pathological range is treatable, resistant, or simply not treatable at all. The inherent limitations of assessment are rarely expressed in an individual case. For example, assessments conducted for legal purposes are extreme oversimplifications in order to address the particular requirements of a legal standard (Bersoff 1992; Menzies 1989, especially chapter 3). As well, systems of categorization fail to recognize the historical and cultural basis of assessments, taxonomy, and the resulting conclusions about normalcy and pathology.[4] Compressing a complex picture into a straightforward category is one way of legitimizing the practice of diagnosis and prognosis. Paradoxically, at the same time that psychiatrists have narrowed the complexity of human experience to sharpen diagnoses, they have taken on a broader range of problems (Miles 1988; Scheff 1984; Wood 1983). The result has been to medicalize and pathologize a wider range of human experience under such diagnoses as 'anxiety' or 'depression' and to extend psychiatric influence and power (Busfield 1986; Scull 1979; Ussher 1991).

Fourth, this approach assumes that predictions or prognoses may be made on the basis of current assessments. In the mental health area, psychiatrists and psychologists were long viewed as uniquely competent to make predictions about such matters as an individual's dangerousness, general stability, and intellectual development, despite overwhelming evidence of the frailty of their predictions (Cocozza and Steadman 1976; Diamond 1974; Hinton 1983; Rosenhan 1973; Webster, Ben-Aron, and Hucker 1985). More recent work on risk assessment characterizes predictions of recidivism as an actuarial exercise and de-emphasizes the importance of psychiatrists as experts (Menzies, Chunn, and Webster 1992). The same line of criticism has not developed about assessments in child welfare and custody determinations. Whether or not there is any connection between the diagnosis of a mother and the interest of the child is a critical conclusion by a particular professional, but because assessments are conducted under a rubric of scientific objectivity, the potential biases of assessors are not calculated into the quality of an assessment (Caplan and Wilson 1990).

Finally, psychology and psychiatry purport that what is observable or obvious in human functioning is not necessarily a complete or even reliable version of what a person is really thinking, feeling, or likely to do. Repression, the important legacy of psychoanalytic theory, suggests that the hidden portion of a person's motivation, feeling, or thought is the darker, more negative aspect of personality. While at first blush, this idea seems inconsistent with psychiatry's reliance on assessments and observations to make scientific predictions about people, this contradiction serves to increase the mystification of psychological or psychiatric practice. What is submerged is not apparent to just anyone, but it can be detected by a psychologist or a psychiatrist who has the requisite knowledge and power to understand and interpret.

Relying on these tenets, psychiatric evidence operates quite bluntly in the child welfare context as scientifically based expert evidence that dovetails with the ideology of motherhood to undermine fitness. The evidence of professionals usually is presented as monolithic, specialized knowledge consistent with the state's suspicion that a woman is an inadequate mother.[5] On the surface, the so-called private child custody hearings contain psychiatric evidence in a more 'balanced' way, since both parties may raise mental health issues. Here, however, as we shall see, the tenets of the psychiatric paradigm allow the aura of scientific objectivity to legitimate a gendered interpretation of parenting and family life.

Case Studies[6]

The Children's Aid Society of Niagara Region v W.(C.A.): A 'Public Contest'

As is typical for child welfare cases, the Ontario decision in *The Children's Aid Society of Niagara Region v W.(C.A.)*[7] is short, unreported, and was not appealed. The mother, Ms W, came to the attention of the Children's Aid Society (hereinafter CAS) before the birth of her child because of the concerns of a public health nurse. Her alleged 'paranoia' was directed mostly at 'the helping agencies,' including hospitals and doctors. When the CAS worker visited the mother's home before the birth, she found few preparations for the child and learned that the mother had received an eviction notice. Even more worrisome to the social worker, the mother planned to have the baby in her apartment because she felt that a home birth would be healthier than a hospital birth. Concerned about the situation, the worker 'demanded' that the woman go to hospital 'under threat of obtaining an order under s.10 of the Mental Health Act,' an order that could lead to her involuntary commitment. 'After much persuasion' the woman went to hospital and gave birth to her child one week later.

The next day the child was apprehended. A series of court appearances followed. At one point the CAS agreed to return the child to the mother on condition that the mother have a psychiatric assessment, meet with a social worker weekly, have regular visits from a public health nurse, work with a parent aide, and see a pediatrician with the baby. According to the court, the mother did not carry out her part of the bargain. She rejected all of the help she had agreed to accept and displayed 'irrational' behaviour. Ms W had no support from her family or her common-law partner, who was with her briefly during this period and took no part in the legal proceedings. Eventually the CAS removed the baby over the mother's resistance during which police were used to assist. Subsequent to the apprehension, supervised access visits went poorly and Ms W became more distrustful of all the helping agencies. She worried about her baby's health and believed that the police, the community agencies, and the legal and health authorities were united in their efforts to separate her from her son. Eventually, home visits were terminated. Various workers continued to be involved with Ms W to help her with budgeting and parenting. Psychiatric and psychological assessments resulted in different diagnoses, but they agreed that long-term drug therapy was Ms W's best course. She refused the recommended medication. In the end, the court found that Ms W's psychiatric disability would be lifelong and granted a permanent order of custody to the CAS.

Lapierre v Lapierre: A 'Private Contest'

In the Saskatchewan case *Lapierre* v *Lapierre*,[8] the mother, Patricia Lapierre, was the primary caregiver for most of the lives of the two children, boys aged 10 and 7, at the time of the proceedings. Phillip Lapierre, an RCMP officer, had a second wife and lived in a different part of Saskatchewan than Patricia and the boys. He brought an application in 1991 to vary a custody order that had originally been made in favour of the mother in a 1983 divorce decree, on the basis of a change in circumstances. A homestudy[9] indicated that the children had a very negative view of their father and wanted to be with their mother. At the time of the variation hearing, the boys lived with Patricia, who also took care of her own elderly mother and attended classes at the University of Saskatchewan. The court described the boys as 'her life.' In the past Patricia had been diagnosed with a mood disorder, hospitalized for her condition, and prescribed Lithium and Prozac. The court ordered that custody be varied and given to the father, finding that the change in circumstances was that the children were older and more aware of the mother's unusual behaviour. One important and somewhat unusual feature of this case was that no psychiatric evidence was entered at the hearing. However, as will be shown, the absence of such evidence was central to the decision.

Power of Psychiatric Evidence in Deciding 'The Best Interests of the Child'

Credibility

Typically, the evidence of a psychiatrist or psychologist conflicts with the evidence of a mother who has been diagnosed as mentally ill, but there is really no contest as to who the court will believe. Despite the problems mentioned above with labels that may be either too wide or too simple, the mother's mental health status is often the central issue in a child welfare proceeding[10] or a custody case.[11] In *W.(C.A.)*, the child welfare case, the court acknowledged that Ms W had the right to refuse medication on her own behalf, but the refusal was significant in deciding whether she was a proper mother. Her failure to follow psychiatric advice was viewed as relating to what was in the best interests of the child. Any suspiciousness a woman might express about the helping professionals in her life is interpreted as further indication of the symptoms that characterize her mental illness.[12] When a woman disagrees with her psychiatrists about whether she requires treatment at all or what sort of treatment is best, her evidence is usually discounted. Refusing to take recommended psychotropic medication,[13] or even missing counselling appointments,[14] have been found to be indications that it is not in a child's best interests to remain with the mother.

Even when a judge hears evidence from a mother who has been labelled mentally disordered and the evidence seems to indicate that she would be fit to parent, psychiatry suggests that what is heard or seen from a person who is mentally disordered is not the whole picture. Ms W gave evidence over the better part of three days and clearly impressed the trial judge. She 'had a wide vocabulary and was well-able to express herself,' 'handled the strain very well,' and although she would accept other help, she rejected drug therapy. Nevertheless, her evidence that she was depressed because of separation from her child was rejected outright by the trial judge, who preferred the evidence of the expert psychiatrist and psychologist. They said that her condition was not situationally determined but rather indicated symptoms of an underlying mental disorder.

In *Lapierre*, the child custody case, the court considered it very important to evaluate Patricia Lapierre's parenting abilities by understanding her as a person 'in the context of her diagnosed mental illness.' The court seized on the issue of correct diagnosis, particularly a discrepancy between the diagnosis of depression made by the family doctor who gave evidence and a diagnosis of manic-depression apparently made by a psychiatrist and accepted by the judge at the hearing through 'consensual hearsay.' Just why the particular label was so important to the custody decision was completely unexplained.

What seemed to make Goldenberg J, the judge in *Lapierre*, virtually apoplectic was the absence of psychiatric evidence to assist him at trial. He stated: 'After much deliberation, I cannot conceive of one valid reason as to why I should have been prevented from seeing the whole picture of Patricia from a medical point of view.' The decision not to call psychiatric evidence was itself considered significant. According to Goldenberg J, each parent has a 'positive duty' to tell the court 'all about himself or herself.' To determine the best interests of the child, 'the good of the parent is certainly to be brought out. But so is the bad, so is the ugly.' In assessing the decision not to call psychiatric evidence, the judge seemed to feel that he had to decide whether Patricia was a rational litigant whose decision was calculated to prevent the court from making adverse findings about her, or whether her mental illness accounted for both the strategic decision and the substance of her evidence which he disbelieved. Either way, Patricia was unlikely to be perceived positively. Goldenberg J could not say 'that Patricia was in control of her actions,' and he was 'reluctant to say, absent psychiatric evidence, that she has lied,' but the 'failure to lead psychiatric evidence may cause me to have inclinations in that direction.' Without the official psychiatric translation of Patricia's evidence, the court was at sea as to whether the mother was sick or simply a liar. In Goldenberg J's own words: 'Were it not for the professional glimpses through wispy veils, I would have without any hesitation whatsoever, labelled Patricia as an out and out liar.'

Information about mental health is compelling to the court only when it comes from a properly qualified source. Although having insight about one's own mental illness is considered positive, too much psychiatric talk by the woman herself may be considered inappropriate and as a further symptom of her mental disorder.[15] Neither qualification as a medical doctor nor the professional credentials of a psychologist are, however, necessarily sufficient to ensure objectivity. The only medical evidence at trial about Patricia Lapierre's psychiatric condition came through her family doctor. Goldenberg J found that Dr Danilkewich did not have the specialized expertise that was required. Besides, the doctor was problematic because she was a close friend of Patricia's and godmother to one child. Because of the personal connection, the court gave little weight to Dr Danilkewich's evidence that Patricia was a good mother. A psychologist was not viewed as an appropriate expert because, like Dr Danilkewich, he was Patricia's friend. These witnesses were perceived not to be objective enough to carry scientific weight. They were disqualified to describe her parenting because they knew her and liked her, although the decision is silent about whether they were part of her support network.

Mental health information that comes from an explicitly feminist source may be particularly ambiguous for the courts. Although the expert may have the requisite qualifications, a feminist analysis is seen as biased and unscientific. In *G.E.C.* v *M.B.A.C.*,[16] Dr Susan Penfold, a well-known feminist psychiatrist, was consulted on questions of alleged sexual abuse by the father and a possibility that the mother had a 'borderline personality disorder and consciously misinterpreted or unconsciously fabricated events' to limit the father's access to the young girl. In her written report to court, Dr Penfold found little support for such motivations by the mother. Instead, Dr Penfold proposed another dimension for the court's consideration: that 'gender bias' or 'mother-blaming' was operating in this case. Seemingly offended by such a suggestion, the court said: 'With all due respect to Dr Penfold, it may be that her "suggestion" for the Court on this point was itself motivated by bias on her part ... The value of Dr Penfold's evidence was also limited by the fact that her report was prepared from a perspective that was more political than professional. In accordance with her feminist viewpoint she gave the benefit of every doubt to Ms D but accorded the opposite treatment to Mr C. She stopped short of reaching conclusions or recommendations that would come to grips with the particular people and issues before her, taking the easier option of throwing up a "suggestion" based on her experience as a member of a task force on family violence.'

Despite the fact that in *viva voce* evidence Dr Penfold was conservative in her opinion and urged caution in reaching conclusions about sexual abuse in such questionable circumstances, her expertise was completely undermined. By being explicit about gendered dynamics, Dr Penfold violated a cardinal ideological rule. According to the court, she was not 'objective' and not an acceptable expert. Not surprisingly, her power as a psychiatrist was assumed to be apolitical. However her feminist analysis so tainted her opinion that it was rendered into political rhetoric.

Motherhood Versus Patienthood

The law presumes the natural healthy family to be a private, self-reliant, autonomous unit that is heterosexual, able-bodied, and nuclear (Chunn 1988, 138; Gavigan 1988, 293). Whenever there is a need for assistance from the state, the family is considered less than ideal. The ideology of motherhood embodies the notion that a good mother is entirely unselfish and prescribes an ideal motherly temperament that is patient at all times and never angry (Wearing 1984, 72). Ideological demands for autonomy and selflessness create special problems for mothers with psychiatric disabilities because of conflicting requirements of being a 'good' mother and a 'good' patient. In contrast to the expectation of motherly selflessness, an ideal patient of the mental health system should be introspective and self-absorbed in an effort to get better. To this end a person must be dependent on the mental health system at least to the extent prescribed by the authorities.

The stark reality is that mothers with psychiatric disabilities are rarely able to meet the demands of autonomy and selflessness. They are almost certainly poorer than their male partners, or they are typically single parents who rely on financial support from the state. At the *Lapierre* hearing, Patricia had a Legal Aid lawyer while Phillip had private counsel. In *W.(C.A.)*, Ms W lived on a modest disability pension. Walmsley, ACJ remarked: 'Often she would find herself out of funds a few days after getting her cheque. Her rent is often unpaid and Carrie routinely receives eviction notices.' What is considered 'selfish' when a mother is labelled mentally ill is an interpretation that fuses ideas about motherhood with a judgment about a woman's compliance with psychiatric opinion. According to Walmsley ACJ, Ms W related to her son 'in terms of her own emotional needs, was impatient of his needs.' In *Lapierre* the court found that by taking herself off medication, Patricia was at best exercising very bad judgment and, at worst, putting herself first. In the opinion of the court she was 'unable to put the needs of the children ahead of her own.' For women with psychiatric disabilities, the requisite selflessness may mean extreme self-sacrifice, including the possibility of relinquishing children for their benefit.

This romanticized aspect of motherhood is demonstrated by *Re: Brown* where the court commented on parental sacrifice of children to the state: 'Perhaps out of their love for these children someday will come an understanding that this sacrifice was made for their benefit. Sometimes love demands extreme sacrifice; the mother who uses her body as a shield to protect her young ones from the bombs of war, the parents who endure starvation in order to feed their children.'[17]

Is there a resolution to this conundrum? Probably not. A classic 'sick role' exempts people from blame for their deviance temporarily, but the exemption depends on the person actively seeking to recover (Parsons 1979, 176–7). 'Actively seeking to recover' means that a woman must act in ways that may be antithetical to ideal motherhood. Already perceived as dependent, patienthood demands even more reliance on the state by way of the supports of the mental health system. As well, the required therapeutic process may mean that a woman will disclose her true, ambivalent, and perhaps not-very-nice-feelings about her children and her role as mother. Admitting these feelings is fatal to the woman as a 'good mother.' This 'damned if you do' and 'damned if you don't' scenario inevitably results in alternating mother-blaming and patient-blaming.

Although widely held ideas of mothering may account for mother-blaming in general, mental health professionals engage in 'mother-blaming' because of certain fundamental aspects of the paradigm in which they work (Caplan and Hall-McCorquodale 1985; Chesler 1972). Psychological and psychiatric theories of motherhood have explained and blamed mothers for such diverse things as asthma, schizophrenia, and autism in children (Penfold and Walker 1983, 124–40). By relying on empirical evidence generated by a 'scientific method,' psychiatry concludes that 'maternal deprivation' is an objective answer to why children are maladjusted.

A good example is John Bowlby's early 'scientific' work on attachment and maternal deprivation that used children who had experienced long-term hospitalization (Bowlby 1969; Tizard 1986). Despite its flaws, widespread criticism, and bizarre ultimate applications, this research is still used to criticize day care for young children. Bowlby concluded that families failed because full-time employment of the mother was on a par with such conditions as the death or imprisonment of a parent, social calamity, war, or famine. Clearly overreaching, Bowlby concluded that maternal deprivation meant anything less than full-time motherhood. While there may be some minor commentary on how fathers affect their children's development, and a new ideological construction of fatherhood may influence social scientific research on fathers in different directions than on mothers (Drakich 1989), there is simply no male equivalent for 'the schizophregenic mother' or 'the overprotective mother.' The schizophregenic mother has been defined as inadequate, domineering, more involved in pursuits outside the home, cold, and emotionally detached. The overprotective mother is seen to be as rejecting of her child as the schizophregenic mother, but she demonstrates her hostility in another way by excessively coddling or pampering the child (Penfold and Walker 1983, 129).

Gendered Dynamics

Most child custody disputes are between a mother and a father and gendered power dynamics often arise (Fineman 1988). There has been heightened attention in recent years to the importance of preserving fathers' relationships with children with a corresponding onus on mothers to facilitate these relationships (Bourque 1995; Drakich 1989). When evidence indicates that children are not interested in spending time with their father or when a mother may expose her children to 'severe domestic disharmony,'[18] or the court finds that a mother's suspicions that a father abused children are unfounded,[19] judges tend to process the findings through psychiatric discourse.

In *Lapierre*, for example, the court found that the children's love for the father was being eroded by the mother and that Patricia's attitude towards Phillip had severely impaired her ability to function as a parent. Phillip was portrayed very differently. When Phillip described the financial and logistical difficulties in exercising access, Goldenberg J 'noted his sadness, his anguish.' As to the entire custody proceeding, 'Phillip was prepared to give up the custody claim and settle for more access if she would stop making him look bad to the boys. To me this is an indicator of a parent who is prepared to put the interests of the boys first.'

Ms Birbeck, author of a homestudy in the *Lapierre* case, reported that the older child, Brett, had told her that the father had pushed him off a ski-doo and laughed when he picked up the child. Phillip's common-law wife, Barbara, had said she heard Kurt, the younger child, make disparaging comments about his father, and Kurt said his mother had used this language. Within this web of hearsay, Goldenberg J made rather extraordinary findings about the significance of this evidence. The ski-doo incident was an accident that happened in the course of father-son 'rough and tumble' play, but Brett's interpretation of the accident came from Patricia's influence. It was 'admissible evidence to support Ms Birbeck's conclusion that Patricia's parenting has been such that the boys have been denied the right that every child should have, the right to feel loved by, and to love, both of his or her parents.' The alleged disparaging comment by Kurt was simply 'another example of Patricia's parenting being directed at depriving the boys of their natural right to love and be loved by their father,' because Goldenberg J rejected 'even a suggestion that Phillip is a heartless uncaring father.' There are, clearly, other possible interpretations of the boys' stories to Ms Birbeck. How is it that Goldenberg J was so sure that the stories originated in the mother's attitude and actions?

When mothers are unhappy with their children's contact with the father or refuse to facilitate access because they worry about how the father treats them, they are viewed as contributing to the downfall of already fractured family relations. A readily available and culturally acceptable explanation for such behaviour is an existing diagnosis such as paranoia, borderline per-sonality, or some other psychiatric designation. Phillip had a practical problem seeing the boys because he lived in a different part of the province than they did, a not unusual scenario. The decision did not identify any obstacles that Patricia had put in the way of Phillip's access to the boys during their separation, but she had not told him that during the court pro-ceedings the boys were staying within walking distance of their father. Despite Patricia's unremarkable record in relation to Phillip's access in the past, Goldenberg J saw her failure to disclose where the boys were staying during the trial as another startling indication of Patricia turning the boys against their father. He stated that he could not 'comprehend how any liv-ing human being who really cared for the boys could do such a thing to them. I am left to wonder if such a person really cared, or if such a person was in touch with reality.' Without the benefit of a proper psychiatric translation of her actions, he was torn between questioning her mothering or her sanity.

Where the gender dynamics are altered, the interpretation is different. If a father whose mental health is at issue interferes with access to a mother, he can expect a slap on the wrist from the courts but little more. In *Beck* v *Beck*,[20] both a clinical social worker and the author of a homestudy sug-gested that the father had a psychiatric disorder. For all of their lives, the mother had been the primary caregiver, but the children (then 14, 11, and 9 years of age) wanted to live with their father. With the exception of Mr Beck and one other witness who was a friend of the father, all witnesses described Mrs Beck as a competent parent, but many raised concerns about the father. In granting sole custody to the father, Mullally J noted that although it may be true that the children had turned against their mother because of their father's influence, 'Mrs Beck has failed to maintain their love, affection and respect.' Unlike the warnings that judges regularly give to women who are viewed as turning their children against their father, Mullally J refused to police the father's behaviour and said that 'neither the Court, nor anyone else can stand guard over Mr Beck in order to have him refrain from criticizing his wife.'

Summary

Mental health experts are entrusted with an individual's most 'private' thoughts, feelings, and memories in their role as therapists. By invoking mental health experts and the courts to resolve matters about children, the otherwise private relationship is moved to the public domain whether the matter is child welfare or custody. As state actors, psychiatrists interpret and translate the words of their patients for the courts. It is difficult to imagine a more silencing process.

In child welfare cases, the private therapist–client relationship coexists with the public responsibility to report risk to children. The courts must decide whether a mother is unfit where the other option is that the state assumes the role of parent. One apparently less radical step than to disqualify the mother is for the court to order the family to be monitored by the watchful eye of the mental health system (Mosoff 1995). On the surface these cases represent 'victories' for women compared with decisions that their children must be taken into care, but in reality, they amount to a different way for public authorities to regulate the family. Rather than a court order that the formal child protection authority assume the parental role and remove the child from the private sphere of the family, the court perpetuates an illusion that the privacy of the family is intact. However, the integrity of that family is obviously tenuous and depends entirely on the opinion of state-sanctioned experts authorized to scrutinize the family on an ongoing basis. They are officially qualified to look beyond an unremarkable exterior.

In a so-called private custody case, the proceeding resembles the 'public' child protection process when a mother's psychiatric status is raised. Expert opinion is invoked or relied upon in this public sphere to speak to a mother's fitness. The public/private line is further blurred by the potential use of private financial resources to purchase psychiatric opinions. Because men usually earn more money, they are able to buy more psychiatric opinions, therapies, and resources. Mothers may therefore be discredited as mentally ill in custody hearings even when there is no previous psychiatric history because of the wealthier party's easier access to resources. In short, the 'best interests of the child' standard is such a pliable concept that decisions are almost inevitably shaped by the input of mental health professionals when a mother has a mental health label. The same malleability characterizes the concept of 'fitness' that is linked to the primary caregiver presumption.

The Primary Caregiver Presumption: In Whose Best Interests?

In response to concerns about the 'best interests of the child' standard, some feminists have suggested that the primary caregiver presumption be used in custody disputes (e.g., Boyd 1990; Smart and Sevenhuijsen 1989). This strategy grew out of a concern that mothers' caregiving was overlooked and undervalued, particularly when any aspersions were cast against her, relating to, for example, her sexuality, financial stability, employment, mental stability, or promiscuity. The primary caregiver presumption provides an advantage in law to the parent who presents better evidence of a history of caring for the child. Part of the rationale for adopting the presumption in the custody context is to avoid severing the fundamental caregiving relationship (Neely 1985). A critical caveat is that the primary caregiver must be found to be 'fit' by the court.

This strategy may be useful for many women involved in private custody disputes. However, it does little to strengthen the position of women with mental health histories who are engaged in child protection or custody battles. Ideas about fitness will remain fundamentally unchallenged with this presumption, and assumptions about the type of mothering engaged in by women with mental health histories are likely to continue to permeate judicial decision making. Judges have particular views of women with psychiatric histories and both the best interests test and the primary caregiver presumption provide a vehicle to expound these views. What might otherwise be considered intensely 'motherly' comments or actions may be considered to be further evidence of irrationality and unfitness in the context of a psychiatric diagnosis.[21] For example, excessive worry about a child's health is probably epidemic in mothers. However, according to the judges in their cases, both Ms W and Patricia Lapierre had irrational concerns about their children's health that were especially significant because of their psychiatric labels.[22] Ms W's concerns about her child's food and health were symptomatic of her paranoia, pathologized even more because she refused to accept medical reassurance. Although Goldenberg J was 'left with the understanding that when the children were younger, perhaps Phillip did not pay as much attention to their allergies as he might have,' the discussion about Patricia Lapierre's worries about her children's allergies to bee stings attributed her concerns either to her illness or her animosity to Phillip.

In its brief on *Child Custody and Access Policy*, the Canadian Advisory Council on the Status of Women (hereinafter CACSW) supports in principle the presumption of the primary caregiver in Canada and anticipates the way that the 'fitness' question may become a 'gaping hole' (Sack 1992) in the strategy. The report recommends that the presumption not be based on a 'list of tasks' as in the leading U.S. case, *Garska* v *McCoy*,[23] but should take into account 'all of the physical, emotional, social, and relational tasks of parenting' (CACSW 1994, 14). This departure from the list of factors approach is intended, in part, to avoid undervaluing the parenting work that women with physical disabilities perform in managing others who carry out certain tasks. In addition, the report says that the primary caregiver presumption should not be rebutted simply because a woman is receiving psychiatric care. Although such an effort to limit the legal vulnerability of women with mental health histories to being deemed unfit because they have received psychiatric care are laudable, it is not enough. It will not, for example, help those mothers who are criticized for not accepting psychiatric treatment. It was Ms W's refusal to accept the psychiatric paradigm that led to threats of her civil commitment and the apprehension of her baby almost immediately after birth.

It may also be harder for women with disabilities to establish that they were or are, in fact, the child's primary caregiver. A disabled mother's caregiving in such activities as 'planning and preparing meals' or even 'teaching elementary skills' may be construed as less important if others assist her, regardless of whether the requisite help is physical because a mobility impairment makes it difficult to tie a toddler's shoes or mental because an intellectual handicap makes it difficult to teach arithmetic. Academic literature on parenting complicates matters further by dividing caring functions into two categories: physical labour and nurturing functions (Bernard 1974, 112). The physical-nurturing caring distinction is especially problematic for women with mental disabilities.[24] Using the physical-nurturing distinction of caring work, women with physical disabilities might successfully argue that supplementary care could accommodate their needs: as long as the physical aspects of caring are done through supplementary care, they are able to perform the more important nurturing component. The woman with a physical disability just might, then, overcome the dissonance between her situation and the ideal of the self-reliant family. She may keep her child with state assistance because supplementary care, a legitimate function of social work (Swift 1991), can provide a discrete answer to a specific need. The same is not true of mental disability. The length and type of supplementary care that would accommodate the needs of mothers with mental disabilities is less predictable and courts are more likely to challenge their capacity to provide adequate nurturing to their children. For this reason, women with mental disabilities are more likely to find agencies and courts expressing more severe reactions to concerns about caring by acting to protect children in child welfare matters or finding another caregiver in custody cases. In the words of Walmsley ACJ, Ms W was seen to have 'a *lifelong psychiatric pensionable* disability that would prevent her from *ever* caring for Simon' (emphasis added).

Exactly how the presumption of the primary caregiver will affect women, especially mothers with disabilities, may also be different in the 'private' and 'public' spheres. Custody disputes, while ostensibly private in nature, become more public for women with mental health histories, because of the power of psychiatry and the ideology of unfit mothers surrounding the proceeding. In custody decisions, an emphasis on primary caregiving may be used easily against mothers with mental health histories. Although caregiving by mothers is undervalued in general (Boyd this volume), caregiving by mothers with mental health histories may either be completely discounted or may be interpreted as a further symptom of mental disorder. The latter result is especially likely when there is psychiatric evidence to deem caregiving obsessional or when there is another woman in the father's life who can assume the caregiving role, as was the case with Phillip Lapierre's common-law wife. For eight years Patricia Lapierre was the primary caregiver of the children, yet her work was summarily dismissed. In fact, there was a negative connotation to the children being 'her life.'

The implications of the primary caregiver presumption for child welfare cases involving women with mental health histories is less clear. On the one hand, the concept seems to make little sense in this context because there are not two parents competing to show which is the more 'fit' parent. The mother *is* usually the primary caregiver, often the only caregiver, with the state buttressed by psychiatry trying to terminate the relationship. Conceivably, the primary caregiver presumption could assist mothers with mental health histories by supporting the importance of maintaining the primary relationship. However, this interpretation is unlikely. The overwhelming power of a psychiatric label and the nuances of how judges perceive child rearing through the lens of an ideology of motherhood are likely to disadvantage mothers with mental health histories in child protection proceedings.

Perhaps the only presumption that would aid a mother with a mental health history is an explicit presumption in favour of mothers. For obvious reasons, that is not a realistic option. Among other things, it has no application to same-sex parents. A different approach would see these cases, not through the applications of rules or presumptions, but rather as questions involving equality and human rights. The duty not to discriminate against women on the basis of mental disability may require judges to see that mothering and nurturing may be performed in different ways. Particularly in the context of child welfare proceedings, where the public nature of the dispute is more obvious and the resources of the state are rallied against the women in her role as mother, judges should bear in mind section 15 of the

Canadian Charter of Rights and Freedoms. A vision of substantive equality, that looked beyond the surface to equality of conditions,[25] would give rise to the responsibility to attempt to accommodate the differences of women with mental disabilities wherever possible, in order to allow them to raise their children. While this resolution will not always be possible, an equality approach would mean that judges should not be quick to decide against a women with a mental health history.

Conclusion

The cultural standards for being an ideal mother are difficult for anyone to meet. For women with disabilities they present special difficulties. A common thread between child welfare and custody matters is a strong view of the ideal mother and family, around which psychiatric discourse and legal standards coalesce. One of the tenets of the ideology of motherhood is that being a mother is a fundamental part of being a woman. However women are required to be mothers, or permitted the privilege (Molloy 1992) of motherhood, only if they are deemed to be 'fit.' Women with disabilities have had a painful history of dangerous experimental contraceptives, non-consensual sterilizations, coercive abortions, and social policies about family life that do not contemplate women with disabilities as mothers (Asch and Fine 1988, 297; Blackford 1993; Goundry 1994). This wide-ranging interference with fertility, pregnancy, and parenting attests to the social presumption that women with disabilities are not fit mothers. A psychiatric disability is especially problematic because of 'the riches English gives to scientific officialdom for expressing its uncertainty, doubt, reservation, its lack of commitment to "fact" while it ponderously asserts privileged truth' (Mays 1995, 172). The judicial focus on diagnosis, the lingering stigmatizing labels of psychiatry, and reliance on mental health professionals to explain what behaviour 'really' means, all generate continuing questions about a mother's fitness, often long after the events that lead to the original diagnosis.

The power of psychiatry obliterates the distinction between public child welfare and private custody disputes for women with mental disabilities. In contests over their children, the voices of mothers with mental health histories are both absent in the courts and overlooked in feminist strategizing. In using the best interests of the child standard, the courts defer to mental health experts when confronted with a mother with a mental health label. The previously private relationship between a mother and her therapist is subject to public scrutiny. Besides being unable to rebut the presumption

of unfitness to mother that a psychiatric label creates, the woman is faced
with the conflict of being at once a good patient and a good mother. The
presumption of the primary caregiver, in an effort to be gender neutral, is
not much better in that it does nothing to displace the presumptions created by a psychiatric label.

Mothers with mental health histories are unlikely to benefit from any
presumption designed to benefit the 'average' woman in custody disputes:
they are not 'average,' and their differences are repeatedly used to disadvantage them in their attempts to raise their children. In determining questions about children where mothers have a mental health label, the courts
should be keenly aware of the bases of psychiatric opinion and its powerful
impact. Judges should test this evidence scrupulously, bearing in mind the
constitutional guarantees of equality before the law for all persons with
disabilities. Otherwise, decisions about children where mothers have psychiatric labels will continue to be made by a jury dressed in medical white
as well as judicial black.

NOTES

I would like to thank Isabel Grant, Fiona Kay, Marilyn MacCrimmon, and Jim
Russell, all of whom read earlier drafts of this chapter and made helpful suggestions,
and especially Susan Boyd, who has been a painstaking, gentle, and ever-patient edi-
tor. As well, I am grateful for the invaluable research assistance of Chantal Morton,
Debra Parkes, and Gillian Calder.

 1 British Columbia: Family and Child Service Act, 1980, c. 11. In Ontario, the
   Child and Family Services Act, RSO 1990, c. C11, amended by SO 1992, c. 32, s.
   3, 1993, c. 27, s. 37 states that children will be apprehended if in need of protection and that need will be determined in the best interests of the child defined
   within the Act. The Ontario Act, s. 14(3)(a) refers to 'a parent's emotional condition, mental condition, mental deficiency or use of alcohol or drugs' in its definition.
 2 Divorce Act, RSC 1985, c. 3 (2nd Supp.), ss. 16 and 17; in British Columbia the
   Family Relations Act, RSBC 1979, c. 121, s. 24; and in Ontario, the Children's
   Law Reform Act, RSO 1990, c. C12, amended by SO 1992, c. 32., s. 4, 1993, c.
   27, s. 24.
 3 I use the terms 'psychiatrist/psychologist' and 'psychiatry/psychology' inter-
   changeably to refer to a range of mental health personnel and models. There are,
   however, important distinctions between psychiatrists and other mental health
   personnel because of psychiatry's explicit training in a medical model and the

important duties delegated to physicians or psychiatrists in mental health legislation.

4 For a pointed example of the ways that pathology is socially defined and the
roles of experts in contributing to social consensus, see the American Psychiatric Association (1974) 'Position Statement on Homosexuality and Human
Rights,' *American Journal of Psychiatry* 131, 497, describing the American Psychiatric Association polling its members about removing homosexuality from
the diagnostic system.

5 In the rare cases that a particular mental health professional confirms the
mother's evidence to the court, and disagrees with other experts where the
state's evidence is that she is unfit, courts may make some effort to integrate the
favourable mental health professional's view with the overall state psychiatric
evidence. See *New Brunswick (Minister of Health and Community Services)* v
N.J.C. (1990), 239 APR 316 (NBQB).

6 My observations in this chapter are based on a review of approximately 200
Canadian reported and unreported child welfare and custody decisions between
1985 and 1994 where there was an issue relating to a mother's mental health.

7 [1987] OJ No. 1838 (Ont. Gen. Div.).

8 [1991] SJ No. 387 (Sask. QB).

9 Used in the generic sense, a homestudy refers to an investigation and analysis of
a home environment for the purpose of a decision about children, such as to
provide information for determinations of custody, access, foster placement, or
adoption. Homestudy reports, usually carried out by social workers or counsellors, vary widely in what is considered to be pertinent information. In some
cases the term is used in a more legal sense and refers to a statutory provision or
court ordered investigation, e.g., the Family Relations Act, *supra* note 2, s. 15.

10 See *N.B.* v *N.J.C. supra* note 5; *N.P.* v *B.C. (Superintendent of Family and Child
Service)* [1992] BCJ No. 1828; *Minister of Social Services* v *V.S.* (1985) 69 NSR
435 [mother diagnosed with schizophrenia]; *CAS (Pictou)* v *L.P. and R.P.*
(1986), 72 NSR (2d) 164 [mother diagnosed with manic-depression].

11 See *Galay* v *Bott*, [1994] BCJ No. 155 [bi-polar disorder]; *G.E.C.* v *M.B.A.C.*,
[1993] BCJ No. 1393 (BCSC) [paranoia]; *Kaemmele* v *Jewson*, [1992] OJ No.
970 (Gen. Div.) [cyclothamic disorder]; *Mitchell* v *Mitchell*, [1994] OJ No. 1311
(Ont. Gen. Div).

12 In my experience as a mental health lawyer representing people at civil commitment hearings, persons who express distrust of their 'treatment team' are likely
to be labelled as even more 'paranoid.'

13 *CAS Niagara* v *W.(C.A.) supra* note 7; *N.B.* v *N.J.C. supra* note 5; *New Brunswick (Minister of Health and Community Services)* v *C.(N.)* (1987), 9 RFL (3d)
332 (NBQB).

14 *P.E.I. (Director of Child Welfare)* v *H.(D.)*, [1989] PEIJ No. 60.

15 *Turner* v *Turner*, [1991] NSJ No. 104 (NSSC – Trial Div.).

16 *Supra* note 11.

17 (1975) 2 RFL 315 at 316.

18 See *R.J.* v *D.J.* [1993] SJ No. 590 (QB), where the court found that although a highly intelligent mother with a psychiatric disability diagnosed as a 'personality disorder' alleged that their father had sexually abused the two daughters, loved her children, and had never physically abused them, she was unable to care for them without impairing their functioning or exposing them to 'severe domestic disharmony.'

19 *G.E.C.* v *M.B.A.C.*, *supra* note 11; *Rodgers* v *Rodgers* [1987] BCJ No. 739 (BCSC); *G.(G.L.)* v *G.(S.P.)* [1986] BCJ No. 2334 (BCSC).

20 [1992] PEI N9. 43 (PEISC).

21 In *H.(D.)*, *supra* note 14, e.g., the mother's evidence about her child was interpreted through the lens of a psychiatric diagnosis rather than heard as the expression of the sentiments of any number of mothers. She further stated that 'she would kill herself if she lost F, she had nothing else to live for. She considers suicide to be a rational act on her part because F is her life.'

22 An extreme example is when overattentiveness to a child's health is given a psychiatric diagnosis. In *Guppy* v *Guppy* [1992] NJ No. 133 (Fam. Ct.), the child had severe asthma. The possibility was raised that the mother had Münchhausen syndrome by proxy, a condition where the person becomes convinced that a child has a certain sickness and by persuasion induces in the child the reality of it so that she can seek medical attention.

23 278 SE 2d 357 (W. Va. 1981). According to this leading American case, the caring and nurturing duties that the trial court must determine in deciding who the primary caregiver was include (1) preparing and planning of meals; (2) bathing, grooming, and dressing; (3) purchasing, cleaning, and care of clothes; (4) medical care, including nursing and trips to physicians; (5) arranging for social interaction among peers after school; (6) arranging alternative care, i.e., babysitting, daycare, etc.; (7) putting child to bed at night, attending to child in the middle of the night, waking child in the morning; (8) disciplining, i.e., teaching general manners and toilet training; (9) educating, i.e., religious, cultural, social etc.; and (10) teaching elementary skills, i.e., reading, writing, and arithmetic.

24 See American neglect cases that forbid a presumption that a physical disability creates an inadequacy but do not apply the same rule to mental disability. In *Re Jeannie Q.* 31 Cal. App. 3rd 709 [2nd Dist Ct. App. 1973].

25 See *Andrews* v *Law Society of B.C.* (1989) 10 CHRR D/5719 (SCC), at 5738–44, where McIntyre J rejected formal equality as an inadequate idea of equality.

REFERENCES

American Psychiatric Association. 1974. 'Position Statement on Homosexuality and Human Rights.' *American Journal of Psychiatry* 131(4), 497

Arnup, Katherine. 1989. '"Mothers Just Like Others": Lesbians, Divorce and Child Custody in Canada.' *Canadian Journal of Women and the Law* 3(1), 18–32

Asch, Adrienne, and Michelle Fine. 1988. 'Shared Dreams: A Left Perspective on Disability Rights and Reproductive Rights.' In Michelle Fine and Adrienne Asch, eds., *Women with Disabilities: Essays in Psychology, Culture, and Politics*. Philadelphia: Temple University Press, 297–305

Begum, Nasa. 1992. 'Disabled Women and the Feminist Agenda.' *Feminist Review* 40, 70–84

Bernard, Jessie Shirley. 1974. *The Future of Motherhood*. New York: Dial Press

Bersoff, Donald N. 1992. 'Judicial Deference to Nonlegal Decisionmakers: Imposing Simplistic Solutions on Problems of Cognitive Complexity in Mental Disability Law.' *Southern Methodist University Law Review* 46, 329–72

Blackford, Karen A. 1993. 'Erasing Mothers with Disabilities through Canadian Family-related Policy.' *Disability, Handicap and Society* 8, 281–94

Bourque, Dawn M. 1995. '"Reconstructing" The Patriarchal Nuclear Family: Recent Developments in Child Custody and Access in Canada.' *Canadian Journal of Law and Society* 10, 1–24

Bowlby, John. 1969. *Attachment and Loss, vol. 1–3*. New York: Basic Books

Boyd, Susan B. 1994. '(Re)Placing the State: Family, Law and Oppression.' *Canadian Journal of Law and Society*, 9, 39–73

– 1990. 'Potentialities and Perils of the Primary Caregiver Presumption.' *Canadian Family Law Quarterly* 7, 1–30

– 1989. 'Child Custody, Ideologies and Employment.' *Canadian Journal of Women and the Law* 3(1), 111–33

Busfield, Joan. 1986. *Managing Madness: Changing Ideas and Practice*. London: Hutchinson

Butler, Judith. 1989. *Gender Trouble: Feminism and the Subversion of Identity*. New York: Routledge

Canadian Advisory Council on the Status of Women. 1994. *Child Custody and Access Policy: A Brief to the Federal/Provincial/Territorial Family Law Committee*. Ottawa: Canadian Advisory Council on the Status of Women

Caplan, Paula J., and Ian Hall-McCorquodale. 1985. 'Mother-blaming in Major Clinical Journals.' *American Journal of Orthopsychiatry* 55, 345–53

Caplan, Paula J., and Jeffery Wilson. 1990. 'Assessing the Child Custody Assessors.' *Reports of Family Law* 27(3d), 121–34

Chesler, Phyllis. 1972. *Women and Madness*. New York: Avon

Chunn, Dorothy. 1988. 'Rehabilitating Deviant Families Through Family Courts: The Birth of "Socialized" Justice in Ontario, 1920–1940.' *International Journal of the Sociology of Law* 16, 137–58

Cocozza, Joseph J., and Henry J. Steadman. 1976. 'The Failure of Psychiatric Predictions of Dangerousness: Clear and Convincing Evidence.' *Rutgers Law Review* 29, 1084–1101

Diamond, Bernard L. 1974. 'The Psychiatric Prediction of Dangerousness.' *University of Pennsylvania Law Review* 123, 439–52

Drakich, Janice. 1989. 'In Search of the Better Parent: The Social Construction of Ideologies of Fatherhood.' *Canadian Journal of Women and the Law* 3(1), 69–87

Durkheim, Emile. 1938. *The Rules of Sociological Method.* London: Collier Macmillan

Fineman, Martha Albertson. 1990. 'Images of Mothers in Poverty Discourses.' *Duke Law Journal* 2, 274–95

– 1988. 'Dominant Discourse, Professional Language and Legal Change in Child Custody Decision-making.' *Harvard Law Review* 101, 727–74

Gavigan, Shelley A.M. 1988. 'Law, Gender and Ideology.' In Ann Bayefsky, ed., *Legal Theory Meets Legal Practice.* Edmonton: Academic Printing and Publishing, 283–95

Goundry, Sandra A. 1994. *Women, Disability and the Law: Identifying Barriers to Equality in the Law of Non-Consensual Sterilization, Child Welfare and Sexual Assault.* Manitoba: Canadian Disability Rights Council

Harding, Sandra. 1991. *Whose Science? Whose Knowledge?* Ithaca: Cornell University Press

Hinton, John. 1983. *Dangerousness: Problems of Assessment and Prediction.* London: Allen and Unwin

Ingleby, David. 1982. *Critical Psychiatry: The Politics of Mental Health.* Harmondsworth: Penguin

Kline, Marlee. 1993 'Complicating the Ideology of Motherhood: Child Welfare Law and First Nation Women.' *Queen's Law Journal* 18, 306–42

– 1992. 'Child Welfare Law, "Best Interests of the Child" Ideology and First Nations.' *Osgoode Hall Law Journal* 30, 375–425

Mays, John Bentley. 1995. *In the Jaws of Black Dogs: A Memoir of Depression.* Toronto: Penguin

Menzies, Robert J. 1989. *Survival of the Sanest: Order and Disorder in a Pre-Trial Psychiatric Clinic.* Toronto: University of Toronto Press

– Dorothy E. Chunn, and Christopher D. Webster. 1992. 'Risky Business: The Classification of Dangerous People in the Canadian Carceral Enterprise.' In Kevin R.E. McCormick and Livy Visano, eds., *Canadian Penology: Advanced Perspectives and Research.* Toronto: Canadian Scholars Press, 61–93

Miles, Angela. 1988. *The Neurotic Woman: The Role of Gender in Psychiatric Illness*. New York: New York University Press

Molloy, Maureen. 1992. 'Citizenship, Property and Bodies: Discourses on Gender and the Inter-War Labour Government in New Zealand.' *Gender and History* 1, 293–304

Morris, Jenny. 1991. *Pride against Prejudice*. London: Women's Press

Mosoff, Judith. 1995. 'Motherhood, Madness and Law.' *University of Toronto Law Journal* 45, 107–42

Neely, Richard. 1985. 'The Primary Caretaker Parent Rule: Child Custody and the Dynamics of Greed.' *Yale Law and Policy Review* 3, 168–86

Oakley, Ann. 1979. *Becoming a Mother*. Oxford: Martin Robertson

Parsons, Talcott. 1979. 'Definitions of Health and Illness in the Light of American Values and Social Structure.' In E. Gartly Jaco, ed., *Patients, Physicians and Illness: A Sourcebook in Behavioral Science and Health*. New York: Free Press, 120–44

Penfold, P. Susan, and Gillian A. Walker. 1983. *Women and the Psychiatric Paradox*. Montreal: Eden Press

Piercy, Marge. 1976. *Woman on the Edge of Time*. New York: Ballantine

Prilleltensky, Isaac. 1989. 'Psychology and the Status Quo.' *American Psychologist* 44(5), 795–802

Riley, Denise. 1988. *'Am I that Name?' Feminism and the Category of 'Women' in History*. London: Macmillan

Rose, Nikolas. 1987. 'Beyond the Public/Private Division: Law, Power and the Family.' *Journal of Law and Society* 14, 61–76

Rosenhan, D.L. 1973. 'On Being Sane in Insane Places.' *Science* 179, 250–8

Sack, Laura. 1992. 'Women and Children First: A Feminist Analysis of the Primary Caretaker Standard in Child Custody Cases.' *Yale Journal of Law and Feminism* 4, 291–328

Sarason, Seymour. 1981. *Psychology Misdirected*. New York: Free Press

Scheff, Thomas. 1984. *Being Mentally Ill: A Sociological Theory*. New York: Aldine

Scull, Andrew. 1979. *Museums of Madness: The Social Organization of Madness in Nineteenth Century England*. London: Allen Lane

Smart, Carol. 1989. *Feminism and the Power of Law*. London, New York: Routledge

Smart, Carol, and Selma Sevenhuijsen, eds. 1989. *Child Custody and the Politics of Gender*. London and New York: Routledge

Spelman, Elizabeth V. 1988. *Inessential Woman: Problems of Exclusion in Feminist Thought*. Boston: Beacon Press

Swift, Karen. 1991. 'Contradictions in Child Welfare: Neglect and Responsibility.' In Carol T. Baines, Patricia M. Evans, and Sheila M. Neysmith, eds., *Women's*

Caring: Feminist Perspectives on Social Welfare. Toronto: McClelland and Stewart, 234–71

Thompson, Rollie A. 1989. 'Why Hasn't the Charter Mattered in Child Protection?' *Canadian Journal of Family Law* 8, 133–63

Tizard, B. 1986. 'The Care of Young Children.' In *Thomas Coram Research Unit Working and Occasional Papers*. London: University of London Institute of Education

Toope, Stephen J. 1991. 'Riding the Fences: Courts, Charter Rights and Family Law.' *Canadian Journal of Family Law* 9, 55–96

Ussher, Jane M. 1991. *Women's Madness: Mysogyny or Mental Illness*. Amherst: University of Massachusetts Press

Wearing, Betsy. 1984. *The Ideology of Motherhood: A Study of Sydney Suburban Mothers*. Sydney: Allen and Unwin

Webster, Christopher, M. Ben-Aron, and S. Hucker. 1985. *Dangerousness, Probability and Prediction: Psychiatry and Public Policy*. New York: Cambridge University Press

Wood, Garth. 1983. *The Myth of Neurosis*. London: Macmillan

Zylberberg, Philip. 1992. 'Minimal Constitutional Guarantees in Child Protection Cases.' *Canadian Journal of Family Law* 10, 257–81

10

Looking beyond *Tyabji*: Employed Mothers, Lifestyles, and Child Custody Law

SUSAN B. BOYD

In March 1994 a high-profile member of the British Columbia legislature lost custody of her three children to her estranged husband. The custody decision rested mainly on the grounds that Judy Tyabji had a more 'aggressive' career-oriented lifestyle than the father, Kim Sandana, who lived in the rural outskirts of Kelowna and worked in a grocery store. Tyabji had left Sandana after she became intimately involved with Gordon Wilson, then leader of the B.C. Liberals. Wilson eventually was ousted as leader, and Tyabji resigned as Liberal house leader. They then began their own political party, the Progressive Democratic Alliance, and subsequently married.

Tyabji's 'public' life was viewed as impeding her ability to function adequately in the 'private' sphere, an interesting reversal of the oft-quoted fact that women's role in the 'private' family sphere impedes them from moving into 'public' office. The case invoked considerable discussion in the media and elsewhere of the repercussions for mothers who work in demanding careers. Some female journalists who interviewed me about the case were apprehensive about its implications for their own potential custody disputes. Other commentators applauded this type of case[1] for entertaining the possibility that men could be recognized as appropriate custodial parents in an apparently gender-neutral fashion.[2] In mid-October 1994 Tyabji appeared on the Oprah Winfrey show to discuss her case and, according to newspaper accounts, portrayed herself as a working woman unfairly penalized by the courts for having a political career. She said that 'she would have quit her job in order to keep custody of her three children.'[3] In a related development, the female prosecutor in the O.J. Simpson case was challenged for custody of her children by their father who argued that her career was too demanding (Mayer 1995).

These fact situations raise difficult questions concerning caregiving in heterosexual families, work outside the home, law, and social change. All of these questions are related to the gendered aspects of public/private ideology. Feminist research on child custody law has revealed that women's caregiving labour in heterosexual families has tended to be undervalued at the same time as it is expected and taken for granted under the ideology of motherhood (Boyd 1989a; Fineman 1995; Smart and Sevenhuijsen 1989). This contradictory dynamic prevails even in the current era of ostensibly gender-neutral family law. An ideology of motherhood continues to be reproduced in custody and access decision making, albeit in a more subtle and contradictory manner than in earlier decades (Boyd 1995).

By reviewing the relationship between labour force participation and familial roles, I consider in this chapter whether the *Tyabji* case represents a progressive new era of gender-neutral custody law, or whether it reinforces earlier trends that undervalue women's labour. This question is related to another issue: has the gendered nature of the public/private, work/family divide been transcended as women's labour force participation and visibility in careers such as politics have increased, or is the divide reasserting itself in more complex and subtle ways? Although Judy Tyabji is not necessarily a 'typical' mother, the dynamics in her case reveal the contested nature of concepts such as 'mother,' 'father,' and 'gender,' and the difficulty that law has in dealing with those shifting discourses.

One question that I will *not* try to answer is whether Tyabji should or should not have received custody. Custody judgments are very stylized, so that by reading them we learn more about the way that judges rationalize their decisions than about the best interests of the (particular) children (Millbank 1994). As well, the highly indeterminate nature of the 'best interests of the child' principle has been clearly revealed (Mnookin 1975). This statutory principle relies heavily on the discretion of individual judges for elaboration with reference to particular fact situations. Researchers have demonstrated the extent to which factors such as race and sexual orientation affect the application of the best interests principle: families and individuals who depart from a white, middle-class, heterosexual normative model generally have not been treated neutrally by legal decision makers (e.g., Arnup 1989; Chunn 1992; Kline 1993, 1992). This research raises serious questions about whether the best interests principle ever can be applied neutrally. It also suggests that the purportedly protected value of family privacy is highly contingent on factors such as race, sexual orientation, class, and disability. As Mosoff points out in this volume, once custody affairs reach the stage of judicial decision making, little remains private, particularly once a mother's 'fitness' becomes the focus. As well, the *Tyabji* case illustrates the extent to which we live in an era where less and less of people's lives can be private (Thompson 1990, 238), especially in the case of public figures such as Judy Tyabji and Gordon Wilson. The open-book nature of their lives and the role of the media in constructing their personalities were instrumental in this case.

The judge in *Tyabji* spent a lot of time explaining why Tyabji was unreliable, why her testimony was not credible, and why she had acted against the best interests of the children. These assessments are related to her dramatic entry as a mother of young children into the 'public' sphere of politics: the expectation that mothers should be selfless in the private sphere of family was flouted by Tyabji. Men who enter politics, on the other hand, may leave employment in the private sphere, but are not viewed as abandoning their families in the same way as women, precisely because the expectations of them in the family realm are lower. Neutrality in this context becomes an oxymoron, and it is often impossible in analysing judicial decision making in the custody realm to 'really' know what the 'correct' decision would have been. It is, then, at the level of discourses on the relationship between paid work, lifestyles, gender, credibility, and parenting – and the disciplining effect of these discourses – that the *Tyabji* case is of importance to my analysis.

Gender Relations, Gendered Work, and Custody Law

In the modern Canadian custody statutes that have emerged since 1970 judges are directed to make decisions in contested child custody cases by considering what arrangement will be in the best interests of the child(ren) in question.[4] Without the help of guidelines such as the paternal preference of the nineteenth century, or the earlier twentieth century presumption that children of tender years should be with mothers unless they were 'unfit,' judges of necessity must exercise a great deal of discretion in making custody decisions. Value judgments related to expectations of appropriate maternal and paternal behaviour can often be detected in judicial efforts to clarify the indeterminacy of the best interests principle in any given case. These value judgments are connected to the ideologies of motherhood and fatherhood embedded in the normative model of 'family' that characterizes Western industrialized countries such as Canada (Boyd 1989a, 1989b; Girdner 1986). This model of family in turn reproduces power relations related to race, class, sexual orientation, and disability, as well as gender (Kline 1993; Millbank 1992, 1994; Mosoff 1994; Roberts 1993).

Mothers who are employed in the 'public' sphere outside the home tend to be assessed by judges and other legal actors as less than ideal, unless it is felt that they have no choice but to work because of their class position. In that case they may be excused from the normative exigencies of motherhood (Boyd 1989a; Teghtsoonian 1995). Other mothers who in some way depart from that idealized image, such as lesbian mothers or mothers with disabilities, also encounter difficulties in measuring up to the ideal (Arnup 1989; Millbank this volume; Mosoff 1994). The 'ideal' mother remains a middle- or upper-class, stay-at-home mother who devotes herself to her children's interests (and probably those of their father's), who puts her own interests second, or third, and who therefore performs her role within the context of the patriarchal heterosexual nuclear family (Boyd 1996; Fineman 1995). Her work in the private sphere of the heterosexual family, although ideologically valued as a key aspect of womanhood, remains unpaid and undervalued (Armstrong and Armstrong 1994). While in a relationship with a man, mothers' roles in the public sphere therefore tend to be viewed as inconsistent with those in the self-sacrificing private sphere, in that they challenge a mother's exclusive devotion to her children and their father. At the same time, post-divorce mothers may be expected to become self-sufficient by seeking work in the public sphere, rather than relying on their ex-partners for support. The contradictions of the ideology of motherhood and the ideology of equality become clear in this context (Boyd 1989a).[5]

Employed mothers are often constructed as selfish and as putting their own interests first, despite the fact that many two-parent, heterosexual families today have both parents in the labour force at least partly in order to make ends meet. The notion of a family wage – one wage that could support a family – no longer exists, if it ever did, and its applicability was always limited (Armstrong and Armstrong 1994; Gavigan 1993, 598–600). In Canada in 1988 both parents were employed in 58 per cent of two-parent heterosexual families with children under age 13. In 1991, 4.6 per cent of dual-earner families had incomes that fell below Statistics Canada's low income cut-off points, and thus they were likely living below the poverty line. Without the contribution of the female partner's earnings, the low-income incidence among these families would have been almost 18 per cent. Earnings of women were even more crucial (to avoid poverty) in young families with the female partner under 35 years of age (Lero and Johnson 1994, 12; Statistics Canada 1995, 35). Even the analysis in this paragraph, implying that mothers work because they need to rather than because they want to, is derived from an expectation that mothers will normally devote themselves to their families (Teghtsoonian 1995).

If mothers demonstrate a willingness to compromise their public sphere activity, for example, by taking part-time work instead of full-time (which women do disproportionately to men) (Ghalam 1993, 21), they may be regarded somewhat more positively by judges in custody cases (Boyd 1989a). Judicial reinforcement of the ideology of motherhood thus accommodates changes in the external conditions of mothering. It is often assumed, however, that the male partners of mothers who participate in the public sphere of the paid labour force share child care more or less equally; in other words, that they reciprocate by turning their attention away from the public sphere, to some degree, and towards the private sphere of family. Any preference for mothers on the basis that they are primary caregivers of the children may thus dissipate. This phenomenon occurs *despite* the studies demonstrating that women – whether employed or not – are still overwhelmingly responsible for child care and domestic labour in heterosexual households. Ninety-five per cent of women with children under 5 provide primary child care on a daily basis, compared with 69 per cent of men (Lero and Johnson 1994, 8). In dual-earner married couples in which both parents were employed full-time, the majority of wives (52 per cent) retained all responsibility for daily housework (some of which is related to child care), while 28 per cent had most responsibility. Equal sharing of housework was reported in 10 per cent of these families, and in the remaining 10 per cent the husband had all or most of the responsibility (Marshall 1993, 26; see also Hessing 1993). Armstrong and Armstrong pointed out that many of the time-budget studies that produce these figures do not take account of the constant responsibility that caregiving of children involves (1994, 114). Women's responsibility for child care and household labour may therefore be consistently underreported.

At another level, men have not been assessed as parents from the same starting point as women, either legally or culturally. Men are, as fathers, *expected* to be in the public labour force. The normative assumption is that men contribute to their family and children in this way. Any activity that they perform in the private sphere of home and family is therefore regarded as somewhat 'extra' to the normal expectations of them (Girdner 1986, 174) and is often applauded in judicial decision making (Boyd 1989a), as well as by neighbours and casual observers. There is tremendous pressure on women to prove that they care *about* children by caring *for* them. Men can more easily convince others, such as judges and mediators, that they care about their children without necessarily doing the service work (Smart 1991). They can more easily show, without appearing to abdicate their responsibilities, that the service work will be covered by offering a new female partner, a grandmother (as in *Tyabji*) or a sister (Boyd 1989a).

Objectivity or neutrality in the assessment of maternal and paternal behaviour is, therefore, very difficult to achieve, and, I suggest, far more difficult than the judiciary is prepared to admit. The *Tyabji* case provides a focus for examining whether gender neutral assessment of mothers and fathers in the realm of custody law is possible, even where they apparently have swapped their public and private gender assignments.

The *Tyabji* Case

Judy Tyabji and Kim Sandana had agreed before the custody trial that the children (a son aged 5 and two daughters aged 4 and 1)[6] should not be split up by a court award. An interim order awarded temporary custody to Tyabji for the six-month period before the final judgment. Two court-appointed expert witnesses (Dr Baerg, a family court counsellor, and Dr Lea, a registered psychologist) recommended that custody should stay with Tyabji.

The trial judge, Spencer J, did not directly address the fact that Judy Tyabji left her four-year marriage with Kim Sandana in a public and dramatic way to live with Gordon Wilson, an act that had invoked considerable public disapproval. As he pointed out, a custody award is not supposed to punish the parent who receives access rather than custody. He did, however, say that a parent's behaviour might affect the award: 'Responsibility for breaking up the marriage, where it lies clearly with one side more than the other, is not necessarily a test for awarding custody. It is relevant only if it shows that one parent or the other pursued, and will continue to pursue, his or her self-interest to the detriment of the children, or if it shows that one or the other is less believable on oath, it may result in that parent's evidence bearing upon custody receiving less weight' (*Tyabji*, 269). Tyabji failed on both counts, as we shall see.

In keeping with recent trends in custody law, Spencer J attempted to write gender out of his decision making altogether: 'Stereotypical gender views have no place in an award of custody ... Custody will not be awarded on the basis of any pre-conceived idea about daughters being with mothers and sons with fathers, or about age-appropriate placements, or about the rights of working parents of either sex not to be deprived of custody simply because they have a particular career path. In every case the court must determine the best interests of the children and all else must give way to that' (ibid. 270). However, Spencer J went on to say that he was nonetheless 'alive to the common sense suggestion that, often, small children will have formed a stronger emotional and physical bond with their mothers' (ibid.). This notion must be weighed against any evidence to the contrary as well as any evidence showing that 'as strong a bond has since formed with the other parent, or that the probable futures of the parents puts one, rather than the other, in a position better to serve the best interests of the children from the time of the trial onwards' (ibid.).

On both factors of 'subsequent bonding' and 'probable futures,' Spencer J determined that bonding with Tyabji had diminished in importance. This determination led him to decide the case in direct contradiction to the opinions of the expert witnesses, which is relatively unusual, although the ultimate decision always rests with the court (Bala 1990, 219). Spencer J said that, like himself, the experts had found it difficult to choose between the parents, both of whom had deep love for the children and had much to offer them, albeit in quite different ways. Therefore, the experts had made their recommendations based on 'theoretical principles' (*Tyabji*, 271). These principles were somewhat problematic because they included the tender years doctrine and a preference for a two-parent (opposite sex presumably) norm, at least in the case of expert Dr Lea.[7] In general, however, the experts appeared to decide on the basis of Tyabji's role as the 'historical emotional caregiver' and her 'broader perspective on the children's needs.'[8] Spencer J departed from their opinions for five main reasons that I analyse in detail below (my numbering differs slightly from his in order to organize the discussion more clearly): (1) involvement in child care and 'bonding'; (2) probable futures and stability; (3) mother exaggerates complaints: cats and in-laws; (4) characters and careers; and (5) lifestyles.

Spencer J was satisfied that each parent offered a more than satisfactory level of love, guidance, and security to the children, and he therefore felt that there was little to differentiate between them. It is often in the apparently hard custody cases such as this one that the ideological dimensions of custody decision making emerge more visibly. In Spencer J's rationalization of his decision to grant custody to Sandana, despite the expert opinions, the issue of Tyabji's 'career and ambition' enters the scene.

Involvement in Child Care and 'Bonding'

Spencer J found that although Kim Sandana was relatively uninvolved in the oldest child's care until he was about 1 year old, he had since that time been actively involved with the boy and the other children. Tyabji disagreed with this assessment of the father's involvement (as many women do),[9] but Spencer J preferred Sandana's evidence. This preference was partly because of Tyabji's earlier comments to the press about her role as an MLA being 'more than a full-time job,' 'almost a 24 hour-a-day, seven-days-a-week job' (ibid. 272). Tyabji protested that the quote was taken out of context, but Spencer J concluded: 'That quote, taken with the other evidence from both sides, satisfies me that the demands of her work as an MLA have resulted in the mother spending less time with the children from her election in October 1991 up to the interim custody order of September 3, 1993, than did the father' (ibid. 272).

In addition, Tyabji's earlier efforts to calm her political public – not all of whom were happy with her entry into politics as a young mother – about the implications of her career for the care of her children were held against her in the custody determination. In particular, her statements to the public that the children were growing 'much closer to [her] husband as a result of [her] work' were used. She said that while her 'first priority always has and always will be my family,' her husband was 'at home with them almost every minute that I am away.' Later she added, 'I find myself happier with my role, and therefore a better mother, because I am doing something suited to my nature' (ibid. 272). The overall impact of these quotes on Spencer J was to demonstrate Sandana's involvement in child care, not Tyabji's commitment as a mother nor her pleasure in combining public and private roles.

Further, Tyabji's role in organizing care for the children by locating a nanny was negated by the fact that Spencer J found that the father primarily instructed the nanny about the children's needs in their Kelowna home. Sandana was found to have been 'actively involved in caring for the children in a hands-on way' (ibid. 273). As well, based on a detailed counting of days in which the children were in the father's care and in the mother's care after her election, Spencer J found that 'the children were more used to being in the family home with their father and the nanny than with their mother and that it was of assistance to the mother in her career that they be there' (ibid. 274). He also found that Tyabji's credibility as a witness was deficient (ibid. 273–4) and that the evidence of her friends was less reliable than that of Mrs Brown, the nanny who worked in the Kelowna home (and who admitted that she was disenchanted with Tyabji) (ibid. 276). He was 'persuaded that Mrs Brown's recollection that the mother, when at home in Kelowna, spent a great deal of time in and about her constituency business while the father was responsible for the children's care, is correct' (ibid. 274).

Probable Futures and Stability

Spencer J's other main reason for awarding custody to Sandana was a consideration of the children's future, although he noted that it is always difficult to predict. He chose to look at the short term rather than the long term. The fact that Sandana could offer the family home and community that the children had lived in until the interim order was key: 'If they are in their father's custody, the children can look forward to staying at his home in the rural outskirts of Kelowna for the foreseeable future' (ibid. 274).

The apparent flexibility of Sandana's schedule was also viewed as a benefit. He worked full-time at a grocery store from 2:00 p.m. to 10:00 p.m. five days a week, with Tuesdays and Thursdays off. The former nanny would provide care on weekends when he worked. He would also be helped by his mother who lived next door, except when her market garden business consumed her energies from approximately April until an undefined date (presumably in the fall). At that point, Sandana would obtain another nanny for three days a week in addition to the weekend nanny. One of the expert assessors had pointed out that Sandana was out of the house for some nights of the week in addition to those when he was working, because of his involvement in various sports activities in the community (apparently without the children).[10] However, in Spencer J's assessment of Sandana's availability to the children, the father was simply assumed to be available to the children as a result of his less demanding job.

In contrast, Spencer J noted that, while in Tyabji's custody, the children had moved from Sechelt to Victoria and that the future was vague given the political careers of both Tyabji and Wilson. 'Granted the vagaries of political life, those careers are uncertain ... I accept that geographic stability is less important to small children than is the stability of their family context, but it is an advantage the father has to offer' (ibid. 275). Spencer J did not mention that an assessor found that Sandana disliked change, and for that reason valued routine, and that he was marginally less accepting of the children's foibles than Tyabji.[11] As well, Tyabji was found by expert witness Lea to be more actively involved with the children during play activities than Sandana.[12] Expert witness Dr Baerg found that the youngest daughter appeared to be more content in the home of her mother and Wilson, where both Tyabji and Wilson participated in caring for the children in a relaxed routine. The children appeared to be generally more relaxed and less demanding of attention when with Tyabji.[13]

The 'stability' offered by Sandana was viewed by Spencer J as overriding the (alleged) benefit that Tyabji could offer of having both female and male influences in her household, a factor that is often a benefit to fathers in custody disputes because they tend to repartner more often than mothers. He agreed that, all other things being equal, that would be an advantage (failing to comment on the heterosexist nature of this argument on role-modelling offered by one of the experts). But here all things were not equal. That Tyabji's career path entailed her absence from her home to a much greater degree than the father's occupation was bad enough. Worse still, her new partner was in the same career. Comments of both Tyabji and Wilson to the press were used to illustrate the demanding lives of politicians.[14]

Spencer J also questioned the viability of Wilson's relationship with Tyabji, noting a comment made by Wilson to the press 'that the stress of politics on a marriage is extreme' (ibid. 276). But he tried to avoid potential criticism that he was implying that some jobs preclude obtaining custody of children: 'This factor should not be seen as disentitling all who serve in public office to the custody of their children. In many cases, probably most, where one partner follows a political or any other demanding occupation, the other partner is available to assume the family role' (ibid. 275). Embodied in this comment is the problematic assumption that politicians are usually coupled with a partner who is available to assume the family role, which may be more apt for male than female politicians (Sawer and Simms 1993, 141, 143). In addition, Spencer J failed to mention the gendered nature of the phenomenon he described, in other words, that women more often 'assume the family role.' Nor did he pursue the logic of implying that the parent in public office in this scenario (more often a man) should not necessarily lose custody. Spencer J went on to characterize the 'problem' of two parents who both have demanding careers as being 'by their choice': 'They are then faced with the task of providing for their children in their absences. In such a case there is no question of choosing between alternative custodial regimes' (*Tyabji*, 275).

But here, Spencer J needed only to choose between the parent with the apparently less demanding occupation and the one with the more demanding one. It was apparently irrelevant that the parent with the more demanding career was a woman, who had already breached social taboos by having a very public affair that caused a scandal with a politician she met in the course of pursuing her career. Yet lying beneath the surface of the judgment is disapprobation of her behaviour. Nor was it considered by Spencer J that the demanding nature of jobs is relative to factors such as the energy level and ambition of the individual worker. In this case, it seems that Tyabji had considerable energy and ambition in regard to both her career and her children. No matter what Tyabji did, she was arguably doomed: 'I find that although the mother spent whatever time she could with the children in the midst of her busy political career, her time with them was, and will continue to be, limited because of her career agenda' (ibid. 275). In contrast to both Tyabji and Wilson, Sandana 'although lacking the support of anyone to compensate for his wife's absence, as a surrogate mother, will have far fewer compelling distractions to interfere with his attention to the children' (ibid. 277).

Mother Exaggerates Complaints: Cats and In-Laws

A theme in Spencer J's judgment was that Tyabji's evidence was 'at times exaggerated by her perception of a conspiracy against her' (ibid. 280). Tyabji raised health concerns about cleanliness and the number of cats in the Kelowna home and the home of the paternal grandmother next door. These concerns were viewed as exaggerated and an exercise in self-justification (as a reason for the breakdown of her marriage, along with other sources of tension with Sandana's family). The homes of both parents were evaluated by Spencer J as 'perfectly acceptable,' with 'the father's offering more scope for young children to run and play' (ibid. 278). Not only was Tyabji's evidence discounted, but it was held against her because she was constructed as a woman who exaggerated selfishly for her own benefit.

Characters and Careers

Although Spencer J did not appear to count this factor as a separate reason for departing from the experts' opinions, it was evidently of key importance to him. Psychological tests apparently suggested that 'the father is less assertive than the mother. He is more inclined to a contemplative, philosophical outlook whereas the mother is more action-oriented' (ibid.). Although Sandana was found to have a tendency to procrastinate, Spencer J found that he did not procrastinate in everything. In general, the judge 'prefer[red] the sort of influence [that the father has] to the influence, valuable as it may be, that the mother presents at this stage' (ibid.). The father was 'a person who is relaxed and philosophical, who is highly intelligent although he has little post-secondary education, and who will spend time with his children, both caring for them and entertaining and educating them. They are his primary concern.' Although Sandana had interests outside the home such as teaching judo and playing soccer, these 'do not present him with as demanding an agenda as the mother's political ambition presents to her' (ibid.). Sandana's difficulty in coping with the need for attention of all three children at once – commented on by the experts – could be dealt with in time and indeed might diminish 'as the children reaccustom themselves to being permanently with him' (ibid.).

In contrast, Tyabji's character was described by Spencer J as 'strong and assertive,' characteristics that are not usually viewed as part of the ideology of motherhood. Although he assessed her as 'intensely interested in her children's well-being and able to offer them love and quality guidance,' she 'has an intense interest in the advancement of her own career, which will compete with the children's needs for her attention' (ibid. 279). Her intense interests appeared to be incompatible. Two 'minor incidents' – involving the older children's accidents in or near water – were cited to support this concern. While parents clearly should be attentive to children's activities around water, the fault was attributed to Tyabji's political 'obsession': 'What is of concern is that on both occasions the mother was engrossed in her political activities without taking adequate care to watch the children or to see that some responsible person was watching them' (ibid.).

Any notion that Tyabji placed the children's interests at the centre of her life was questioned at another level. For example, she had registered the son in kindergarten under her surname rather than 'the family name' Sandana. Spencer J was also troubled by a photograph session in which Tyabji, Wilson, and Tyabji's three children were portrayed together. Tyabji's moves to distance herself from her previous relationship were taken to indicate an overlooking of the interests of the children (ibid.), a trend that is typical of custody and access developments in recent years (Bourque 1995).

Lifestyles

Spencer J explained that 'the children will find a calmer, less aggressive lifestyle with the father than they would with the mother. *They are less likely to learn that other people's views may be ignored.* At this stage of their lives I think that is in their best interests. There will be time in the future for them *to be spurred by their mother's ambition*' (*Tyabji,* 279–80, emphasis added). The relationship between Tyabji's lifestyle and ignoring other people's views or being spurred by ambition remained unexplained. Tyabji was also condemned for being adversarial in her testimony, for example, being 'unwilling to concede that [Sandana] played any substantial role in their nurturing' (ibid. 280). This adversarial tendency was apparently related to her 'aggressive lifestyle' generally.

In summary, Spencer J said that the father would provide more continuity of care, whereas the mother's attention as a custodial parent would be 'to a degree, sidetracked by her career agenda,' as would that of Wilson. 'At their present ages, the children will benefit more from their father's lower-key approach to life than from the mother's wider ranging ambition' (ibid. 281). In contrast, the experts emphasized the 'socio-emotional' area, with Dr Baerg concluding that Tyabji was the 'historical emotional caregiver' and Dr Lea noting that the tender years doctrine (which favoured giving custody of young children to mothers) had relevance at least for nursing children.

Assessment of the *Tyabji* Case

Regardless of whether Tyabji should or should not have received custody, it is possible to identify some troubling themes in Spencer J's decision. Overall, although he deemed it quite proper that Tyabji took her infant child to Victoria while she attended the spring 1992 session of the provincial legislature (ibid. 271), he took a dim view of her dedication to her career in relation to her parenting dedication. This dim view prevailed despite the experts finding that Tyabji went out of her way to prioritize her children's interests in the organizing of her work life. Spencer J ultimately favoured the conservative, quiet, lifestyle of Sandana in a more rural environment. This assessment did not, however, reflect a neutral value judgment.

Mothers who depart from the norm – whether sexually or in terms of work or lifestyle – often have trouble persuading judges that it is in the best interests of their children to be with them. This difficulty may be particularly acute when they wish, as Tyabji did, to move away from a rural 'safe' environment that evokes a romantic image of the perfect old-fashioned upbringing for children to a more urban life that evokes images of promiscuity, instability, and danger. Ideological assumptions concerning what is 'best' for children are bound up in idealized notions of family units with traditional 'normal' gender roles and support networks that are imagined to be more typical of country life. In a period when 'family values' are being (re)invoked, the ideological purchase of these images cannot be underestimated, as a 1992 lesbian custody case shows.

In S. v S., the mother wished to move to Vancouver, having moved to the interior of British Columbia because of her husband's preference. This perhaps understandable decision for a woman beginning to self-identify as a lesbian was constructed not only as selfish, but as depriving her children of the safe, stable, country environment that the father offered. She lost custody on the grounds that her 'adventure' was not one that 'the children should be part of at this point in time.' The status quo was deemed to be in 'the totality of the environment which [the children] have in Cranbrook and the regularity or normality which that connotes.'[15]

Most judges insist that custody decisions should not take into account factors such as sexual identity, political beliefs, type of work, or class. Nevertheless, it is clear that all of these factors can be (re)introduced if they are constructed as bearing on the best interests of children, as they frequently are. In that context, if a parent's way of life challenges what is viewed as 'normal,' and the other parent offers a more 'stable' option, the parent living outside the norm may be constructed as placing their children's interests secondary to their own (Boyd 1992). Gendered expectations related to ideologies of family, motherhood, and fatherhood influence the assessment of each parent by judges and others.

A number of related questions can be asked about the *Tyabji* decision:

1 Was it gender neutral, as Spencer J insisted? Can custody decision making ever be gender neutral in the current conjuncture, and if so, how?
2 Does the emphasis on involvement in caregiving in *Tyabji* follow the recommendations of those who advocate attention to patterns of primary caregiving for the purposes of custody determinations?
3 How does the *Tyabji* case fit with other recent decisions and policy debates on custody law and gender?

Does the Gender-Flip Work? Is Sandana a 'Mother'?

In *Tyabji*, Spencer J bent over backwards to insist that he was being neutral in his determination. He did so in part by reversing the facts in his mind at the end of his judgment, as a test of his decision: 'If the facts as they relate to the mother related instead to the father, and vice versa, I have no doubt at all that she would be awarded custody. As it is, I am satisfied that custody should be awarded to him' (*Tyabji*, 281). Perhaps the decision really did turn on which parent had the time to assume the admittedly time-consuming responsibilities of (single) parenting in a society that relegates parenting to the private sphere of family (Boyd 1994; Fudge 1989). Perhaps Sandana fell sufficiently into the passive psychological norms of womanhood that he was effectively viewed as the mother – or at least the primary caregiver – in this case.

Still, even Spencer J's gender flip may not be capable of being neutral, as the following questions indicate. If Sandana had been a woman, with shift work in a grocery store, spending three nights a week out on sports activities in addition to the evenings she worked, would she have been constructed as a mother who put her children's interests first? (Also, would she have earned as much as Sandana?) Or would she have been viewed as selfish and as having an inflexible work schedule and lifestyle? Would having a large number of cats in her house and her mother's house have been regarded as a neutral factor? Or would she have been viewed as a sloppy housekeeper? Would the fact that she was nervous of change and had felt consumed by her husband be viewed neutrally, or would she have been viewed as neurotic? If Tyabji had been a male politician, offering a new female role model (politician) and caregiver, would he have been viewed as excessively ambitious? Or would he have been viewed as being in a position to offer his children the benefits of his class? Would his complaints about the cat urine on the child's bed have been viewed as exaggerated, or might he have been viewed as a concerned father? Would his marriage to an educated, successful woman with children of her own have been viewed as a liability? These evaluations quite possibly cannot be applied neutrally in a gendered society where the standards of accountability for parenting are gendered. Woman and men in equal positions *may* receive equal treatment in courts, but they rarely are in the same position.

Did Mr Justice Spencer Apply a Primary Caregiver Standard in Tyabji?

One strategy to redress the undervaluing of women's caregiving labour in the private sphere, as well as to address other gendered power plays in the custody field, has been to argue for a primary caregiver presumption. Under such a presumption, it is assumed that it is in the best interests of the child(ren) to grant custody to the parent who has been the primary caregiver in the past, unless that parent is clearly unfit (Boyd 1990; CACSW 1994; Fineman 1991; Neely 1984; Smart and Sevenhuijsen 1989). This presumption has been criticized on a number of counts. It has the potential to reproduce an ideology of motherhood based on a narrow conception of family and privatized responsibility for children, which in turn reinforces gendered relations in both private and public spheres (Olsen 1984; Pulkingham 1994). As well, it may exacerbate the difficulties experienced by women with disabilities, First Nations women, and other women in showing that they are 'good mothers,' given that their patterns of parenting may not resemble primary caregiving as it is currently conceptualized (Kline 1993; Mosoff this volume). In general, the presumption may not be capable of addressing the fundamental gendered problems of custody determination. The primary caregiving emphasis does, however, potentially allow decision makers to notice and revalue what has been viewed as women's work in the home: child care, nurturing, and the domestic labour associated with it. As well, it insists that this work be prioritized in custody determinations instead of factors such as sexual orientation, labour force participation, and so on, which so often detract attention from women's work.

It may, however, be easier said than done to ensure that the primary caregiver emphasis is applied without engaging problematic ideological assumptions (Mosoff this volume). Primary caregiving *has* been taken into account by judges in some U.S. jurisdictions, only to be subverted in a manner that defeats its original purpose. For example, excessive attention may be paid to the sexual conduct of mothers, their survival of domestic abuse, or the paucity of their economic resources (Sack 1992, 292–3). As well, just as primary caregiving language started to be used in Canadian courts in the 1980s (Boyd 1990), other trends have operated to obscure women's primary responsibility for caregiving. Fathers have been constructed as having a vital role to play in the raising of children (Drakich 1989; Fineman 1995). Mothers who are viewed as 'depriving' fathers of this opportunity – for example, by limiting access to children by moving away or by breaking up a relationship 'unnecessarily' – are viewed increasingly negatively in society and in law (Bourque 1995; Boyd 1996).[16] Simultaneously, as mothers have entered the labour force in increasing numbers, it becomes difficult for judges and other legal actors to 'see' that caring for children remains a privatized, gendered phenomenon, with women continuing to take more responsibility on the whole. The gender neutrality of the primary caregiver presumption may preclude its application in a gender-sensitive manner (see Erickson 1984, 449–50).

Arguably, when a mother is viewed as an active, ambitious, career woman, this difficulty becomes an impossibility. In the context of the *Tyabji* case, we may never know the answer to the question of whether there was a primary caregiver when her relationship with Sandana was intact, and if so, who it was. This case may illustrate the kind of fact situation where that sort of determination is simply not possible because of the ways the parents organized their lives. However, some troublesome questions remain. Is it possible that Tyabji carried out the role of organizing her children's care and ensuring that they were with her as much as possible *despite* the demands of her career? Is it possible that this possibility cannot be seen because it is assumed that she pursues her political career in the same way as a man? Tyabji *may* have been breaking new ground in this field. She often took the children with her to political functions and set up offices to accommodate the children.[17] Without wishing to reinforce 'Supermom' expectations of mothers with multiple work responsibilities and commitments in a society that fails adequately to support them, this possibility should not be overlooked.

The more popular view, endorsed by the *Tyabji* decision, was that Sandana was breaking new ground in fatherhood. Most feminists working on custody have wanted to develop a standard of decision making that allows for a recognition of fathers who *have* taken key responsibility for care giving. The concern has been that judges often leap to hasty conclusions about, or exaggerate, the extent of paternal participation in caregiving. In so doing they ignore the continuing gendered nature of caregiving and the differing ideological assumptions of men and women as parents and workers.

In *Tyabji*, Sandana was effectively viewed as the primary caregiver, although this language was not used. This view was constructed despite the fact that one of the expert assessors determined that Tyabji was the 'historical emotional caregiver.'[18] This psychological bond may not be the same as a primary caregiver tie, but it is often related to the primary caregiver role. Apparently the judge who made the 1993 interim judgment in favour of Tyabji also believed that the children were more emotionally bonded to her than to their father.[19] As well, the family doctor reported that the children were brought to his office by both parents, but more so by Tyabji, especially when they were younger.[20] Tyabji reported to expert witness Dr Baerg that she feared 'a disruption in her children's lives from the primary care that she has always given or arranged for' and that 'she and her husband have always agreed on child rearing matters only because it was directed almost entirely by herself.'[21] Both experts reported that the children were less demanding and somewhat more at ease with Tyabji than Sandana, although neither expert drew adverse conclusions concerning Sandana as a result.

Instead of discussing this evidence that may have been related to caregiving responsibilities, Spencer J counted the days that the children spent with each of Tyabji and Sandana (*Tyabji*, 274). This approach was somewhat unusual. The relevant period for counting was defined to be the period of time *before* the interim order (after which the children spent more time with Tyabji) and *after* the oldest child was 1 year old (before which Sandana was not very involved in child care). Yet in other cases, usually where the mother was found to be the primary caregiver while the family was intact, the relevant period has sometimes been defined to be that during which the father had interim custody. In two recent British Columbia cases, where the mothers were acknowledged to have been primary care-givers, good caring by the mother was either said not to count, because the mother was seen as selfish or self-serving,[22] or, primary caregiving was said not to be a matter of counting.[23] In both cases, the mothers lost custody despite the fact that they had been primary caregivers. If the standard of primary caregiving is to contribute to determination of custody decisions, it needs to be assessed more consistently and in a more thoughtful manner than merely counting days, or women will feel that (their) child care labour is still irrelevant unless men do it.

Regardless of whether Judy Tyabji should or should not have received custody, the fall-out of the *Tyabji* case for employed mothers who are in less high-profile positions than Tyabji is of concern. Tyabji's case received extensive publicity because of her public profile, but on a routine basis many employed mothers encounter difficulties in persuading judges of the validity of their custody claims. Their voices on caregiving and also on issues such as sexual abuse of children are increasingly unheard in a gender-neutral era of custody law that places a high priority on the preservation of ties with fathers, almost no matter what (Bourque 1995).[24] As mentioned before, there is an increasing but mistaken tendency to assume that women in the labour force share caregiving more or less equally with the fathers of their children. The trumpeting of *Tybaji* as a gender-neutral victory for fathers plays into the assumption that fathers have been discriminated against, at least until now, in courts. This assumption in turn aggravates the existing problems that many women have in convincing assessors, lawyers, judges, and others that they have taken primary responsibility for ensuring that their children's needs are met and that, in a custody dispute, they may be best suited to doing so in the future. The disciplinary effect of these messages on women as they negotiate familial relations, and family break-down, should not be underestimated.

Other Recent Trends

Two 1993 decisions of the British Columbia Supreme Court and Court of Appeal[25] shed light on the trends that contribute to the difficulties that women experience in affirming their caregiving work and bond with children. The judge in *Doise*[26] relied on several principles for custody determination set out by the trial judge in *Van Gool*. These principles were left undisturbed by the Court of Appeal in *Van Gool* and were hailed as putting fathers on an equal footing with mothers:[27]

1 'The fact that the petitioner will work outside the home, leaving the children to be cared for by others for a large part of the time, should not be decisive against him [*sic*?] so long as he [*sic*?] can "provide a good home".'

2 'The "tender years" doctrine has little application in present society, nor is the fact that one of these children is a young girl of much significance.'

3 'Conduct by the parent with interim custody which tends to poison the relationship of the children with the other parent or hinder an on-going relationship with their father [*sic*?], may be a factor in the award of permanent custody.'

4 'The court is entitled to consider a parent's propensity for honesty or dishonesty, and his or her social responsibility, in relation to the ultimate welfare of the child ... and to favour the party who has not exaggerated or overstated his or her case.'

On the surface, these principles seem to constitute a progressive affirmation of gender neutrality (unless the sexist language in (1) and (3) is read literally). In their application, however, they may favour men by not considering the context of caregiving or reasons for conduct that appears to 'poison' a relationship (such as fear of abuse). As well women's 'credibility' may be viewed as more suspect in court than men's (Schafran 1995; 1994, 28).

In both *Doise* and *Van Gool* the mothers were apparently competent primary caregivers of the children. Nonetheless, they were found to put their own interests ahead of the children's and lost custody. Mrs Van Gool was viewed as being inflexible 'in respect of any access other than what was specified.' In other words, although she obeyed the law, she did not go beyond this to facilitate the father's contact with the children. She was deemed, therefore, to be 'quite capable of using the children as a weapon in her "war" with the petitioner.' Similarly, Mrs Doise's act of taking the children to Germany and depriving Mr Doise of contact counteracted any evidence that she was the primary caregiver and that the status quo clearly rested with her.

Is it a coincidence that whereas in *Tyabji* the father's apparent primary caregiving was valued, in *Van Gool* and *Doise* the mother's primary caregiving was viewed as a secondary consideration, the mothers were constructed as exaggerators or liars, and they were viewed as unfriendly to the other parent? Spencer J in *Tyabji* apparently ignored the first *Van Gool* principle above, that working outside the home should not prejudice a parent's custody claim. As well, principle (2) concerning hindering ongoing relationships between access parent and child was not viewed as important in *Tyabji*, where one expert and a mediator/counsellor said that Tyabji was more likely to facilitate Sandana's contact with the children than Sandana was to facilitate Tyabji's contact.[28]

The primary caregiver factor *has* been used in some Canadian cases to acknowledge the primary caregiving labour of women.[29] However, when evidence of a woman's career or educational commitment comes into play – or some other evidence of the mother's self-interest – it tends to be assumed that she no longer has an interest in caregiving, or that she was not in fact the primary caregiver. The dichotomy of primary caregiver and 'careerist' tends to be noted mainly in relation to mothers, and not fathers. The primary caregiver emphasis seems to apply mainly in favour of mothers only when they do not disqualify themselves in some other way from the expectations of 'good motherhood' (cf. Iyer this volume). This point supports the argument that approaches to parenting, in law at least, are nowhere near being gender neutral.

Where Do We Go from Here?

To the extent that the above-mentioned cases (falsely) herald a new era of gender-neutral custody decision making, they may exacerbate the gendered power relations in the child custody realm. The political economy of paid work, family relations, and gender relations (Armstrong and Armstrong 1994) shows that, in Canada today, there is still women's work and men's work. Furthermore, the work that most women do has changed remarkably little over the last fifty years. The nature of women's work in the home and in the labour force reinforces and perpetuates, in many complex ways, the division of labour by sex. Although the *nature* of women's work in the labour force has not changed dramatically, their *rate* of participation has risen. But women seem to have relatively little choice in terms of who provides care for their children, care that continues to be relegated to the private sphere (see Teghtsoonian this volume). Armstrong and Armstrong showed that 'those who stay home with children are almost all women; those with paid employment who are primarily responsible for arranging child care are almost all women (unless they are lone-parent fathers); and many more employed women than employed men participate in the various aspects of child care' (1994, 109). Although there has been enormous growth in the labour force participation rates of women with young children, the *actual* number of women in the labour force with children under the age of 6 has declined since

1971. Women may well be solving child care problems by not having children (ibid. 184).

Children remain a contested terrain within this political economy. It is highly problematic and undesirable to assert a 'special' claim for mothers in the custody realm. But the reality is that women's experience of reproduction and mothering remains different from men's of fathering, as a result of socially constructed and economically influenced differences that are deeply embedded in the structures of Canadian society (Arnup and Boyd 1995). Attempting to determine neutrally what the best interests of children are in this context is arguably virtually impossible, as when factors such as race and sexual orientation come into play.

Yet child custody law moves inexorably on in a direction that tries to eliminate gender from decision making (Bala and Miklas 1993; Department of Justice 1993). Many of the gender-neutral trends and initiatives seem innocent in and of themselves. In fact, however, they may diminish the ability of women's voices to be 'heard' in custody and access determinations (Boyd 1995). Women are not seen to be primary caregivers any longer, despite evidence that they are. Women are not permitted to seek distance or independence from unsatisfactory relationships if they are viewed as depriving children of their fathers. Fathers are permitted to be full-time labourers as long as they provide a good home, whereas mothers continue to juggle multiple roles in a social and legal context that reproduces the publicly unsupported nature of their private sphere work.

This analysis demonstrates the short distance that Canadian law and society has moved in shifting the sexual division of labour in heterosexual families, including the labour involved in child care. It also illustrates the continuing influence of public/private ideology, despite the manner in which it has been blurred by women's increased presence in the public sphere of work. Optimistic efforts of the 1970s and 1980s to shift the ways in which law reinforced gendered expectations of women and men have resulted in cosmetic changes to statutory provisions on parenting and families. However, these changes both obscure the extent to which material changes in these relations have been resisted *and* cast the onus on judges and assessors to grapple with the contested nature of gendered identities (woman/man; mother/father) in the 1990s. The *Tyabji* decision represents one such effort to do so and reveals the persistence of gendered concerns in determining questions of custody and parenting, *despite* the judge's effort to insist on gender neutrality. The decision also raises questions about the effectiveness of the (gender neutral) primary caregiver emphasis in dealing with the undervalued nature of women's work.

In the end, custody decisions such as these are a lesson in the impossibility of tackling issues such as the sexual division of labour through law alone. They also raise complex questions for feminists as we grapple with the problem of how to release women from the ideology of motherhood while recognizing the particular and gendered relationship that women have to children. This conundrum will be difficult to resolve without structural changes in society that shift the privatized nature of child care and other caring responsibilities (Boyd 1994). Some of these changes may be foreshadowed by economic restructuring and levels of unemployment of both men and women, which may in some cases lead to the assumption by men of more child care responsibilities than they traditionally have performed.[30] However, without structural change reversing privatization trends (see Armstrong, Kline, Young this volume) these few changes in men's responsibilities in the 'private' sphere are likely to remain limited and conducted on an individual basis only.

Postscript

On 24 June 1996 Judy Tyabji's application to vary the custody order was refused by Madam Justice Sinclair Prowse (Vancouver Registry No. F950017). Although the fact that she had lost her seat in the British Columbia Legislative Assembly and could now devote most of her time to the children was deemed a material change in circumstances, a variation in the order was not deemed to be in the best interests of the children. Sinclair Prowse J noted that Tyabji's full-time employment in a demanding career was a significant factor in the trial judgment, but decided that other factors such as the father's 'calmer, less aggressive lifestyle' and the fact that 'the mother and Mr. Wilson are not always ready to consider the children's best interests' had not changed. Custody should therefore remain with Sandana.

NOTES

Earlier versions of this chapter were presented at the University of Windsor, Humanities Research Group, 9 Nov. 1994; the University of Victoria Faculty of Law, 2 Dec. 1994; and a workshop called Challenging the Public/Private Divide, Faculty of Law, U.B.C., 11–12 May 1995. Thanks to Doris Buss, Joan Brockman, Dorothy Chunn, Nitya Iyer, Katherine Teghtsoonian, Claire Young, and the audience at the three presentations for helpful comments, and to Gillian Calder for research assistance.

1 *Tyabji* v *Sandana* (1994), 2 RFL (4th) 265 (BCSC), Spencer J; *Van Gool* v *Van Gool* (1993), 1 RFL (4th) 20 (BCCA), Lambert, Wood, and Rowles, JJA, affirming the judgment of MacDonald J of the BCSC in *Van Gool* v *Van Gool*, [1993] BCJ No. 180, Vancouver Registry No. D081601 (QL). Page numbers cited subsequently for the *Tyabji* case are taken from the RFL report.

2 Ean Maxwell, Sandana's lawyer, said that the *Tyabji* case was a model of a ruling that is blind to gender and appropriate to the realities of a day in which both men and women are involved in being parents: Alanna Mitchell, 'Busyness of Parent a Custody Issue,' *Globe and Mail*, 5 March 1994, A1, A2. Vancouver family lawyer Robert DeBou has applauded this and the *Van Gool* case. See Mitchell (5 March 1994) and on the *Van Gool* decision, Phil Needham, 'Ruling Puts Fathers on an Equal Footing,' *Vancouver Sun*, 9 Feb. 1994, A2. See also, the column by Peter Raeside on 'Men,' *Globe and Mail*, 2 March 1994, A24, applauding the *Van Gool* decision that 'puts fathers on an equal footing with mothers in custody matters.'

3 Doug Ward, 'Judy Tyabji Takes Child-Custody Woes to Oprah Winfrey Show,' *Vancouver Sun*, 18 Oct. 1994, A3.

4 See, e.g., the Divorce Act, RSC 1985, c. 3 (2nd Supp.), s. 16(8); Family Relations Act, RSBC 1979, c. 121, s. 24.

5 See, e.g., these contradictions in earlier judgments of Spencer J, the judge in the *Tyabji* case: *R.* v *R.*, [1994] BCJ No. 618 (QL); *W.J.R.C.* v *M.P.C.*, [1991] BCJ No. 3598 (QL); *Corrado* v *Corrado*, [1989] BCJ No. 1902 (QL).

6 Justice Spencer described the son as almost six and the younger daughter as almost two. This language arguably diminished the maternal link with the children.

7 See Testimony of Dr G.W. Lea (on file with the author), p. 22.

8 See Testimony of Dr J.M. Baerg (on file with the author), p. 9.

9 Among employees in dual-income full-time earner families, men were extremely satisfied with their spouse's parenting: 90 per cent reported high satisfaction with their spouse's ability and performance as a parent. When women were asked about such things as their spouse's involvement with the children, the amount of help he offered with them, and his child-rearing skills, women in dual-income families were significantly less happy with their husband's performance as a parent: only 63 per cent reporting a high level of satisfaction: Christopher Higgins, Linda Duxbury, and Catherine Lee, 1992, *Balancing Work and Family: A Study of Canadian Private Sector Employees* (London: Western Business School, University of Western Ontario), 72–3, Appendix, p. 16. Summarized in Lero and Johnson (1994, 54).

10 Testimony of Dr G.W. Lea, p. 21; Testimony of Dr J.M. Baerg, pp. 5, 9.

11 Ibid., p. 21.

12 Ibid., p. 16.

13 Testimony of Dr J.M. Baerg, pp. 7–9.

14 See Kenneth Whyte, 'Tyabji Custody Case Shows Context Is All When Considering the Words of Politicians,' *Globe and Mail*, 12 March 1994, D2. Whyte argued that the quotes were taken out of context, that Tyabji and Wilson often 'blow hard' around reporters, and that the thought that 'giving weight to a couple of cheap quotes might have tipped the balance is unsettling.'

15 *S. v S.*, [1992] BCJ No. 1579, Cranbrook Registry No. 02278, BCSC (QL), Mr. Justice Melnick, filed 30 Nov. 1992.

16 See Kathy Tait, 'Hung Out to Dry: Tyabji Didn't Get Support She Wanted from Oprah,' *[Vancouver] Province Showcase*, 23 Oct. 1994, B12, arguing that Tyabji should have lived in her riding, which was home to her children, and found a way for herself and Sandana to co-parent. Recent media reports indicate that she may in fact have decided to follow this advice.

17 Testimony of Dr G.W. Lea, pp. 15, 20.

18 See Testimony of Dr J.M. Baerg, p. 9. The Testimony of Dr G.W. Lea, indicated different grounds for recommending that Ms Tyabji receive custody, including the fact that the youngest child was only 17 months old, that two of the three children were girls, and that Tyabji could offer a 'two-parent' home. These grounds for showing a more significant connection between Tyabji and the children are problematic, but they do parallel the views of Dr Baerg. Dr Lea added that it would be discriminatory to suggest that a young woman with children should not enter politics.

19 See Ward *supra* note 3 at A3.

20 Testimony of Dr J.M. Baerg, p. 6.

21 Ibid., p. 4.

22 *Van Gool* v *Van Gool* (1993), 1 RFL (4th) 20 (BCCA), Lambert, Wood, and Rowles, JJA, affirming the judgment of MacDonald J of the BCSC in *Van Gool* v *Van Gool*, [1993] BCJ No. 180, Vancouver Registry No. D081601 (QL); note that this opinion went against that of the expert assessor.

23 *Doise* v *Doise*, [1993] BCJ No. 2867, Vancouver Registry No. A930461, (SC) (QL), Dorgan J. filed 10 Dec. 1993.

24 See the decisions of Spencer J in *Papalia* v *Papalia*, [1995] BCJ No. 203 (QL); *Rotenbush* v *Rotenbush*, [1992] BCJ No. 1552 (QL); *R.* v *R.*, [1991] BCJ No. 791 (QL); *McMahon* v *McMahon*, [1990] BCJ No. 1075 (QL); *Gosal* v *Gosal*, [1990] BCJ No. 797 (QL); *Avaliotis* v *Massoutis*, [1986] BCJ No. 1164 (QL); *Rutherford* v *Rutherford* (1986), 4 RFL (3d) 457 (BCSC); *Foote* v *Foote*, [1986] BCJ No. 2206 (QL), where at least supervised access was awarded to fathers even where allegations or direct evidence of sexual, physical, or mental abuse by the father existed.

25 *Van Gool* v *Van Gool* (1993), 1 RFL (4th) 20 (BCCA), Lambert, Wood, and
    Rowles, JJA, affirming the judgment of MacDonald J of the BCSC in *Van Gool*
    v *Van Gool*, [1993] BCJ No. 180, Vancouver Registry No. D081601 (QL).
26 *Supra* note 23.
27 See Needham, *supra* note 2 and Raeside, *supra* note 2.
28 See testimony of Dr J.M. Baerg, pp. 4, 9.
29 E.g., *K. (M.M.)* v *K.(U.)* (1990), 28 RFL (3d) 189 (Alta. C.A.); *Levesque* v
    Lapointe (1993), 44 RFL (3d) 316 (BCCA).
30 Some research indicates that while women may be expanding their roles to
    include market skills, men may not yet be assuming private-sphere caregiving
    responsibilities. See Suzanne Mackenzie, (1986), 'Women's Responses to Eco-
    nomic Restructuring: Changing Gender, Changing Space,' in Roberta Hamilton
    and Michèle Barrett, eds., *The Politics of Diversity* (Montreal: Book Center),
    81–100.

REFERENCES

Armstrong, Pat, and Hugh Armstrong. 1994. *The Double Ghetto*, 3rd ed. Toronto:
    McClelland and Stewart
Arnup, Katherine. 1989. '"Mothers Just Like Others:" Lesbians, Divorce, and
    Child Custody in Canada.' *Canadian Journal of Women and the Law* 3(1),
    18–32
– and Susan Boyd. 1995. 'Familial Disputes? Sperm Donors, Lesbian Mothers, and
    Legal Parenthood.' In Didi Herman and Carl Stychin, eds., *Legal Inversions*.
    Philadelphia: Temple University Press, 77–101
Bala, Nicholas. 1990. 'Assessing the Assessor: Legal Issues.' *Canadian Family Law
    Quarterly* 6, 179–226
– and Susan Miklas. 1993. *Rethinking Decisions about Children: Is the 'Best Inter-
    ests of the Child' Approach Really in the Best Interests of Children?* Toronto: Pol-
    icy Research Centre on Children, Youth, and Families
Bourque, Dawn M. 1995. '"Reconstructing" the Patriarchal Nuclear Family:
    Recent Developments in Child Custody and Access in Canada.' *Canadian Jour-
    nal of Law and Society* 10, 1–24
Boyd, Susan B. 1996. 'Is There an Ideology of Motherhood in (Post)Modern Child
    Custody Law?' *Social and Legal Studies* 5(4), 495–522
– 1995. 'W(h)ither Feminism? The Department of Justice Public Discussion Paper
    on Custody and Access.' *Canadian Journal of Family Law* 12(2), 331–65
– 1994. '(Re)Placing the State: Family, Law and Oppression.' *Canadian Journal of
    Law and Society* 9(1): 39–73
– 1992. 'What Is a "Normal" Family?' *Modern Law Review* 55, 269–78

- 1990. 'Potentialities and Perils of the Primary Caregiver Presumption.' *Canadian Family Law Quarterly* 7(1), 1–30
- 1989a. 'Child Custody, Ideologies and Employment.' *Canadian Journal of Women and the Law* 3(1), 111–33
- 1989b. 'From Gender-Specificity to Gender-Neutrality? Ideologies in Canadian Child Custody Law.' In Carol Smart and Selma Sevenhuijsen, eds., *Child Custody and the Politics of Gender*. London: Routledge, 126–57

Canadian Advisory Council on the Status of Women (CACSW). 1994. *Child Custody and Access Policy: A Brief to the Federal/Provincial/Territorial Family Law Committee*. Ottawa

Chunn, Dorothy E. 1992. *From Punishment to Doing Good: Family Courts and Socialized Justice in Ontario, 1880–1940*. Toronto: University of Toronto Press

Department of Justice, Canada. 1993. *Custody and Access: Public Discussion Paper*. Ottawa

Drakich, Janice. 1989. 'In Search of the Better Parent: The Social Construction of Ideologies of Fatherhood.' *Canadian Journal of Women and the Law* 3(1), 69–87

Erickson, Nancy S. 1984. 'The Feminist Dilemma over Unwed Parents' Custody Rights: The Mother's Rights Must Take Priority.' *Law and Inequality* 2, 447–72

Fineman, Martha Albertson. 1995. *The Neutered Mother, the Sexual Family and Other Twentieth-Century Tragedies*. New York and London: Routledge
- 1991. *Illusion of Equality: The Rhetoric and Reality of Divorce Reform*. Chicago and London: University of Chicago Press

Fudge, Judy. 1989. 'The Privatization of the Costs of Social Reproduction: Some Recent Charter Cases.' *Canadian Journal of Women and the Law* 3(1), 246–55

Gavigan, Shelley A.M. 1993. 'Paradise Lost, Paradox Revisited: The Implications of Familial Ideology for Feminist, Lesbian, and Gay Engagement to Law.' *Osgoode Hall Law Journal* 31, 589–624

Ghalam, Nancy Z. 1993. *Women in the Workplace*, 2nd ed. Ottawa: Statistics Canada. (cat. no. 71-534E)

Girdner, Linda K. 1986. 'Child Custody Determination: Ideological Dimensions of a Social Problem.' In E. Seidman and J. Rappaport, eds., *Redefining Social Problems*. New York: Plenum, 165–83

Hessing, Melody. 1993. 'Mothers' Management of their Combined Workloads: Clerical Work and Household Needs.' *Canadian Review of Sociology and Anthropology* 30, 37–63

Kline, Marlee. 1993. 'Complicating the Ideology of Motherhood: Child Welfare Law and First Nation Women.' *Queen's Law Journal* 18, 306–42
- 1992. 'Child Welfare Law, "Best Interests of the Child" Ideology, and First Nations.' *Osgoode Hall Law Journal* 30, 375–425

Lero, Donna S., and Karen L. Johnson. 1994. *110 Canadian Statistics on Work and Family*. Ottawa: Canadian Advisory Council on the Status of Women

Marshall, Katherine. 1993. 'Employed Parents and the Division of Labour of Housework.' *Perspectives on Labour and Income*. Ottawa: Statistics Canada. (cat. no. 75–001E, Autumn), 23–30

Mayer, Jane. 1995. 'Motherhood Issue: Marcia Clark Isn't the Only One Who's Got Troubles.' *New Yorker*, 20 March 1995, 9–10

Millbank, Jenni. 1994. 'What Do Lesbians Do? Motherhood Ideology, Lesbian Mothers and Family Law.' LLM Thesis, University of British Columbia

– 1992. 'Lesbian Mothers, Gay Fathers: Sameness and Difference.' *Australian Gay and Lesbian Law Journal* 2, 21–40

Mnookin, Robert H. 1975. 'Child-Custody Adjudication: Judicial Functions in the Face of Indeterminacy.' *Law and Contemporary Problems* 39(3), 226–93

Mosoff, Judith. 1994. 'Motherhood, Madness and the Role of the State.' LLM Thesis, University of British Columbia

Neely, Richard. 1984. 'The Primary Caretaker Parent Rule: Child Custody and the Dynamics of Greed.' *Yale Law and Policy Review* 3, 168–86

Olsen, Frances. 1984. 'The Politics of Family Law.' *Law and Inequality* 2(1), 1–19

Pulkingham, Jane. 1994. 'Private Troubles, Private Solutions: Poverty among Divorced Women and the Politics of Support Enforcement and Child Custody Determination.' *Canadian Journal of Law and Society* 9(2), 73–97

Roberts, Dorothy E. 1993. 'Racism and Patriarchy in the Meaning of Motherhood.' *American University Journal of Gender and the Law*, 1–38

Sack, Laura. 1992. 'Women and Children First: A Feminist Analysis of the Primary Caretaker Standard in Child Custody Cases.' *Yale Journal of Law and Feminism* 4, 291–328

Sawer, Marian, and Marian Simms. 1993. *A Woman's Place: Women and Politics in Australia*. St Leonards, Australia: Allen and Unwin

Schafran, Lynn Hecht. 1994. 'Gender Bias in Family Courts: Why Prejudice Permeates the Process.' *Family Advocate* 17(1), 22–8

– 1995. 'Credibility in the Courts: Why Is There a Gender Gap?' *Judges' Journal* 34(1), 5–9, 40–2

Smart, Carol. 1991. 'The Legal and Moral Ordering of Child Custody.' *Journal of Law and Society* 18(4), 485–500

– and Selma Sevenhuijsen, eds. 1989. *Child Custody and the Politics of Gender*. London and New York: Routledge

Statistics Canada, Household Surveys Division. 1995. *Characteristics of Dual-Earner Families, 1993*. Ottawa. (cat. no. 13–215)

Teghtsoonian, Katherine. 1995. 'Work and/or Motherhood: The Ideological Construction of Women's Options in Canadian Child Care Policy Debates.' *Canadian Journal of Women and the Law* 8(2), 411–39

Thompson, John B. 1990. *Ideology and Modern Culture: Critical Social Theory in the Era of Mass Communications*. Cambridge: Polity Press

11

Lesbians, Child Custody, and the Long Lingering Gaze of the Law

JENNI MILLBANK

Do they hug each other?
Do they kiss each other?
Do they tell each other that they love each other?[1]

A number of feminists have articulated the illusory nature of the public/
private divide and also shown how constructs of 'the private' have been
used to justify a lack of legal protection for women in the 'domestic' realm
(e.g., O'Donovan 1985; Olsen 1985, 1983; Thornton 1995). Other feminists
have revealed the limited nature of 'the private' realm of marginalized
groups of women, because of excessive state regulation such as intervention
in the lives of First Nations mothers in the name of child welfare (Kline
1993, 1992; Monture 1989). The shifting nature of the public/private divide
as it applies to lesbians has been less well explored. Moreover, arguments
for a 'right to privacy' for lesbians and gay men have tended to reinscribe
the public/private divide, particularly in the United States. A similar trend
is evident in international human rights jurisprudence which has tended to
emphasize privacy rather than equality in lesbian and gay rights claims (see
Pritchard 1995).[2]

Without endorsing a rights-based claim to 'privacy,' I am interested in
interrogating the absence of any space conceived by the law as 'private'
where lesbians, or at least lesbian mothers, are concerned. As African-
American theorists such as Patricia Williams have argued (in response to a
strand of critical legal theory asserting that rights are intangible and obfus-
catory) rights *do* exist as tangible entities *when you don't have them* (see
Williams 1991); the notion of a private space – if not necessarily a 'right' to
privacy – becomes a critical issue when its absence is so total. For example,

when a lesbian custody decision opens with the 'fact' that the mother and her partner have oral sex twice a week, the jolt of shock and sense of invasion that I feel as a reader stems at least in part from a belief that such things should be private. The 'private,' a construct that I know to be fallible, inconsistent, and often contrary to the interests of women, becomes desperately solid and positively desirable at that moment.

This chapter explores the relationship between a demonization of lesbians and the denial of private space to lesbians. This connection is well illustrated by the questions put to a 9-year-old girl about her mother and her mother's partner in a 1988 Tennessee child custody case: 'Do they hug each other? Do they kiss each other? Do they tell each other they love each other?'[3] The child responded 'yes' to each question, and she was also asked whether the women slept together in 'the same bed as well as the same bedroom.' The child had lived with her mother since her father and mother separated when she was a 1-year old, and she wished to remain with her mother. The trial court awarded the father custody, and granted the mother access only on the ground that her lover was barred from the house. In affirming the trial judgment, the court of appeal quoted the child's examination in order to 'shed additional light on the nature and extent of Mother's activities,' and then again as proof of what the daughter had been 'exposed' to. Hugging and kissing – well, well, well.

Collins is remarkable only in the sense that it was the child who was required to give evidence on these points – usually it is the mother, her lover, friends, the father, neighbours, social workers, court-appointed and partisan psychologists, other family members, work mates, and sometimes, still, private investigators. The focus of the questions – hugging, kissing, holding hands, terms of endearment, and who sleeps where – continue to be a commonplace of child custody decisions involving lesbians from the 'dark ages' of the 1970s to the 'enlightened' present day.

At first blush such a focus seems not only irrelevant (what does holding hands have to do with raising children?) but also somewhat indelicate (don't lesbian mothers have *any* privacy?). The existing case law from Australia, Canada, the United Kingdom, and the United States of America[4] reveals a context in which *the lesbian* (for she is almost always viewed as emblematic) is not permitted to shield any part of her life from the judicial gaze. The welfare of children is construed as almost inevitably threatened by lesbianism (it will make the children homosexual, will confuse their gender identities, will traumatize them generally, will expose them to sexual abuse, will expose them to harassment from peers), necessitating concern and intervention. As a legal and social subject in this context, the lesbian is too dangerous to deserve privacy or any other private right. As a mother, she should place the welfare of the child above her own just as the law does; any attempt to claim privacy or to assert rights as a subject separate from her child therefore will prove her to be a bad mother. There is no private realm that can be claimed, nor will it be granted.

In the first section of this chapter I discuss the dangerous lesbian as embodied in cultural discourses and as she appears in legal judgments. In the second section I explore how fear and fantasies about the dangerous lesbian are projected by judges onto children, such that children are seen to be at risk and in need of protection. This context provides the backdrop for what is demonstrated in the third section – that no stone can be left unturned in judicial scrutiny of the mother's sexuality. Courts can and must take a good long look at every (lesbian) thing the (lesbian) mother has ever done, in order to protect her children. The fourth section examines two different aspects of 'the private' that arise from the case law. The first is where lesbian mothers claim that their sexuality is private in the sense that although it is open to judicial scrutiny, it is contained or hidden in real life and thus will not be harmful to the children. The second is where lesbian mothers claim that their sexuality is private, in order to assert a right to privacy, and argue that the courts cannot take it into account, or have done so improperly. Although the first strategy has not always been successful for lesbian mothers, the second strategy has been universally unsuccessful, and the reasons for this discrepancy will be explored.

The Dangerous Lesbian

That a lesbian mother is a danger, or a potential danger, is the starting point of nearly all of the approximately eighty child custody cases analysed as the basis for this chapter. This sense of danger then justifies a judicial erasure of any pre-existing sense of a public/private divide in family law discourses.

Lesbian Danger is so unquestioned as to appear, in culture as in law, 'common sense.' A series of shorthand 'types' of lesbians appear in medical and cultural discourses, are taken to be 'true' or representative, and are then reinscribed by law. Such types commonly include lesbians as male identified/masculine or 'butch,' lesbians as manhating, and lesbians as immature or in a schoolgirl phase. Lesbian relationships commonly appear as butch/femme or sadist/masochist configurations.[5] These projected attributes are an integral part of popular discourses on lesbianism, notably those emanating from the mental health professions (Faderman 1991, 1982; O'Connor and Ryan 1993), and they are reproduced (or, perhaps, translated) in popular cultural forms such as film (see, e.g., Creed 1993; Dyer 1993, 1992, 1990, 1984; Merck 1993; Weiss 1992). The gleeful ease with which the Australian and international press seized upon Tracey Wigginton, a lesbian who stabbed and killed a man in Queensland in 1991, as 'the lesbian vampire killer' (Verhoeven 1993) illustrates the extent to which lesbianism, pathology, violence, and monstrousness are inexplicably intertwined in the popular imagination. The 1990s phenomenon of 'lesbian chic' may have served to make many of these images more glamorous and sexually appealing to the public at large, but has not appreciably changed other elements of representations of lesbianism (see hooks 1993).[6]

The unifying thematic link in much cultural representation of lesbianism is that lesbianism is almost always represented as pathological, dangerous, or otherwise suspect – very rarely does it appear as a neutral factor and almost never as a positive factor. The same point can be made of legal judgments where lesbians appear. I do not suggest a linear progression from cultural to legal knowledge, but agree with Richard Dyer: 'How a group is represented, presented over again in cultural forms, how an image of a member of a group is taken as representative of that group, how that group is represented in the sense of being spoken for and on behalf of (whether they represent, speak for themselves or not), these all have to do with ... how others see members of a group and their place and rights, others who have the power to affect that place and those rights. How we are seen determines in part how we are treated; how we treat others is based on how we see them; such seeing comes from representation' (1993, 1).

In most child custody cases involving a lesbian mother, a court is faced with a mother who has left the father and family structure for a recent lesbian relationship. Lesbianism is thus readily viewed as the cause of family rupture and marital breakdown. Female sexuality and male dispensability are foregrounded in this situation in such a way that 'Lesbian' is often construed as a symbol of aggression, sexuality, hatred of men, sterility, and disease. *Obiter dicta* in a number of judgments regarding the 'threat' posed by lesbian (or gay) parenting to the traditional family form and the continuance of society as we know it suggest a strong thread of the 'public interest' in preventing lesbians from parenting, regardless of the relative dangers or merits of the lesbian mother at hand. A notorious example was provided by Justice Tamillia, writing for the majority of the Pennsylvania Superior Court in *Constant A.* v *Paul C.A.*: 'The essence of marriage is the coming together of a man and a woman for the purpose of procreation and the rearing of children, thus creating what we know to be the traditional family. A goal of society, government and law is to protect and foster this basic unit of society ... Simply put, if the traditional family relationship (lifestyle) were banned, human society would disappear in little more than one generation, whereas if the homosexual lifestyle were banned, there would be no perceivable harm to society ... A primary function of government and law is to preserve and perpetuate society, in this instance, the family' (U.S.A. 1985, at 6). (No prizes for guessing who won custody there.) In three other American cases[7] judges quoted with approval a law review article that reads in part:

The most threatening aspect of homosexuality is its potential to become a viable alternative to heterosexual intimacy ... Young people form their sexual identity partly on the basis of the models they see in society. If homosexual behaviour is legalized, and thus partly legitimized, an adolescent may question whether he or she should 'choose' heterosexuality ... If society accords more legitimacy to expressions of homosexual attraction, attachment to the opposite sex might be postponed or diverted for some time, perhaps until after the establishment of sexual patterns that would hamper development of traditional heterosexual family relationships. For those persons who eventually choose the heterosexual model, the existence of conflicting models might provide further sexual tension destructive to the traditional marital unit. (Wilkinson and White 1977, 595–6)

Likewise a generalized view of lesbianism as inherently pathological was clearly apparent in cases where the court referred to the mother as 'deviate' or her relationship as 'abnormal' or 'unhealthy'[8] or placed emphasis upon houses that were 'unclean' or 'chaotic' as a metaphor for the mother.[9]

In numerous cases, the mother or her partner was characterized by the court as masculine, or their relationship as butch/femme. Explicit examples include judges who actively strove to find 'role definition' between the partners and to masculinize one of them, for example, by finding that the woman who most often drove the car or paid for meals was the 'dominant' one.[10] Use of profane language, raised voices, suggested or actual physical violence, or an 'aggressive' attitude on the part of either the mother or her partner (towards the court or towards professionals involved in the matter) were also construed as evidence of masculine identification, and from there butch/femme inferences about the couple were often drawn. Such 'facts' (or fantasies) always appeared in the case law as a negative finding to the lesbian mother. If lesbian relationships are viewed as an imitation of heterosexual relationships, they are therefore lesser, and quite possibly disturbed. If lesbians are viewed as masculine, then they are aberrant, not really women, and therefore not proper mothers.

A characterization of the mother/partner relationship as one of sexual-ized power abuse paralleled butch/femme assumptions about the women. For example, in an early Australian case the judge found that: 'The wife, however, I find is an emotional and I believe still immature person. Prior to [her current relationship] she was largely ignorant about homosexuality. Miss Argue was not; she had been a committed lesbian for a number of years. I believe the wife did not then and does not now fully perceive exactly what took place ... I believe that Miss Argue from the time of that weekend onwards [a period of two years] has deliberately educated the wife about homosexuality ... Argue deliberately took the wife to see at least one lesbian couple bringing up children. I believe that the wife, then or now, has no real appreciation of what Argue was doing' (*P.C. and P.R.*, Aust. 1979, 78,608).

In such cases the mother was positioned as submissive, passive, or imma-ture; not really responsible for the relationship. It was therefore the partner who presented the real danger, but by implication the mother was incapa-ble of being protective or properly nurturing towards her children and so was a danger by extension.[11] Once the mother or her partner was viewed as powerful and manipulative, the 'butch' half of a butch/femme pair or the sadist half of a sadist/masochist pair, she could then be seen as having an inherent interest in sexual partners less powerful than herself. As her power in her relationship with her partner was often perceived and expressed in terms of age and 'dominance,' it was no large step to then characterize such a woman as having a propensity to abuse children sexually, a point that is explored further in the next section.

Lesbians also appear in the judgments as manhaters, another quality that is implicitly antisocial, dangerously unwomanly, and unmotherly. It is pos-sible that the oft-used epithet 'militant' in the case law (see Millbank 1992) referred to a fear that lesbians hate men and would try to turn their chil-dren against men.[12] In a recent English case the mother was successful and the judge emphasized that this result was because she was not 'militant.' As evidence of this 'non-militancy,' it was noted that both the mother and her partner had previously had heterosexual relationships – marriage and engagement, respectively (*B.* v *B.*, U.K. 1991).

Lesbian identity was seen by the courts as a dangerous thing. It was also viewed as inherently, and excessively, sexual. Such sexuality was an unequivocally negative factor – as sexuality or sexual orientation was inter-preted judicially to mean *sex*. In cases where the mother's relationship was referred to in sexual terms, with words such as 'lover,' 'sexual partner,' 'affair,' 'paramour,' and 'active' or 'practising homosexual,' with very few exceptions, the mother lost. By way of contrast, in cases where non-sexual terms and blatant euphemisms were used, such as 'companion,' 'friend,' and the ubiquitous 'roommate' (also an 'association' or 'arrangement' rather than a *relationship*), mothers were generally successful in winning custody. Moreover, if in characterizing the relationship between the mother and her partner, the judge found that there was not a 'great deal' of sex in the relationship, the mother's chances of gaining custody improved.

Awards of custody and access frequently have required that the mother's partner move from the house or not be present when the children are, and breaches of these conditions, have resulted in revocations of custody or access.[13] Although this type of order was never popular in the United Kingdom and has diminished recently in Canada and Australia, it continues to appear in U.S. decisions – underscoring the persistent theme that lesbianism is a danger against which children must be protected. Courts must usually find some way of connecting the dangerous lesbian with a danger to children. Such connection need not involve evidence or even specific allegations, however, as the next section illustrates.

The Process of Projection: Children in Danger

No matter how dangerous the lesbian mother was seen to be, lesbianism in itself was generally insufficient to deny custody, as the 'best interests of the child' principle that currently dominates child custody law and decision making demands that the focus of the decision, at least ostensibly, be on the welfare of the child(ren). Courts therefore strove in their reasoning to show how the mother's lesbianism spilled over into, or vitiated, her mothering – for instance, by finding that her relationship was unstable or likely to result in abuse or trauma to the child. Because evidence of any of these factors was generally notable by its absence, such factors most likely arose from 'common sense' understandings of lesbianism as dangerous. These fears were then projected onto children who were seen as inevitably 'at risk.'

One of the clearest examples of the judiciary unconsciously projecting its own fears and beliefs onto children occurred in *Eveson* (U.K. 1980). In that case, despite the 6-year-old boy being happy and well balanced, according to all concerned, the trial judge continually reiterated that he would 'instinctively' feel his mother's relationship to be 'strange or unusual' and 'would learn more and more and it would fill him with dismay and would be very worrying and upsetting for him.'

The belief that lesbian relationships are necessarily unstable and, therefore, not in the interests of children, could form a case study of judicial notice all by itself. A typical example is the following remark: 'Experience shows, just as in the case that took place, that homosexual relationships do tend to be even more unstable than heterosexual relations' (*Re D.*, U.K. 1983). Such beliefs entitle judges to undertake laborious examinations of how many female sexual partners the mother had been involved with, a common thread of inquiry and even a major focus of numerous cases. Mothers were typically subjected to cross examination about their relationships, which were sometimes recorded at length. For example, in *Collins* (U.S.A. 1988) one judge quoted testimony as to lovers named by the questioner as 'number two' and 'number three' and so on (of a possible four), in order to illustrate instability. The combination of the mother's and her partner's past relationships was used to determine that the current relationship between the mother and her partner could not possibly be stable. Such findings were made notwithstanding evidence that the relationship between the women was indeed of longstanding and regarded by the parties and expert witnesses as stable. The judicial projection involved is further highlighted by the fact that in the cases generally, mothers' relationships with men prior to, or even following, the marriage were never in issue. Moreover, the number of relationships in which the father had engaged was very rarely noted, and his current partner's sexual history was universally absent from consideration. The (often unstated) premise was that children would be harmed by instability, and so the (potential? inevitable?) instability of the mother's (lesbian) relationship was a danger to them. The actual happiness of the children in question, or the upheaval and instability that a grant of custody to the father could cause, were irrelevant within such a framework.

Another fear projected onto children was that they were at risk of sexual abuse from lesbian mothers, or more commonly, their partners. Although this issue occasionally arose at the behest of the father, it more usually appeared as a 'common sense' concern of the judges. References to the possibility of child sexual abuse were usually oblique, such as referring to the 'physical' as well as 'moral' impact on a child of growing up in a lesbian household, mention of unspecified risks, the possibility of 'corruption,' the mother's sexuality as 'deviate,' emphasizing the youth of the mother's lover(s), or questioning the mother about the safety of leaving the child(ren) alone with gay and lesbian friends.[14] There were also a few direct references to the possibility of child sexual abuse at the hands of the mother's partner. In a recent American case the partner's statement that too many victims of sexual abuse become abusers was taken by the court to mean that she herself had a propensity to abuse (*Williams*, U.S.A. 1990). In an earlier American case the mother's partner was subjected to a series of questions as to whether she had ever had a physical relationship with the 11-year-old daughter or any other child, and the testimony of a psychiatrist that homosexuals 'sometimes switch affection to another partner' was taken as evidence that the child was at risk of sexual advances from her (*Re Jane B.*, U.S.A. 1976). In yet another American case it was suggested by the judge that the daughter's letters to the partner were too 'passionate' and 'adult' to be healthy and that the partner's close relationship with the daughter was suspect, as she had exerted a 'direct and baleful' influence on the child (*N.K.M.* v *L.E.M.*, U.S.A. 1980). Moreover, the plethora of orders barring partners from living in the house with the mother and children, or from being present during overnight access, contain an undercurrent of fear of sexual abuse from the partner. Evidence that sexual abuse by lesbians generally, or the mother/partner in particular, was extremely improbable was generally accepted on the face of the record, but persisted at a subliminal level.

Far more frequent was the equally erroneous assumption that lesbian and gay parents produce homosexual children – a 'common knowledge' proposition that again betrays a projection of judicial fear of lesbian danger, in this instance of lesbians as contagious or converting. Expert evidence was often introduced by mothers to combat this view and assert that the children of lesbians have been shown time and again to be as likely as the children of heterosexuals to grow up heterosexual (for a comprehensive review of such literature, see Tasker and Golombok 1991).[15] Yet in the cases under review, research studies or specialist psychiatrists supporting the lesbian mother, or asserting that lesbian mothers generally did not make children homosexual or emotionally harm them, were frequently dismissed.[16] When judges found, to the contrary, that children of lesbians *would* be influenced to be homosexual, the reasons for doing so were manifold. In a few cases, the father produced his own psychiatrist or psychologist to say that the children would be 'influenced' or 'harmed,' and whatever the comparative levels of experience and expertise, the court chose to accept the doctor advocating the contagion theory (see also Brophy 1992). However, in numerous cases the court simply asserted that it was *common sense* that the child *would* be influenced to be homosexual, regardless of any evidence.[17] Alternately, the court contended that whatever the children's sexual identity, they would nevertheless be 'harmed,' 'disturbed,' or 'traumatized' in some other, unspecified way, by the mother's lesbianism. No evidence was necessary to prove such assertions.

Indeed, the children could be demonstrably happy and still harm was predicted by the court and weighed against the mother: the courts need not wait 'until the damage is done' (*N.K.M.* v *L.E.M.*, U.S.A. 1980).

Such 'common sense' knowledge of danger and the projection of all manner of threats onto poor innocent children – who were often characterized as only momentarily happy and well balanced because they did not yet understand what was in store for them – implicitly justified the intense, minute, and unlimited scrutiny of the lesbian mother that followed, as she had to prove herself an exception to these already established rules.

Everything Is Sexual: Nothing Is Private

With the welfare of innocent children clearly endangered, in the judicial mind, judges not only could, but must, examine every facet of the lesbian mother's life to evaluate the extent of the threat (see *L. and L.*, Australia, 1983 for a 'handy check list' still being applied in the 1990s). Moreover, if sexuality is taken to mean sex, as this section will demonstrate, then the lesbian mother – defined as she is by her sexuality – brings sex with her wherever she goes. In the case law, an astounding range of behaviour, when done by a lesbian, constitutes a sexual display or an actual sex act. Within this paradigm it is logical that nothing the lesbian mother does is innocuous, and so, nothing can be private.

Actual sexual activity was occasionally the subject of direct inquiry, usually if the mother denied being lesbian. In this case the father typically brought photographs, alleged lesbian lovers, eyewitness testimony of sexual exchanges, love letters, taped conversations, and private investigators' reports into evidence, all of which were then pored over to determine whether the mother was, in fact, lesbian.[18] However, even when the mother admitted that the relationship was lesbian, judges sometimes wanted to know *just how lesbian*, by assessing how 'much' sex there was.[19] A discussion of how often, how loudly, and where the mother had sex was also brought into evidence under the rubric of the child's welfare – presumably because overhearing it would constitute 'exposure' of the child to lesbian sex and be harmful. At the furthest extreme of judicial prurience were the U.S. cases of *Lundin*, 1990, which contained lengthy discussions as to whether the mother had ever had (lesbian) sex while the 2-year-old child was asleep in the house, and *Chicoine*, 1992, which described with considerable disapproval the mother's behaviour in a nightclub (dancing and kissing) as sexual and 'public,' before noting that the children were absent. (*Chicoine* was recently cited, incorrectly, in *Van Driel*, 1994, as an instance in which a lesbian mother took her children to lesbian nightclubs. Such a misreading is intriguing: it suggests both an implicit acceptance of the lesbian-as-demon-mother – from which the mother in *Van Driel* was being distinguished as an exception – and also an unintentional critique of the decision in *Chicoine*, because if the children were not *there*, then why was the nightclub even mentioned?)

More usually, the mother actually having sex took second place to a variety of other activities that were viewed as intrinsically sexual and monitored closely to register their impact. The mother sleeping in the same bed, or same room as her partner, for instance, was noted in literally dozens of cases, and described, universally, as a *sexual display* which amounted to 'subjecting' the children to the relationship or 'exposing children to sexual activities.' Likewise, the mother and her lover spending time in the bedroom together during daylight or walking around the house with their dressing gowns on ('partially clad') was treated as a sexual display. More commonly, holding hands, hugging, or exchanging kisses of greeting and departure were scrutinized at length, always with the implicit or explicit understanding that such gestures were *sexual conduct* or a *sexual display*, which would, inevitably, be inappropriate in front of children. In only one case that I have found did a judge disagree with the focus on affection and the presumption that it was sexual. The mother had lost custody and had her access restricted, supervised, and on occasion denied over a four-year-period, largely as a result of allegations that she and her lover had once shared a bed while on holiday with the child and had shown affection in front of the child. The appellate court overruled the access restrictions saying that 'seeing two consenting adults hug and kiss in a friendly manner is not harmful' (*Pleasant*, U.S.A. 1993).

The lengths to which judges in numerous cases went to inquire whether affection was shown, judges' readiness to see anything as sexual (e.g., a shower curtain adorned with naked female forms, presumably innocuous enough to be sold freely to the general public, was discussed as though it was lesbian pornography in *L. v D.*, U.S.A. 1982), and the lengths to which they were prepared to go to protect children from even a glimpse of the terrible sight of affectionate lesbians, is one of the most striking, even definitional, features of the case law. Custody and access were sometimes conditional on the mother undertaking not to touch her partner in any way, or in any 'inappropriate' way, near the child(ren) (see, e.g., *Parsons*, U.S.A. 1995). The judgments effectively suggest that hugging and holding hands are sexual acts because lesbians are doing them, and are damaging to children because lesbians being sexual is perverse and perversity harms children.

In this way an enormous range of the lesbian mother's behaviour is constructed as dangerous or potentially so, without the need for any evidence of harm or even discomfort on the part of the children. The scrutiny of the courts of every aspect of the mother's sexualized life is not only justified in this scheme, but positively demanded. The pervasiveness of such a scheme raises the question: Can anything in the life of a lesbian mother seeking custody or access be private?

Private Lesbians Versus Lesbians Claiming Privacy

The concept of privacy appeared in the cases in two very different ways. The first was when the lesbian mother (often on advice of counsel) claimed that her lesbianism would not be harmful because she kept it 'private' and did not allow the community or her child(ren) to know of it. The second was when the lesbian mother (sometimes with the assistance of *Amicus Curiae* intervention by lesbian and gay or civil liberties groups) claimed that her sexuality could not be taken into account by a court in a negative fashion, or inquired into, by virtue of her right to privacy. These strategies produced drastically different results and are worth exploring before comparing the conceptions of privacy embodied in each.

Generally the mothers who were 'private' and endeavoured to conceal their sexuality had greater chances of success than lesbians who were 'out.' The most blatant application of this standard was in *B. v B.* (U.K. 1991), where the judge made it clear that the mother won because she and her partner were 'private persons' and not 'militant lesbians where the risks ... may be so much greater.' Numerous commentators have noted that 'discreet' mothers who do not 'flaunt' their lesbianism have a better chance of success than those who are openly lesbian (see, e.g., Arnup 1991; Boyd 1991; Millbank 1992; Polikoff 1986; Robson 1992.)

Such discretion could involve concealment of a mother's sexual identity in either or both of two apparently distinct spheres: the world at large (the public) and the children (the private). In the 'public' arena, the mother, by staying closeted in the community, not joining organizations, and not seeking support from other lesbians was seen as exercising self-discipline and proving herself capable of altruism (ostensibly to prevent teasing or ostracism of the child, often noted by the dramatic nomenclature 'peer trauma'). Such an approach also made the mother more acceptable in that it fitted within a traditional liberal framework of 'tolerance' for difference, providing that such difference does not impact negatively on others. In the 'private' arena of her own home the mother, by remaining closeted with the child(ren), by not 'looking' like a lesbian or leading a lesbian 'lifestyle,' removed the 'pornography' of her life from the children's view. Kissing her lover goodbye was no longer sexual because it was not, apparently, done by a lesbian. Her everyday actions were once again everyday, and no harm was done by viewing them.

The doubly private mother was not always successful, however. The mother's 'discretion' was occasionally read as slyness and deception by the judges, thereby creating an unwholesome atmosphere harmful for children – and so, in a Catch-22 situation, the discreet mother lost.[20] Furthermore, courts sometimes held that the doubly discreet mother could 'never be private enough' for their satisfaction (lesbianism lurks and will burst forth at some stage). Such cases suggest that there is, effectively, no private realm for the lesbian no matter how far she retreats. In a recent Canadian case the mother literally was a lesbian virgin, yet in an incredible stretch of logic, the court nevertheless managed to sexualize her. The mother's present celibacy was reconfigured in such a manner as to display her *future* sexual availability. The court assumed that she would find a string of lovers once she moved to the city, and these women would have an unknown (but presumably sinister) effect on the children, which was all the more troubling because the court was unable to assess the risks for itself (*S.* v *S.*, Canada 1992). Effectively then, the mother's celibacy in that case stood as proof of the promiscuity to come and there was no way to keep it private because it had not even happened yet.

Promising to be private involved privacy as a negative concept – something to be retreated to rather than asserted. Promising to be private did not exclude the court or reject the court's right to assess and supervise the mother's privacy, nor did it deny the basic premise at the heart of the court's inquiry – that lesbianism is a danger. In this sense, a promise to be private could more properly be described as a containment of, or exception to, the lesbian danger. This strategy constitutes a sharp contrast to the situation where mothers positively asserted privacy as rights-bearing subjects.

Claiming privacy entailed a positive assertion on behalf of the mother that the court was not entitled to take the mother's sexuality into account as a negative factor, or was not entitled to make orders that restricted her private life, for instance, by banning her lover or other lesbians and gay men from her house. Such a claim was usually framed in terms of 'the right to privacy,' but also sometimes in terms of a right to equal protection under the law or to freedom of association. Rights arguments asserting that the private realm of the lesbian mother's life was entitled to legal protection were raised exclusively in U.S. cases, most likely reflecting the constitutional 'civil rights' culture in that country, as well as the relative newness of the Canadian Charter of Rights and Freedoms (or its more 'public' application to challenge legislative action rather than judicial discretion) and the absence of a codified bill of rights in Australia and the United Kingdom.

Although rights-based arguments arise frequently in articles and case notes on issues in lesbian and gay family law (e.g., Bateman 1992; Beargie 1988; Clemens 1984; Dooley 1990; Fajer 1992; Gross 1986, Leopold and King 1985; Notes 1989; Rosenblum 1991), in the available case law such arguments were met with outright hostility. In all fourteen appellate decisions in which rights claims were argued on behalf of lesbian mothers in the United States between 1976 and 1992, such arguments either were disregarded completely or dismissed after discussion. In not one case did such an argument succeed.[21] A typical dismissal is the judgment in *Re Jane B.* (U.S.A. 1976) which closed a review of constitutional cases raised in the mother's brief with the following statement: 'These cases do not, however extend the protection to innocent bystanders or children who may be affected physically and emotionally by close contact with homosexual conduct of adults ... This is not a matter of constitutional rights of Respondent or [her lover] to be homosexuals or a violation of their freedom of choice of actions. The fundamental question is whether, in the sound discretion of the Court, this type of living environment is detrimental to the child and in her best interest' (at 857, 858). Likewise in *Bottoms* (U.S.A. 1995), although it is unclear from the judgment whether or not the mother made a rights claim, the Supreme Court of Virginia held that 'while the legal rights of a parent should be respected in a custody proceeding, those technical rights may be disregarded if demanded by the interests of the child.'

The premise of the immutability of sexual orientation is central to many gay and lesbian rights claims to equal protection under the law (see, e.g., Bateman 1992; Dooley 1990; but *contra* Notes 1989) in that it places lesbians and gays within the discrete minority paradigm of classic human rights jurisprudence (see Herman 1994). This is not to say that lesbian and gay rights claims *must* be based on immutability, but rather that to date they mainly have been. In the context of child custody, this strategy has backfired: courts have responded that whereas it may indeed be beyond the mother's control to be a lesbian, living with a lesbian lover and exposing one's child to lesbianism was nonetheless a choice, and a very selfish one at that. Such an approach was mirrored in numerous cases that likened the mother's sexuality to a vice, for example, by comparing it to addictive behaviour such as drug use, or likening it to the father's substance use. In such instances the mother was expected to conquer or repress her sexuality, or 'give up' her partner as proof that she could mother. So, for example: 'Just as an alcoholic overcomes the habit and becomes a non drinker, so this mother should attempt to dissolve her 'alternate lifestyle' of homosexual living. Such is not too great a sacrifice to expect of a parent in order to gain or retain the custody of his or her child' (*Collins*, U.S.A. 1988, concurring judgment at 29).

In custody cases where lesbian or gay rights claims were raised, a common thread of 'equality with a vengeance' (MacKinnon 1987) emerged. In the United States the criminality of lesbian sexual acts in some states was used by judges to place lesbian mothers in the position of 'criminals' to be treated 'equally' with other criminal parents such as drug dealers and murderers. (Intriguingly, heterosexuals in these states are presumed not to engage in 'deviate' criminalized acts such as oral sex, in order to prop up the facade of equal treatment.) The most recent, and notorious, case is that of Sharon Bottoms, who was found to be an 'unfit' parent by reason of her (once or twice weekly) oral sex. The trial court stated: 'I will tell you first that the mother's conduct is illegal. It is a Class 6 felony in the Commonwealth of Virginia. I will tell you that it is the opinion of this Court that her conduct is immoral. And it is the opinion of this court that the conduct of Sharon Bottoms renders her an unfit parent.' Bottoms's own mother (the grandmother) was granted custody of the 3-year-old boy. Sharon successfully appealed to the court of appeals which overturned the decision (although custody remained with the grandmother pending the next appeal). The grandmother appealed to the Supreme Court of Virginia where she again won. The court held that the criminality of the 'conduct inherent in lesbianism' was an 'important consideration in determining custody.' Such reasoning sounds implausibly antiquated, but it happened on 21 April 1995 (*Bottoms*, U.S.A. 1995).

The general tone of judicial responses to right claims was that the welfare of the child, or children's rights, were always to be valued above and seen as separate from parental claims. Thus, the very act of claiming a right in this forum was seen to imply a lack of concern by the mother for the child's welfare. A Good Mother puts her child first: a claim to rights is a self-interested, and therefore un-motherly, act. In only two of the fourteen cases containing rights claims did the mother win custody, both on other grounds.

The lack of success and outright condemnation of mothers who claimed privacy as a positive right provides a stark contrast to the relative success of mothers who promised to be private. Mothers who promised to be private admitted the power of courts to scrutinize such private space while simultaneously shielding it from others. This concept of the private was neither a gain for the mother, nor a territory over which she had any control: the court delineated who she could tell about her lesbianism, who she could allow in her house, who she could kiss, and when. It could thus be seen as contiguous with all the other denials of private space to lesbian mothers explored in this chapter, with the exception that such surrender sometimes guaranteed success.

Conclusion

This chapter has attempted to illustrate the lack of any (tangible or conceptual) private arena for lesbian mothers involved in child custody cases and to explore the processes by which this situation has come about. Lesbianism has been the subject of demonization in Western culture. These representations exist also in legal judgments, where they become a source of 'common sense' from which judges draw knowledge. They also form the substance of fears, risks, and dangers that are projected onto vulnerable children, whom the court is then duty bound to protect. Not all lesbian mothers lose custody, but they must face and negotiate their way around the demonization of lesbianism, often by proving themselves to be exceptions to 'the rule.'

In this context, courts can and must scrutinize the lesbian mother to the fullest extent: there is no part of her life that can be held back as private. The relative success of 'discreet' or private lesbian mothers represents an extension of such a lack of privacy, as such mothers permit courts to view or even construct the space in which she exists as lesbian. Lastly, a claim to rights or to privacy in this context is disastrous, and not only because of welfare discourses and the 'child centred' focus of family law – although these factors are operative (Brophy 1992; Smart 1989). Rather it is because lesbians are not viewed as rights-bearing subjects or as having an entitlement because of the extent to which they have been pre-configured as dangerous, criminal, or pathological. Lesbian mothers cannot claim privacy because there is no permissible private space for them in such a legal framework.

NOTES

Thanks to Susan Boyd and Regina Graycar for their helpful and incisive comments on earlier versions of this chapter.

1 *Collins* v *Collins* No. 87–238–II, 1988 Tenn App LEXIS 123 (Tenn App, 30 March 1988), at 2 and 15.

2 See in particular the 1994 decision of the United Nations Human Rights Committee in the *Toonen* case, *Communication No. 488/1992*, (reported by Ivan Shearer (1995) 69 *Australian Law Journal* 600–9). The committee declared admissible Nicholas Toonen's complaint that sections of the Tasmanian Criminal Code criminalizing gay male sex breached Articles 17 (privacy) and 26 (equality) of the *International Covenant on Civil and Political Rights*. However, the committee based its decision in his favour on the privacy ground and left the equality ground undecided.

3 *Collins, supra* note 1, at 2 and 15.

4 This chapter is based on an analysis of cases from these countries, spanning the period 1974–95 (current to Aug. 1995) reported either in conventional law reports or through the computer case databases Quicklaw, Westlaw, and Lexis. All cases involve a lesbian mother versus heterosexual father custody dispute situation unless otherwise specified.

Australia: *A. and J.* (1995) 19 Fam LR 260, *Brook and Brook* (1977) FLC 90–325, *Cartwright and Cartwright* (1977) FLC 90–302, *G. and G.* (1988) FLC 91–939, *Harvey and Creswell* (1988) (unreported, No. ACT G2, Full Court of the Federal Court of ACT, 23 Dec. 1988, before Davies, Kelly, and Neaves, JJ), *Jarman* v *Lloyd and Ors* (1982) 8 Fam LR 878 (maternal grandmother also a party, but not hostile to mother), *Kitchener and Kitchener* (1978) FLC 90–436, *L. and L.* (1983) FLC 91–353, *N. and N.* (1977) FLC 90–208, *O'Reilly and O'Reilly* (1977) FLC 90–300, *P.C. and P.R.* (1979) FLC 90–676, *Schmidt and Schmidt* (1979) FLC 90–685, *Shepherd and Shepherd* (1979) FLC 90–729 (mother ex-lesbian, father gay), *Spry and Spry* (1977) FLC 90–271.

Canada: *Adams* v *Woodbury* [1986] B.C.J No. 2725 (unreported, Quicklaw, BC SC, Vernon, Lamperson LJSC, 26 June 1986) (contested adoption of lesbian mother's child by unrelated couple), *Re (L.A.) B.* [1989] BCJ No. 2431 (unreported, Quicklaw, B.C. Prov Ct, Auxier Prov Ct J 14 December 1989) (wardship), *Re Barkely and Barkely* (1980) 108 DLR (3d) 613 (Ont), *Bezaire* v *Bezaire* (1980) 20 RFL (2d) 358 (Ont CA), *Bernhardt* v *Bernhardt* (1979) 10 RFL (2d) 32 (Man QB), *Case* v *Case* (1974) 18 RFL 132 (Sask QB), *Children's Aid Society of Halifax* v *A.(M.)* [1986] NSJ No. 423 (unreported, Quicklaw, NS Fam Ct, Neidermayer JFC, 25 Nov. 1986) (wardship), *Collins* v *Collins* (1994) (unreported, 15 June 1994, Ont CJ LEXIS 1148) (lesbian mother seeking to deny access to gay father), *Daller* v *Daller* (1988) 18 RFL (3d) 53 (Ont HC), *Elliott* v *Elliott* [1987] BCJ No. 43 (unreported, Quicklaw, BC SC, Vancouver, MacKinnon J, 15 Jan. 1987), *Ewankiw* v *Ewankiw* (1994) 52 ACWS 3d 575 (Man QB), *K.* v *K.* (1975) 23 RFL 58 (Alta), *Monk* v *Doan and Aitken* (1991) 94 Sask R 315 (Sask QB) (lesbian seeking custody of her sister's children), *N.* v *N.* [1992] BCJ No. 1507 (unreported, Quicklaw, BC SC, Vancouver, Warren J,

2 July 1992), *Robertson* v *Geisinger* (1991) 36 RFL (3d) 261 (Sask QB) (father also gay), *S.* v *S.* [1992] BCJ No. 1579 (unreported, Quicklaw, BC SC, Cranbrook, Melnick J, 30 Nov. 1992), *Seselja* v *Seselja* [1994] OJ No. 639 (unreported, Quicklaw, Ont CJ, Prov Div, Brampton, Karswick Prov Div J, 9 March 1994), *Steers* v *Monk* [1992] OJ No. 2701 (unreported, Quicklaw, Ont CJ, Prov Div, Brampton, Wolder Prov Div J, 1 Dec. 1992), *Tomanek* v *Tomanek* [1993] OJ No. 1371 (unreported, Quicklaw, Ont CJ, Gen Div, Sault Ste Marie, Noble J, 10 June 1993).

United Kingdom: *Re A.* (wardship: children in care) (1979) 1 FLR 100, *B.* v *B.* [1991] 1 FLR 402, *C.* v *C.* [1991] 1 Fam LR 223 (CA), *Cummins* v *Vassallo* (1981) (unreported, Ct App, Ormrod, Shaw LJJ, Purchas J, 4 Feb. 1981) (lesbian sought custody of her young half-brother and sister vs children's father or wardship), *Re D. and D.* (unreported, CA, Eveleigh LJ and Ormrod, Sir R, 16 Feb. 1983), *Re E.* (unreported, CA, Gibson LJ and Braewell J, 1 July 1993) (lesbian seeking to adopt unrelated child), *Eveson* v *Eveson* (unreported, CA, Arnold, Sir J and Lane, Dame E, 27 Nov. 1980), *Holder* v *Holder* (unreported, CA, O'Connor CJ and Lately J, 12 Dec. 1985), *Re M.* (judicial continuity) [1993] 1 FLR 903 (CA), *Re N.* (1994) (unreported, CA, Neill, Saville LJJ, 2 Sept. 1994), *Re P.* (1983) 4 FLR 401 (CA), *Re S.* (unreported, CA, Glidewell LJ and Cazelet J, 22 July 1993), *S.* v *S.* (1978) 1 FLR 143 (CA), *Walker* v *Walker* (unreported, CA, Ormrod and Brandon JJ, 17 June 1980) (father somewhat gay).

United States: *Ashling* v *Ashling* 599 P. 2d 475 (Or App 1979), *Anonymous* v *Anonymous* 503 NYS 466 (AD 4 Dept 1986), *Barron* v *Barron* 594 A 2d 682 (Pa Super 1991), *Bennett* v *O'Rourke* (1985) (unreported slip opinion, LEXIS, Tenn App, 5 Nov. 1985), *Bezio* v *Patenaude* 410 NE 2d 1207 (Mass 1980) (lesbian mother versus unrelated adult who had guardianship by consent), *Black* v *Black* 1988 Tenn App LEXIS 167 (Tenn App, 10 March 1988), *Blew* v *Verta* 617 A 2d 31 (Pa Super 1992), *In re Breisch* 434 A 2d 815 (Pa Super 1981) (wardship), *Bottoms* v *Bottoms* 457 SE 2d 102 (VA Supreme 1995), 444 SE 2d 276 (Va App 1994) (maternal grandmother versus mother), *Chicoine* v *Chicoine* 479 NW 2d 891 (SD 1992), *Collins* v *Collins* No. 87–238–II, 1988 Tenn App LEXIS 123 (Tenn App, 30 March 1988), *Constant A.* v *Paul C.A.* 496 A 2d 1 (Pa Super 1985), *D.H.* v *J.H.* 418 NE 2d 286 (Ind App 1981), *Dailey* v *Dailey* 635 SW 2d 391 (Tenn App 1981), *In re Marriage of Diehl* 582 NE 2d 281 (Ill App 2 Dist 1991), *DiStefano* v *DiStefano* 401 NYS 2d 636 (NY App 1978), *Doe* v *Doe* (Adoption) 284 SE 2d 799 (Va 1981) (father and new wife sought adoption contested by mother), *Doe* v *Doe* 452 NE 2d 293 (Mass App 1983), *Fox* v *Fox* 1995 WL 22057 (Okla) (14 July 1995), *G.A.* v *D.A.* 745 SW 2d 726 (Mo App 1987), *Hembree* v *Hembree* 1995 WL 326951 (Ala Civ App) (2 June 1995) (mother vs maternal grandfather and maternal step-grandmother), *Jacobson* v *Jacobson* 314 NW 2d 78

(ND 1981), *In Re Jane B. an infant* 380 NYS 2d 848 (NY 1976), *Kallas v Kallas* 614 P 2d 641 (Utah 1980), *L. v D.* 630 SW 2d 240 (Mo App 1982), *Large v Large* 1993 Ohio App LEXIS 5810 (Ohio App 10 Dist, 2 Dec. 1993), *Larson v Larson* No. CA 94–154, 1995 WL 407108 (Ark App) (5 July 1995), *Lundin v Lundin* 563 So 2d 1273 (La App 1 Cir 1990), *M.J.P. v J.G.P.* 640 P 2d 966 (Okl 1982), *M.P. v S.P.* 404 A 2d 1256 (NJ App 1979), *In re Martins* 269 Ill App 3d 380 (Ill App 1995), *Mohrman v Mohrman* 565 NE 2d 1283 (Ohio App 1989), *N.K.M. v L.E.M.* 606 SW 2d 179 (Mo App 1980), *In re Parsons* 1995 WL 442587 (Tenn App) (27 July, 1995), *Peyton v Peyton* 457 So 2d 321 (La App 2 Cir 1984), *Phillips v Phillips* 1995 Ohio App LEXIS 1030 (Ohio App 1995), *In re Marriage of Pleasant* No. 1-91-3835, 1993 Ill App LEXIS 1810 (Ill App 1 Dist, 8 Dec. 1993) (access restricted following loss of custody to mother), *S. v S.* 608 SW 2d 64 (Ky App 1980), *S.E.G. v R.A.G.* 735 SW 2d 164 (Mo App 1987), *S.L.H. v D.B.H.* 745 SW 2d 848 (Mo App 1988), *S.N.E. v R.L.B.* 699 P 2d 875 (Alaska 1985), *Schuster v Schuster* (joined with *Isaacson v Isaacson*) 585 P 2d 130 (Wash 1978), *Thigpen v Carpenter* 730 SW 2d 510 (Ark App 1987), *Townend v Townend* 1 FLR (BNA) 2830 (Ohio 1975) (paternal grandmother granted custody), *Tucker v Tucker/Calvin* 910 P 2d 1209 (Utah SC 1996), 881 P 2d 948 (Utah App 1994), *Van Driel v Van Driel* 525 NW 2d 37 (SD App 1994), *Werneburg v Werneburg* 6 FLR (BNA) 2280 (NY 1980), *White v Thompson* 569 So 2d 1181 (Miss 1990) (mother versus father and paternal grandparents), *In Re Marriage of Williams* 563 NE 2d 1195 (Ill App 3 Dist 1990). See also Millbank (1994).

5 None of these types are 'true,' in that while some lesbians may be accurately described by them, this would be no more so than women in any other section of the population. See Hanscombe and Forster (1982), Lewin (1993), O'Connor and Ryan (1993), Pollack and Vaughan (1987).

6 The phenomenon of 'lesbian chic' is a concept coined by the print media, primarily glossy magazines, in describing representations of lesbianism in the U.S.A., mixing both lesbian characters in fiction and real 'personalities' in life. Although 'lesbian chic' is novel in depicting lesbianism (or, more frequently, bisexuality) as sexy and 'interesting,' it is not necessarily devoid of the numerous negative pre-chic characteristics imputed to lesbians – they are simply more beautiful, and thus arguably titillating to a heterosexual audience. Moreover, 'chic' lesbian characters, when they appear, are often swiftly destroyed, converted back to heterosexuality, or written out – differing only from earlier representations in that 'chic' lesbians are universally *attractive* (see, e.g., Nancy's swift recantation of lesbianism in *Rosanne* in 1993 and the virtually instantaneous near-lethal burning of the lesbian character Allison on *Beverley Hills 90210* in 1995).

7 *Schuster* (U.S.A. 1978) (dissent), *M.J.P. v J.G.P.* (U.S.A. 1982) and *Collins* (U.S.A. 1988) (concurring), *supra* note 4.

8 See, e.g., United Kingdom: *Eveson* 1980, *Re P.* 1983, *Re D.* 1983. U.S.A.: *Werneburg* 1980, *S. v S.* 1980, *N.K.M. v L.E.M.* 1980, *Doe* 1981, *L. v D.* 1982, *Constant A. v Paul C.A.* 1985, *S.E.G. v R.A.G.* 1987, *G.A. v D.A.* 1987, *Collins* 1988, *Chicoine* 1992, *Larson* 1995. Australia: *Cartwright* 1977, *supra* note 4.

9 See, e.g., Canada: *Elliott* 1987, *Bernhardt* 1979. U.S.A.: *D.H. v J.H.* 1981, *Diehl* 1991, *supra* note 4.

10 See, e.g., Australia: *P.C. and P.R.* 1979, *L. and L.* 1983, *G. and G.* 1988. U.S.A.: *N.K.M. v L.E.M.* 1980, *Dailey* 1981, *supra* note 4.

11 On a few occasions such characterization was reversed, with the mother positioned as the abuser. The most overt example of characterizing lesbianism as a form of sexual vampirism occurred in *Williams*, where the court stated: 'Here the evidence reveals that the mother exhibited gross character defects. The mother, while a nurse at Lifeway, actively recruited a patient who was a minor [17 or 18 years of age, disputed, mother's age not noted] to engage in an illicit and criminal relationship ... In doing so, the mother showed her propensity to feed her sexual appetite without regard to morals, ethics or law. As an employed nurse at this drug treatment program, Marian abused her position in order to take advantage of an underage drug addict whom she desired as a sexual partner (U.S.A. 1990, *supra* note 4, at 1199).

12 For a recent example, see *A. and J.* (Aust. 1995), *supra* note 4, where although the court regarded both parents as being equally capable of parenting, and the mother had retained interim custody, it held that the child required a 'balancing' male influence to counter having a lesbian mother. As the father planned to move interstate, he was granted custody to preserve this 'balancing' influence. This finding was upheld on appeal to the full court.

13 Cases where restrictions have been ordered are – Canada: *Elliott* 1987, *Bezaire* 1980 (both losing custody when condition breached). United Kingdom: *S. v S.* 1978, *Re P.* 1983. U.S.A.: *Re Jane B.* 1976, *Schuster and Isaacson* 1978, *DiStefano* 1978, *Ashling* 1979, *M.P. v S.P.* 1979, *Dailey* 1981, *N.K.M. v L.E.M.* 1980, *L. v D.* 1982, *Anonymous* 1986 (restriction too broad, limited on appeal to homosexual contact or conduct), *S.E.G. v R.A.G.* 1987, *Diehl* 1991, *White v Thompson* 1990, *Chicoine* 1992, *Blew v Verta* at trial, overturned on appeal (access only) 1992, *Collins* 1988, *Pleasant* at trial, overturned eventually on appeal (access only) 1993, possibly also *Larson* 1995 at trial. Australia: *Spry* 1977 at interim hearing but removed at trial, *Kitchener* 1977, *P.C. and P.R.* at interim hearing but removed at trial, *G. and G.* 1988 at interim but removed at trial, *supra* note 4. The period between interim hearing and trial was usually around one year.

14 See, e.g., U.S.A.: *S. v S.* 1980, *D.H. v J.H.* 1981, *Collins* 1988, *Pleasant* 1993. United Kingdom: *Eveson* 1980, *B. v B.* 1991, *supra* note 4.

15 The unstated premise is that if the child were to grow up homosexual she or he (or society as a whole) would be 'harmed' by the award of custody to the lesbian mother. A vigorous assertion of the heterosexuality of lesbians' children becomes complicit in this framework, as it is intended as evidence that the children are, in effect, unharmed. Nancy Polikoff (1986) is one of few commentators to express reservations about these tactics.

16 Likewise, in cases where a court-appointed or partisan psychologist, psychiatrist, or counsellor had interviewed the mother and/or child and recommended in the mother's favour, the mother still had a far less than even chance of winning custody.

17 See, e.g., United Kingdom: *B.* v *B.* 1991. U.S.A.: *M.J.P.* v *J.G.P.* 1982, *S.E.G.* v *R.A.G.* 1987, *Black* 1988, *Collins* 1988, *Chicoine* 1992, *Pleasant* 1993. Australia: *Cartwright* 1977, *supra* note 4.

18 See, e.g., Canada: *Bernhardt* 1979. U.S.A.: *N.K.M.* v *L.E.M.* 1980, *D.H.* v *J.H.* 1981, *S.L.H.* v *D.B.H.* 1988. United Kingdom: *S.* v *S.* 1980. Australia: *N. and N.* 1977, *supra* note 4.

19 See, e.g., Canada: *Daller* 1980. U.S.A.: *Doe* 1981. Australia: *P.C. and P.R.* 1979, *supra* note 4.

20 See, Canada: *Ewankiw* 1994. United Kingdom: *Eveson* 1980, *supra* note 4.

21 The cases were, U.S.A.: *Ashling* 1979, *DiStefano* 1978, *M.P.* v *S.P.* 1979, *Dailey* 1981, *S.E.G.* v *R.A.G.* 1987, *Mohrman* 1989, *Blew* v *Verta* 1992, *Collins* 1988, *Re Jane B.* 1976, *Schuster and Isaacson* 1978, *L.* v *D.* 1982, *Constant A.* v *Paul C.A.* 1985, *Thigpen* v *Carpenter* 1987, *Diehl* 1991, *supra* note 4. In a single case, an argument for freedom of speech made by the mother under the state constitution in question was successful in overturning a 'gag order' that had banned the parties from speaking to any person, in public or private, about the matter: see *S.N.E.* v *R.L.B.* 1985, *supra* note 4.

REFERENCES

Arnup, Katherine. 1991. '"We Are Family": Lesbian Mothers in Canada.' *Resources for Feminist Research* 20, 101–7
– 1989. '"Mothers Just Like Others": Lesbians, Divorce and Child Custody in Canada.' *Canadian Journal of Women and the Law* 3(1), 18–32
Bateman, Margaret. 1992. 'Lesbians, Gays and Child Custody: An Australian Legal History.' *Australian Gay and Lesbian Law Journal* 1, 47–71
Beargie, Robert. 1988. 'Custody Determinations Involving the Homosexual Parent.' *Family Law Quarterly* 22, 71–86
Boyd, Susan. 1992. 'What Is a Normal Family? C v C (A minor) (Custody: appeal).' *Modern Law Review* 55, 269–78

- 1991. 'Potentialities and Perils of the Primary Caregiver Presumption.' *Canadian Family Law Quarterly* 7, 1–30

Brophy, Julia. 1992. 'New Families, Judicial Decision Making and Children's Welfare.' *Canadian Journal of Women and the Law* 5(2), 484–97

Clemens, Margaret. 1984. 'In the Best Interests of the Child and the Lesbian Mother: a Proposal for Legislative Change in New York.' *Alberta Law Review* 48, 1021–44

Creed, Barbara. 1993. *The Monstrous-Feminine: Film, Psychoanalysis, Feminism.* Routledge: London

Dooley, David. 1990. 'Immoral Because They're Bad, Bad Because They're Wrong: Sexual Orientation and Presumptions of Parental Unfitness in Custody Disputes.' *California Western Law Review* 26, 395–424

Dyer, Richard. 1993. *The Matter of Images: Essays on Representation.* London: Routledge

- 1992. *Only Entertainment.* London: Routledge
- 1990. *Now you See It: Studies on Lesbian and Gay Film.* London: Routledge
- ed. 1984. *Gays and Film*, rev. ed. New York: Zoetrope

Faderman, Lillian. 1991. *Odd Girls and Twilight Lovers.* New York: Columbia University Press

- 1982. *Surpassing the Love of Men: Romantic Friendship Between Women from the Renaissance to the Present.* London: Women's Press

Fajer, Marc. 1992. 'Can Two Real Men Eat Quiche Together? Storytelling, Gender-role Stereotypes, and Legal Protection for Lesbians and Gay Men.' *University of Miami Law Review* 46, 551–651

Gross, Wendy. 1986. 'Judging the Best Interests of the Child: Child Custody and the Homosexual Parent.' *Canadian Journal of Women and the Law* 2, 505–31

Hanscombe, Gillian, and Jackie Forster. 1982. *Rocking the Cradle: Lesbian Mothers, a Challenge in Family Living.* Boston: Alyson

Herman, Didi. 1994. *Rights of Passage: Struggles for Lesbian and Gay Legal Equality.* Toronto: University of Toronto Press

hooks, bell. 1993. 'Power to the Pussy: We Don't Wannabe Dicks in Drag.' In Lisa Frank and Paul Smith, eds., *Madonnarama: Essays on Sex and Popular Culture.* Pittsburgh: Cleis Press, 65–80

Kline, Marlee. 1993. 'Complicating the Ideology of Motherhood: Child Welfare and First Nation Women.' *Queen's Law Journal* 18, 306–42

- 1992. 'Child Welfare Law, "Best Interests of the Child" Ideology and First Nations.' *Osgoode Hall Law Journal* 30, 375–425

Leopold, Margaret, and Wendy King. 1985. 'Compulsory Heterosexuality, Lesbians, and the Law: The Case for Constitutional Protection.' *Canadian Journal of Women and the Law* 1, 163–86

Lewin, Ellen. 1993. *Lesbian Mothers: Accounts of Gender in American Culture.* Ithaca: Cornell University Press

MacKinnon, Catharine. 1987. *Feminism Unmodified: Discourses on Life and Law.* Cambridge: Harvard University Press

Merck, Mandy. 1993. *Perversions: Deviant Readings.* London: Virago

Millbank, Jenni. 1994. 'What do Lesbians Do? Motherhood Ideology, Lesbian Mothers and Family Law.' Masters In Law Thesis, University of British Columbia, Vancouver

– 1992. 'Lesbian Mothers, Gay Fathers: Sameness and Difference.' *Australian Gay and Lesbian Law Journal* 2, 21–40

Monture, Patricia. 1989. 'A Vicious Circle: Child Welfare and the First Nations.' *Canadian Journal of Women and the Law* 3(1), 1–17

'Notes: Custody Denials to Parents in Same Sex Relationships: An Equal Protection Analysis.' 1989. *Harvard Law Review* 102, 617–36

O'Connor, Noreen, and Joanna Ryan. 1993. *Wild Desires and Mistaken Identities: Lesbianism and Psychoanalysis.* London: Virago

O'Donovan, Katherine. 1985. *Sexual Divisions in Law.* London: Weidenfeld and Nicolson

Olsen, Frances. 1985. 'The Myth of State Intervention in the Family.' *Journal of Law Reform* 18, 835–64

– 1983. 'The Family and the Market: A Study of Ideology and Legal Reform.' *Harvard Law Review* 96, 1497–1578

Polikoff, Nancy. 1986. 'Lesbian Mothers, Lesbian Families: Legal Obstacles, Legal Challenges.' *New York University Review of Law and Social Change* 14, 907–14

Pollack, Sandra, and Jeanne Vaughn. 1987. *Politics of the Heart: A Lesbian Parenting Anthology.* Ithaca: Firebrand

Pritchard, Sarah. 1995. 'The Jurisprudence of Human Rights: Some Critical Thought and Developments in Practice.' *Australian Journal of Human Rights* 2(1), 3–38

Robson, Ruthann. 1992. *Lesbian (Out)law: Survival Under the Rule of Law.* New York: Firebrand

Rosenblum, David. 1991. 'Custody Rights of Gay and Lesbian Parents.' *Villanova Law Review* 36, 1665–96

Smart, Carol. 1989. *Feminism and the Power of Law.* London: Routledge

Tasker, Fiona, and Susan Golombok. 1991. 'Children Raised by Lesbian Mothers: The Empirical Evidence.' *Family Law* May, 184–7

Thornton, Margaret, ed. 1995. *Public and Private: Feminist Legal Debates.* Melbourne: Oxford University Press

Verhoeven, Deb. 1993. 'Biting the Hand that Breeds: The Trials of Tracey Wigginton.' In Helen Birch, ed., *Moving Targets: Women, Murder and Representation.* London: Virago, 95–126

Weiss, Andrea. 1992. *Vampires and Violets: Lesbians in the Cinema.* London: Jonathan Cape

Wilkinson, J. Harvie III, and G. Edward White. 1977. 'Constitutional Protection for Personal Lifestyles.' *Cornell Law Review* 62, 563

Williams, Patricia. 1991. *The Alchemy of Race and Rights.* Cambridge: Harvard University Press

PART 4
CURRENT CHALLENGES: RESTRUCTURING,
PRIVATIZATION, AND GLOBALIZATION

12

Public Taxes, Privatizing Effects, and Gender Inequality

CLAIRE F.L. YOUNG

As this book demonstrates, there are many aspects of the public/private divide, and these different aspects have various effects in many legal spheres. In this chapter I focus primarily on the construction of the state (as represented by the federal government) as the public sphere and the family as the private sphere. I also discuss the role of the market and the ambiguity of its position as part of the public/private dichotomy. In contrast to the state, the market is the private sphere but, when juxtaposed with the family, it becomes part of the public sphere (Olsen 1983). From a feminist tax perspective, any discussion of the public/private divide has tended to focus on the role that the tax system plays as a disincentive to women's participation in the paid labour force (the public sphere) and the consequent reinforcement of their primary responsibility for child care and household labour in the heterosexual (private) family (Kitchen 1986; Lahey 1985; Maloney 1989). Building on this work, I focus on the role of the tax system as a tool in funding social and economic programs.

I analyse three examples: the deduction for child care expenses; the rules that require the inclusion and permit the deduction of child support payments; and the preferential tax treatment for contributions to private pension plans and registered retirement savings plans. Using tax expenditure analysis as my theoretical base, I concentrate on the privatizing effect of funding social and economic programs through the tax system and the detrimental consequences of this policy for women. This privatization is manifested primarily by the use of tax incentives to encourage reliance on the family (rather than the state) for matters such as the support and care of children and the financial welfare of elderly women. Despite the fact that public funds are being directed by the tax system towards such matters as child care and the support of the elderly, the structure of the tax system results in an abdication by the state of much of the responsibility for these matters and places it on the family and, in some instances, the market. This shift in responsibility is accomplished in different ways and with differing results for each of the areas I discuss, but in all three cases women are disadvantaged as a result.

The tax system is not merely a revenue-raising instrument. It is also a massive spending program. This concept of the tax system as a spending program had its genesis in the United States in 1969 (Surrey 1969). Tax expenditure analysis recognizes that any departure from a normative tax system, by way of measures such as income exclusions and tax deductions, deferrals, or credits, is a tax expenditure (Surrey 1973). That is, rather than delivering a direct subsidy for a particular activity or endeavour by way of, for example, a direct grant, the government delivers the subsidy through the tax system. Tax expenditure analysis has been recognized by the Canadian federal government and incorporated into its tax policy-making process (Poddar 1988); indeed the publication of tax expenditure accounts detailing the cost of all tax expenditures has become entrenched in the Canadian budget process.[1] The debate about whether the tax system is the appropriate tool by which to deliver subsidies for social and economic activity has been vigorous. I contend that in many instances the tax system is a very blunt instrument by which to deliver sophisticated social programs. For example, a deduction in the computation of income is one type of tax measure often used to deliver a subsidy, but a deduction is worth more to those who pay tax at a high rate than to those who have less income and pay tax at a lower rate. An 'upside down effect' in terms of tax equity is thereby produced because the value of a deduction is tied to the rate at which a taxpayer pays tax. Even if the subsidy is delivered as a tax credit and is therefore worth the same in terms of tax dollars saved to all taxpayers, those who pay no tax (frequently the poor) do not receive the subsidy unless it is a refundable tax credit.

The discriminatory impact of the tax system on women has been discussed elsewhere (Dulude 1979; Kitchen 1986; Lahey 1985; Maloney 1989, 1987; National Association of Women and the Law 1991; Woodman 1990; Young 1994b). This discrimination takes many forms and includes the deleterious effect on women (who form the majority of the poor in Canada) of the recent trend towards less progressivity in the tax system, as well as the reliance on tax deductions to deliver subsidies. The discriminatory effect of the tax system on women is the background to the issues that I shall discuss in this chapter. It is exacerbated in many instances by the tax system's designation of the private sphere (as repre-

sented by the family and sometimes the market) as the primary benefi-
ciary of tax subsidies.

Child Care

The lack of affordable, accessible child care in Canada has been well documented (see, e.g., Lero et al. 1992; Pence 1992). It has been estimated that
only 15 per cent of children 12 years of age or younger who require care
for 20 hours a week are served by licensed child care arrangements (Health
and Welfare Canada 1991). The unavailability of child care is a significant
impediment to entry or re-entry into the paid labour force for women with
children (Duffy and Pupo 1992; Maloney 1987; National Action Committee on the Status of Women, (NACSW) 1993; Status of Women Canada
1986). For some women it means not working outside the home, and for
others it means part-time work, shift work, or work at a location close to
home. Indeed women form 70 per cent of the part-time labour force and
one-quarter of women working part-time cite family responsibilities as the
reason (CACSW 1994, 49). Lack of child care is clearly an economic issue
for women. In 1991 women's earnings (full-time and part-time) were only
61.5 per cent of men's earnings (Statistics Canada 1993b, Text Table II, 13).
A contributing factor to this inequality in earnings is that part-time work is
less remunerative than full-time work. Another contributing factor is that
women with children may be required to work in jobs that require fewer
overtime hours or that allow them unpaid leave during school vacation
times (NACSW 1993). Women without child care often are not able to take
advantage of educational opportunities that would lead to higher-paying
jobs.

The primary method of funding child care in Canada is through the tax
system. Section 63 of the Income Tax Act[2] permits a deduction in the
computation of income for child care expenses and in 1993 (latest figures
available) the cost of this deduction was over $305 million (Canada,
Department of Finance 1995). The amount of the deduction under section
63 is limited to $5,000 for an eligible child under 7 (or who has a prolonged
mental or physical impairment) and $3,000 for an eligible child aged 7 to
15. Allowable child care expenses include amounts paid for babysitting services, day nursery services, and boarding school or camp fees, although
there are weekly maximums prescribed in the latter two categories. The
child care expense must have been incurred to enable the taxpayer or supporting person who resided with the child to perform the duties of
employment, carry on a business, undertake certain occupational training,

or carry on grant-funded research. An eligible child is a dependent child of the taxpayer or the taxpayer's spouse.[3] The deductible amount is limited to the lesser of the amounts described above or two-thirds of the taxpayer's earned income for the year. In two-parent families the deduction must be claimed by the person earning the lower income, except where she or he is a full-time student, in prison, incapable of caring for the children, or living apart from the other person for at least 90 days by reason of the breakdown of their relationship.[4]

The policy underlying the deduction is to enable women with children to work outside the home by reducing their costs of child care.[5] In theory the deduction facilitates the movement of women from the private sphere (the family) into the public sphere (the workplace). The problem is that, at the same time, the deduction has a privatizing effect with respect to the child care services that are intended to reduce the impediment to women's participation in the paid labour force. Put simply, public funds allocated to child care are, through a combination of factors, being directed towards financing child care in the private sphere, that is, the family or the private market. Unlike direct subsidies paid in the form of operating or capital grants to non-profit child care facilities, tax subsidies are received by individuals and may be in respect of any child care expense. There are no limits on the forms of the child care that qualify for the subsidy. That is, they may be any child care service provided by any person, other than – in the case of the current section 63 deduction – the parent of the child or a relative under 18 years of age. But it is irrelevant for tax purposes whether the child care is provided by the private sector (through the family or other in-home care-givers) or the public sector (through licensed day care facilities) or, indeed, in unlicensed day care facilities that may be run for profit or not. This method of funding may serve to privatize child care and is one example of the general trend towards privatizing the costs of social reproduction (Fudge 1989).

The lack of spaces for children in child care facilities has already been discussed. Indeed the majority of parents report difficulties in finding child care for their children (Pence 1992). Taken together, the lack of spaces and the non-accountability for the nature of the child care that gives rise to the tax deductible expense results in recourse in many instances to family members as the providers of child care (ibid.). Although this state of affairs may be acceptable to some, it presents problems for others, including those without family members able to provide child care and those who prefer not to have to resort to their families for child care. The role of the state in this scenario is complex. It does provide a subsidy for child care and in that respect takes some responsibility for the provision of child care and recognizes that it is not the sole responsibility of the family. But at the same time the state ceases to play a direct role once that subsidy has been provided, leaving the availability and nature of child care to the private sector, that is, the family or the private market. By channeling the subsidy in this manner rather than towards the construction and operation of licensed child care facilities, the state limits the options women have with respect to child care. Women who do not meet the strict requirements of section 63, because they require child care to attend school or university or have no 'earned income' against which to apply the deduction, must rely even more heavily on child care provided by family members because they receive no subsidy through the *Act*.

Many of those who lobby for improved child care have been careful to stress the need for a system that involves more participation by the state – participation that goes beyond funding. The Canadian Day Care Advocacy Association (CDCAA) has lobbied strongly for both increased funding for public non-profit child care facilities and increased government regulation of child care. Studies show that parents prefer to use licensed, regulated child care, if it is available (Pence 1992). The National Council of Welfare (1988) also recommended the creation of more licensed child care spaces and less reliance on informal arrangements such as care by family members. None of these recommendations have been implemented. Although the current Liberal government has declared an intention to work with the provinces to increase the number of child care spaces, this initiative is tied to a rate of economic growth that has not yet been met (Human Resources Development Canada 1994). The 1995 budget was silent on the issue of child care, but did propose a dramatic cut in funding to the provinces and the replacement of the Canada Assistance Plan with new arrangements (see Teghtsoonian this volume). The likely result is a continued reliance on private arrangements such as the use of family members, nannies, and domestic workers employed in the home.

Reliance on the private sector to provide child care contributes to an undervaluation of the labour involved in child care. In 1991 the average salary for child care workers (of whom 96.6 per cent are women) was $13,252, placing them last in Statistics Canada's list of the lowest paid professions (Statistics Canada 1993a). The inordinately low salaries paid to child care workers are somewhat surprising given the lack of child care spaces and the high demand for child care services. One might expect market forces to push the salaries upwards. The fact that an increase has not occurred can be attributed to several factors, including the fact that child care work is performed primarily by women and is viewed as a 'woman's issue' and the belief that women are the natural carers for children (Ferguson 1991; Teghtsoonian this volume). The invisibility of child care labour because of its frequent provision in the home (private sector) also contributes to its undervaluation. This invisibility and undervaluation are exacerbated both by the method of funding provided, that is, through the tax system, and by the inadequate amount of the tax subsidy. Although many factors contribute to the undervaluation of child care work, an increased role by the state through the provision of more licensed child care spaces, thereby decreasing reliance on the private sector and increasing the visibility of child care work, would be a good first step towards redressing the problem of undervaluation.

Many child care workers are immigrant women, often women of colour, who work for low wages in conditions in which they are subjected to racism and other forms of exploitation (Macklin 1992). They are required by regulations made under the Immigration Act[6] to live in the home of their employer, increasing their vulnerability to abuse. The use of the tax system to provide a subsidy that will be used in the private sector serves to reinforce the subordination and oppression of these women. One cannot, however, assume that a less private child care system such as one that relies primarily on publicly funded licensed day care facilities would automatically redress the problems of racism and the oppression of immigrant domestic workers. The issue is complex and many factors, such as current immigration policies and the undervaluation of child care work, contribute to the present state of affairs.

In an ideal world there would be a child care program through which the state and society generally would take more responsibility for the regulation and provision of the service. Child care is, after all, a societal issue and not only an individual choice. However, given that the tax system is currently the primary method of funding child care, it is important to ensure that steps are taken to recognize its weaknesses and to improve the tax measures so that they do not exacerbate the existing privatization and consequent invisibility and undervaluation of child care. One way to redress this problem would be to provide accelerated capital cost allowance for initial and ongoing capital expenditures with respect to child care facilities. Further, the availability of the deduction could be dependent upon specific criteria being met by the operators of the child care facility, which in turn would ensure that certain minimum standards were met. This mechanism could be used to subsidize both the creation of the child care spaces and the ongoing operation of child care facilities (see Young 1994a, 1994b).

Child Support Payments

The taxation of child support payments has been the focus of much public attention as a result of the constitutional challenge by Suzanne Thibaudeau to the requirement that amounts received as child support be included in the recipient's income. In this section, I review the operation of the tax rules that apply to child support payments, the policy underlying those rules, and the decision of the Supreme Court of Canada in *M.N.R* v *Thibaudeau.*[7] My conclusion is that the tax rules contribute to and reinforce the privatization of economic responsibility for children, a responsibility that falls disproportionately on the custodial parent, usually the mother. The majority of the court in *Thibaudeau* also implicitly reinforced this concept of child support as a private matter.

Paragraphs 60(b) and (c) of the Act provide a deduction in the computation of income to those who pay child support. The deduction is available if the payment is made on a periodic basis, is for the maintenance of the child, and is made pursuant to court order or written agreement. If an amount is deductible by the payor, paragraphs 56(1)(b) and (c) require that the amount be included in the income of the recipient (whether or not the payor actually takes the deduction), and this is known as the inclusion/deduction system.[8] The gendered dimensions of these rules are straightforward; 98 per cent of those paying child support, and thereby entitled to the deduction, are men, and 98 per cent of those receiving child support payments that they must include in their income are women (Martel 1993). The *Thibaudeau* case brought to the forefront the disproportionate hardship this imposes on women. Suzanne Thibaudeau argued that the requirement that she include in her income child support payments received from her ex-spouse discriminated against her on the basis of her status as a single custodial parent in contravention of section 15 of the Canadian Charter of Rights and Freedoms. By a majority of five to two (with the men on the court in the majority and the only two women on the court in dissent), the Supreme Court of Canada held that the requirement to include child support payments in income did not discriminate against Thibaudeau on the basis of either sex or family status. In brief, the majority concluded that there was no burden imposed by the inclusion/deduction system on the group consisting of separated or divorced parents.[9] Also Cory and Iacobucci JJ found that if there was any disproportionate displacement of tax liability as between the ex-spouses, that was a problem for family law, rather than tax law, to remedy.

The federal government offers several rationales for the inclusion/deduction policy with respect to the taxation of child support payments (Zweibel and Shillington 1993). Two of them are particularly relevant to this chapter.[10] They are that the tax deduction for child support payments acts as an incentive for the non-custodial parent to pay, and that the inclusion/deduction system results in a tax subsidy that benefits custodial families by resulting in higher support payments. While these rationales indicate a willingness on the part of the state to take some public responsibility for the welfare of children after the breakdown of their parents' relationships, the tax rules are ineffective in this regard. The reality is that despite the appearance of some public responsibility, the welfare of these children is left to the private sphere as represented by their separated parents, and in particular to their mothers. As mentioned, 98 per cent of the recipients of child support are women, so it is they who are at a significant disadvantage as a result of a system requiring them to include child support in their income.

Although enforcement of child support awards is primarily a matter of provincial jurisdiction, one of the stated policy reasons for the current tax deduction for child support payments is to encourage individuals (primarily fathers) actually to make the payments.[11] Despite provincial legislation such as the Family Maintenance Enforcement Act[12] in British Columbia and the Family Support Plan Act[13] in Ontario, as well as the tax deduction given to those who pay child support, there has not been a significant improvement in compliance with child support orders (Douglas 1993). Indeed, in spite of these measures, it has been said that 'enforcement is so haphazard that the economic burden of children is inequitably borne by custodial parents, usually mothers' (Durnford and Toope 1994, 13).

Using the tax system and public funds to encourage economic activity is commonplace, and in many cases quite effective. Nevertheless, there appears to be little correlation between the entitlement to a tax deduction and compliance with support orders. As Zweibel and Shillington stated: 'Non-compliance has been linked to many factors including resentment towards former spouses, dissatisfaction with access and custody arrangements, a general sense of having been mistreated by the legal system and a gradual loss of connection with the children' (1993, 18). Because the tax system is not an effective incentive, and given the limited effectiveness of provincial efforts, enforcement remains a relatively private matter; in many cases it is up to the woman to seek out and attempt to enforce payment from her ex-partner. If the father does not comply with a support order, the economic responsibility for the child is the mother's alone. The only recourse then is to public social assistance, and there is evidence that many custodial parents avail themselves of it (Douglas 1993). Stigmatization of the custodial parent as someone who is incapable of providing for her children frequently results, and the role that the non-custodial father who has not complied with the support order has played in this situation tends to go unnoticed.

The preceding discussion has focused on the ineffectiveness of the tax system as a child support enforcement incentive. But we must recognize that even if the tax system (a public tool) is effective in this regard, the result is a 'private' solution. Family law in Canada is based increasingly on a private model that has been described as the individual responsibility model of the family (Eichler 1990–1). This model bears a striking resemblance to the older patriarchal model in that the economic status of women and children is viewed as the individual responsibility of the spouses and parents, rather than a social responsibility (ibid. 69). Any improvement to the enforcement of child support through measures such as tax deductions will simply reinforce this private model. The custodial mother remains dependent on her ex-spouse for the support of her child and the 'family' is treated as one unit. As Eichler said of the individual responsibility model, 'the great problem with it is that it actually allows for a *decrease* in societal contributions to families' (ibid. 67). It cannot, therefore, adequately address female and child poverty.

The main justification for the current tax treatment of child support payments is that it provides a subsidy that benefits custodial families by resulting in higher support payments. The subsidy supposedly arises when the payor is in a higher tax bracket than the recipient because the monetary value of the deduction to the payor exceeds the amount of tax payable by the recipient. In theory, this subsidy permits a higher support award. It has been estimated that the amount of this tax subsidy is approximately $300 million a year (Federal/Provincial/Territorial Family Law Committee 1995). Certainly the objective of providing such a subsidy is laudable and reflects a desire by the state to take some responsibility for the support of children after the breakdown of their parents' relationships. The problem is, however, twofold. First, the subsidy only arises in the limited number of cases where the payor is in a higher tax bracket than the recipient. If both pay tax at the same rate or the recipient pays at the higher rate there is no subsidy. Second, as I shall explain, even when there is a subsidy, it often results in more after tax dollars for men who make child support payments rather than higher support awards.

Several studies have examined how frequently a subsidy arises by reason of the payor being in a higher tax bracket than the recipient, with estimates ranging from 34 per cent (Zweibel and Shillington 1993) to 59 per cent (Martel 1993). Regardless of the exact figures, the Federal Court of Appeal in *Thibaudeau* v *M.N.R.* recognized that 'even on the government's own figures the inclusion/deduction system, whose alleged purpose is to benefit single custodial parents and their children, cannot do so in at least one third of the cases. There is no guarantee that it actually does so in the remaining two thirds of the cases and there is evidence to suggest that it does not.'[14] In those cases where no subsidy arises, the state does nothing to alleviate the extra expenses incurred with respect to children whose parents are living apart. Indeed, the tax rules impose a significant burden on women who receive child support by requiring them to pay tax on the child support they receive. In *Thibaudeau* at the Supreme Court of Canada level, McLachlin J described the problems with the tax legislation this way: 'It focused solely on improving the financial situation of the non-custodial parent and ignored the tax position of the custodial parent. It contained no provisions to ensure that the custodial parent receiving payments for children would not see her personal tax burden increased' (at 415). Given this tax burden, the onus is placed on custodial mothers to ensure that the tax burden is accounted for when the amount of the support is set in family law negotiations. This onus frequently results in private negotiation between the separated individuals about public funds at a time that is not particularly conducive to cooperation, that is, at the end of a relationship.

Regardless of whether or not the respective tax rates of the payor and recipient produce a subsidy, women face a significant problem as a result of the requirement that they include child support in income. In order that the recipient not be at a disadvantage because of the tax liability, she must request an adjustment (the 'gross up') to the amount of the child support award to take her tax liability into account. As Ellen Zweibel pointed out: 'The system increases the vulnerability of the custodial parent, who must now bargain for the income tax gross-up in order to protect the effective value of the child support payment' (1994, 342). Family law is thus relied upon to compensate for the imposition of a tax liability. But such compensation is not always forthcoming. Studies have shown that either the amount is not grossed up to take tax consequences into account, or if an attempt is made to gross up the award, it is frequently not done accurately (Zweibel and Shillington 1993, 12). For example, to include the full tax liability of the recipient of child support, the amount of the award must be grossed up more than once, so that the gross up itself is then grossed up again to take account of the tax liability. Without this second adjustment, the tax payable on the gross up is not taken into account, resulting in a failure to compensate the recipient fully for her tax liability. Also, because entitlement to refundable tax credits such as the Goods and Services tax credit and the Child Tax Benefit decreases as income increases, the inclusion in income of an award may have the adverse result of reducing the amount of those credits for the recipient of the child support. If the award is grossed up to reflect the tax liability, the gross up itself may trigger a reduction in the amount of the refundable credits. It should also be noted that none of these adjustments to the amount of the child support payments mean that the subsidy is in fact shared by the parties.

The issue of grossing up is not a simple mechanical matter. In many cases, child support awards are very subjective, and consequently inequitable, with judges basing the amount of the award on their perception of how much the payor can afford. In fact, studies show that the average child support order is for less than one-half of the expenses incurred with respect to the child (Douglas 1993, 3). In these cases women receive less than they should, and at the same time bear the cost of the inclusion in their income of the amount. The cost of child rearing is therefore borne primarily by these women. It must also be recognized that one of the most significant flaws in the current tax rules is that they operate on the assumption that the parents of the child have a common interest in setting the amount of these awards in an equitable manner. Yet this assumption is not always or indeed often accurate. Very little pooling of income occurs even in ongoing relationships (Philipps and Young 1995, 283), so that it is highly unrealistic to expect separated individuals to pool the tax subsidy. Furthermore, negotiations about the amount of child support to be paid to the custodial parent do not take place in isolation. Frequently they are part of ongoing negotiations or disputes about issues such as custody or property division, with resulting trade-offs. It is important in this regard to recognize that the parties cannot be assumed to be in an equal position with respect to bargaining power. As Durnford and Toope noted: 'Women are not infrequently pressed to bargain away economic advantages in order to avoid legal battles over their children' (1994, 28).

Despite this evidence, the *Thibaudeau* decision created a false dichotomy between tax policy and family law, at least with respect to child support payments. In finding that there was no discrimination, Cory and Iacobucci JJ stated that, in their view, the problems encountered by Thibaudeau and other women did not lie in the tax system, but rather with family law. They said: 'If there is any disproportionate displacement of the tax liability between the former spouses (as appears to be the situation befalling Ms Thibaudeau), the responsibility for this lies not in the Income

Tax Act, but in the family law system and the procedures from which the support orders originally flow' (at 410). Given that without the inclusion/ deduction rules there would be no need for family law to compensate with respect to the amount of child support orders, this logic is flawed. It also indicates that, to the extent that family law is private law and the negotiation of separation agreements which provide for child support a private matter, the Supreme Court of Canada is suggesting a private solution to the problems presented by the tax system.

A key to understanding the decision reached by the majority in *Thibaudeau* is that the relevant group for the purposes of their *Charter* analysis was separated or divorced 'couples' or, as Cory and Iacobucci JJ put it, the 'post-divorce "family unit"' (at 410). This approach is in contrast to that of the two women judges on the Court (McLachlin and L'Heureux-Dubé JJ), who found that the issue to be resolved was whether *custodial parents* are discriminated against in comparison to non-custodial parents. Viewing separated or divorced individuals as part of a couple for tax purposes (or indeed as part of a Charter analysis) reinforces the role of the privatized family as exclusively responsible for the support of children, even when the family, as such, no longer exists. Considering custodial mothers to be part of one unit with their ex-spouses does not reflect the reality of their lives. It also places them in a position of dependence on their ex-spouses for the support of their children at a time when presumably they have no other ties to them.

The poverty endured by many women and their children after the end of their relationships with the fathers of their children is well documented. Statistics show, for example, that in 1991, 82 per cent of lone-parent families were headed by women (Lero et al. 1992), and of those almost 62 per cent lived below the low income cut-off (Statistics Canada 1992a). Furthermore, a study by the Department of Justice in 1990 found that the economic effects of divorce or separation are much more severe for women than men with, for example, a poverty rate of 58 per cent for women after divorce in contrast to that of 9 per cent for men (National Council of Welfare 1990). Both the tax burden faced by custodial mothers and the private model of child support that requires women to seek child support from their ex-spouses contribute in part to this poverty. As Eichler demonstrated, however, problems such as the poverty experienced by custodial mothers and their children cannot be solved by recourse solely to private family law (1990–1, 82). Such an approach would mean that women will continue to be dependent on men, and it does nothing to challenge the structural problems that result in inequalities for women, such as the fact that they tend to earn less than men. As I have discussed, the role of the tax system as a public tool is currently that of a buttress to the family law rules. It builds on and supports the model of individual as opposed to societal responsibility for the financial support of children after their parents separate or divorce. We need to question whether, given the problems I have outlined with both the current tax rules and the policy underlying them, it is time to repeal the inclusion/deduction system. The current tax rules are a state tool that hinders any progress away from the current private model and towards a child support model that recognizes both societal and parental responsibility as desirable.

Pension Plans

In its report on Women and Taxation, the Women and Taxation Working Group of the Ontario Fair Tax Commission said that 'the current system of tax-assisted savings for retirement results in systemic discrimination against women, as the benefits are disproportionately enjoyed by men' (1992, 22). In this part I discuss the operation of the rules and consider their privatizing effects and their impact on women.

Retirement income in Canada takes many forms. Indeed the Canadian pension system can be described as a pyramid.[15] At its base is the Old Age Security (OAS), a flat rate monthly amount paid to all persons over 65, and supplemented by the Guaranteed Income Supplement (GIS).[16] The next level is the Canada Pension Plan (CPP), which is intended to provide retirement income for those who have participated in the paid labour force, although it should be noted that in 1986, for example, only 60 per cent of women over 18 contributed to CPP (Statistics Canada 1990, 110). Near the apex of the pyramid, are the two pension programs on which I shall focus. They are the Registered Pension Plan (RPP), an employment-based pension plan, and the Registered Retirement Savings Plan (RRSP), a personal retirement plan. Both plans are subsidized heavily by the tax system, and both owe their position at the top of the pyramid to the fact that they are 'private' plans of which only a limited number of Canadians are able to take advantage.

Retirement saving is subsidized extensively by the tax system through tax breaks for both contributions to, and income earned by, RPPs and RRSPs. For example, sections 147.2(1) and (4) of the Act permit the deduction by employers and employees of their contributions to RPPs. Section 149(1)(o.1) provides that the income earned by funds in the registered pension plan is not taxable. For 1993 (latest figures available) the value of this preferential tax treatment was in excess of $12 billion, making it the single largest tax expenditure that year (Canada, Department of Finance 1995). Contributions to RRSPs (up to a maximum of $12,500 for the 1995 taxation year) are also tax deductible and the income earned by the funds accumulates within the plan on a tax-free basis. A taxpayer is also permitted to claim a deduction (subject to limitations as to amount) for contributions to an RRSP in the name of the taxpayer's spouse. There are limits on the amount that can be contributed to RRSPs that take into account any contributions made to an RPP.

The privatizing effect of these rules is significant. The rules operate in a manner that places great emphasis on the role of both the market and the family in retirement saving. An RPP is a retirement saving vehicle which is dependent on the market (as represented by private employers) for its establishment. Giving a tax deduction for contributions to RPPs and sheltering the income earned by the plans is an example of the tax system being used to encourage private market activity. When the market does not or cannot respond to this encouragement, the tax system looks next to the family to fill the gap by permitting RPPs to provide spousal benefits after the death of the contributor and spousal contributions to be made to RRSPs.

This policy of looking to the private sector to meet the needs of the elderly in retirement is highly flawed. By encouraging retirement savings through contributions to RPPs (private employment pension plans), the state delivers a publicly funded subsidy in a manner that excludes many from entitlement. Only those who work for relatively large employers who are economically able to provide a pension plan will benefit; those who work part-time, in non-unionized jobs or for small employers unable to finance these plans, or those who are self-employed or unemployed, usually do not benefit from this scheme. Women are disproportionately represented in the group that is unable to take advantage of the tax benefits. For example, between 1976 and 1991 women consistently represented at least 70 per cent of part-time workers (Ghalam 1993), and, although women have been entering the workforce in increasing numbers, in 1991 42 per cent of women did not participate in the paid labour force (Statistics Canada 1992b, Table 1).

Women who do not have access to work-related pension plans may contribute to RRSPs, but the ability to take advantage of the preferential tax treatment afforded contributions to these plans depends on having funds with which to make the contribution. Given that women earn considerably less than men, they tend to have less discretionary income to contribute to

RRSPs. Indeed, statistics show that in 1992 men contributed an average of $1,065 per person a year more than women (Revenue Canada 1994, calculations based on figures at 106–7), and, in Ontario in 1988, for example, approximately two-thirds of the contributions to RRSPs were made by men (Women and Taxation Working Group 1992, 20).

Neither RPPs nor RRSPs are of benefit directly to women who work in the home and do not participate in the paid labour force. These women do not have access to RPPs and, with no income, are unable to contribute to an RRSP. The tax system recognizes this problem and attempts to redress it partially by including special rules that apply to spouses. For example, RPPs may provide survivor benefits (either pre- or post-retirement) that ensure that pension payments made to an individual can, on the death of the individual, be received by the individual's spouse. This provision is, however, problematic because section 252(4) of the Act defines a 'spouse' as a person living in a conjugal relationship for at least one year with a person of the opposite sex. (Indeed, until 1994 the definition of spouse only included persons who were legally married.) 'Spouse' does not include the same-sex partners of lesbians and gay men. The regulations made under the Act state that if an RPP provides survivor benefits to anyone other than a spouse (as defined in the Act) the Minister of National Revenue may refuse to register a pension plan or may deregister an already registered plan. The result is a loss by the plan of all the preferential tax treatment, so that it becomes financially impossible for employers to include lesbian and gay employees in the same employment pension plan as heterosexual employees. Therefore, lesbians and gay men have to look to their employers (the private sector) to set up separate pension plans for them and their partners. Because those plans receive no public funding, the costs are high, and, consequently, very few employers provide them (Young 1994c, 541).[17]

Some relief for women who are unable to contribute to an RPP or RRSP is also provided by a rule that allows an individual to contribute to an RRSP in their spouse's name. This benefit is not available in respect of the same-sex partners of lesbians and gay men. Together with the provision of survivor benefits, this rule highlights a general problem with the tax subsidization of pension plans and RRSPs. State-subsidized benefits are being provided to individuals solely on the basis that they are in a particular defined relationship with another person. Single persons and those whose relationships are not recognized by the tax system are discriminated against. The tax system has viewed some forms of dependency as deserving of tax relief, and the result is a privatization of economic responsibility for dependent persons.[18] As with the previous examples of child care and child support, even though the tax system (public funding) is used to deliver a subsidy, it does so in a problematic manner. For example, the subsidy is delivered to the economically dominant person in the relationship and not the 'dependent' person who needs it. This manner of delivery assumes that income will be pooled and redistributed equitably in the relationship, but, as discussed earlier with regard to child support, such pooling does not occur in the majority of relationships.

As Donnelly stated: 'A pension system which assumes a "world composed of only two categories of people: full-time participants in the labour market (husbands and fathers), and the people they support (women and children)" does not fit the experience of women today' (1993, 423). Making the only access to the tax-subsidized pensions such as RPPs and RRSPs for many women dependent on their relationship with a man is unacceptable. The reality is that more women than ever before are living without a spouse or partner, and 82 per cent of lone-parent families are headed by women (Lero and Johnson 1994, 14). Furthermore, elderly single women are disproportionately represented among the poor in Canada. In 1991, 47.4 per cent of unattached women over 65 lived below the poverty line, and the depth of their poverty was on average $2,546 below that line (CACSW 1994, 55).

A pension system that is more universal and less exclusionary is desirable. Even if one recognizes that there are constraints on the state with respect to the amount of funding available for pensions, steps could be taken to make the system fairer. Because tax relief is provided as a deduction in the computation of income, it is worth more to a taxpayer with a higher income who pays tax at a high rate than to those with less income. This system benefits men more than women by virtue of their higher incomes. Converting the deduction to a tax credit would make it worth the same in terms of tax dollars saved to all taxpayers.[19] Converting the deduction to a refundable tax credit would mean that even a person who does not pay tax could benefit from the tax advantage if they had funds to contribute to the RPP or the RRSP.

None of these suggestions, however, address the problems of those excluded from the system. More radical measures such as greater access to private employment pension plans for part-time workers and improvements to the CPP to include those currently excluded would go some way to redressing the inequities I have discussed. But the problems caused by the general relegation of the issue of retirement savings to the private sphere must not be underestimated. In particular, this relegation contributes to the poverty experienced by so many elderly women. By making tax subsidies for retirement saving dependent, in many cases, on being in a heterosexual familial relationship, the state reinforces the private family as responsible for the financial welfare in retirement of many women. This policy choice has been made very clear by successive federal governments, both Liberal and Conservative. In endorsing this policy Marc Lalonde (formerly the Canadian Finance Minister) put it this way: 'Private arrangements provide the individual with greater flexibility and personal control over pension saving than are possible under public pension programs, with their fixed schedules of contributions and benefits.'[20] Yet, as I have demonstrated, many women do not have access to private retirement tax subsidies. Even for those women who might gain access to these tax subsidies through spousal relationships with men, making their welfare in retirement dependent on having been in, and remaining in, a heterosexual relationship with a man is highly problematic. It imposes significant limitations on them by restricting their choices about how and with whom they live their lives.

Conclusion

As I have demonstrated in this chapter, the tax system has a significant privatizing effect in three very different spheres. In general, that privatizing effect is a consequence of tax expenditures being directed towards the family and, to a lesser extent, the private market. In particular, the limitations of the child care expense deduction combined with a lack of licensed child care spaces result in considerable recourse to private child care arrangements such as the reliance on family members or in-home domestic workers. The inclusion/deduction rules for child support payments, upheld constitutionally by the *Thibaudeau* decision, reinforce the position of the 'family' as responsible for the support of children after the separation or divorce of their parents. This responsibility is borne disproportionately by women who often do not receive enough child support to compensate for the tax liability they face. Indeed, frequently they also do not receive any of the tax subsidy, the existence of which is one of the federal government's rationales for requiring child support payments to be included in income. Finally, the tax expenditures for RPPs and RRSPs also result in a reliance on the private sector, as represented by the market or the family, for retirement saving. These three examples share one common theme: in each case women tend to be seriously and disproportionately disadvantaged. These women include women with children, women who work in the home and not in the paid labour force, women who are child care workers, separated and divorced women, women who do not have access to employment pension plans, lesbians, elderly women, and poor women.

It is time to rethink the role of the tax system as a tool by which to deliver the subsidies I have discussed in this chapter. Removing the provisions from the tax system and redirecting the funds currently spent by the tax system would provide the opportunity to refashion these expenditures in a manner that would have less of a privatizing effect. For example, in the case of child care, funds could be spent directly on the creation and operation of licensed child care facilities. In the case of child support, the subsidy intended to defray some of the costs associated with the support of children from families that have separated, could be delivered directly to the custodial parent, thereby eliminating the need for any increase in the amount of the child support payment. In the case of retirement saving, there could be a reduction in the amount of tax relief for private pension plans such as RPPs and RRSPs and a redirection of those funds to a more universal pension system that would include those currently excluded from the system. These measures would result in a shift away from the current privatization of these social programs, towards increased state responsibility.

NOTES

The financial assistance of the Social Sciences and Humanities Research Council of Canada is gratefully acknowledged. Also many thanks to Nitya Iyer, Katherine Teghtsoonian, and Margot Young for their helpful comments on an earlier draft, to Kristin Graver for her excellent research assistance, and to Susan Boyd for her insightful comments on this chapter, and her patience.

1 The federal government recognizes the concept of tax expenditure analysis by publishing tax expenditure accounts. These have been released in 1979, 1980, 1985, 1992, 1993, 1994, and 1995. See Canada, Department of Finance (1979). *Government of Canada Tax Expenditures Account: A Conceptual Analysis and Account of Tax Preferences in the Federal Income Tax and Commodity Tax Systems* (Ottawa: Department of Finance; Canada, Department of Finance 1980). *Government of Canada Tax Expenditure Account: An Account of Tax Preferences in Federal Income and Commodity Tax Systems, 1976–1980* (Ottawa: Department of Finance; Canada, Department of Finance 1985). *Account of the Cost of Selective Tax Measures* (Ottawa: Department of Finance; Canada, Department of Finance 1992). *Government of Canada Personal Income Tax Expenditures* (Ottawa: Department of Finance; and Canada, Department of Finance 1993). *Government of Canada Personal and Corporate Income Tax*

Expenditures (Ottawa: Department of Finance). *Government of Canada Tax Expenditures* (Ottawa: Department of Finance 1994) and *Government of Canada Tax Expenditures* (Ottawa: Department of Finance 1995).

2 RSC 1985, c. I–5 (hereinafter the Act).

3 Provided that the child's income does not exceed the basic personal amount, which for 1994 was $6,456.

4 It should be noted that the child care deduction is not considered to be a tax expenditure by the Department of Finance (Canada, Department of Finance 1993, 57). The reasoning is that the deduction is an expense of earning taxable income. This interpretation is at odds with the definition of tax expenditures as 'deviations from a benchmark tax system' (at 4). According to the Department of Finance the benchmark includes the existing tax rates and brackets, the unit of taxation, time-frame of taxation, treatment of inflation for calculating income, and those measures designed to reduce or eliminate double taxation. Therefore, by their own definition of the benchmark, the child care expense deduction is a deviation therefrom.

5 The proposal to include a deduction for child care expenses in the Act was explained in the following manner: 'Costs of looking after young children when both parents are working, or when there is only one parent and that parent is working, would be allowed as a deduction subject to certain conditions. This new plan is intended primarily to benefit mothers who need to work to support their families': Benson, Edgar J, 1969, Minister of Finance, Canada, *Proposals for Tax Reform* (Ottawa: Queen's Printer), 10.

6 Immigration Regulations, CRC, c. 940, s. 2(1) (definition of 'live-in caregiver').

7 [1995] 1 CTC 382 (hereinafter *Thibaudeau*).

8 The March 1996 budget proposed changes to these rules. The existing inclusion/deduction system will not apply to child support orders made on or after 1 May 1997. Furthermore, new child support guidelines will be introduced which will apply when a child support order is made in a divorce proceeding. It is important to note, however, that the inclusion/deduction system will continue to apply to all existing child support orders, unless they are varied on or after 1 May 1997.

9 The majority consisted of Justices Gonthier, Sopinka, LaForest, Cory, and Iacobucci, with L'Heureux-Dubé J and McLachlin J in dissent. It should be noted that Cory and Iacobucci JJ disagreed with the Charter analysis of Gonthier J. They preferred to adopt the Charter analysis of McLachlin J, although they reached a different conclusion on the facts.

10 The other rationales are (a) symmetry, that is, where a deduction has been claimed by the payor the recipient should pay tax on that amount; (b) equity for custodial mothers not receiving support, that is, taxpayers with the same

incomes from different sources should pay the same amount of tax; and (c) the decreased ability of non-custodial parents to make these payments where they have a new family.

11 In a letter dated 8 April 1991 to Glenda Simms, president, Canadian Advisory Council on the Status of Women, Michael Wilson, then minister of finance, said: 'the tax assistance ... provides an incentive for the payor to make regular and complete payments.'

12 SBC 1988, c. 3.

13 SO 1991, c. 5.

14 [1994] 2 CTC 4 at 19.

15 This metaphor is used in an excellent article (Donnelly 1993) discussing the discriminatory effect of the Canadian pension system for women and analysing many of its privatizing effects.

16 Currently, the OAS is subject to a clawback under the Act as income increases, although it is proposed that the current tax clawback be replaced by a deduction at source.

17 This discriminatory treatment of lesbian and gay employees is the subject of a s. 15 Charter challenge being brought by the Canadian Union of Public Employees. In *Rosenberg* v *Canada (Attorney General)* (1995), 127 DLR (4th) 738, 25 OR (3d) 612 Ontario Court (General Division) held that the definition of 'spouse' in the Act as it applies to pension plans discriminates on the basis of sexual orientation in contravention of s. 15 but is saved by s. 1 of the Charter. The case is currently under appeal.

18 The tax provisions that are intended to assist taxpayers in spousal relationships in which one taxpayer is economically dependent on the other include the spousal tax credit and the rules that permit the transfer of certain unused tax credits of one spouse to the other, who may use them to offset their tax payable. For a discussion of these provisions, see Young (1994c).

19 This recommendation was made by the now disbanded Canadian Advisory Council on the Status of Women: Townson 1995.

20 Canada, Department of Finance 1984, 6–7.

REFERENCES

Benson, Edgar J. 1969. Minister of Finance, Canada, *Proposals for Tax Reform*. Ottawa: Queen's Printer

Canada, Department of Finance. 1995. *Government of Canada Tax Expenditures*. Ottawa: Department of Finance

– 1985 *Account of the Cost of Selective Tax Measures*. Ottawa: Department of Finance

- 1984. *Building Better Pensions for Canadians: Improved Tax Assistance for Retirement Saving*. Ottawa: Department of Finance
- 1980. *Government of Canada Tax Expenditure Account: An Account of Tax Preferences in Federal Income and Commodity Tax Systems, 1976–1980*. Ottawa: Department of Finance
- 1979. *Government of Canada Tax Expenditures Account: A Conceptual Analysis and Account of Tax Preferences in the Federal Income Tax and Commodity Tax Systems*. Ottawa: Department of Finance
Canada, Department of Justice, Bureau of Review. 1990. *Evaluation of the Divorce Act – Phase II: Monitoring and Evaluation*. Ottawa: Queen's Printer
Canadian Advisory Council on the Status of Women (CACSW). 1994. *Work in Progress: Tracking Women's Equality in Canada*. Ottawa: Canadian Advisory Council on the Status of Women
Donnelly, Maureen. 1993. 'The Disparate Effect of Pension Reform on Women.' *Canadian Journal of Women and the Law* 6(2), 419–54
Douglas, Kristen. 1993. *Child Support: Quantum, Enforcement and Taxation*. Ottawa: Research Branch, Library of Parliament
Duffy, Ann, and Norene Pupo. 1992. *Part-Time Paradox: Connecting Gender, Work and Family*. Toronto: McClelland and Stewart
Dulude, Louise. 1979. 'Joint Taxation of Spouses – A Feminist View.' *Canadian Taxation: A Journal of Tax Policy* 1(4), 8–12
Durnford, John, and Stephen Toope. 1994. 'Spousal Support in Family Law and Alimony in the Law of Taxation.' *Canadian Tax Journal* 42(1), 1–107
Eichler, Margrit. 1990–1. 'The Limits of Family Law Reform or, the Privatisation of Female and Child Poverty.' *Canadian Family Law Quarterly* 7, 59–84
Federal/Provincial/Territorial Family Law Committee. 1995. *Report and Recommendations on Child Support*. Canada: Minister of Public Works and Government Services
Ferguson, Evelyn. 1991. 'The Child-Care Crisis: Realities of Women's Caring.' In Carol Baines, Patricia Evans, and Sheila Neysmith, eds., *Women's Caring: Feminist Perspectives on Social Welfare*. Toronto: McClelland and Stewart, 73–105
Fudge, Judy. 1989. 'The Privatisation of the Costs of Social Reproduction: Some Recent Charter Cases.' *Canadian Journal of Women and the Law* 3(1), 246–55
Ghalam, Nancy. 1993. *Women in the Workplace*, 2nd ed. Ottawa: Statistics Canada
Health and Welfare Canada. 1991. *Status of Day Care in Canada*. Ottawa: National Day Care Information Centre
Human Resources Development Canada. 1994. *Improving Social Security in Canada: A Discussion Paper*. Ottawa: Minister of Supply and Services Canada
Kitchen, Brigitte. 1986. 'The Patriarchal Bias of the Income Tax in Canada.' *Atlantis* 11(2), 35–46

Lahey, Kathleen A. 1985. 'The Tax Unit in Income Tax Theory.' In E. Diane Pask, Kathleen E. Mahoney, and Catherine Brown, eds., *Women, the Law and the Economy*. Toronto: Butterworths, 277–310

Lero, Donna S., and Karen L. Johnson. 1994. *110 Canadian Statistics on Work and Family*. Ottawa: Canadian Advisory Council on the Status of Women

Lero, Donna S., Alan R. Pence, Margot Shields, Lois M. Brockman, and Hillel Goelman. 1992. *Canadian National Child Care Study: Introductory Report*. Ottawa: Statistics Canada

Macklin, Audrey. 1992. 'Foreign Domestic Workers: Surrogate Housewife or Mail Order Servant?' *McGill Law Journal* 37, 682–760

Maloney, Maureen. 1989. 'Women and the Income Tax Act: Marriage, Motherhood, and Divorce.' *Canadian Journal of Women and the Law* 3(1), 182–210

– 1987. *Women and Income Tax Reform*. Ottawa: Canadian Advisory Council on the Status of Women

Martel, Nathalie. 1993. Affadavit, cited in *Thibaudeau* v *M.N.R.* [1994] 2 CTC 4, 18–19

National Action Committee on the Status of Women. 1993. *Review of the Situation of Women in Canada* by Punam Khosla. Toronto: National Action Committee on the Status of Women

National Association of Women and the Law. 1991. *Women and Tax Policy*. Ottawa: National Association of Women and the Law

National Council of Welfare. 1990. *Women and Poverty Revisited: A Report*. Ottawa: Supply and Services

Olsen, Frances. 1983. 'The Family and the Market: A Study of Ideology and Legal Reform.' *Harvard Law Review* 96(7), 1497–1578

Pence, Alan R., ed. 1992. *Canadian National Child Care Study: Canadian Child Care in Context: Perspectives from the Provinces and Territories*, vol. 1. Ottawa: Statistics Canada

Philipps, Lisa, and Margot E. Young. 1995. 'Sex, Tax and the Charter: A Review of *Thibaudeau* v *The Queen*.' *Review of Constitutional Studies* 2(2), 221–304

Poddar, Satya. 1988. 'Integration of Tax Expenditures into the Expenditure Management System: The Canadian Experience.' In Neil Bruce, ed., *Tax Expenditures and Government Policy*. Kingston: John Deutsch Institute for the Study of Economic Policy, Queen's University, 260–68

Revenue Canada. 1994. *Taxation Statistics, 1994 Edition: Analyzing 1992 Individual Tax Returns and Miscellaneous Statistics*. Ottawa: Revenue Canada

Statistics Canada. 1993a. *The Daily*, 13 April 1993.

– 1993b. Household Surveys Division. *Earnings of Men and Women 1991* Ottawa: Minister of Indusry, Science and Technology

- 1992a. Housing, Family and Social Statistics Division. *Income Distributions by Size in Canada, 1991* Ottawa: Dominion Bureau of Statistics
- 1992b. Household Surveys Division. *Labour Force Annual Averages 1991.* Ottawa: Statistics Canada
- 1990. Housing, Family and Social Statistics Division. *Women in Canada: A Statistical Report,* 2nd ed. Ottawa: Statistics Canada

Status of Women Canada. 1986. *Report of the Task Force on Child Care* (the 'Cooke Report'). Ottawa: Supply and Services Canada

Surrey, Stanley. 1973. *Pathways to Tax Reform.* Cambridge: Harvard University Press

- 1969. *Annual Report of the Secretary of the Treasury for the Fiscal Year 1968* (Speech to Money Marketeers). Washington, DC: U.S. Government Printing Office

Townson, Monica. 1995. *Women's Financial Futures: Mid-Life Prospects for a Secure Retirement.* Ottawa: Canadian Advisory Council on the Status of Women

Woodman, Faye. 1990. 'The Charter and the Taxation of Women.' *Ottawa Law Review* 22(3), 625–89

Women and Taxation Working Group, Ontario Fair Tax Commission. 1992. *Women and Taxation.* Toronto: Ontario Fair Tax Commission

Young, Claire. 1994a. 'Child Care and the Charter: Privileging the Privileged.' *Review of Constitutional Studies* 2(1), 20–38

- 1994b. 'Child Care – A Taxing Issue?' *McGill Law Journal* 39(3), 539–67
- 1994c. 'Taxing Times for Lesbians and Gay Men: Equality at What Cost?' *Dalhousie Law Journal* 17(2), 534–59

Zweibel, Ellen. 1994. '*Thibaudeau* v R.: Constitutional Challenge to the Taxation of Child Support Payments.' *National Journal of Constitutional Law* 4, 305–50

- and Richard Shillington. 1993. *Child Support Policy: Income Tax Treatment and Child Support Guidelines.* Toronto: Policy Research Centre on Children, Youth and Families

13

Blue Meanies in Alberta: Tory Tactics and the Privatization of Child Welfare

MARLEE KLINE

The Canadian state is undergoing a historic transformation (Brodie 1995; Panitch 1994; Teeple 1995). The postwar compromise on which the welfare state rested has now crumbled and societal expectations about provision for social need appear to be swiftly changing. Central to current political struggle over the fate of the institutions of the welfare state is a renegotiation of the appropriate division between public and private responsibilities (Armstrong and Armstrong 1994a, 32; Brodie 1995, 47, 53). Even the traditional public role in protecting the welfare of children has become subject to such reconceptualization. The increasingly dominant view is that the state has inappropriately taken over activities best left to the family, the community, and the market.[1] A contraction and restructuring of the public sector through privatization and other means of dismantling social programs is presented as the solution.

This trend towards privatization, one of several foundational principles of an emerging neoliberal state (see, e.g., Brodie 1995, 49ff; Teeple 1995, 75ff),[2] is increasingly mirrored in public policy at both the federal and provincial levels. The Conservative government of Ralph Klein in Alberta provides the most extreme example, although federal Liberal fiscal and social welfare policies promoted in 1995, and those of the Conservative government elected in Ontario in 1995, reflect similar tendencies. The income security, social service, health, and education systems are being seriously eroded as a result, with greatest impact on those who are economically marginalized, in particular racialized, immigrant, elderly and/or disabled women and their children. What is equally distressing is how successfully current governments have achieved and maintained legitimacy and the perception of public support for their fundamentally regressive changes.[3] In the spring of 1995, for example, despite two years of massive deficit-reduction driven cuts to social spending (Adkin 1995), the Klein government in Alberta still attracted 73 per cent popular support (Denis 1995, 370).⁴ This chapter explores some of the discursive tactics employed by neoliberal governments to promote their regressive policies. In particular, I analyse reliance on emergent ideology and dominant ideology, as well as the appropriation of oppositional discourse.⁵ I take as a case study a December 1994 decision by the Tory government in Alberta to privatize the delivery of child welfare services.⁶

The New Alberta Action Plan for Delivery of Child Welfare Services (the 'Action Plan')

The new plan for child welfare in Alberta is to transfer the design and management of child welfare-related services from government departments to voluntary boards, based in local communities, and the delivery of child welfare service to local agencies. The 'local authorities' will rely on jurisdiction over funding allocation to oversee the delivery of child welfare services by private agencies. Government itself will maintain only 10 per cent of its current mandate at the end of the three-year implementation process. Such remaining involvement will consist of responsibility for overall policy direction and the monitoring and evaluation of funding allocation decisions made by the local authorities. The stated goal behind this new organizational structure is to 'redirect ... resources [from internal government administration] to where they are needed most and where they will be most effective [i.e., direct services].'⁷ This 'realignment of roles and responsibilities [will],' according to the government, 'let parents and communities do what they do best – care for children – and let government support change, define key results, and facilitate the process.'⁸

Privatization⁹ measures such as this one are certainly not new phenomena in the social welfare context. Since the early 1980s the delivery of social welfare services has increasingly been transferred from government to the non-public sector in a variety of jurisdictions in Canada and elsewhere (Ismael and Vaillancourt 1988; Kamerman and Kahn 1989; McBride and Shields 1993: Rekart 1993; Suleiman and Waterbury 1990; Veljanovski 1987). Several disparate factors have been identified as converging behind this trend. Privatization has most often been associated with neoliberal concerns to reduce the size of government, decrease government spending, and dismantle the welfare state. But such policies have also been promoted to serve more progressive goals to undermine the overly bureaucratic, centralized, universalized, and often fragmented nature of service delivery, in favour of grassroots control over and design of more wholistic and integrated services appropriate to the diversity of local needs (Azim 1987; Mishra, Laws, and Harding 1988; Rekart 1993). Opportunities for progressive transformation have sometimes been presented by privatization policies at the same time as regressive consequences (Armstrong and Armstrong 1994a; Christiansen-Ruffman 1990, 102; Shragge 1990, 172). Most fundamentally, however, the privatization measures of the 1980s across Canada were linked to the desire to reduce government responsibility for social welfare programs, and correspondingly increase the investment of public funds in the private sector to facilitate service delivery (Ismael and Vaillancourt 1988).

Child welfare services have been somewhat less vulnerable than other social programs to privatization measures of the last and current decade, likely because of the historic and unique responsibility accorded to the state to oversee the welfare of children. This role is rooted in the eighteenth century *parens patriae* right of the state to intervene in families and exercise authority over children and their parents or guardians if deemed in the best interests of the child(ren) involved (Macintyre 1993, 22). This right has since been encoded in statute in every province. As a result, even in jurisdictions where dismantling and retrenchment of the welfare state have been general goals, child welfare departments have often escaped relatively unscathed.[10]

Governments have been particularly loath to privatize child *protection* services that involve performance of statutory mandates to apprehend children in need of protection. Protection services can be distinguished from *support* services, which involve such things as the provision of homemakers and respite child care to mothers and other caregivers of children who are deemed to be 'at risk.' Prior to 1994 some provincial child welfare departments and children's aid societies had begun to privatize the delivery of child-related support services by contracting those services out to the voluntary and commercial sectors (Mishra, Laws, and Harding 1988; Rekart 1993). The Action Plan in Alberta, however, represents the first time that delivery of child *protection* services will be transferred entirely from a government department to the non-public sector.[11] This new trajectory signals, more than any other previous move towards privatization, that the postwar consensus on the appropriate divide between public and private provision has been fundamentally eroded.[12]

Anticipating the Action Plan's Regressive Effects

Services do not simply remain intact when they are transferred from one realm to another through privatization. Rather, in the process of transfer, 'the things moved ... become differently encoded, constructed and regulated' (Brodie 1995, 54). The new framework for child welfare services contemplated by the Action Plan in Alberta is ultimately a regressive one. This is reflected in its fundamental goal – namely, for 'fewer children and their families ... [to be] dependent on public support' (Alberta 1994a, 35). The bottom line here, in other words, is the bottom line. The Action Plan recognizes that more and better quality services are needed.[13] At the same time, however, the government states that no additional money is available to support such development. The only way that newly recognized needs can be met within this framework is out of existing resources in the revamped Ministry of Family and Social Services (the 'ministry'). Clearly it is contemplated that something will have to give – but what?

The answer lies in the ominous assurance by the government that current ministry front-line social workers (1900 staff FTE) will be 'assisted' to find new employment opportunities in the new community-based services that appear as a result of the Action Plan (Alberta 1994a, 10). The proposed changes, in other words, will have a very serious impact on social work jobs, and consequently, on women, who perform most social work jobs (71.9 per cent in 1991) (Armstrong and Armstrong 1994b, 38; Statistics Canada 1993). Although the Alberta government has insisted that the plan is not a cost-saving measure,[14] it will result in the loss of higher-paying, more secure public sector jobs with benefit packages, in favour of increased reliance on the volunteer, non-profit, and for-profit sectors. This shift will effectively break public service unions and civil service standards and facilitate the creation of non-unionized, lower-paid, or even unpaid social work jobs (Alberta Association of Social Workers 1986, 6; Armstrong 1994, 46; Bell-Lowther 1988, 103; Bowlby et al. 1994, 26; Hurl 1984, 397). The considerable savings in wages that results will ensure that child welfare is made more 'affordable' (Alberta 1994b, 10).

It is also unlikely that the ministry, at only 10 per cent of its original capacity, will have the ability, let alone the staff resources, to carry out the oversight functions required by decentralization (see, Azim 1987). Governments have generally had great difficulty establishing effective monitoring systems for alternative care services such as group homes contracted out to the private sector (Hurl 1984, 401). In 1986 the Alberta Association of Social Workers (1986, 5–6) presented evidence that much less complicated oversight functions than those now contemplated were being inadequately carried out by the relevant government department. It is difficult to see, therefore, how effective monitoring will be established, particularly when overseeing child protection services is added to the mix.

The significant reduction of government responsibilities will also result in the loss of accumulated expertise in province-wide specialized children's services. For example, the Action Plan contemplates the decentralization of specialized programs for children with disabilities. Although it is possible that, by this change, more or better services may be made available in greater proximity to those who need them, the diversity of needs of children with disabilities may not be so easily met in localized contexts. As well, when public sector front-line social work jobs are made obsolete, it is questionable whether the government will continue to play a role in providing practical training for newly hired child protection social workers.[15] This result would be completely contrary to recent trends such as a key recommendation of the Gove Inquiry into Child Protection in British Columbia (1995) to fast-track the development of a longer, more comprehensive 20-week employee training program for child protection social workers.

Finally, the 'extra' $50 million allocated to children's services by the Action Plan will not come without great cost. It is to be redirected from the budgets of existing programs in 'other areas' within the Ministry of Family and Social Services. Some of it may come from money saved by the province by slashing its welfare rolls.[16] The Action Plan also implies that funding for 'adult programs' may be diminished. Programs such as Day Care (costing $74.2 M) and the Office for the Prevention of Family Violence (costing $8 M) are therefore placed in potential jeopardy.

Problematic Discursive Tactics

The Alberta government has attempted to obscure and distract attention from these anticipated regressive results by employing a number of interesting and effective discursive tactics. To begin with, the government incorporates into its discourse, and thus reinforces, the emergent view that measures such as those contemplated in the Action Plan are an inevitable, natural, and necessary result of economic globalization. It also incorporates, and thus reinforces, dominant ideology regarding the family and the public/private divide. As a further tactic, the Alberta government appropriates oppositional discourse to support its regressive ends. I will consider each of these mechanisms in turn and, finally, analyse the contradictions that have resulted from the juxtaposition of dominant ideological discourse and oppositional discourse within the Alberta government's emphasis on delivery of child welfare services by the 'community.'

Emergent Ideology: Inevitability because of Economic Globalization

Janine Brodie argued that the emergence of the neoliberal state is being driven by what she termed 'restructuring discourse': 'The central theme of restructuring discourse is that we have no political choices left about how to shape our collective lives and futures other than to follow a market-driven approach to the globalization of the international economy. We are told that there is simply no escaping "adjustment," which restructuring discourse defines exclusively as reducing fiscal and regulatory burdens on business and lowering expectations about the role of the state' (Brodie 1995, 49). To the extent that restructuring discourse is attaining greater legitimacy and wider acceptance, it represents an aspect of what Raymond Williams has referred to as 'emergent culture' (1980, 40–5).

In this context, the Alberta government draws on restructuring discourse to justify changes to the delivery of child welfare services. It argues that 'economic realities have drawn to a close the long history of growth in federal and provincial programs.' Given this 'era of declining resources,' it follows that governments and other organizations 'have no choice but to reexamine their objectives and the ways in which they meet them.' 'Dramatic readjustments' are required 'in order to succeed, indeed to survive, in today's age of rapid [economic, political, social, and technological] change' (Alberta 1994b, 3). The Action Plan, the government insists, is linked to its more general concern to 'see that its revenues and resources are applied in a cost-effective manner' (ibid. 5). A re-examination of the structure of children's services is thus presented as an inevitable, natural, and necessary result of new and incontestable 'economic realities' (ibid. 7).

In relying on restructuring discourse, the Alberta government both supports its own agenda and also plays a part in the incorporation of this emergent discourse into dominant culture. That such incorporation has occurred relatively quickly over the last few years is not surprising given the nature of this discourse. It represents particular forms of fiscal and regulatory change as inevitable, thereby de-legitimating political opposition to such change. Though subject to increasing challenge by critical scholars (e.g., Brodie 1995; Philipps 1996; Teeple 1995), restructuring discourse is thus uniquely difficult to counteract.

Reliance on Dominant Public/Private and Familial Ideology

The Action Plan developed in Alberta represents a shift in conceptualizing the appropriate public role in protecting the welfare of children, a result consistent with the goal of restructuring discourse to lower expectations about the role of the state. The shift is accomplished by first reaffirming and reinscribing, and then reinterpreting, the traditional public/private divide between government responsibility, on the one hand, and family/community responsibility, on the other. In the context of care for children, dominant public/private ideology translates into a presumption of privatized responsibility and a residual public role in child protection when private mechanisms of the family and community break down.[17]

The Alberta government reaffirms this dominant public/private framework by adopting it as a main organizing principle: 'Parents and extended families are expected to assume primary responsibility and accountability for their children' (Alberta 1994b, 6). To support this approach they refer to evidence that many Albertans desire 'a reaffirmation of the value of families and communities as the basic support systems in our society' (ibid. 6). By reinforcing a traditional public/private framework in this manner, the Alberta government draws strength for some of the more radical aspects of its Action Plan.

It is in interpreting and applying this traditional framework, in deciding where to draw the line between public and private responsibility for child welfare, that the Action Plan in Alberta deviates somewhat from the postwar conception of the state's collective responsibility for child protection. The central argument of the Alberta government is that the current system has inappropriately shifted the public/private divide, allocating too much responsibility to government 'for "solving" *social* problems and concerns,' and ignoring in the process 'the important roles which have traditionally been played by the family and by the community' (ibid. 5). This misalignment, in turn, has given rise, according to them, to serious problems, most importantly 'a growing dependence on government' (ibid. 6). Thus, a transfer of the administration and delivery of child welfare services, including child protection, to local communities is required on the basis that government has gone too far into, and performed poorly, a role to which it is not suited and one that is best carried out by the family and the community. 'It is time,' the Action Plan concludes, 'to let the community and the family resume their irreplaceable roles' (ibid. 8).

This reassertion of family and community responsibility for child welfare, and concomitant re-alignment of the public/private divide, must be challenged on a number of levels. In this section I want to consider problematic aspects of the invocation of 'family'; an interrogation of the Alberta government's reliance on the concept of 'community' is developed below.

The reinvigoration of 'family' represents, first of all, a naturalizing strategy: child-related services are constructed as being returned to their natural place. Even more significantly, the Alberta government invokes 'family' in quite an abstract and decontextualized manner. Its applications of the concept, however, are neither gender- nor race- nor class-neutral. For example, the reassertion of family responsibility, and the suggestion that the traditional role of the family has been ignored and displaced (ibid. 5), implies that families, meaning women, do not *already* carry the burden of providing and caring for their children which is inherent in the residual nature of the current child welfare system.[18] Moreover, promoting the transfer of some child welfare services from public provision to 'family' will mean, in practice, the further offloading of collective responsibility for child welfare (albeit now limited) onto individual women's generally invisible and unpaid domestic labour.[19]

A further implication of the Alberta government's invocation of family is that this institution lies entirely outside the state. On the contrary, the role of family in society is partially constructed through state regulation and through the reinforcement of dominant familial ideology by state institutions and processes (Boyd 1994; Chunn 1992; Gavigan 1993; Olsen 1985; Robertson Elliot 1989; Ursel 1992). In the case of Alberta the state is attempting to 'reconstitute the domestic' (Brodie 1995, 53) by inscribing an even greater role for family in providing for the welfare of children than had been expected in the postwar period. In this manner the Alberta state is purporting to minimize its role in child welfare; in practice, however, the new system proposed by the Action Plan indicates that state intervention will continue, albeit in new forms.

At first glance the Alberta government's understanding of family appears to challenge one aspect of the dominant ideological conception – its nuclear nature. Although the (nuclear) family is identified as important to children, reference is also made to the role of the extended family (Alberta 1994b, 6). Recognition of extended family involvement in child welfare, particularly in regard to First Nations people, would certainly be welcomed (Indian Association of Alberta 1987; Kline 1993, 331–5). In this case, however, the extended family is identified by the Alberta government, not as crucial to development of appropriate solutions for child welfare problems, but rather as 'part of the child's problem' (Alberta 1994b, 6). The government thus overlooks the positive and necessary caregiving role played by extended family members in many cultural contexts – for instance, in First Nations communities (Indian Association of Alberta 1987). In the end, dominant familial ideology is left unchallenged, if not reinforced.

Also of concern is the Alberta government's view that the current mix between government (public) and family (private) responsibility has led to an overdependence by individuals on government services. The Action Plan insists that people have become too reliant on government and will 'grow stronger' if they 'deal with their *own* problems.'[20] This reflects a classic individualistic blame-the-victim approach to understanding the sources of economic and social problems and inequality (e.g., Djao 1983). It implies that families (read: women) and the community (again read: women) can easily resolve problems that are grounded in much wider social relations of oppression and inequality. The Alberta government suggests, for example, that social problems such as 'family violence,' 'substance abuse,' 'low income,' and 'illiteracy' (all of which are correlated with child welfare involvement) are primarily 'family and community issues' (Alberta 1994b, 18) and, thus, not the business of government. The role of the state in creating, reproducing, and reinforcing the relations of social and economic inequality that contribute to these factors is thereby obscured. As a result, conditions of oppression, exploitation, and inequality that determine when, how, and which people can exercise 'individual' responsibility are entirely submerged by the Alberta government. The particular construction of dependence in the Alberta Plan also helps to obscure government support (via tax expenditures, deductions, deferrals, and the like) of high-income individuals and corporate entities that generally are represented as operating without public assistance.

Appropriation of Oppositional Discourses

The most problematic tactic of the Alberta government is its appropriation of oppositional discourses to support and legitimate its regressive transformation of child welfare service delivery. Reliance on oppositional discourses, however, presents an interesting contradiction: official reinforcement offers some potential for progressive transformation as well. Such prospects, in turn, are themselves limited by the way the ideas are reformulated and redirected in the official discourse. I want to illustrate this dynamic by identifying the implications of the Alberta government's reliance, first, on First Nations discourses on self-government and cultural specificity, and, second, on other progressive critiques of the child welfare system.

Appropriation of First Nations Discourses
Especially problematic is the significant reliance by the Alberta government on the 'particularly strong endorsement' (Alberta 1994b, 23) by First

Nations of the idea of community delivery of child welfare services to justify the government's more general privatization agenda. No attempt is made to situate the First Nations emphasis on self-government within the context of the historically specific and disproportionately destructive impact that dominant child welfare regimes have had on First Nations people and communities (see, e.g., Armitage 1993; Hawthorn 1966; Hudson and McKenzie 1981; Johnston 1983; Kline 1992; Monture 1989; Sanders 1975).[21] This experience precipitated the long and continuing struggle by many First Nations to regain control over child protection from the provinces, but the Alberta government neither acknowledges nor bases its reference to First Nations support on this history. It simply implies that First Nations 'share the *same* goal of ... community-based services' (Alberta 1994a, 5) as it does.

On the one hand, the Action Plan goes further than any preceding Alberta government initiative to recognize First Nations concerns with respect to child welfare. Indeed, extending 'Aboriginal services' is identified as a primary goal of the Action Plan. In the past, in contrast, 'real commitment [to First Nations] ... ha[d] been consistently minimal and frequently after the fact' (Walter 1993, 236). On the other hand, this recognition of the importance of Aboriginal child welfare matters appears to be driven more by the legitimacy that such association accords to the Alberta government's own child welfare agenda than by a genuine change in approach and attitude towards First Nations. But such appropriation of First Nations discourse may well be of contradictory effect for the Alberta government. In recognizing the aspirations of First Nations in the child welfare context, the government may have set itself up for political backlash from First Nations if it now fails to facilitate realization of those aspirations.

For a variety of reasons, however, the various measures in the Action Plan supposedly designed to facilitate the transfer 'of responsibility for planning and delivering services for Aboriginal children and families ... to Aboriginal communities' (Alberta 1994a, 10) are unlikely to make a substantial difference to the First Nations women[22] and their children who suffer the brunt of the system. The Action Plan identifies First Nations people as requiring 'services which recognize, respect and honour their culture, values, treaties and self-government initiatives' (Alberta 1994b, 26). Yet effective self-government is unlikely to be realized through the framework established in the Action Plan. For one thing, little accommodation is made for the specificity of the needs and context of First Nations. For example, First Nations communities will have to satisfy the same general criteria for obtaining block funding as will 'local authorities.' These criteria will include demonstrating that services have been integrated, 'child-focused services' developed, administration streamlined, and crisis and early intervention services balanced (Alberta 1994a, 21). The necessity to meet such requirements will provide the government with overriding control over First Nations service design. Similarly, the provincial statutory scheme will continue to regulate child protection, with authority under it simply delegated to First Nations communities. This structure will also serve to constrain the creative application of traditional First Nations mechanisms for child protection (Kline 1992).[23] Finally, the Alberta government is not likely to follow through with what is required to facilitate the development of separate management structures for First Nations because of concerns about cost. For example, Aboriginal authorities are warned not to work 'in isolation' in order to 'ensure effective use of available resources and to reduce duplication' (Alberta 1994a, 25). For the same reasons, the Action Plan contemplates that the government will continue to play a role in identifying opportunities for joint ventures between Aboriginal authorities, and between Aboriginal authorities and local authorities (ibid.). This continuing role may serve to impede rather than facilitate genuine First Nations self-governance of child welfare.

The Alberta government also appropriates First Nations arguments about the importance of cultural specificity in the child welfare context to its own regressive ends. It recognizes, for example, that First Nations people have 'identified a need for a culturally responsive shift in perspective, away from one in which problems are seen simply as private issues among individuals and families' (Alberta 1994b, 30). For First Nations people the concern is to recognize the cultural context within which First Nations individuals and families operate so as to develop more traditional, holistic, non-individualized approaches to resolving child welfare problems. The government, however, draws on the First Nations emphasis on community to reach a very different conclusion. First Nations communities are identified not as resources for solving child welfare problems, but as themselves *the* problem: 'The community, more so than the individual, can be seen as the primary *client* requiring services' (ibid.). This characterization not only misrepresents First Nations recommendations, it also implicitly constructs First Nations communities as problematic environments for the raising of children.

The problematic and regressive nature of the appropriation and distortion of First Nations views on cultural specificity is further highlighted in the identification of First Nations children and their communities as particularly 'high risk.' First Nations are characterized in the Action Plan as the only identifiable high needs group, on the basis that 50 per cent of children in care are First Nations, whereas only 9 per cent of Alberta children are First Nations (Alberta 1994a, 4). On this basis, half of the extra $50 million committed to child-related services from within the Ministry of Family and Social Services will be dedicated specifically to Aboriginal children's programs. On one level, this categorization purports to respond to First Nations claims about the specificity of their child welfare needs. Such targeting, however, also corresponds with neoliberal concerns to back away from collective provision and universal entitlement towards the distribution of scarce resources to only those who need them most (Brodie 1995, 73).

The targeting approach in the Action Plan is highly problematic, not least because it constructs the child welfare issues currently faced by First Nations as individually or community-based, rather than largely the result of colonialist processes and intersecting relations of economic and social inequality in which the Canadian state has been implicated (Hudson and McKenzie 1981; Kline 1994, 1992; Monture 1989). The Action Plan explicitly identifies lack of caregiving ability of individual parents, or of entire communities in the case of First Nations, as the source of child welfare problems. 'Skills training' is then held out as the solution (Alberta 1994a, 22). But what those deemed 'at risk' need more immediately and fundamentally than skills training is adequate and affordable housing, sufficient levels of social assistance or wages, protection from racism and/or other forms of discrimination, educational opportunities, and so on. Rather than revealing the wider social relations of oppression that affect the capacity of First Nations women and others to care for their children, the targeting of groups such as First Nations 'serves to pathologize and individualize differences as well as to place the designated group under increased state surveillance and administrative control' (Brodie 1995, 74).

Appropriation of Progressive Critiques and Research
The Alberta government also appropriates extensive and powerful critiques of the current regime of government delivery of child welfare services to justify the demise of the system under their Action Plan. For example, critiques of the sexist, ethnocentric, and racist aspects of mainstream social work practice (e.g., Swift 1991; Wharf 1993) are appropriated to disparage 'the very systems and services established to help children and families' – namely, 'the helping professions and the government's service systems' – as having themselves 'taken their toll on the family' (Alberta 1994b, 5). More

specifically, the Action Plan condemns the system for *imposing* solutions rather than developing solutions 'with families' (ibid. 5–6). This condemnation is used to support the government's conclusion that 'the family' itself and 'community networks of support' (ibid. 7) should be relied on to develop a response to child welfare concerns, rather than professional social workers from outside a community. This argument for deprofessionalization, however, also supports the implicit goal to decrease the cost of social work labour discussed above. Thus, progressive critiques of public sector child protection practice are being relied on to achieve ultimately regressive ends.

This approach ignores the continuing need for professional training even for those people taking on child welfare work from within a community. The quick leap to a solution involving deprofessionalization also obscures government accountability for some of the problem. For many years government departments failed to hire front-line workers from the communities disproportionately involved in the system. They also failed to provide adequate training for social workers in their departments. In contrast to the deprofessionalization solution posed by the Alberta government, others who have conducted critical analyses of social work practice and government service departments have called instead for greater representation in hiring and more extensive and effective training for front-line child protection workers (e.g., Gove Inquiry into Child Protection 1995, vol. 3, 63–6; Walter 1993).

Also deprofessionalizing in result is the Action Plan's emphasis on much greater participation of the volunteer sector – including volunteer organizations, charities, religious organizations, and service clubs – in delivering child welfare services (Alberta 1994b, 7). Increased reliance on volunteer labour would ultimately reduce the need for costly professional social workers. This policy shift is justified in the Action Plan on the basis that volunteer organizations have been particularly successful in designing effective support services, ones that better meet local needs (ibid. 6–7).

The Alberta government supports these arguments for deprofessionalization with reference to progressive research on the capacity and ingenuity of specific communities to design and implement their own child welfare services with limited resources. The Action Plan refers approvingly to various child welfare 'success stories' identified by progressive scholars involving community organizations that 'overcame various obstacles in order to supply much-needed services' (ibid. 39–40). For example, a mutual-aid group providing support to parents of children at risk is lauded as having decreased the number of children placed in foster care and thus reduced child welfare costs for that group by 30 per cent. Other examples include an Aboriginal community centre offering employment and support that depends on multiple sources of funding from different levels of government and private funding agencies; an urban agency offering weekly, self-help support groups to parents experiencing conflict with their teenaged children; and an agency providing 'a parent-owned, home-based program of early education to children with severe and multiple disabilities' (ibid. 39–40). These examples identified in the research are used to reinforce the view that costly professional social work services are unnecessary, as well as less effective.

Reference to this progressive research also helps the Alberta government demonstrate that communities have the capability to deliver their own child welfare services (ibid. 41), and that sufficient and adequate community resources exist to begin the process immediately.[24] Even the Alberta Association of Social Workers (1986) conveniently advanced this position in a position paper submitted to the Alberta government in June 1986.[25] Such arguments have unwittingly provided a convenient rationale for government withdrawal from service delivery (Mishra, Laws, and Harding 1988, 120). Although there is explicit recognition of the contradictory implications of their work by some progressive scholars (e.g., Shragge 1990, 167), this has not hindered interests like the Alberta government from relying on progressive research to problematic ends.

The necessity for reliance on existing community-based services, however, also has some potential to serve progressive goals. Successful implementation of the Alberta government Action Plan for community delivery is dependent on the participation of the very same community resources identified in the research referred to above. These are the groups that have accumulated some expertise in the field in addition to government service departments. The government's dependence on these groups will, in turn, grant them some measure of bargaining power in contract negotiations (Rekart 1993, 130; Shragge 1990, 173), thus providing some progressively transformative potential as well. Such participation in the new scheme will, however, carry its own contradictions by also serving to legitimate generally regressive, cost-cutting measures (Shragge 1990, 172).

On a more practical level, it is not at all clear whether the 'community strengths and resources' the Alberta government expects to 'build upon'[26] will in fact support the full range of child welfare services required by the end of the three-year implementation period. The community-based agencies now in existence likely provide support services to families (usually mothers or other female caregivers) identified as at risk, but not statutorily mandated apprehension services. Certainly some of the established agencies as well as new ones may be enticed into the delivery of apprehension services once government service contracts become available. There are a number of reasons, however, why grassroots organizations such as immigrant women's centres, anti-poverty networks, and battered women's services, which have direct knowledge of the situation of various child welfare client groups, may choose not to become so involved.

Considerable research now demonstrates the negative transformative impact of government service contracts on community-based organizations. For example, the necessity to fit within particular funding criteria can limit the freedom groups would otherwise have to establish their own agendas and practices (Shragge 1990, 138). Advocacy and political reform work, in particular, may go by the wayside if not mandated under a service contract or if contract administration work with government takes precedence (Rekart 1993, 127). Indeed, in British Columbia, conflicts of interest were found to arise for staff previously engaged in government lobbying whose jobs became dependent on government funding.[27] The documentation and tracking requirements of funding contracts can also lead to problematic reorganization of the internal processes of community-based agencies (Ng, Walker, and Muller 1990, 178). Additionally, the provision of short-term funding can serve to destabilize an otherwise viable organization if funding is suddenly taken away (Shragge 1990, 149). There is risk, therefore, of grassroots agencies being co-opted by a system 'designed to serve state interests and not arising out of the communities' needs and struggles' (Christiansen-Ruffman 1990, 101).

It is also apparent that previous privatization measures in Alberta (which by 1993 had resulted in at least 35 per cent of child welfare services being delivered by community-based organizations via service contracts and agency grants rather than government departments) have not provided adequate resources for communities to develop more relevant and appropriate child welfare services (Walter 1993, 302).[28] There is no evidence in the Action Plan that funding the wider range of services contemplated will result in more adequate provision. Indeed, the very narrow framework of principles against which the success of community organizations in delivering children's services was measured in the search for appropriate role models, dictates against this. One of these – 'diversity in resource base' (Alberta 1994b, 40) – indicates that the government does not expect to fund completely the community resources in question.[29]

The general focus on lowering costs evident in the Action Plan also does not bode well for the provision of adequate funding. For example, the 'open, competitive' basis (Alberta 1994a, 10) on which funding will be allocated to community-based agencies reinforces the argument that cost reduction is a significant aspect of the shift to community delivery. The competitive framework may pressure agencies to underbid, with salaries being the most likely to suffer in the process. It would not be surprising, therefore, if community organizations were pessimistic about the prospects for community development offered by the Action Plan. They, along with the previous children's advocate, will be concerned that the measures are 'synonymous with the shrinking of program mandates; withdrawal of services; and budget-driven "downloading,"' rather than representative of a serious effort to listen to or meaningfully engage with the community (Walter 1993, 303). In the end the majority of services will likely be 'tendered to private entrepreneurs and corporate chains as ... happened with the privatization of daycare and nursing homes' (Alberta Association of Social Workers 1986, 3).

Progressive research on the importance of early intervention to long-term success in maintaining families and extended families intact is also relied on extensively by the Alberta government, but to problematic ends. On a general level, the adoption of early intervention as a primary goal signals an important shift towards facilitating the development of more preventive services, as opposed to mere crisis intervention. In application, however, as discussed above, preventive action translates primarily into individual skills training, thus greatly oversimplifying the sources of child welfare problems. The early intervention rationale thereby serves to legitimate the problematic construction of child welfare needs as fundamentally the result of individual aberration.

Finally, the Action Plan appropriates progressive discourse in support of its identification of service integration as a primary goal. Children's services, writ large, are to be integrated at the local level across ministerial and departmental boundaries. The programs identified for integration include Child Welfare, Handicapped Children's Services, Children's Mental Health, Public Health, Education, Special Education, Early Childhood Development, and Young Offender Programs. Greater coordination and more wholistic provision of services for children have long been identified as important by left critics and front-line workers (e.g., Alberta Association of Social Workers 1986, 4; Wharf 1993). The official stated purpose of the Alberta initiative – namely, 'to remove organizational barriers, budget conflicts and gaps in service' (Alberta 1994a, 5) – however, speaks more to administrative efficiency and budgetary concerns. Efficient administrative processes are certainly important. However, the focus on organizational change also serves to limit conflict by defining issues in non-political terms (Handler 1993, 245) and to deflect attention away from more complex and difficult systemic concerns such as those identified above in regard to First Nations child welfare (Hurl 1984, 399; Walter 1993, 312; Wharf 1993). The potential benefits of organizational integration might also be undermined eventually by the increased fragmentation likely to result from the process of dealing out responsibility to greater numbers of independently functioning service providers (Bell-Lowther 1988, 103).

Contradictions of 'Community' Discourse

My final example illustrates how some of the discourse adopted by the Alberta government has both dominant and oppositional resonance and is, thus, effective for drawing support from a wide range of different sources. The core element of the Action Plan – namely, the transfer of management and delivery of child welfare services to the *'community'* – is key in this regard.

What distinguishes the Action Plan in Alberta from previous initiatives in that province (Kinkaide 1987), and in other jurisdictions (e.g., Ontario) (Mishra, Laws, and Harding 1988), is the transfer to the *'community'* of responsibility not only for service delivery, but also for the design and management of services, and most importantly, funding allocation. In no other jurisdiction in the child protection context has the role of government been so attenuated. The geographically based 'local authorities' will be run by 'small, volunteer board[s],' determined through consultation with 'communities.'[30] They will have the authority to design and manage all children's services in their areas as well as responsibility to ensure that such services are 'integrated, streamlined and responsive to local children's needs.'[31]

The call for community management dovetails to some extent with recommendations of progressive critics for decentralization and de-bureaucratization of the child welfare system and the location of control in local communities (e.g., Shragge 1990). For example, social work scholar Brian Wharf (1993, 1992) argued for 'community governance' of child welfare as a means to shift *power* to the groups that have been affected most destructively by child welfare services. Community-based agencies, in Wharf's view, have the greatest knowledge and expertise to adapt services to local needs, and yet in the past they have seldom been consulted, let alone provided control (Wharf 1993, 99, 121). What ultimately distinguishes the Alberta approach from that of progressive critics, however, is the meaning attached to the notion of 'community.'

In regard to the current struggle over the meaning of public and private, the Alberta government invokes the concept of community to inscribe private responsibility as opposed to public, that is, collective, responsibility for provision of social needs. Community responsibility, however, can also carry a collective meaning. For progressive critics such as Wharf, community stands in for a revived public, a less rigid and bureaucratized, more democratic mechanism for collective provision for social need.[32] From this perspective, government is not replaced; its role, rather, is shifted to that of funding source and regulator and away from that of direct service provider. The Alberta government attempts to obtain support for *its* initiative by appropriating a progressive understanding of community as a collective mechanism of support. For example, it adopts the view that communities 'are in a much better position than large government organizations to understand the needs of children and families, and to design flexible, effective responses to those needs' (Alberta 1994a, 4). However, the government does not follow through with what the progressive understanding entails, and the organizational structure dictated for local authorities ensures that genuine and meaningful community participation and control will be subverted.

The concept of 'community' appears to have been relied on in the Alberta Action Plan primarily for its dominant ideological power. The dominant conception of community is a problematic one: a state of 'existing together with others in relations of mutual understanding and reciprocity' (Young 1990, 235). It assumes 'a homogeneous group of people who basically relate ... to each other in a caring and non-alienated fashion' (Yuval-Davis 1994, 410). This understanding is misrepresentative as well as reductionist; it obscures the social relations of race, gender, class, sexual orientation, disability, and so on, that fragment as well as construct communities (see Walker 1990, 42). It cannot simply be assumed that community activities necessarily serve the interests of all community members, in particular the most vulnerable and disempowered (Ng, Walker, and Muller 1990, 309). The best way to confront and minimize power relations between and within groups that compose communities is to establish an explicit system of representation for disempowered groups in any decision-making process (Young 1990, 253).

Unfortunately, the Action Plan's proposed structure dictates against effective representation and, thus, against significant control of service delivery being transferred to the constituencies most negatively affected by the current system, namely, poor women and their children, especially First Nations and racialized immigrant women. Each local authority will be composed of fourteen members, each a representative of a different group purportedly with some connection to child welfare issues within a geographically defined community. Yet only *one* of the intersecting groups overrepresented in the child welfare system is explicitly recognized: namely, 'Aboriginal groups.' Even this recognition is itself limited. First Nations, which are extremely diverse and constitute over 50 per cent of children under the care of child welfare authorities, are collectively provided with only *one* seat out of fourteen on local authorities. This does not bode well for First Nations children and their caregivers living off-reserve and/or in urban contexts, whose only avenue for input into the system may be through the local authorities.

The other groups overrepresented in the child welfare system disappear within the depoliticized and degendered categories allocated representation on the local authorities – parents, volunteer associations, elders, police departments, business people, religious organizations, charitable organizations, service clubs, citizens at large, sports groups, cultural organizations, youth groups, and local government.[33] It is not immediately clear why it is considered important for some of these groups to have decision-making power in regard to child welfare services. Moreover, women, who compose the great majority of consumers (Kline 1993, 318, n44; Marshall 1993, 136; Stairs 1989) as well as workers (Armstrong 1994; Statistics Canada 1993) within the child welfare system, will have no explicit role to play on local authorities. It is not unusual for women to disappear in mainstream community discourse (Walker 1990). They are simply assumed to be present within 'families,'[34] or in this context, perhaps, within the category of 'parents.' But there is no reference in the Action Plan to women in and of themselves, let alone to feminist organizations. Women are also unlikely on an ad hoc basis to fill many of the allotted spots on the local authorities. Empirical evidence demonstrates that men more often than women volunteer to sit on such boards. Women tend instead to be involved in advocacy work and direct service provision (Armstrong 1994, 101; Dehli 1990). Other groups that have particular knowledge of people overrepresented in the system, such as anti-poverty groups, anti-racist organizations, and battered women's shelters and advocacy groups, will also have difficulty fitting within the established categories.

Local authorities constituted on a more representative basis might have had the potential to put increased pressure on government to provide the necessary resources to fulfil unmet local needs. Indeed, this has been the experience in other jurisdictions. In the late 1970s and early 1980s, for example, the Ontario government experimented with similar bodies –

'local children's services committees (LCSC)' – providing them with a mandate to establish priorities and allocate funding. Plans for full implementation were cancelled, however, when it became clear that the program had actually resulted in greater pressure on government to increase funding and expand services to meet local needs (Hurl 1984, 400). Similarly, in Winnipeg in the mid-1980s, an NDP experiment in decentralizing administrative bodies in the child welfare context was 'instrumental in influencing service innovation and in pressing for the necessary resources to meet new service demands' (Wharf 1993, 117). To avoid this result, the Progressive Conservative government that inherited the program in 1991 decided to collapse the regional community-based agencies into one.

The structure of the local authorities in the Alberta Action Plan is such that similar pressure is unlikely to be brought to bear on government for increased resources or influence on overall policy. Transferring authority over most decision making to a community-based body, moreover, will effectively insulate the government from political accountability for the results of those decisions. The community-based decision-making bodies themselves, in turn, will be unlikely to produce progressive decisions, given their unrepresentative nature. In the end, those groups with most at stake will be left with less influence on policy direction and less potential to contest problematic decisions affecting the delivery of child welfare services.

Conclusion

It is crucial to understand how and why fundamental institutions of the welfare state are being rapidly eroded and transformed. This chapter has demonstrated that this transformation is as much ideological as infrastructural. And at the core of this ideological change is a renegotiation of the appropriate division between public and private responsibilities. This examination of the privatization of child welfare in Alberta has served to illustrate some of the mechanisms facilitating this process.

Most importantly, the Tory government in Alberta is having some success re-aligning, in practice, the divide between public and private responsibility for child welfare. This is partly a result of its discursive tactics. Although the Action Plan to privatize the delivery of child welfare services will be extremely regressive in effect, these implications are obscured by the government's reliance on dominant and emergent ideology, as well as oppositional discourses. The Alberta government affirms generally the notion of allocating responsibility for child welfare between public and private institutions (dominant public/private ideology), but then re-aligns the traditional postwar divide by shifting the burden of service delivery, including child protection, from public to non-public bodies. This shift is justified partly on the basis of cost effectiveness and new global economic demands (emergent ideology). More insidiously, the popular appeal of this measure is greatly increased by its resonance with progressive ideas for transformation of the system (oppositional discourses). The Alberta government unabashedly exploits this coincidence by drawing on First Nations demands and critical research on the child welfare system to support its own agenda. These ideas are accorded political legitimacy in the process. Ultimately, however, each progressive insight is transposed into a politically regressive result.

The analysis in this chapter suggests that an appeal to oppositional viewpoints, as well as dominant and emergent ones, is being relied on to legitimate regressive political change. It remains to be seen how effective such discursive strategies will be for neoliberal governments in the long term. It is not clear, for example, whether the current policies in Alberta will in fact help to shift public/private ideology to the extent sought by the Tory government. This will depend in part on the effectiveness of strategies of resistance engaged by those on the left.

It is crucial for those on the left to interrogate official discourse and reveal the regressive social, economic, and political relations it supports. This exercise will also help to identify the points of contradiction within official discourse where struggle for progressive change would be most fruitfully directed. In the end, struggle by those active within feminist, anti-racist, anti-poverty, and First Nations movements must occur on a number of discursive as well as other fronts simultaneously. Attention must be paid not only to challenging dominant and emerging ideology, but also to limiting the ways that oppositional ideas can be turned against the interests of their advocates.

NOTES

This chapter benefited from comments on earlier drafts provided by Susan Boyd, Dorothy Chunn, Judith Mosoff, Lisa Philipps, Kathy Teghtsoonian, and Margot Young. I am also grateful for feedback received while presenting the paper on which the chapter is based at the Socio-Legal Studies Conference, Leeds, U.K., 27–29 March 1995; American Law and Society Association Meeting, Toronto, 1–4 June 1995; and the Canadian Law and Society Association Meeting, Montreal, 5–7 June 1995. Thanks also to Evelyn Ackah, Melanie Ash, Rachel Edgar, and Chantal Morton for helpful research assistance. This research was supported by a grant under the 'Women and Change' program of the Social Sciences and Humanities Research Council.

1 The concepts of family, community, and market are encoded in this discourse in particular and complex ways, with important political, social, and economic implications. The 'market,' for example, is posited as above politics, as an inevitable and neutral process beyond our control (Brodie 1995, 50) with the result that state buttressing and regulation of market forces remain largely invisible (Teeple 1995, 80–1). Some of the problematic ways in which the concepts of 'family' and 'community' are invoked, particularly their gendered, racialized, and class-related meanings and implications, will be considered in the course of the argument developed below.

2 Related aspects of an emerging neoliberal state include emphasis on the primacy of the market in generating a new social order, a belief in self-regulating market forces, and the elevation of economics over politics (Brodie 1995, 50). This entails a general reorientation of economic and social policy to the perceived needs of the private sector, particularly the demands of new forms of monopolistic global competition (Jessop 1993, 29–30).

3 This question of how popular support is achieved and maintained was also of particular interest to Stuart Hall (1988) in his analysis of Thatcherism in Britain. I am grateful to Dorothy Chunn for reminding me of the relevance of Hall's work on 'authoritarian populism' to this discussion of politics in Alberta. For an analysis of the thematic organization of Klein's populism, see Denis (1995, 374).

4 See also Scott Feschuk, 'Success Spoils Alberta PCs' Re-election Plan,' *Globe and Mail*, 23 May 1995, A1, A3. Adkin (1995) argued, however, that significant opposition to the Klein government does exist, but is seldom reported partly because of people's fear to voice their opposition. In addition, a national survey recently found that, overall, Canadians 'seem to reject the minimalist model of government being pursued in Alberta': Edward Greenspon, 'Maintain Services, Canadians Tell Survey,' *Globe and Mail*, 25 Feb. 1995, A1. The study also revealed important class differences. When asked to choose among 19 possible priority areas for government, e.g., the general public ranked all but two of them – defence and foreign aid – highly (ibid.). In contrast, the top goals of elite Canadians were those such as prosperity, competitiveness, and minimal government. These were ranked as three of the four lowest concerns by the general public.

5 For an analysis of how progressive, i.e., oppositional, discourse is used to legitimate regressive practices in the context of health-care reform, see Armstrong (1996).

6 Scott Feschuk, 'Alberta Planning Transfer of Child-welfare Services,' *Globe and*

Mail, 1 Dec. 1994, A6. The new Alberta Action Plan for delivery of child welfare services (the 'Action Plan') is contained in a document produced by the
Alberta Commissioner of Services for Children (Alberta 1994a). The results of
consultations and a research analysis undertaken by the Commissioner of Services for Children in the preceding year are contained in a supporting document
(Alberta 1994b). It must be deliberate that no mention is made of an incisive,
comprehensive, critically constructive yet hard-hitting review of Alberta's child
welfare system mandated by the previous Conservative government and conducted by Bernd Walter (then Children's Advocate) (Walter 1993). In addition
to the main government documents, the following analysis is also based on
News Releases issued by the Alberta government at 9:00 a.m. and 10:30 a.m.
30 Nov. 1994 and attached background material: A three-page question-and-
answer format 'Backgrounder'; an information sheet entitled 'The Role of Local
Authorities'; and two charts entitled respectively 'Children's Services Budget
and Manpower 1994/95 Forecast' and 'Child Welfare Budget.'

7 Backgrounder, *supra* note 6, Q.15.
8 Alberta News Release, 30 Nov. 1994, 9:00 a.m.
9 Privatization can encompass a variety of approaches ranging from the transfer
of particular services out of government departments through purchase-of-
service agreements, to the withdrawal of government departments from entire
service areas.
10 In Alberta, for example, the Department of Alberta Social Services underwent a
privatization process in the early 1980s which involved decentralization and
regionalization of program administration as well as various 'efficiency' measures designed to downsize the number of full-time staff and control departmental growth (Hornick, Thomlison, and Nesbitt 1988). The Child Welfare
program was substantially unaffected by these measures, however, likely
because of the statutory basis of the program and thus stronger departmental
mandate, and the longer-term historical inertia of many of its services (ibid.). It
is possible that anticipated caseload reductions from greater constraints on state
intervention in the family incorporated in the revised Child Welfare Act of 1984
also reduced the perceived need for more drastic measures (ibid.). This pattern
continued through the mid-1980s in Alberta. For example, though grants for 7
out of 11 programs in the Alberta Department of Social Services were decreased
during that period, the Child Welfare program (as well as Services for the Handicapped, Community Social and Health Services, and Alcohol and Drug Abuse)
experienced a funding increase (Azim 1987). Nonetheless, as a result of privatization measures instituted in the 1980s, by 1994 about three-quarters of the
government's funding for childen's services was directed to service contracts and
agency grants (Alberta 1994b, 6).

11 This observation applies to provinces where the state took on direct delivery of child welfare services. The situation is different in Ontario, for example, where responsibility for both child protection and support services has always been delegated to government-funded semi-public children's aid societies. In that context, privatization discourse has provided a new rationale for old partnerships and facilitated further devolution of services (Mishra, Laws, and Harding 1988). In more recent years, in many provinces, both child protection and support services have been delegated in particular instances to First Nations communities and agencies, and to particular regions (see, e.g., the Winnipeg example discussed below).

12 This is not to say that the previous understanding of the appropriate divide between public and private provision in the child welfare context was unproblematic. Indeed, the state was understood to play only a residual protective role, stepping in only after private care mechanisms failed. See text at note 17.

13 Four specific objectives are identified as guiding the Action Plan: community delivery, focus on early intervention, aboriginal services, and integration of services.

14 Backgrounder, *supra* note 6, Q.15.

15 The Alberta Ministry of Family and Social Services currently provides a 4-week intensive training course that new social workers take during their first 6 months on the job: Telephone interview with Joyce Armstrong, Training Resources Consultant, Staff Development, Ministry of Family and Social Services, 12 Dec. 1995.

16 Feschuk, *supra* note 6.

17 Importantly, this presumption of privatized responsibility has tended to be easily disregarded when faced by other concerns such as the desire to assimilate First Nations (e.g., Kline 1994, 1993, 1992; Monture 1989), or impose dominant bourgeois familial ideology upon the dependent and working poor (Chunn 1992). In these cases, the government often takes an interventionist role in the 'private' realm of family and community care for children.

18 Residual means that the state intervenes only after other institutions such as the family or market have failed (Wilensky and Lebeaux, 1965).

19 Many more women than men participate in child care and other forms of domestic work (Armstrong, this volume; Harvey, Marshall, and Frederick 1991).

20 Backgrounder, *supra* note 6, Q.11.

21 From the time provincial child welfare schemes were first extended to First Nations on reserves in the late 1950s, vastly disproportionate numbers of First Nations children have ended up in the custody of child welfare authorities. In addition to the tragic effects this has had on individual children, their mothers,

and extended family members, the continuous removal of children has also hindered the transmission of First Nations culture and traditions from elders to younger generations, thereby threatening the very survival of First Nations.

22 Very few men appear as parties in child welfare cases involving First Nations children. This may reflect the central role played by First Nation women in child care. The practice of many child protection agencies and departments to track child protection files through the mother (Marshall 1993, 236; Stairs 1989) may also be partly responsible for this result (Kline 1993, 318 n44).

23 Other provinces have pursued similar policies, facilitating the delegation of statutory mandates to First Nations communities: e.g., Child and Family Services Act, RSO 1990, c. C.11, part 10; Child, Family and Community Service Act, SBC 1994, c. 27, s. 90–2; Child and Family Services Act, SS 1989–90, c. C-7.2, s. 61–2.

24 See, e.g., Shragge (1990, 154) who has concluded that the diversity of alternative service organizations (ASOs) 'demonstrates the capacity of local communities to carry out these mandates.'

25 They referred to 'the important role Alberta ... voluntary organizations have had and continue to have in the delivery of personal social services,' providing an example of a program which 'enabled the development of many needed and successful services, such as home care and day care, subsequently taken over by the Alberta Government in 1978 and 1980 respectively' (Alberta Association of Social Workers, 25 June 1986, 3). See also the brief of the Canadian Association of Social Workers to the McDonald Commission, which urged the commission to 'consider voluntary organizations and associations of employers and employees as vehicles for the administration of social benefits. Community-based voluntary associations are a long-established tradition in Canada. They are nonprofit in nature [and] ... deliver a broad range of human services. They are capable of doing more' (Mishra, Laws, and Harding 1988, 120).

26 Alberta News Release, 30 Nov. 1994, 9:00 a.m.

27 Telephone interview 14 Aug. 1995 with Josephine Rekart, Social Planning and Research Council of British Columbia, who is continuing to study the effects of privatization on voluntary agencies that provided social services in British Columbia during the 1980s. There is evidence of similar conflicts of interest arising in Alberta as well. Adkin has observed that 'many people feel silenced and intimidated – afraid to speak out against the government for fear of losing their jobs, or their institutional funding' (1995, 42).

28 The Alberta government asserts that by 1994, about 75 per cent of its funding for children's services was directed to service contracts and agency grants (Alberta 1994b, 6).

29 The other key factors that received approval were flexible programming, inno-

vative programming, and existence of the 'right stuff' (meaning attitude, skills, and enthusiasm of staff) (Alberta 1994b, 40–1).

30 Backgrounder, *supra* note 6, Q.6.

31 Role of Local Authorities, *supra* note 6.

32 I am grateful to Margot Young for helping me to clarify this point.

33 One service professional and one local service provider are also included to serve in an advisory capacity.

34 Mary Jane Mossman has analysed problematic aspects of the conjunction of women as individuals with their role in families and concluded that the 'individual women's needs are mediated by a notion of the family, broadly-defined, which undermines financial security for women, while preserving the head-of-the-household role for men in the community of the family unit, both in theory and in practice' (1989, 216). Thanks to Susan Boyd for drawing my attention to this link.

REFERENCES

Adkin, Laurie E. 1995. 'Life in Kleinland: Democratic Resistance to Folksy Fascism.' *Canadian Dimension* April–May, 31–42

Alberta. 1994a (Nov). *Focus on Children: A Plan for Effective, Integrated Community Services for Children and their Families*. Edmonton: Commissioner of Services for Children

– 1994b (Nov). *Finding a Better Way: The Consultations and Research Leading to the Redesign of Children's Services in Alberta*. Edmonton: Commissioner of Services for Children

Alberta Association of Social Workers. 1986. *Alberta Association of Social Workers' Position Paper on the Alberta Government Policy of Privatizing Public Social Services (The Commercialization of Caring)*. A brief submitted to the ministers of Alberta Social Services and Alberta Occupational and Community Health, and the members of the Legislative Assembly, 25 June

Armitage, Andrew. 1993. 'Family and Child Welfare in First Nations Communities.' In Brian Wharf, ed., *Rethinking Child Welfare in Canada*. Toronto: McClelland and Stewart, 131–71

Armstrong, Pat. 1996. 'Unravelling the Safety Net: Transformations in Health Care and Their Impact on Women.' In Janine Brodie, ed., *Women and Canadian Public Policy*. Toronto: Harcourt Brace, 129–49

– 1994. 'Closer to Home: More Work for Women.' In Pat Armstrong, Hugh Armstrong, Jacqueline Choiniere, Gina Feldberg, and Jerry White, *Take Care: Warning Signals for Canada's Health System*. Toronto: Garamond, 95–110

– and Hugh Armstrong. 1994a. 'Health Care as a Business: The Legacy of Free

Trade.' In Pat Armstrong, Hugh Armstrong, Jacqueline Choiniere, Gina Feldberg, and Jerry White, *Take Care: Warning Signals for Canada's Health System*.
Toronto: Garamond, 31–51

– 1994b. *The Double Ghetto: Canadian Women and their Segregated Work*, 3rd ed.
Toronto: McClelland and Stewart

Azim, A.N. 1987. 'Privatization of Social Services: Potential Implications and Consequences.' In Jacqueline S. Ismael and Ray J. Thomlison, eds., *Perspectives on
Social Services and Social Issues*. Ottawa: Canadian Council on Social Development, 39–64

Bell-Lowther, Erica. 1988. 'Privatization: Increasing Government Efficiency or
Dismantling the Welfare State?' *Social Worker* 56(3), 101–4

Bowlby, Ken, Peter C. McMahon, Pat Bradshaw, and Victor Murray. 1994. 'Privatization and the Delivery of Personal Social Services: Is the Voluntary Board of
Directors Up to the Task?' *Philanthropist* 12(1), 21–43

Boyd, Susan. 1994. '(Re)Placing the State: Family, Law and Oppression.' *Canadian
Journal of Law and Society* 19(1), 39–73

Brodie, Janine. 1995. *Politics on the Margins: Restructuring and the Canadian
Women's Movement*. Halifax: Fernwood

Christiansen-Ruffman, Linda. 1990. 'On the Contradictions of State-Sponsored
Participation: A Case Study of the Community Employment Strategy Program
in Labrador, Nova Scotia and Prince Edward Island.' In Roxana Ng, Gillian
Walker, and Jacob Muller, eds., *Community Organization and the Canadian
State*. Toronto: Garamond, 85–107

Chunn, Dorothy. 1992. *From Punishment to Doing Good: Family Courts and
Socialized Justice in Ontario, 1880–1940*. Toronto: University of Toronto
Press

Dehli, Kari. 1990. 'Women in the Community: Reform of Schooling and Motherhood in Toronto.' In Roxana Ng, Gillian Walker, Jacob Muller, eds., *Community
Organization and the Canadian State*. Toronto: Garamond, 47–64

Denis, Claude. 1995. 'Government Can Do Whatever It Wants: Moral Regulation
in Ralph Klein's Alberta.' *Canadian Review of Sociology and Anthropology*
32(3), 365–83

Djao, Angela. 1983. *Inequality and Social Policy: The Sociology of Welfare*.
Toronto: Wiley

Gavigan, Shelley. 1993. 'Paradise Lost, Paradox Revisited: The Implications of
Familial Ideology for Feminist, Lesbian and Gay Engagement to Law.' *Osgoode
Hall Law Journal* 31, 589–624

Gove Inquiry into Child Protection. 1995. *Report of the Gove Inquiry into Child
Protection*. Victoria, BC: Ministry of Social Services

Hall, Stuart. 1988. 'The Toad in the Garden: Thatcherism among the Theorists.' In

Cary Nelson and Lawrence Grossberg, eds., *Marxism and the Interpretation of Culture*. Urbana and Chicago: University of Illinois Press, 35–57

Handler, Joel. 1993. 'The Politics of Decentralization and Empowerment.' *Windsor Yearbook of Access to Justice* 13, 239–63

Harvey, Andrew S., Katherine Marshall, and Judith A Frederick. 1991. *Where Does Time Go?* Ottawa: Ministry of Industry, Science and Technology

Hawthorn, H.B., ed. 1966. *A Survey of the Contemporary Indian of Canada: A Report on Economic, Political, Educational Needs and Policies*. Ottawa: Indian Affairs Branch

Hornick, Joseph P., R.J. Thomlison, and Lynne Nesbitt. 1988. 'Alberta.' In Jacqueline S. Ismael and Yves Vaillancourt, eds., *Privatization and Provincial Social Services in Canada*. Edmonton: University of Alberta Press, 41–74

Hudson, Pete, and Brad McKenzie. 1981. 'Child Welfare and Native People: The Extension of Colonialism.' *Social Worker* 49, 63–88

Hurl, Lorna F. 1984. 'Privatized Social Service Systems: Lessons From Ontario Children's Services.' *Canadian Public Policy* 10(4), 395–405

Indian Association of Alberta. 1987. *Child Welfare Needs: Assessment and Recommendations*. Calgary: Indian Association of Alberta

Ismael, Jacqueline S., and Yves Vaillancourt, eds. 1988. *Privatization and Provincial Social Services in Canada*. Edmonton: University of Alberta Press

Jessop, Bob. 1993. 'Towards a Schumpeterian Workfare State? Preliminary Remarks on Post-Fordist Political Economy.' *Studies in Political Economy* 40 (Spring), 7–39

Johnston, Patrick. 1983. *Native Children and the Child Welfare System*. Ottawa: Canadian Council on Social Development

Kamerman, Sheila B., and Alfred J. Kahn, eds. 1989. *Privatization and the Welfare State*. Princeton: Princeton University Press

Kinkaide, Perry S. 1987. 'The Revitalization of Community Enterprise: The Alberta Case for "Privatizing" Social Services.' In Jacqueline S. Ismael and Ray J. Thomlison, eds., *Perspectives on Social Services and Social Issues*. Ottawa: Canadian Council on Social Development, 19–38

Kline, Marlee. 1994. 'The Colour of Law: Ideological Representations of First Nations in Legal Discourse.' *Social & Legal Studies* 3, 451–76

– 1993. 'Complicating the Ideology of Motherhood: Child Welfare Law and First Nation Women.' *Queen's Law Journal* 18, 306–42

– 1992. 'Child Welfare Law, "Best Interests of the Child" Ideology and First Nations.' *Osgoode Hall Law Journal* 30, 375–425

Macintyre, Ewan. 1993. 'The Historical Context of Child Welfare in Canada.' In Brian Wharf, ed., *Rethinking Child Welfare in Canada*. Toronto: McClelland and Stewart, 13–36

Marshall, Georgina. 1993. *Social Construction of Child Neglect*. MSW thesis, University of British Columbia

McBride, Stephen, and John Shields. 1993. *Dismantling a Nation: Canada and the New World Order*. Halifax: Fernwood

Mishra, Ramesh, Glenda Laws, and Priscilla Harding. 1988. 'Ontario.' In Jacqueline S. Ismael and Yves Vaillancourt, eds., *Privatization and Provincial Social Services in Canada*. Edmonton: University of Alberta Press, 119–40

Monture, Patricia. 1989. 'A Vicious Circle: Child Welfare Law and the First Nations.' *Canadian Journal of Women and the Law* 3, 1–17

Mossman, Mary Jane. 1989. 'Individualism and Community: Family as Mediating Concept.' In Allan C. Hutchinson and Leslie J.M. Green, eds., *Law and the Community: The End of Individualism?* Toronto: Carswell, 205–18

Ng, Roxana, Gillian Walker, and Jacob Muller, eds. 1990. *Community Organization and the Canadian State*. Toronto: Garamond

Olsen, Frances. 1985. 'The Myth of State Intervention in the Family.' *University of Michigan Journal of Law Reform* 18, 835–64

Panitch, Leo. 1994. 'Globalization and the State.' In R. Milliband, and L. Panitch, eds., *Socialist Register 1994: Between Globalism and Nationalism*. London: Merlin, 60–93

Philipps, Lisa. 1996. 'Discursive Deficits: A Feminist Perspective on the Power of Technical Knowledge in Fiscal Law and Policy.' *Canadian Journal of Law and Society* 11(1), 141–76

Rekart, Josephine. 1993. *Public Funds/Private Provision: The Role of the Voluntary Sector*. Vancouver: University of British Columbia Press

Robertson Elliot, Faith. 1989. 'The Family: Private Arena or Adjunct of the State?' *Journal of Law and Society* 16(4), 443–63

Sanders, Douglas. 1975. *Family Law and Native People: Background Paper*. Ottawa: Law Reform Commission of Canada

Shragge, Eric. 1990. 'Community Based Practice: Political Alternatives or New State Forms?' In Linda Davies and Eric Shragge, eds., *Bureaucracy and Community: Essays on the Politics of Social Work Practice*. Montreal: Black Rose Books, 37–173

Stairs, Felicite. 1989. 'Women and the Child Welfare System.' Unpublished paper, Osgoode Hall Law School, York University

Statistics Canada. 1993. *Occupation*. Ottawa: Department of Industry, Science, and Technology Canada (cat. no. 93–327)

Suleiman, Ezra N., and John Waterbury, eds. 1990. *The Political Economy of Public Sector Reform and Privatization*. Boulder: Westview Press

Swift, Karen. 1991. 'Contradications in Child Welfare: Neglect and Responsibility.' In Carol Baines, Patricia Evans, and Sheila Neysmith, eds., *Women's Caring:*

Feminist Perspectives on Social Welfare. Toronto: McClelland and Stewart, 234–71

Teeple, Gary. 1995. *Globalization and the Decline of Social Reform.* Toronto: Garamond

Ursel, Jane. 1992. *Private Lives, Public Policy: 100 Years of State Intervention in the Family.* Toronto: Women's Press

Veljanovski, Cento. 1987. *Selling the State: Privatization in Britain.* London: Weidenfeld and Nicolson

Walker, Gillian. 1990. 'Reproducing Community: The Historical Development of Local and Extra-local Relations.' In Roxana Ng, Gillian Walker, and Jacob Muller, eds., *Community Organization and the Canadian State.* Toronto: Garamond, 31–46

Walter, Bernd. 1993. *In Need of Protection: Children and Youth.* Calgary: Ministry of Family and Social Services

Wharf, Brian. 1993. *Rethinking Child Welfare in Canada.* Toronto: McClelland and Stewart

– 1992. *Communities and Social Policy in Canada.* Toronto: McClelland and Stewart

Wilensky, Harold, and Charles Lebeaux. 1965. *Industrial Society and Social Welfare.* New York: Macmillan

Williams, Raymond. 1980. *Problems in Materialism and Culture.* London: Verso

Young, Iris Marion. 1990. *Justice and the Politics of Difference.* Princeton: Princeton University Press

Yuval-Davis, Nira. 1994. 'Identity Politics and Women's Ethnicity.' In Valentine M. Moghadam, ed., *Identity Politics and Women: Cultural Reassertions and Feminisms in International Perspective.* Boulder: Westview Press, 408–24

14

Going Global: Feminist Theory, International Law, and the Public/Private Divide

DORIS ELISABETH BUSS

In recent years international law has come under the scrutiny of feminist scholars who have challenged its claim to objectivity and neutrality.[1] International law is generally defined as the law governing relations between nation states, and it includes treaties, trade agreements, and United Nations (hereafter U.N.) activity. Looking behind apparently neutral international law principles, such as non-intervention in domestic state affairs, feminist scholars have revealed the uneven and gendered impact of international law on the lives of men and women (Charlesworth, Chinkin, and Wright 1991, 614–15, 644). The burgeoning feminist literature on international law has raised questions about not only the 'male' world of international law (ibid. 621) but also the difficulties of a feminist theory that seeks to analyse women's *global* oppression.

Feminist analysis of international law raises in a very direct way issues of diversity and inclusion within feminist theory. Looking at the gendered nature of international law requires a consideration not only of the ways in which Western women are affected by international law or policy, but also of the marginalized position of Third World women within both law and feminism.[2] Yet placing Third World women at the centre of the analysis can be both the principal strength and the principal weakness of feminist international law theory. By discussing the application of international law to Third World women, Western feminists are able to move beyond their own limited experience to explore the experiences of other women who, being differently positioned, are exposed to international law in different ways. As Brenda Cossman and Ratna Kapur note, however, a Western discourse that theorizes Third World women's subordination carries the danger of reinforcing Western 'positional superiority,' that is, 'the colonialist idea of the superiority of West over East, and in turn, of the superiority of the conditions of Western women over Eastern women' (1993, 279–80).

Implicit in feminist international law theory, therefore, is a construction of 'the' Third World woman and by extension, 'the' Western woman. As Chandra Mohanty argued, gender is not just uncovered by feminist scholarship, it is also produced (1992, 76; Nesiah 1993, 204). To explore and mediate the ways in which feminist international legal theory constructs Third World women, the feminist project and its impact must continually be questioned. In the words of Gayatri Spivak, this vigilance requires that feminists have a 'simultaneous other focus: not merely who am I? but who is the other woman? How am I naming her? How does she name me? Is this part of the problematic I discuss?' (Spivak 1987, 150).

Starting from Spivak's caution, I explore the ways in which feminist international law theory may define Third World women and their engagement with law and legal structures in a narrow and problematic way.[3] The focus of my inquiry is on the use of the public/private divide as an analytical tool within feminist international law theory. Mohanty argued that 'feminist analyses which attempt to cross national, racial and ethnic boundaries produce and reproduce difference' through the 'naturalization of analytic categories which are supposed to have cross-cultural validity' (Mohanty 1992, 75). I therefore consider the extent to which feminist international law theorizing of the public/private divide presumes its cross-cultural application and the impact that this presumption has on the construction of Third World women within the literature.

In this chapter I briefly outline some of the feminist theory that forms the basis of my analysis. I then discuss the literature's reliance on the public/private divide and argue that it is problematic for two reasons. First, it essentializes women's experience along Western lines. Gender becomes the central category of oppression, and women's experiences are predetermined, ahistoric, and denuded of colonialized or racialized context. Second, some of the feminist literature tends to construct the public/private divide in static terms, presuming a rigid division between the spheres. The effect is a tendency to essentialize women's lives based on assumptions about their experience within the private as opposed to public realm. In the final section I consider how feminist critiques of the public/private divide play out in the context of a key concept in international law: state sovereignty doctrine. I argue that feminist critiques of state sovereignty doctrine presume that there is an actual realm of domestic affairs that is immune from international intervention. This approach fails to consider the reality of global inequality that makes some states more susceptible to intervention than others. In addition, by failing to address the complex relationships inherent in state sovereignty, feminist international legal theory fails to account for women's different and sometimes contradictory relationships with international law generally and statehood particularly.[4]

By critically analysing the use of the public/private divide within this literature I do not mean to reject it as a tool of analysis. In certain circumstances the public/private divide provides a useful analytic tool for identifying dominant thinking about men and women and their roles in society, including international society. My objective in this chapter is to raise questions about how the public/private divide is theorized by feminist international law scholars and to challenge its centrality to an analysis that seeks to have cross-cultural application.

In undertaking this analysis, I want to stress that the scholars working in the area of feminist international law theory are very conscious of issues of race, ethnicity, and colonialism, and their effect on international law. Within this body of literature, scholars confront those issues at different levels and in different ways and I do not mean to suggest that many of the problems I identify are not also of concern to other scholars. However, as this body of literature develops there must be a constant interrogation of our means and objectives. I hope to explore the 'constructs, assumptions, and preoccupations' (Bunting 1993, 16) inherent in the international feminist literature so that we can continue the process of critical examination.

Feminist International Law Theory

Within international law, feminist scholarship has developed along two different, but compatible lines. The first has been an examination and critique of international human rights as directed to the needs of men, thereby excluding women from their scope and effect. For example, international human rights law is criticized for creating a hierarchy of rights in which civil and political rights are treated as fundamental rights as opposed to social and economic rights, which are seen as utopian abstractions (Bunch 1990). Recognizing the limitations of international human rights, the focus of this scholarship has been on rethinking human rights to increase their utility in addressing women's inequality.[5] The second area of feminist scholarship, which is the focus of this chapter, has gone beyond looking solely at human rights to a critical analysis of international legal doctrines and structures generally (Charlesworth, Chinkin, and Wright 1991). The work in this area engages broad theoretical questions of women's subordination and the role of international law in facilitating that subordination. In this way, feminist international law theorists have endeavoured to apply feminist theory to international law not only to address women's inequality, but also to inform the development of international law.

Recognizing the diversity of women affected by and involved with international law, feminist international law theory starts from the premise that 'feminist analysis of international law must take account of the differing perspectives of First and Third World feminists' (ibid. 618). This approach means incorporating the 'issues raised by Third World feminists' to reorient feminism 'to deal with the problems of the most oppressed women, rather than those of the most privileged' (ibid. 621).

Charlesworth, Chinkin, and Wright have noted that Third World women have a complex and often conflictual relationship with both feminism and international law. Although feminists and Third World scholars occupy similar positions on the margins of international law, these authors argued that the Western voice of feminism is resisted by both the European–American establishment of international law and the 'intensely patriarchal "different voice" discourse of traditional non-European societies' (ibid. 619). Third World feminists are placed in the difficult position of having to challenge not only the patriarchal voice of the Third World, but also the 'western rationalist language of the law' (ibid.).

The principal focus of feminist international law theory has been on the exclusion of women from international law and legal structures (ibid. 621–2). Frances Olsen noted that exclusion in this context is 'an active verb,' meaning that women are not left out of international law through some oversight, but that international law is structured on and represents the interests of men as the 'embodied subordinators of women' (Olsen 1993, 164–5). For example, Charlesworth, Chinkin, and Wright pointed to several doctrinal and structural aspects of international law that operate to exclude women. These include the method of state representation at the U.N., which is almost exclusively male, the bureaucracy of the U.N., which is also dominated by men, and the process of international law making, which looks exclusively at the actions of male leaders in making treaties and consenting to different international laws (1991, 622–5). Feminist international law scholars, thus, challenge the objectivity and neutrality of international law, arguing that it reflects the concerns of men and ignores and undermines the concerns of women (ibid. 625). By drawing 'various dichotomies between the public and private spheres,' international law, they argue, obscures the ways in which it may affect women differently than men (ibid.).

The Public/Private Distinction in International Law

At a fundamental level, international law rests on and reproduces distinctions between public and private spheres, with the public sphere being regarded as the 'province of international law' (ibid. 625). International law draws distinctions between international and state (termed 'domestic') affairs, state and non-state activities, and public international law (matters between states) and private international law (primarily commercial matters). The principal distinction identified by feminist international law scholars as problematic is between international and state affairs. International law applies only to matters between recognized international actors, primarily nation states, and does not cover matters internal to a state. These internal matters are insulated from external scrutiny unless states agree to regulate aspects of their internal affairs under the terms of treaties and agreements such as the International Covenant on Civil and Political Rights. International law, therefore, constructs a public world of interstate activity which is said to be separate from the private world of domestic or internal state affairs (ibid. 625–7; Charlesworth 1988–9, 194; Olsen 1993, 157–9; Walker 1994, 173–4).

Feminist international law theorists set their public/private analysis in the context of Western feminist theory. That is, they try to do at the international law level what feminist scholars have done at the domestic law level, which is to demonstrate the gendered nature of public/private distinctions inherent in liberal theory and liberal democracies (Charlesworth, Chinkin, and Wright 1991, 626–7).[6] Feminist scholars have noted that the ideological division between public and private spheres provides the framework for differential state regulation of the 'civic' and 'home' arenas and, consequently, the lives of men and women (Olsen 1983). The public/private divide incorporates an ideological matrix that is prescriptive in nature, defining how life *should* be: for example, family life should be 'private.' This prescription may reinforce women's oppression by insulating the family from the effects of legal prohibitions against violence, for example.

Feminist international law scholars have applied a similar analysis, demonstrating that the public/private divide within international law 'privileges the male world view and supports male dominance in the international legal order' (Charlesworth, Chinkin, and Wright 1991, 627). As an example, Charlesworth, Chinkin, and Wright argued that the international prohibition against torture, by incorporating a division between public and private, denies women the same protection as men from torture. Torture is defined in terms of state-sponsored or condoned activity. To come within the ambit of international law, 'a public official or a person acting officially must be implicated in the pain and suffering' (ibid. 628). 'Private' acts of torture, though not condoned, are thought to be the province of domestic as opposed to international law. For most women, however, the torture or cruel and inhuman treatment that they experience occurs in the home or the 'private' sphere.[7] Not only does international law not apply to this sphere, but in many cases, neither does domestic law (MacKinnon 1993b). In this way, women are obscured by multiple layers of the private sphere (Wright 1993, 129) and insulated from whatever protections law may offer.

Karen Engle characterized the feminist international law critique of the public/private divide as taking two forms: either international law is shown to be not universal in scope because it excludes the private sphere and by extension women, or international law – principally human rights law – applies to the private sphere but public/private divide ideology is used as a 'convenient screen to avoid addressing women's issues' (Engle 1993, 143). Engle noted that often feminist international law scholars use both approaches, reflecting their difficult position in simultaneously critiquing women's exclusion from international law while exploring the possibilities for women's inclusion in those same international legal structures (ibid. 145). This ambivalence manifests itself in competing notions about the public/private divide as an analytic tool. The public/private divide is generally recognized as an ideological construct that is implicated in masking inequality between men and women (Charlesworth, Chinkin, and Wright 1991, 629; Wright 1993, 121–2). That analysis is taken further by some theorists to argue that the public/private divide is constructed in all societies and contributes to the global oppression of women (Charlesworth, Chinkin, and Wright 1991, 626; Romany 1993, 111; Walker 1994, 173–4). Finally, the public/private divide is also depicted as an actual divide between separate spheres that approximate the spheres within which men and women lead their lives (Engle 1993, 148). In the following sections I explore these different conceptions of the public/private divide and ultimately argue that the divide is a useful analytic tool for identifying dominant ideological views about men and women and their relationship with law. The public/private divide becomes problematic, however, when it is applied cross-culturally without consideration of its specifically Western orientation (Howe 1995, 86) and when particular forms of the divide are treated as fixed entities. In other words, it is problematic when it is used in an essentialist manner and when it is conceptualized as a static concept.

Essentialist Aspects of Feminist Analysis of Public/Private in International Law

Within some feminist international law theory, the public/private divide is assumed to have universal validity not only in explaining the gendered nature of international law, but also as a way to explain all women's oppression. Although women throughout the world experience oppression differently, because of variations in race, history, culture, and so on, it is argued that we are unified by a universal devaluation of all things female. This universal oppression is manifested through a 'pattern' of privileging the male, public sphere over the private, female sphere (Charlesworth, Chinkin, and Wright 1991, 626). The exclusion of women from the international sphere, it is argued, facilitates their oppression in the domestic sphere (Romany 1993, 111; Walker 1994, 173–4). This analysis is problematic for two reasons. First, it employs a Western analytic concept, in this case the public/private divide, without considering its particular bias. Second, it assumes a commonality of oppression based on gender that fails to recognize the differing historical and structural forms of oppression to which women are subject. As a result, Third World women are analysed as similar to Western women but subject to greater oppression.

To the extent that international law draws from a Western, liberal tradition, it is useful to examine ideological assumptions, like the division between public and private spheres, that are inherent in legal and administrative systems. That analysis becomes problematic when the public/private divide is seen as the axis upon which all women's oppression is hinged. As the public/private distinction clearly has its roots in a Western, liberal conception of the world, the categories are heavily imbued with a specific Western meaning and resonance (Stivens 1991, 14–15). Using the public/private distinction as the key to understanding all women's oppression means that 'other' women's experiences will always be filtered through Western analytic categories and Western ways of knowing.

Hilary Charlesworth argued that the public/private divide is a Western construct only to the extent that the 'content of each sphere is defined by western experience' (1994, 69). An analysis of international law premised on the public/private divide essentializes women's experience only if 'women are regarded as always opposed to men in the same ways in all contexts and societies' (ibid.). According to Charlesworth, 'it is not the activity which characterizes the public/private, but rather the actor: that is women's subordination to men is mediated through the public and the private dichotomy' (ibid. 70).

The difficulty with this approach is that it starts from the premise that women's subordination, everywhere and for all time, can be understood through an analysis of a public/private dichotomy. This analysis therefore assumes that (1) all cultures construct public and private spheres that are recognizable as such, and (2) the private sphere, or women, will be devalued within that society. Implicit in this approach is an assumption about the structure of women's lives and the nature of their oppression. That is, women everywhere will inhabit a private sphere, and their experience of oppression can be linked to a devaluation of that sphere. As Jennifer Koshan notes (this volume), this analysis does not necessarily apply, for example, to Aboriginal women living in Canada, whose lives traditionally were not ordered by a hierarchical division between public and private spheres (see also Greatbatch 1989, 523; Howe 1995, 86–7).

The public/private divide used in feminist international law theory also identifies gender as the defining feature of all women's oppression. Although Charlesworth argued that public and private spheres are defined in terms of their particular context, this approach still insists on a dichotomous world-view that sees women as always apart from, and opposed to, men (Rosaldo 1980, 409). This analysis accepts rather than challenges an 'understanding [of] social forms as the creation of the lives and needs of men' (ibid.). Missing from this analysis is a way of exploring the 'relationships of women and men as aspects of a wider social context' in which asymmetrical gender relations are produced as well as incorporated (ibid. 414).

In addition to homogenizing women's experiences along Western lines (Howe 1995, 84), the reliance on Western analytic categories without first accounting for their differential application to Third World women can be destructive for women whose lives do not conform to the Western model. Anne Marie Goetz argued, for example, that there has been 'a tendency in western feminism to employ oppositional categories in culturally disjunctive ways' (1991, 141) which has had an adverse impact on Third World women through development policies that define problems in terms of gender rather than structural inadequacies (ibid. 142).

Also absent from some of the feminist international law literature is an appreciation of the intersection of factors such as race, class, culture, religion, and gender in producing women's oppression. By focusing on the social construction of gender as the source of oppression, feminist international legal theory makes it difficult to consider the multiple structures of oppression that women negotiate in their daily lives. The category 'woman' becomes the central characteristic from which presumed incidences and structures of oppression necessarily flow. Thus, we look for certain forms of oppression inherent in the subject 'woman' rather than looking for women defined through their interaction with various systems of oppression (Mohanty 1992, 84). Focusing on patriarchy as the cause of women's subordination misses the pernicious effects of colonialism and monopoly capitalism on the lives of Third World women (Mohanty 1991a) and their privileging effect on the lives of Western women. For example, much of the literature explores the ways in which women have been left out of international legal regulation. The objective then becomes bringing women *into* the public realm of international law without considering if *in* is where they want to be (Engle 1993, 149–50).

The lives of Third World women have never been immune from regulation or international interference. Starting with colonialism, Third World women's lives have been regulated by imperialist powers, foreign intervention, capital exploitation, and, ironically, destructive development policies based on false assumptions about women's activities.[8] For some Third World women, therefore, the prospect of further intervention through international law, which has arguably contributed to their continuing oppression, may not be seen as a progressive development.

To the extent that Third World women can be said to inhabit a private sphere, it may be that in some cases that private sphere is seen as a place of refuge or security. Koshan argues, for example, that even in the West, for women of colour, the private world of the family, while sometimes a place of violence, may be a site of resistance against the dominant culture (this volume). Aida Hurtado (1989, 849) and Zillah Eisenstein (1994, 202–3) have made similar arguments in the context of some Black American women, who may see the family as a potential place of refuge from a racist society (Howe 1995, 86–7). In a related way, some Third World women, reflecting their different and complex experiences of oppression, may not see the private world as always oppressive. For example, Lama Abu-Odeh argued that for some women, wearing the veil can be an 'empowering and seductive' choice (1992, 1527). The veil may offer Arab women security and social respectability. Thus, the decision to wear the veil may be a way for some Arab women to negotiate the daily effects of public/private ideology (Engle 1993, 148–9).

Because feminist international law theory starts from an assertion of women's commonalties, there is a tendency to focus on women's shared experiences of oppression, rather than pursuing their differences. For example, Charlesworth argued that it is 'possible to describe women as having "a collective social history of disempowerment, exploitation and subordination extending to the present"' (1993, 5). By focusing on women's shared position of disempowerment, the important context of women's different cultural and historical experiences is lost. Stripped of colonial, historical, and cultural context, the category 'woman' gets defined in the image of Western women (Duclos 1990, 357; Spelman 1988, 166).

Using analytic categories developed in the context of Western experience carries the risk of constructing the West as the norm; the standard against which all else is judged. Applying these analytic categories cross culturally means that all women's oppression is discussed in terms that mirror Western experiences. Constrained by bounded categories, it becomes difficult to talk about Third World women's different experiences of oppression. As Vasuki Nesiah noted, focusing on women's shared oppression 'translates into the power to define and produce "Third World" women – typically as passive victims of male oppression' (1993, 204).

For example, the recent war in the former Yugoslavia has drawn the attention of many feminist international law theorists to the tragedy of mass rapes committed in Bosnia-Herzegovina (Chinkin 1994; Copelon 1994; Gibson 1993a, 1993b; Wing and Merchan 1993). One of the most vocal feminist scholars and activists in this area is Catharine MacKinnon (1994a, 1994b, 1993a). A key theoretical issue raised by MacKinnon is how to discuss the mass rape of women as a crime under international law while accounting for the fact that these rapes were used as a weapon of war directed at women of certain ethnic backgrounds, in most cases Muslim women. For MacKinnon, it is essential to locate mass rape within the reality of everyday violence against women. 'The rapes in the Serbian war of aggression against Bosnia-Herzegovina and Croatia are to everyday rape what the Holocaust was to everyday anti-semitism ... As it does in this war, ethnic rape happens everyday' (1994b, 74).

Mass rape, therefore, represents one end of a continuum of violence. The ethnic-specific dimension of the rapes adds a further layer of oppression to the everyday violence suffered by women: 'Rape is a daily act by men against women and is always an act of domination by men over women. But the fact that these rapes are part of an ethnic war of extermination ... means that Muslim and Croatian women are facing twice as many rapists with twice as many excuses, two layers of men on top of them rather than one, and two layers of impunity serving to justify the rapes' (MacKinnon 1993a, 89).

MacKinnon's graphic imagery of 'layers of men' points to an understanding of oppression as layered. Muslim and Croatian women are rape victims *first* because of their gender, *then* because of their race or ethnicity.

Grounds of oppression become hierarchical, with gender the most important, defining characteristic, while other grounds, such as race, aggravate the oppression. However, viewing the oppression of women as layered fails to account for the complex and interdependent relationships within which women interact (Gavigan 1993). Women's different experiences of oppression become matters of degree (Harris 1990, 595–6); 'we' all experience violence, 'they' just experience more violence. We are all oppressed, they simply have more oppressors.

MacKinnon's understanding of women's differences in terms of layers not only depicts, in this case Muslim women, as the super-oppressed, it also implies that Western European and North American white women have no religious or cultural identification. White, Western women are represented as the norm of gender oppression. Muslim women are portrayed as exceptional because they *also* have a religious and cultural identification. This analysis obscures the position of relative advantage occupied by white, Western women and the difference that this advantage will have to our experience of gender oppression.

Reducing questions of difference to issues of degree not only essentializes women's oppression along Western lines, but it also exacerbates the problem of 'positional superiority' (Cossman and Kapur 1993, 279–80) discussed earlier. Within some feminist international law theory, the emphasis on women's shared history (Charlesworth 1993, 5) is coupled with a 'reorientation' of international feminism to address 'the problems of the most oppressed women rather than those of the most privileged' (Charlesworth, Chinkin, and Wright 1991, 621). The 'most oppressed women' are clearly Third World women who live within 'intensely patriarchal ... traditional non-European societies' (ibid. 619). From the vantage point of Western women, Third World women are constructed as the super-oppressed. If women everywhere are equated with subordination (Mohanty 1991b, 64) then Third World women are *really* subordinated.

Static Construction of the Public/Private Divide

Feminist analysis of the public/private divide, whether in domestic or international law, has looked not only at the physical dimensions of the public/private spheres, but also at the ideological matrix, or 'shared vision of the social universe' (Olsen 1983, 1498), that underlies and supports them. In feminist international law theory, for example, the division between public and private has been described as 'an ideological construct rationalizing the exclusion of women from the sources of power' (Charlesworth, Chinkin, and Wright 1991, 629) and as being 'crucial to the extension of power from the state to other centers of authority' (Wright 1993, 121). Despite this recognition of the ideological dimensions of a division between public and private worlds, much of the feminist international law theory tends to focus on actual spheres in which men and women are said to lead their lives. In this way, the public and private spheres are reified.

For example, violence against women, and the international prohibition against torture are discussed almost exclusively in terms of the public, male world of torture versus the private, female world of violence in the home. International law, and the law against torture specifically, are criticized for failing to address the sexual violence 'which is a defining feature of women's lives' (Charlesworth 1994, 73). Not only does this analysis presume that sexual violence, as opposed to racial or ethnic violence, is the defining feature of all women's lives, it also assumes that violence against women necessarily takes place in the home. This analysis overlooks women who are subjected to violence in the public sphere, whether as soldiers, political activists, or because of their cultural, ethnic, and sexual orientation (Amnesty International 1991). Wartime rape, for example, is a pervasive form of violence that in many respects occurs in the public world of international conflict (Brownmiller 1975) and is subject to international prohibition (Geneva Convention IV, Article 27).

Violence against women, therefore, cannot be characterized as necessarily occuring in one sphere and not the other. An analysis that looks at violence against women solely in terms of a gendered public/private divide overlooks the complex forms of violence and international legal regulation to which women are subject. I am not suggesting that the public/private divide is not a useful analytic tool in the case of violence against women. However, it may be more helpful to consider how separate sphere *ideology*, as opposed to concrete public and private spheres, affects the nature and extent of international legal prohibitions to violence against women. Such an approach might ask, for example, how public/private ideology affects the international law definition of wartime rape? Does public/private ideology influence how wartime rape is understood and treated? For example, wartime rape, though prohibited by the Geneva Conventions and other international agreements, was not prosecuted at Nuremberg, but now is being prosecuted by a tribunal for war crimes committed in the former Yugoslavia. Why were the 'simple' wartime rapes of the Second World War and other conflicts not considered a war crime but the mass rape of women in Bosnia were? What does this differential treatment of rape tell us about how rape is seen by and constructed through international law?[9]

By assuming that there are actual spheres in which women and men lead their lives there is a tendency not only to treat public and private as static spheres, but also to accept an impermeable division between them. That is, the feminist international law literature tends to overlook the interrelationship between public and private domains: the extent to which 'the "private" is necessarily circumscribed by the "public" just as the "public" is partially defined by those areas of "private" rights which are excluded from it' (Wright 1993, 121).

Karen Engle, for example, while arguing that the public/private divide should be collapsed (1993, 151), implicitly accepted that division in her analysis of the divide between public international law and the private world of international trade. She takes the position that feminist scholarship needs to reconsider its characterization of the private sphere as necessarily bad for women. She argued that women's position at the margins of international law should be compared with the position of market actors who also operate at the margins (ibid. 149–50; 1994, 107). Market actors, Engle argued, wish to avoid application of public international law, reasoning that they have more power in the informal world of international trade than in the regulated world of international law (1994, 107). In contrast, many feminist scholars and activists work to bring women into the core of international law believing that 'it may offer them protection that is unavailable in the family or even in municipal law' (ibid. 107–8). Engle concluded her analysis by arguing that the different positions of market actors and women on the margins of international law should serve as a 'reminder' to feminist international law scholars that 'fleeing the margins for the core is not necessarily the best way to attain power' (ibid. 118).

The difficulty with Engle's analysis is that while she argued for the collapse of the public/private divide, she tends to reconstruct it through her own conception of the core/margin and regulated/unregulated spheres of international law. That is, Engle assumed that there are separate spheres – the regulated and the unregulated – that approximate the public/private divide. The public arena is equated with regulation by international law, while the private world of international trade remains relatively free from regulation. In this analysis, market actors operate in an unregulated world of international trade located at the margins of international law. Far from being unregulated and marginal, however, international trade operates within numerous legal limitations and may exercise influence over aspects of international law. In addition to the obvious example of the General Agreement on Tariffs and Trade, international trade is regulated by different types of other formal measures 'designed to overcome perceived abnormalities or unfair practices' (Kennedy 1994b, 11) within international markets and economies. International law, in this context, is not seen as repressive, but as necessary to the effective conduct of international trade. Thus, international trade and legal regimes are not so much separate as interdependent. If public and private are thought of as interdependent rather than separate spheres, the margins of international law appear not as *unregulated*, or free from interference, but as subject to different types of regulation (Wright 1993, 121–2). In a similar way, women's position at the margins of international law does not mean that their lives are untouched by international law, only that they are subject to different types of legal regulation.

In the next section I consider feminist analysis of state sovereignty doctrine which has become central to much of this literature. Equated with patriarchy, state sovereignty is seen by many feminist international law scholars as the source of women's exclusion from international law. This analysis, however, presumes a definition of state sovereignty that is ahistoric and fails to account for the power imbalances inherent in the state system. In addition, by focusing on state sovereignty as the cause of women's marginalized position in international law, feminist theory fails to account for women's different and sometimes contradictory relationships with international law and, therefore, with sovereignty.

State Sovereignty

For many feminist international law scholars, the principal embodiment of the gendered public/private distinction is state sovereignty doctrine that mandates against external interference in the internal affairs of individual states. The formal notion of state sovereignty doctrine with which feminist scholars take issue is described by David Kennedy: 'Sovereignty establishes states as public subjects, concentrating public will in a single voice, absolute within its delimited sphere and formally equal in its relations with other sovereigns. This is the sovereignty which divides international from national competence and public from private action' (1994b, 6).

State sovereignty doctrine, therefore, is seen as the arbiter between the public world of international activity and the private world of state/domestic affairs. Some feminists have argued that by upholding the sanctity of domestic state affairs, state sovereignty doctrine supports structural relationships of power and domination of men over women (Charlesworth 1994, 73); it reinforces 'oppression against women through its complicity in systemic male oppression and violence' (ibid. 75–6). States 'are patriarchal structures' excluding 'women from elite positions' and concentrating 'power in, and control by, an elite' (Charlesworth, Chinkin, and Wright 1991, 622). 'A feminist transformation of international law' therefore, requires a 'revision of our notions of state responsibility' and 'the centrality of the state in international law' (ibid. 644).

Shelley Wright has developed perhaps the most nuanced analysis of state sovereignty doctrine, arguing that it is analogous to the patriarchal nuclear family (1993, 128). State consent – the 'glue which binds states' in the international arena – is based on the same notion of consent that underlies social contract theory (ibid.). State sovereignty presumes that all states are independent, autonomous bodies equally consenting to treaties and customary international law. This notion of consent, Wright argued, is based on the paternalistic nuclear family model in which the man is the only legitimate person capable of giving consent on behalf of his wife, children, and slaves (ibid.). At the international level, the state government or authority occupies the same position as the family patriarch. In both instances, men are positioned as the relevant political actors, operating in the public sphere on behalf of (their) women who remain hidden in the private sphere. In addition, the principle of non-intervention in the domestic affairs of states is analogous to the arguments about the 'sanctity' of the home, justifying its immunity from external regulation (ibid. 128–9).[10]

Ongoing engagement with state sovereignty doctrine is central to much feminist international law theory. Because state sovereignty is pivotal to the ideological division between public and private spheres, its deconstruction is essential to an international feminism that seeks to make the private more public. As such, state sovereignty forms a case study of feminist theorizing on international law and specifically the public/private divide. Feminist analysis of state sovereignty tends to construct a limited notion of gender oppression that is not always representative of the experiences of all women. It does this in two ways. First, it assumes that state sovereignty is the key reason for women's exclusion from international law, thereby missing other unequal structures that define some women's oppression. Second, it assumes that all women will desire, and benefit from, a redefined sovereignty.

Within some feminist international law theory, the patriarchal state is depicted as a principal actor in women's marginalization in international law. The implication of this argument is that, but for state sovereignty doctrine, the international community would address women's ongoing subordination. This argument presumes a political commitment to women's equality that is perhaps not demonstrable at an international level. In addition, it constructs patriarchy – and the nation state – as a monolithic entity equally benefiting men at the expense of women (see, e.g., Charlesworth, Chinkin, and Wright 1991, 615); a sort of international male conspiracy (Engle 1993, 150–1). This approach presumes that there is a rigid division between the public world of international law and the private world of domestic affairs. State sovereignty is depicted as an absolute; the international community does not interfere in the domestic concerns of other states. This picture, of course, overlooks the many formal and informal ways states, and other actors, interfere in the domestic matters of neighbouring states. Intervention can include overt state acts like military invasion, trade embargoes, or official protests, or, more subtle measures like diplomatic pressure or the actions of international financial actors.

In addition, the argument that sovereignty is the manifestation of patriarchal authority overlooks the unequal power structures among states. For many states, sovereignty, defined as the freedom to govern without external interference, is significantly attenuated. World Bank and International Monetary Fund loans and repayment plans, the influence of foreign capital, and the conduct of superpowers often have more effect on domestic policy than the exercise of sovereign authority (Ghai 1991, 420–1; Jackson 1990). For many Third World countries, sovereignty, in the sense it is used in feminist and other international literature, has been an unattainable ideal.

The rejection of state sovereignty doctrine by many feminist scholars assumes not only that all men necessarily benefit from its continuation, but also that all women will rejoice in its demise. Charlesworth argued, for example, that while state sovereignty embodies complex relationships, it is 'simply irrelevant to most women's experience' (Charlesworth 1993, 9). This perspective ignores the legal and symbolic importance that state sovereignty may have for different people, including women. Perry Dane noted that because sovereignty is 'tied to power, cohesion, culture, faith, community and ethnicity,' it embodies a complex of ideas that can have, at the very least, metaphoric significance for some people (1991, 966). Similarly, Stephen Toope argued that sovereignty is an important rallying cry because it has come to include 'concepts of culture, peoplehood and nation' (1992, 294).

For some Third World women, who, as colonized peoples, have experienced marginalization in the power politics of global affairs, the prospect of state sovereignty and the legitimating power of that doctrine may be extremely important. The argument that state sovereignty needs to be renegotiated in the name of politicizing women's lives will have little purchase with women who have developed their feminist consciousness in the context of national liberation movements (Mohanty 1991a, 10; Sedghi 1994, 93). These women may see the state as an embodiment of their ethnic representation in the global arena. The Western feminist focus on limiting state sovereignty places Third World women's identity as women in conflict with their national or ethnic identities. Characterizing state sovereignty doctrine as oppressive of all women also overlooks women's varying experiences of oppression. In some feminist international law literature, state sovereignty doctrine tends to get constructed as a barrier to meaningful law reform. This analysis, however, fails to consider that some women, principally those in the West, are able to draw on financial and political resources to circumvent state sovereignty. For example, some Canadian women have used both domestic and international courts to pursue legal remedies to address their unequal position: Sandra Lovelace, a Maliseet Indian, brought a complaint under the International Covenant on Civil and Political Rights successfully challenging the discriminatory definition of Indian status under paragraph 12(1)(b) of the Indian Act (RSC 1970, c. I–6) (Bayefsky 1983). These avenues are not always available to women who do not share the same access to financial and practical resources.

Also implicit in much feminist analysis of state sovereignty is an assumption that this doctrine is an unexamined mainstay of international law, equally supported by Western and Third World elites. Charlesworth, for example, argued that state sovereignty, and the statist system, is an 'explicit commitment of the current international legal order' (1993, 8) which feminists must challenge for its institutionalization of male perspectives (ibid. 7). State sovereignty, however, has been the subject of extensive discussion by international lawyers and scholars. As Martti Koskenniemi noted, the argument that state sovereignty needs to be limited in the pursuit of a just, international community has a long tradition in mainstream, Western international law scholarship and is premised on an 'inherently universalizing' notion of sovereignty (1991, 40–1; Kennedy 1994a, 9).

If state sovereignty is not the universal hegemonic apparatus depicted by feminist international theorists (among others), where does that leave the analysis? First, the reality of women's oppression becomes much more complex. State sovereignty is not necessarily the principal source of women's subordination nor the only barrier to meaningful reform. Second, recognizing the contingent position of Third World states, and Third World women, requires examining other oppressive structures. That is, the lack of reforms benefiting women cannot be attributed solely to the intractability of state sovereignty and patriarchal systems of oppression, but must require an examination of other inequalities, including sustained economic marginalization. I do not mean to suggest that there is a cause of women's oppression – economic marginalization – that is worse than another – gender inequality. Rather, I wish to emphasize that women's oppression is a product of multiple structures that women encounter and engage with on a daily basis. By focusing on state sovereignty doctrine as a principal component of women's global subordination, feminist international legal theory loses sight of 'First World complicity' in the economic marginalization of Third World women (Razack 1995, 48). The role of the West in producing and maintaining the conditions of some women's enduring hardship is left untheorized. Third World women are presumed to share the interests of Western women in dismantling state sovereignty, and Western women's position of relative advantage is ignored.

Conclusions

In this chapter, I have raised questions about how feminist international law theory constructs both women and law. My objective has been to participate in a continuing conversation about the norms and assumptions inherent in feminist theories of international law. To truly embrace cultural diversity – a central requirement of any theory that seeks to be relevant to all women – feminist international law theorists must 'be careful in our assumptions, critical of our paradigms of analysis, and aware of our position in the debate' (Bunting 1993, 18).

The focus in feminist international law theory on the public/private divide is problematic not simply because it relies on a primarily Western model, but because it is used as a central paradigm for understanding women's gender oppression. As I have argued, this approach tends towards universalizing and essentialist assumptions about women and their experience of oppression, rather than engaging in local, contingent, and historically specific analysis. Feminist international legal theory must move beyond simply recognizing difference to 'living' it (Duclos 1990, 359), which means incorporating insights gleaned from women's diversity to challenge dominant assumptions about our essential characteristics and social norms (ibid. 370; Phillips 1992, 27).

NOTES

In writing this chapter I benefitted enormously from the insights of several people who reviewed my earlier drafts: Dorothy Chunn, Nitya Iyer, Marlee Kline, Jennifer

Koshan, Karin Mickelson, Kathy Teghtsoonian, Margot Young, and Claire Young. In particular, I would like to thank Susan Boyd who spent considerable time and effort editing various drafts of this and other work. Her insights and tremendous support were, and still are, invaluable. This chapter was written while I was a graduate student at the Faculty of Law, University of British Columbia. I appreciate the supportive and intellectually stimulating community I found there.

1   See especially Charlesworth, Chinkin, and Wright (1991) and Cook (1992). The phrase 'feminist approaches to international law' is taken from an article by the same name, authored by Charlesworth, Chinkin, and Wright. This thorough and provocative article has, in many respects, laid the groundwork for other literature in this area and, in fact, has led to numerous other articles and books. See, in particular, Dallmeyer (1993); 1992 *Australian Yearbook of International Law* 12; Charlesworth (1994); Knop (1993).

2   By 'Western women' I mean white, middle and upper class women from Europe and North America. I use the term 'Third World' to refer to women who are from countries of the south: Asia, Africa, and the Middle East. My use of the terms 'Third World' and 'Western' are not just geographical designations but are references to the asymmetrical relationship between northern and southern countries resulting from colonialism and continuing economic and technological imbalances. By Third World women, I am also referring to women who, for reasons of race, ethnicity, class, and history, are constructed, by international legal and some feminist discourse, as 'other.' I have many misgivings about employing terminology such as 'Third World' and 'Western' by which women are named as cohesive groups (Mohanty 1991a, 1991b). In addition, the boundaries of the categories Third World and Western are not clear. With the decline of the Soviet Union, many countries in Eastern Europe are facing economic, technological, and political marginalization within the international arena that places them in asymmetrical relationships similar to some countries in the Third World. Recognizing the limitations of terms like Third World and Western, I employ them in this chapter to convey the economic, social, and political imbalance between women in different parts of the globe. Recognizing and incorporating a sensitivity to that imbalance is part of the challenge to feminist international law theory that I wish to explore.

3   As a white, Western, feminist, student of international law, I identify myself with the Western feminists who are pursuing work in international law. While I hope to explore and challenge this work, I consider this chapter to be part of the growing international feminist law scholarship and hope that it too will be subject to critical review.

4   After completing the draft of this chapter, I was given a copy of Adrian Howe's

then unpublished article (1995, 70–1) in which she engages critically with Charlesworth, Chinkin, and Wright (1991). Howe structured her commentary as an 'encounter' between Charlesworth, Chinkin, and Wright's article, as the 'landmark text' in white Western feminist law scholarship, and Chandra Mohanty, as representative of postcolonial feminism (1995, 70–1, 74). Howe's observations about the universalizing and essentialist tendencies in feminist international law theory are similar to my own. In addition, she commented on the centrality of the public/private distinction to this literature, arguing that it is 'a perfect example' of 'Eurocentric "methodological universalisms"' (ibid. 86). While I agree with Howe's principal arguments concerning essentialist aspects of feminist international law theory, I do not always agree with her characterization of Charlesworth, Chinkin, and Wright's article as 'impervious' to the critical scholarship of poststructural feminists (ibid. 87).

5 For bibliographic reference, see Cook (1992), and Engle (1992).

6 Although domestic feminist legal theory has considered the variable distinctions drawn between state/civil society and market/family (Olsen 1983), feminist international law theory has focused almost exclusively on the division between international and state arenas, with little or no consideration given to the market/domestic divide. Exceptions to this are Wright (1993) and Engle (1994, 1993) who tend to pursue a more nuanced analysis of public/private divisions within international law and who include tentative analyses of the position of the market within international law and society. These works will be discussed in more detail later in this chapter.

7 The authors' analysis raises some concerns about essentializing women's experiences of the private sphere and the violence they experience there. I explore these concerns more fully later in this chapter.

8 Feminist development theorists have documented the systematic undervaluation within development policies of women's unpaid subsistence and domestic labour. By focusing on men as the sole economic producers, development policies undermined women's contribution to the family income, health, education, and general welfare through subsistence farming and reproduction. As a result, the modernizing efforts of the 1960s and 1970s caused women's social and economic status to decline. See Goetz's discussion of Ester Boserup's work (1991, 137), and generally Charlesworth, Chinkin, and Wright (1991, 641); Sen and Grown (1987).

9 Many of these questions are dealt with in my LLM thesis: 'Crossing the Line: Women, Rape and the War in Bosnia-Herzegovina' (1995) at the University of British Columbia. I conclude that wartime rape is variously constructed as public and private depending on, among other things, the ethnic, national, and cultural construction of the women who were victims of rape. For a discussion of

rape during the conflicts listed in my discussion, see Brownmiller (1975); and Copelon (1994).
10 Wright's analysis of state sovereignty (1993) includes an analysis of the relationship between public/private divisions and the legitimization of inequality between states. She briefly touches on the position of market actors in the international arena, raising questions about public/private ideology and the regulation of the effects of international capital. Her analysis deserves more attention than I can give it in this chapter.

REFERENCES

Abu-Odeh, Lama. 1992. 'Post-Colonial Feminism and the Veil: Considering the Differences.' *New England Law Review* 26 (Summer), 1527–37
Amnesty International. 1993. *Yugoslavia: Women under the Gun.* New York: Amnesty Action
– 1991. *Women in the Front Line: Human Rights Violations against Women.* New York: Amnesty International
Bayefsky, Anne F. 1983. 'The Human Rights Committee and the Case of Sandra Lovelace.' *Canadian Yearbook of International Law* 20, 244–65
Brownmiller, Susan. 1975. *Against Our Will: Men, Women and Rape.* New York: Simon and Schuster
Bunch, Charlotte. 1990. 'Women's Rights as Human Rights: Towards a Re-Vision of Human Rights.' *Human Rights Quarterly* 12, 486–98
Bunting, Annie. 1993. 'Theorizing Women's Cultural Diversity in Feminist International Human Rights Strategies.' *Journal of Law and Society* 20, 6–18
Charlesworth, Hilary. 1994. 'What Are "Women's International Human Rights"?' In Rebecca J. Cook, ed., *Human Rights of Women: National and International Perspectives.* Philadelphia: University of Pennsylvania Press, 58–84
– 1993. 'Alienating Oscar? Feminist Analysis of International Law.' In Dorinda Dallmeyer, ed., *Reconceiving Reality: Women and International Law.* Washington: American Society of International Law, 1–18
– 1988–9. 'The Public/Private Distinction and the Right to Development in International Law.' *Australian Yearbook of International Law* 12, 190–204
– Christine Chinkin, and Shelley Wright. 1991. 'Feminist Approaches to International Law.' *American Journal of International Law* 85, 613–45
Chinkin, Christine. 1994. 'Rape and Sexual Abuse of Women in International Law.' *European Journal of International Law* 5, 326–41
Cook, Rebecca. 1992. 'Women's International Human Rights: A Bibliography.' *International Law and Politics* 24, 857–88
Copelon, Rhonda. 1994. 'Surfacing Gender: Reconceptualizing Crimes against

Women in Time of War.' In Alexandra Stiglmayer, ed., *Mass Rape: The War Against Women in Bosnia.* Lincoln: University of Nebraska Press, 197–230

Cossman, Brenda, and Ratna Kapur. 1993. 'Women and Poverty in India: Law and Social Change.' *Canadian Journal of Women and the Law* 6, 278–304

Dallmeyer, Dorinda, ed. 1993. *Reconceiving Reality: Women and International Law.* Washington: American Society of International Law

Dane, Perry. 1991. 'The Maps of Sovereignty: A Mediation.' *Cardozo Law Review* 12, 959–1006

Duclos, Nitya. 1990. 'Lessons of Difference: Feminist Theory on Cultural Diversity.' *Buffalo Law Review* 38, 325–81

Eisenstein, Zillah, R. 1994. *Reimaging Democracy.* Berkeley: University of California Press

Engle, Karen. 1994. 'Views from the Margins: A Response to David Kennedy.' *Utah Law Review* 7, 105–18

– 1993. 'After the Collapse of the Public/Private Distinction: Strategizing Women's Rights.' In Dorinda Dallmeyer, ed., *Reconceiving Reality: Women and International Law.* Washington: American Society of International Law, 143–55

– 1992. 'International Human Rights and Feminism: When Discourses Meet.' *Michigan Journal of International Law* 13, 517–610

Gavigan, Shelley A.M. 1993. 'Paradise Lost, Paradox Revisited: The Implications of Familial Ideology for Feminist, Lesbian, and Gay Engagement to Law.' *Osgoode Hall Law Journal* 31(3), 589–624

Geneva Convention Relative to the Protection of Civilian Persons in Time of War. Adopted 12 Aug. 1949, 6 U.S.T. 3516, T.I.A.S. No. 3365, 75 U.N.T.S. 287

Ghai, Yash. 1991. 'The Theory of the State in the Third World and the Problem of Constitutionalism.' *Connecticut Journal of International Law* 6, 411–23

Gibson, Suzanne. 1993a. 'On Sex, Horror and Human Rights.' *Women: A Cultural Review* 4(3), 250–60

– 1993b. 'The Discourse of Sex/War: Thoughts on Catharine MacKinnon's *1993 Oxford Amnesty Lecture.' Feminist Legal Studies* 1(2), 179–88

Goetz, Anne Marie. 1991. 'Feminism and the Claim to Know: Contradictions in Feminist Approaches to Women in Development.' In Rebecca Grant and Kathleen Newland, eds., *Gender and International Relations.* Bloomington and Indianapolis: Indiana University Press, 133–57

Greatbatch, Jacqueline. 1989. 'The Gender of Difference: Feminist Critiques of Refugee Discourse.' *International Journal of Refugee Law* 4(1), 518–27

Harris, Angela. 1990. 'Race and Essentialism in Feminist Legal Theory.' *Stanford Law Review* 42, 581–616

Helsinki Watch. 1992. *War Crimes in Bosnia-Hercegovina,* vol I. New York, Washington, Los Angeles, and London: Helsinki Watch

Howe, Adrian. 1995. 'White Western Feminism Meets International Law: Chal-
lenges/Complicity, Erasures/Encounters.' *Australian Feminist Law Journal* 4,
63–91

Hurtado, Aida. 1989. 'Relating to Privilege: Seduction and Rejection in the Subordination of White Women and Women of Color.' *Signs* 14(4), 833–55

International Covenant on Civil and Political Rights. (1966) 999 U.N.T.S. 171 Can.
T.S. No. 47, in force, including Canada, 1976

Jackson, Robert H. 1990. *Quasi-states: Sovereignty, International Relations and the
Third World.* Cambridge: Cambridge University Press

Kennedy, David. 1994a. 'The International Style in Postwar Law and Policy.' *Utah
Law Review* 1, 7–103

– 1994b. 'Receiving the International.' *Connecticut Journal of International Law*
10(1), 1–26

Knop, Karen. 1993. 'Re/Statements: Feminism and State Sovereignty in International Law.' *Transnational Law and Contemporary Problems* 3, 293–344

Koskenniemi, Martti. 1991. 'Theory: Implications for the Practitioner.' In Philip
Allott, ed., *Theory and International Law: An Introduction.* London: British
Institute of International and Comparative Law, 3–45

MacKinnon, Catharine A. 1994a. 'Rape, Genocide, and Women's Human Rights.'
In Alexandra Stiglmayer, ed., *Mass Rape: The War against Women in Bosnia.* Lincoln: University of Nebraska Press, 183–95

– 1994b. 'Turning Rape into Pornography: Postmodern Genocide.' In Alexandra
Stiglmayer, ed., *Mass Rape: The War against Women in Bosnia.* Lincoln: University of Nebraska Press, 73–81

– 1993a. 'Crimes of War, Crimes of Peace.' In Stephen Shute and Susan Hurley,
eds., *On Human Rights: The Oxford Amnesty Lectures, 1993.* New York: Basic
Books, 83–109

– 1993b. 'On Torture: A Feminist Perspective on Human Rights.' In Kathleen E.
Mahoney and Paul Mahoney, eds., *Human Rights in the Twenty-First Century: A
Global Challenge.* Netherlands: Martinus Nijhoff, 21–31

Mohanty, Chandra Talpade. 1992. 'Feminist Encounters: Locating the Politics
of Experience.' In Michèle Barrett and Anne Phillips, eds., *Destabilizing
Theory: Contemporary Feminist Debates.* Stanford: Stanford University
Press, 74–92

– 1991a. 'Introduction: Cartographies of Struggle: Third World Women and the
Politics of Feminism.' In Chandra Talpade Mohanty, Ann Russo, and Lourdes
Torres, eds., *Third World Women and the Politics of Feminism.* Bloomington and
Indianapolis: Indiana University Press, 1–47

– 1991b. 'Under Western Eyes: Feminist Scholarship and Colonial Discourses.' In
Chandra Talpade Mohanty, Ann Russo, and Lourdes Torres, eds., *Third World*

Women and the Politics of Feminism. Bloomington and Indianapolis: Indiana University Press, 51–80

Nesiah, Vasuki. 1993. 'Toward a Feminist Internationality: A Critque of U.S. Feminist Legal Scholarship.' *Harvard Women's Law Journal* 16, 189–210

Olsen, Frances. 1993. 'International Law: Feminist Critiques of the Public/Private Distinction.' In Dorinda Dallmeyer, ed., *Reconceiving Reality: Women and International Law.* Washington: American Society of International Law, 157–69

– 1983. 'The Family and the Market: A Study of Ideology and Legal Reform.' *Harvard Law Review* 96(7), 1497–1578

Phillips, Anne. 1992. 'Universal Pretensions in Political Thought.' In Michèle Barrett and Anne Phillips, eds., *Destabilizing Theory: Contemporary Feminist Debates.* Stanford: Stanford University Press, 10–30

Razack, Sherene. 1995. 'Domestic Violence as Gender Persecution: Policing the Borders of Nation, Race, and Gender.' *Canadian Journal of Women and the Law* 8(1), 45–88

Romany, Celina. 1993. 'Women as *Aliens*: A Feminist Critique of the Public/Private Distinction in International Human Rights Law.' *Harvard Human Rights Journal* 6, 87–125

Rosaldo, M.Z. 1980. 'The Use and Abuse of Anthropology: Reflections on Feminism and Cross-Cultural Understanding.' *Signs* (Spring), 389–417

Sedghi, Hamideh. 1994. 'Third World Feminist Perspectives on World Politics.' In Peter R. Beckman and Francine D'Amico, eds., *Women, Gender and World Politics: Perspectives, Policies and Prospects.* Westport: Bergin and Garvey, 89–105

Sen, Gita, and Caren Grown. 1987. *Development, Crises, and Alternative Visions: Third World Women's Perspectives.* New York: Monthly Review Press

Spelman, Elizabeth V. 1988. *Inessential Woman: Problems of Exclusion in Feminist Thought.* Boston: Beacon

Spivak, Gayatri. 1987. 'French Feminism in an International Frame.' In Gayatri Spivak, ed., *In Other Worlds: Essays in Cultural Politics.* New York and London: Routledge

Stivens, Maila. 1991. 'Why Gender Matters in Southeast Asian Politics.' In Maila Stivens, ed., *Why Gender Matters in Southeast Asian Politics.* Clayton: Monash University, 9–24

Toope, Stephen J. 1992. 'State Sovereignty: The Challenge of a Changing World.' In *Proceedings of the Canadian Council on International Law, 1992,* 294–7

Walker, Kristen. 1994. 'An Exploration of Article 2(7) of the United Nations Charter as an Embodiment of the Public/Private Distinction in International Law.' *International Law and Politics* 26, 173–99

Wing, Adrien Katherine, and Sylke Merchan. 1993. 'Rape, Ethnicity, and Culture:

Spirit Injury from Bosnia to Black America.' *Columbia Human Rights Law Review* 25, 1–48

Wright, Shelley. 1993. 'Economic Rights, Social Justice and the State: A Reappraisal.' In Dorinda Dallmeyer, ed., *Reconceiving Reality: Women and International Law*. Washington: American Society of International Law, 117–42

– 1988–9. 'Economic Rights and Social Justice: A Feminist Analysis of Some International Human Rights Conventions.' *Australian Yearbook of International Law* 12, 241–64

Index

Garska v *McCoy*, 242. *See also* primary
caregiver assumption
gender roles: swapping, 258, 266–7
globalization, 24, 360–84
Gove Inquiry into Child Protection in
British Columbia, 334

Harris, Mike, 54
hegemony, 21–2
heterosexism: and role-modelling, 262
history: of homework, 147–8; relevance of, 77–80
homework (industrial), 14, 21, 46–7,
144–67; and British Columbia, 149,
152–3; and class, 147; cottage industry, 144, 147; devaluation of, 157; as
economic survival tactic, 154;
employment relations and, 150,
155–9; employment standards, 145,
150–2; as feminized and racialized,
144, 145, 152–5; history of, 147–8;
and immigrant women, 148, 152–5,
156, 157; invisibility of, 148, 155; and
organized labour, 149–50; outsourcing of, 147; reasons for taking, 154–5;
and visible minority women, 153.
See also garment industry
household, 49–51; care for the elderly,
50; child care, 50; deregulation, 56;
division of marital property, 51;
domestic work, 50; as site of
women's oppression, 146; wife battering, 51

ideology: dominant, 335–8; emergent,
335. *See also* familial ideology; ideology of motherhood
ideology of motherhood, 237, 274; and
child custody, 254; and compulsory
motherhood, 178–82; employed

mothers and, 253–79, 255–6; and
good mother / bad mother, 169, 177;
in judicial decisions, 257; and patienthood, 236–8; and primary caregiver presumption, 267; and
psychiatric disability, 236–8, 245–6;
Tyabji's departure from, 264; and
working mothers, 178
immigrant women, 14, 48, 144–67, 174,
312; and access to services, 153–4;
attitudes towards, 156; fears of, 157;
as homeworkers, 152–5
Immigration Act, 312
Income Tax Act, 309, 313, 319
international law, 360–84; and feminism, 360–84
intersectionality, 12, 24, 94–100, 152–5,
173–7, 367–70

Klein, Ralph, 330. *See also* Alberta
Action Plan

law: as site of struggle, 22. *See also*
criminal law; family law; social welfare law; taxation law
law reform, 5–7, 92–4; and exclusion of
Aboriginal women, 97–100; feminist
critiques of, 93–4; police and prosecution policy directives and, 92–3
lawyers: work histories, 214–16. *See
also* women in the legal profession
legal profession: demographic changes
in, 197–200; glass ceiling effects in,
201–3; and government as employer,
210, 214–15; lack of flexibility in,
206; racial, class, and ethnic representation by, 200, 202; women's
impact on, 195–6. *See also* women in
the legal profession
lesbian relationships: as unstable, 286–7